European Studies in Social Psychology

Social markers in speech

European studies in social psychology

This series will consist mainly of specially commissioned volumes on specific themes, particularly those linking work in social psychology with other disciplines. It will also include occasional volumes of 'Current Research'. *Social markers in speech* is the first volume to appear; others are in preparation.

The series is jointly published by the Cambridge University Press and the Editions de la Maison des Sciences de l'Homme, in close collaboration with the Laboratoire Européen de Psychologie Sociale of the Maison, as part of the joint publishing agreement established in 1977 between the Fondation de la Maison des Sciences de l'Homme and the Syndics of the Cambridge University Press.

Cette collection est publiée en co-édition par Cambridge University Press et les Editions de la Maison des Sciences de l'Homme en collaboration étroite avec le Laboratoire Européen de Psychologie Sociale de la Maison.

Elle comprend essentiellement des ouvrages sur des thèmes spécifiques permettant de mettre en rapport la psychologie sociale et d'autres disciplines, avec à l'occasion des volumes consacrés à des 'recherches en cours'. *Social markers in speech* est le premier volume à paraître dans cette série. Il s'intègre dans le programme de co-édition etabli en 1977 par la Fondation de la Maison des Sciences de l'Homme et les Syndics de Cambridge University Press.

Social markers in speech

Edited by
Klaus R. Scherer
Professor of Psychology, University of Giessen

and
Howard Giles
Reader in Social Psychology, University of Bristol

Cambridge University Press
Cambridge
London   New York   Melbourne

Editions de la Maison des Sciences de l'Homme
Paris

Published by the Syndics of the Cambridge University Press
The Pitt Building, Trumpington Street, Cambridge CB2 1RP
Bentley House, 200 Euston Road, London NW1 2DB
32 East 57th Street, New York, NY 10022, USA
296 Beaconsfield Parade, Middle Park, Melbourne 3206, Australia
and
Editions de la Maison des Sciences de l'Homme
54 Boulevard Raspail, 75270 Paris Cedex 06

First published 1979

Phototypeset in V.I.P. Palatino by
Western Printing Services Ltd, Bristol

Printed in Great Britain at the University Press, Cambridge

Library of Congress Cataloguing in Publication Data
Main entry under title:
Social markers in speech.
Includes index.
1. Sociolinguistics.   2. Social interaction.
I. Scherer, Klaus Rainer.   II. Giles, Howard.
P40.S545   301.2'1   79–4080

ISBN 0 521 22321 0 hard covers
ISBN 0 521 29590 4 paperback

Contents

Contributors

PENELOPE BROWN
  Social and Political Sciences Committee, University of Cambridge

COLIN FRASER
  Social and Political Sciences Committee, University of Cambridge

HOWARD GILES
  Department of Psychology, University of Bristol

HEDE HELFRICH
  Fachbereich Psychologie, Justus-Liebig-Universität Giessen

JOHN LAVER
  Department of Linguistics, University of Edinburgh

STEPHEN LEVINSON
  Department of Linguistics, University of Cambridge

W. PETER ROBINSON
  Department of Education, University of Bristol

KLAUS R. SCHERER
  Fachbereich Psychologie, Justus-Liebig-Universität Giessen

PHILIP M. SMITH
  Department of Psychology, University of Bristol

DONALD M. TAYLOR
  Department of Psychology, McGill University

PETER TRUDGILL
  Department of Linguistic Science, University of Reading

Preface

The importance of speech as a marker of social identity has been convincingly illustrated by Eliza Doolittle, a Cockney flower girl transformed into a lady of high standing in part by changing some of the social markers in her speech. While Shaw's Professor Higgins in *Pygmalion* slightly exaggerated the propelling power of social class markers for status climbing even in Victorian England, there is little doubt that for most speakers in most cultures and language groups of the world, speech cues provide information about geographical origin, age, sex, occupational roles, group membership, social status, personal dispositions and the nature of the speech situation. The present volume attempts to survey systematically the current state of knowledge concerning the ways in which various biological, psychological and social characteristics of individuals are reflected or 'marked' in speech and the influence of situational and cultural contexts on the occurrence and interpretation of such speech markers. While many disciplines in the social and behavioural sciences have shown a lively interest in the information speech transmits about the speaker over and above the linguistically encoded meaning of his utterances, there has been a remarkable lack of interdisciplinary cooperation in this area of research. Owing to the resulting fragmentation of research efforts and the fact that relevant publications appear in a wide variety of journals and periodicals, there appears to be a great terminological confusion, a lack of comparability of theoretical and operational concepts, and an absence of an accumulation of the research findings. Although these perennial ills cannot be cured simply by providing exposure to relevant approaches in neighbouring disciplines, it is hoped that a selective survey of research in anthropological linguistics, sociolinguistics, and the social psychology of language, will be a first step towards more integrated and cumulative interdisciplinary work in this area. The present volume attempts to provide just that.

The editors are cognizant of the fact that the introduction of the term 'marker' in a very general sense may add to the terminological confusion criticized above. However, the use of alternative terms such as sign, index, symptom, indicator, clue, seemed equally if not more problematical given their history and connotation in different disciplines. Since the term 'marker' has not been extensively used in the social and behavioural sciences (except in linguistics), it was hoped that it could provide a fairly neutral designation of the phenomenon to be studied, which would be acceptable to all disciplines concerned.

Thus, in the chapters to follow, the term 'marker' should be taken in a fairly general sense to mean speech cues that potentially provide the receiver with information concerning the sender's biological, psychological and social characteristics. The term 'social markers' as a superordinate concept was chosen for the title of this work not only to avoid cumbersome enumeration in the title but also to highlight the fact that the markers with which we are concerned play an important role in *social interaction*.

The collection of review chapters in this volume, which in itself is an international and interdisciplinary effort, grew out of a colloquium which the editors organized under the auspices of the Laboratoire Européen de la Psychologie Sociale at the Maison des Sciences de l'Homme in Paris from 6–8 October 1977. All of the participants in the colloquium were interested in and had done work on the social functions of speech markers in terms of interpersonal and intergroup dynamics. In addition to the contributors to this volume, the following social psychologists were active participants in the colloquium: Jean-Léon Beauvois, Guy Fielding, Rodolphe Ghiglione and Jo Kleiven. The editors and contributors to this volume are most grateful for the important contributions of Peter Schönbach, Thomas Luckmann and Serge Moscovici who served as discussants to the colloquium. Special thanks are due to Clemens Heller and Adriana Touraine for their invaluable support in the organization of the colloquium which was supported by grants from the Thyssen Foundation, W. Germany, the DGRST, France, the Fondation de la Maison des Sciences de l'Homme, France and the Social Science Research Council, Great Britain.

While most of the following chapters were originally written for this colloquium, the present volume should not be considered as a publication of the conference proceedings. First, the original papers went through a series of revisions incorporating comments and suggestions from a large number of critical readers. In their final form, chapters were written specifically as contributions to a reference work on social markers in speech. Second, the chapters by Laver & Trudgill (ch. 1) and Brown & Levinson (ch. 8) were commissioned to round off and complement the coverage of the volume.

In spite of exercising considerable editorial influence, the editors have abstained from imposing requirements for absolute uniformity of terminology, approach and style on the authors. Such an attempt would not only have been difficult, given the interdisciplinary nature of the enterprise, but possibly damaging considering that this is a first attempt to explore the nature and the functioning of social markers in speech. The purpose of this volume is to present facts and ideas rather than a tight terminological and conceptual framework. Consequently, the reader will have to be prepared for some conceptual looseness as well as for some degree of dissension concerning the use of the term 'marker'. Furthermore, each of the authors approaches the speaker characteristic with which he or she is concerned from a somewhat different angle reflecting his discipline or the specific problem of the scientific assessment of the characteristics dealt with. This diversity of the approaches taken has an important positive side-effect; it ensures that the reader does not have to cope with a tiring enumeration of speech markers. In the final chapter by Giles, Scherer & Taylor (ch. 9), there is an attempt to integrate wherever possible some of these perspectives. What is presented is not a 'marker theory', given the present state of the art, but rather a heuristic to provide a vocabulary and foundation for the development of interdisciplinary research on speech markers.

The volume should be useful to various classes of readers. Scholars and researchers in anthropology, linguistics, ethology, sociology, psychology and social psychology may find it helpful as an orientation and reference tool for work in the general areas of language and communication. Independently of their specific research interests, many behavioural and social scientists may be interested in the remarkable wealth of information about speakers which is conveyed by various aspects of their speech patterns, and the way in which such information is used in everyday social interaction. Finally, the volume should be useful in graduate and undergraduate courses concerned with the pragmatic aspects of human language.

K. R. SCHERER
H. GILES

Giessen/Bristol, August 1978

1. Phonetic and linguistic markers in speech

JOHN LAVER and PETER TRUDGILL

Many disciplines are professionally interested in the analysis of markers of identity in speech, and in the nature of the listener's performance in attributing particular characteristics to the speaker on the basis of such markers. A necessary prerequisite for the development of research in this area, from the standpoint of any discipline, is the provision of an adequate phonetic and linguistic account of the marking phenomena themselves. The aim of this chapter is to indicate some ways in which concepts already available in phonetic and linguistic theory can help to refine the analysis of markers in speech.

The structure of the chapter begins with a brief discussion of the semiotic basis of how speech can serve a marking function as well as fulfilling its role as a vehicle for linguistic communication. Then the phonetic nature of markers in speech is discussed, in terms of voice features, features of tone of voice, and features of linguistic articulations. This is followed by an account of the way in which phonological differences between accents can mark social aspects of speakers' identities. Syntactic markers are then considered. Recent work in the study of discourse and conversational interaction is touched on, and some aspects of lexical markers are examined. The chapter concludes with some tentative hypotheses about the listener's process of attribution which emerge from the phonetic and linguistic discussion.

1. The semiotic basis of marking

Given that the concept of marking deals essentially with the production and perception of communicative and informative signs, it forms part of a general theory of semiotics (cf. Giles, Scherer & Taylor, this volume: ch. 9, 3.1). In recent years, there has been a surge of interest in semiotic theory (cf. Eco 1976), but the history of semiotics as a discipline can be

1

traced back to Greek medicine. Morris (1946: 285–7) says that it was first used to refer to the theory of medical symptoms used as signs in the diagnosis and prognosis of disease. The Stoic philosophers then used 'semiotic' to mean the general theory of signs. Morris traces the history of semiotics into medieval Europe, through the works of Augustine and Boethius. There, the subject (known as 'scientia sermocinalis') developed in the work of figures such as Petrus Hispanus, Abelard, Roger Bacon, Thomas of Erfurt, Sigur of Courtrai and William of Occam. From them, two divergent traditions developed: one led to the work of the British empiricist philosophers like Francis Bacon, Hobbes, Locke, Berkeley, Hume and Bentham; the other, through the work of Leibniz, led to that of modern symbolic logicians such as Boole, Frege, Peano, Russell, Whitehead, Carnap and Tarski. The philosophical basis of an interest in the notion of marking stands on a very long-established foundation, therefore, and theré is much of value to be gained from these earlier writings on the subject.

One of the most accessible of the semiotic philosophers, and probably the most relevant for the purposes of this volume, is Charles Saunders Peirce, the American pragmaticist philosopher of the late nineteenth century. Six volumes of his collected papers have been edited by Hartshorne & Weiss (1931–5), and Feibleman (1946) provides a useful condensed version of his writings.

Peirce's definition of 'semiotic' was 'the formal doctrine of signs (where) a sign is something which stands to somebody for something in some respect or capacity' (Hartshorne & Weiss 1931–5: II, 227–8). Peirce divided the different sorts of signs into three mutually intersecting trichotomies. The second trichotomy is the most relevant here. Feibleman (1946: 90) gives a compressed quotation of this as follows:

'The second trichotomy of signs consists of the *icon*, a sign which refers to an object by virtue of characters of its own which it possesses whether the object exists or not (2. 247); the *index*, a sign which refers to the object that it denotes by virtue of being really affected by that object (2. 248); and the *symbol*, a sign which refers to the object that it denotes by virtue of a law, usually an association of general ideas, which operates to cause the symbol to be interpreted as referring to that object (2. 249).'

This concept of a symbolic relationship holding between a sign and its referent, where the relationship is conventional and arbitrary, lies at the heart of the linguistic code. But it is Peirce's notion of an index that is the most interesting in any consideration of how speech identifies the speaker. He used the term in a number of rather different senses, but the one most useful for marking purposes is his evidential sense illustrated by the quotation above, where an index was said to refer to its object 'by virtue of being really affected by that object'. The orientation of a weathercock would in this usage be evidence for, or an index of, wind-direction; the height of a column of mercury in a thermometer would be an index of heat. 'Index' can thus be equated with 'marker', and terms derived from 'index', such as 'to indicate', 'indicative' and 'indication', can be used as technical terms in association with 'to mark' and 'marking'. One modification to Peirce's basic concept needs to be accepted, however. For Peirce, the connection between an index and its object was nonarbitrary; we shall find it useful, nevertheless, to allow an arbitrary connection between some markers in speech and the personal characteristics indicated by them, or taken by the listener to be so indicated.

One writer in particular who has developed a quite explicit typology of markers of identity in speech, based partly on some of Peirce's ideas, is Abercrombie (1967). He used Peirce's term 'index', and describes three classes of indices in speech that reveal personal characteristics of the speaker:

(a) those that indicate membership of a group (e.g. a regional or a social group);
(b) those that characterize the individual;
(c) those that reveal changing states of the speaker (e.g. changing affective states (Abercrombie 1967: 7–9).

We shall refer to these three types of indices as *group markers, individuating markers* and *affective markers* respectively. The typology that Abercrombie suggests will be adopted here, in conjunction with a cross-cutting classification of markers into three other categories:

(a) those that mark social characteristics, such as regional affiliation, social status, educational status, occupation and social role;
(b) those that mark physical characteristics, such as age, sex, physique and state of health;
(c) those that mark psychological characteristics of personality and affective state.

We shall call these three types of markers *social markers, physical markers* and *psychological markers* respectively. The two typologies differ chiefly in the way that psychological attributes are handled.

Another linguist who has taken an explicit interest in indexical information in speech is Lyons. His position on the distinction between 'communicative' and 'informative' signs (which is a not uncontroversial distinction) will be followed in this chapter. Lyons suggests that:

'a signal is communicative . . . if it is intended by the sender to make the receiver aware of something of which he was not previously aware. Whether a signal is communicative or not rests, then, upon the possibility of choice, or selection, on the part of the sender. If the sender cannot but behave in a certain way (i.e. if he cannot choose between alternative kinds of behaviour), then he obviously cannot communicate anything by behaving in that way . . . 'Communicative' means "meaningful for the sender".' (Lyons 1977: 33)

This is contrasted with 'informative' in the sense that:

'a signal is informative if (regardless of the intentions of the sender) it makes the receiver aware of something of which he was not previously aware. 'Informative' therefore means "meaningful to the receiver".' (Lyons 1977: 33)

What a speaker says is thus communicative, but his accent, unless he has the possibility of speaking with more than one accent, is informative.

Lyons adopts Abercrombie's classification of indices, but proposes one further category, based on Abercrombie's third type: 'those that reveal changing states of the speaker'. Lyons calls this proposed category a 'symptom', recalling the diagnostic use of signs in medicine, but widens the scope of a symptom beyond the indication of affective information:

'any information in a . . . signal which indicates to the receiver that the sender is in a particular state, whether this be an emotional state (fear, anger, sexual arousal or readiness, etc.), a state of health (suffering from laryngitis, etc.), a state of intoxication, or whatever, [can be] described as symptomatic of that state' (Lyons 1977: 108).

2. Phonetic and phonological markers

In order to be able to discuss details of the phonetic and phonological phenomena that act as markers in speech, it will be helpful briefly to consider the physical and auditory variables involved in speech production and perception. Many good introductions to general phonetic theory are available (e.g. Pike 1943; Abercrombie 1967; Ladefoged 1971, 1976; O'Connor 1973). Ladefoged (1962) offers a lucid, short introduction to the acoustic basis of speech, and Hardcastle (1976) gives a schematic, readable account of the anatomy and physiology of speech. The reader is referred to these sources for a more detailed exposition, and the comments on speech production and perception that are offered here are intended only as an orientation.

We can initially consider speech production from the point of view of the different muscle systems which make up all the vocal apparatus. The muscle systems exploited in speaking are almost all anatomically inter-connected (Laver 1975), so that no muscular action takes place without affecting the activity of many other parts of the vocal apparatus. Each muscular action has to be cooperatively facilitated by all the muscle systems that could potentially counteract the desired effect of its execu-tion. Speaking thus requires the most complex and skilful collaboration between the different muscle systems, whose cooperative actions all have to be precisely and intricately coordinated in time. It is not at all surpris-ing, therefore, that in learning to control such a complex apparatus sufficiently to be able to produce auditorily acceptable imitations of speech patterns heard in one's social environment, speakers should nevertheless develop idiosyncracies of pronunciation that serve to indi-viduate them within their own social group.

The notion of an isolable muscle system is itself something of a fiction. But if we accept the fiction as analytically convenient, then there are seven basic muscle systems whose contributions to speech can be distin-guished. These are: the *respiratory system*, which supplies the driving force that pushes air out of the lungs, up to the larynx and the rest of the vocal tract, for speech purposes; the *phonatory system*, which controls the actions of the vocal folds in producing phonation; the *pharyngeal system*, which controls articulatory activity at the bottom end of the vocal tract; the *velopharyngeal system*, which controls the production of nasality; the *lingual system*, which is responsible for the oral articulations underlying most consonant and vowel segments; the *labial system*, which controls the actions of the lip structures; and the *mandibular system*, which controls movements of the jaw.

From an articulatory and aerodynamic point of view, speech is the joint product of the collaborative interaction of all these muscle systems, as reflected in the continually changing configurations of the vocal tract and larynx, and the pattern of airflow from the lungs to the outside air. These articulatory and aerodynamic changes give rise to associated acoustic changes, which can be described in terms of a number of acoustic para-meters. The acoustic parameters in turn have a statable relationship to perceptual, auditory parameters. The auditory variables in speech are basically of two sorts: quality features and dynamic features.

The acoustic correlates of features of auditory quality are essentially spectral in nature, and include such aspects as formant frequencies and amplitudes, and the frequency and amplitude of aperiodic noise in the spectrum. The acoustic correlates of dynamic auditory features include fundamental frequency as the correlate of *pitch*, intensity as the correlate of *loudness*, and duration as the correlate of *length*. It should be noted, however, that the allocation of fundamental frequency and intensity to the acoustic realization of dynamic auditory features is not always completely valid: pitch 'jitter' and loudness 'shimmer' (that is, aperiodic cycle-to-cycle variability of fundamental frequency or intensity around the mean value) are both heard as contributing to auditory quality, giving a 'rough', 'harsh' auditory texture.

Auditorily, all speech is made up of sounds describable in terms of quality, pitch, loudness and length. All markers in speech thus depend on these variables for their phonetic realization, and the discussion that follows is an attempt to explain the phonetic basis of different types of speaker-characteristics.

There are three different facets of vocal performance to be considered. Each of these facets is subject to a different time-perspective. Firstly, there is the facet of vocal performance that represents the speaker's permanent or quasi-permanent *voice*, by which he is recognizable even when his consonants and vowels are unintelligible, for example, when heard speaking on the other side of a closed door. The other two facets are *tone of voice* and the *phonetic realizations of linguistic units*. The time-perspective of tone of voice is usually medium-term, and that of linguistic articulations very short-term.

Because voice features are by definition long-term, they lie quite outside any possibility of signalling linguistic meaning, so it is appropriate to refer to such voice features as *extralinguistic*. Since they are not normally consciously manipulated by the speaker, voice features are informative but not communicative. The medium-term features that make up tone of voice, and which have the function of signalling affective information, have a rather closer resemblance in some ways to the short-term use of the vocal apparatus for signalling linguistic meaning, and such features are therefore often referred to as *paralinguistic*. They are 'para'linguistic in the sense that they form a communicative code subject to cultural convention for its interpretation; paralinguistic features are not fully linguistic in the sense that they lack the possibility of signalling meaning through sequential arrangement into structures, which is a criterial property of linguistic communication.

Neither extralinguistic nor paralinguistic features are irrelevant to directly linguistic interests, since they constitute a background against which the linguistic articulations can achieve their perceptual prominence. Strictly, each of the three types of vocal feature, extralinguistic, paralinguistic and linguistic, acts as a perceptual ground for the figures of the other two types of figure.

Each of these categories of vocal behaviour will now be discussed in more phonetic detail. A summary of the relationship between these vocal variables and their marking functions is given in table 1.

2.1. Extralinguistic voice features

Long-term speaker-characterizing voice features are of two different sorts. One type of voice feature arises from anatomical differences between speakers. The second type is the product of the way in which the individual speaker habitually 'sets' his vocal apparatus for speaking. Unlike this second type, which will be discussed in a moment, the first type of feature is by definition outside any possibility of control by the speaker. It includes anatomical influences on aspects of voice quality and of voice dynamics.

Anatomical influences on voice quality are due to factors such as basic vocal tract length, dimensions of lips, tongue, nasal cavity, pharynx and jaw, dental characteristics, and geometry of laryngeal structures (Abercrombie 1967: 92). These anatomical factors impose limits on the range of spectral effects (in terms of formant frequency and amplitude ranges, and on the distribution of aperiodic noise through the spectrum) that the speaker can potentially control acoustically.

Anatomical influences on voice dynamics are due to factors such as the dimensions and mass of the vocal folds, and respiratory volume. These influence pitch and loudness ranges, by imposing limits on the ranges of fundamental frequency and amplitude that the speaker can produce.

Listeners' judgements of physical attributes, based on the product of such anatomically derived features, are amongst the most accurate conclusions drawn. This is precisely because they are based on invariant, involuntary aspects of a speaker's vocal performance. Physique, age and sex are all judged with a fair accuracy, and interesting information about a speaker's medical condition is also sometimes accurately inferred.

Physique and height are probably judged accurately because of the good correlation that seems to exist between these factors and the dimensions of the speaker's vocal apparatus. A tall, well-built man will tend to

Table 1. The relationship between vocal variables and their marking functions

	permanent	quasi-permanent	medium-term	short-term
Signalling function	informative		informative and communicative	
Relation to language	extralinguistic voice characteristics		paralinguistic 'tone of voice'	phonetic realizations of linguistic units
Temporal perspective	permanent	quasi-permanent	medium-term	short-term
Vocal variables	vocal features deriving from anatomical differences between individuals influencing both quality and dynamic aspects	voice settings, i.e. habitual muscular adjustments of the vocal apparatus, including voice quality settings and voice dynamic settings	'tone of voice' achieved by temporary use of voice settings, including paralinguistic quality settings and paralinguistic dynamic settings	momentary articulatory realizations of phonological units, including short-term manipulations of phonetic quality features and short-term manipulations of phonetic dynamic features
Marking function	physical markers	social and psychological markers		
Potential controllability	uncontrollable, therefore unlearnable	under potential muscular control, therefore learnable and imitatable		

have a long vocal tract and large vocal folds. His voice quality will reflect the length of his vocal tract by having correspondingly low ranges of formant frequencies, and his voice dynamic features will indicate the dimensions and mass of his vocal folds by a correspondingly low range of fundamental frequency. His large respiratory volume will be reflected in a powerful loudness range. If we then hear such a voice over the telephone, we normally have a confident expectation that the speaker will turn out to be a large, strong male. In general, our expectations are fulfilled, within a reasonable margin of error. Bonaventura (1935) gave subjects pictures and voices to match, and found that fair accuracy was achieved: in terms of Kretschmerian body-types (Kretschmer 1925), judgements of *pyknic* types were most accurate, accuracy was less for *leptosome* types, and least for *athletic* types. Moses (1940, 1941) gives general support to this, and Fay & Middleton (1940a) report a more detailed finding: they found that in judging body-types from voices transmitted over a public address system, the results were 22 per cent above chance for pyknic types, 20 per cent for leptosomes, but only 1 per cent above chance for athletic types. Lass, Beverly, Nicosia & Simpson (1978) report that listeners typically judge weight to within 3–4 lbs (though overestimating the weight of males and underestimating that of females), and that they judge height to within 1.5 inches (though underestimating the height of both males and females). There is one class of voices where the general correlation does not apply, but where listeners nevertheless seem to be able to reach successful conclusions about the physical attributes. That is where the formant ranges of the voice are radically discrepant with the fundamental frequency, as in particular types of dwarfism (Vuorenkoski, Tjernlund & Perheentupa 1972; Weinberg & Zlatin 1970). In these cases, the dimensions of the vocal folds are smaller than their general correlation with vocal tract length would lead one to expect.

Exceptions to the general rule of our ability as listeners to attach a particular size and physique to a given voice are sufficiently rare to take us aback when they occur.

Age is judged accurately (Dordain, Chevrie-Muller & Grémy 1967; Hollien & Shipp 1972; Mysak 1959; Ptacek, Sander, Maloney & Roe Jackson 1966; Shipp & Hollien 1969). Voice quality features probably play their part in marking this characteristic, but voice dynamic features are likely to be the more primary cues. Age is marked by pitch in both males and females: Hollien & Shipp (1972) show a progressive lowering of mean pitch with age for males from 20 up to 40, then a rise from age 60 through the 80s. Mysak (1959) also showed this rise in mean pitch from the 50s upwards. Dordain *et al*. (1967) report a drop in mean pitch for older women, but a rise with extreme age. Ptacek *et al*. (1966) also report a reduced pitch range with extreme age.

Features of auditory quality can signal aspects of the age of a speaker. These include the quality associated with the 'breaking' voice of puberty, and the quality of extreme old age. Vocal indications of puberty, referred to in clinical literature as 'vocal mutation', often include whispery voice. Luchsinger & Arnold (1965: 132) write that 'In addition to the lowering of the average speaking pitch, the voice is frequently husky during mutation, or it may sound weak.' The senescent voice of extreme old age derives from a complex of endocrinal, anatomical and physiological changes. The mucal fluid supply often becomes disturbed, either greatly increasing or decreasing, tissues become increasingly less elastic, and cartilages become calcified and ossified (Fyfe & Naylor 1958; Luchsinger & Arnold 1965; Meader & Muyskens 1962; Terracol & Azémar 1949). Meader & Muyskens (1962: 77) comment that 'Since the rigidity of tissue is one determination of its resonating qualities, the gradual deposition of lime in . . . cartilages (replacing them by bone) helps to explain the shrill voice and thin voice (deficient in harmonics) of age.' Because muscles atrophy, the glottis of old speakers often has a bowed appearance (Luchsinger & Arnold 1965: 136; Tarneaud 1941); this means that, to achieve phonation, greater effort has to be exerted to bring the vocal folds together, and a rather harsh voice is often the result. When this is combined with inefficient phonation because of an excess of mucus, the type of voice that results is a harsh whispery voice, as suggested by the following comment from Luchsinger & Arnold (1965: 136): 'Tracheal and laryngeal mucous secretions are increased, sometimes on an allergic basis. Together with a tendency to chronic bronchitis, this over-secretion of mucus produces the hacking, coughing, throat-clearing, or "moist" hoarseness of the old man.' In old age, fatty tissue can build up in the ventricles in the sides of the upper larynx (Ferreri 1959), and the ventricular folds above the ventricles can shrink towards the sides of the larynx, giving a wider entrance to the ventricles (Luchsinger & Arnold 1965: 136). All these factors can contribute significantly to the fine detail of the auditory quality of the phonation being produced. Luchsinger & Arnold also mention work by Braus (1924), who 'pointed out that the larynx and the entire respiratory and digestive tract are in a lowered position with senility' (1965: 137), because of the loss of elasticity of the muscular and ligmental structures from which these organs are suspended. Any such elongation of the vocal tract tends to lower the ranges of the formant frequencies. A more extensive discussion of age markers in speech can be found in Helfrich (this volume: ch. 3).

One usually forms fairly accurate impressions of a speaker's sex from vocal clues. The clearest indicator is probably pitch range. Hollien, Dew & Philips (1971) measured the mean minimum and maximum fundamental frequency for a group of 332 adult males and 202 young adult females. The male range was 78–698 cs, and the female range 139–1108 cs. Differences of pitch range are directly attributable to different laryngeal dimensions. Kaplan (1960: 144) reports typical dimensions for glottal length in adult males as 23 mm, and in adult females as 17 mm. Differences of spectral quality also contribute to signalling the sex of the speaker, because female vocal tracts are shorter than male tracts, on average, as reflected in higher formant frequency ranges. Fant (1960) gives a list of acoustic values for average male subjects, and compares them with those for females and children. He writes that:

'The natural range of variation of the voice fundamental frequencies for non-nasal voiced sounds uttered by average male subjects is as follows:

F0 – 60–240 cs.
F1 – 150–850 cs.
F2 – 500–2500 cs.
F3 – 1500–3500 cs.
F4 – 2500–4500 cs.

Females have on average one octave higher fundamental pitch but only 17% higher formant frequencies; see Peterson and Barney (1952); Fant (1953). Children about 10 years of age have still higher formants, on the average 25% higher than adult males, and their fundamental pitch averages 300 cs. The individual spread is large.' (Fant 1960: 242)

In an article in 1966, Fant amended this position slightly, when he said that:

'The common concept of physiologically induced differences in formant patterns comparing males and females is that the average female F-frequencies are related to those of the male by a simple scale factor inversely proportional to the overall vocal tract length (i.e. female F-pattern about 20% higher than male). This simple scale factor rule has important limitations.' (Fant 1966: 22)

He points out that the deviations from the rule are obscured if an average is taken over all vowels, and says that female–male relations are

'typically different in (1) rounded back vowels, (2) very open unrounded vowels, (3) closed front vowels . . . The main physiological determinants of the specific deviations from the average rule is that the ratio of pharynx length to mouth cavity length is greater for males than for females, and that the laryngeal cavities are more developed in males.' (1966: 22)

'The scale factor relating average female formant frequencies to those of men is a function of the particular class of vowels . . . The female to male scale factor is of the order of 18% averaged over the whole vowel system . . . The scaling of children's data from female data comes closer to a simple factor independent of vowel class' (Fant 1966: 29).

A further discussion of sex markers in speech can be found in Smith (this volume: ch. 4).

The discussion immediately above concerned universal parameters on which all speakers can be placed. We now turn briefly to consider the case of some physical attributes which can be indicated by voice features which normally apply to smaller sections of the population, in considerations of a speaker's medical state. This covers such aspects as abnormalities of anatomy or physiology, the physical effects of trauma or disease, the noxious effects of alcohol, drugs or smoking, transient effects of endocrinal changes, and signs of fatigue.

Voice features indicate a surprisingly wide range of information about a speaker's medical state (Laver 1968: 49), in both what might be considered 'normal' and 'abnormal' conditions. Abnormalities of anatomy can be revealed by voice features associated with such conditions as unusual patterns of dentition (Lawson & Bond 1968), the use of dentures (Lawson & Bond 1969), and unusual conformations of the jaw. A number of abnormal congenital conditions can also be indicated: vocal fold sulcus (a furrow along the glottal edge of the vocal fold, which gives rise to so-called *diplophonic voice*, a mode of phonation with two different simultaneous fundamental frequencies (Kiml 1962)); some types of cleft palate (Jaffe & de Blanc 1970; Lowry 1970); subglottal bars of tissue in the lower larynx (Howie, Ladefoged & Stark 1961); and anatomical similarities in the voices of monozygotic twins (Alpert & Kurtzberg 1963). More generally, to the extent that any given genetically transmitted condition influences vocal anatomy, then the voice quality and voice dynamic features of the particular speaker will act as markers of his genetic make-up. One might therefore expect that genetic disorders such as sex-chromosome anomalies and autosomal anomalies like Down's Syndrome (mongolism) would be characterized by symptomatic voices, although this is a research area which has not yet been developed.

Abnormal physiological conditions due to pathology and laryngeal paralysis can be indicated by voice features (Luchsinger & Arnold 1965: 218–62). Parkinson's disease, for example, is marked by tremulous pitch (Canter 1963), and chronic laryngitis by a whispery voice (McCallum 1954).

Clues in voice quality to endocrinal abnormalities are found in cases of voice disorders resulting from diseases of the thyroid, adrenal and pituitary glands (Luchsinger & Arnold 1965: 188–217). Laver (1968) suggests that systematic research into the possible use of the voice as a diagnostic marker of these and similar medical states would be extremely valuable. So far, the area has only sporadically attracted investigation (McCallum 1954; Palmer 1956; Punt 1959; Sonninen 1960; Canter 1963).

More transient medical states, which while not permanent are outside the speaker's control, can be indicated by voice features when the speaker is suffering from conditions of local inflammation of his vocal organs, as in laryngitis, pharyngitis and tonsillitis, and from nasal catarrh, adenoids or a cold (Abercrombie 1967: 92; Laver 1968: 49).

Other transient factors in voice quality derive from changes in the copiousness and consistency of the supply of lubricating mucus in the larynx, and in the characteristics of the mucal lining covering the vocal folds, affecting the efficiency of their vibration. One such state is the voice of sexual arousal in both men and women, which is often rather whispery, and in which fine control of pitch becomes more difficult. A similar endocrinal effect is found in the voices of women in the pregnant or premenstrual state, according to Tarneaud (1941) and Perelló (1962). Greene (1964: 80) cites Hildernisse (1956) as reminding us that 'singers often have a clause in their contracts to exempt them from singing during the menstrual period'. See also Amado (1953).

Voice features sometimes reveal aspects of a speaker's medical state as a result of the abusing of his vocal apparatus. The hoarse voice of the chronic smoker (Devine 1960; Myerson 1950) and of the chronic drinker (Luchsinger & Arnold 1965), is a familiar experience.

Lastly, information about more transient states such as fatigue can sometimes be marked by voice features. In extreme fatigue, the mode of phonation can become inefficient, resulting in whispery voice or in weak, breathy voice. It should be noted, however, that in less extreme cases of fatigue, Fay & Middleton (1940b) showed that the ability of listeners to judge a speaker's rested or tired condition from his voice alone appears to be based on stereotypes, in that judges agree with each other in their judgements but are much less often accurate.

Attributions of psychological characteristics of a speaker are sometimes made on the basis of markers which are in fact the product solely of physical characteristics. Listeners are often ready to believe that a speaker with a loud, low-pitched voice that is due to a large, robust physique is also thereby endowed with an authoritative personality (cf. Scherer, this volume: ch. 5, 4). Misattributions of this sort, where anatomically derived information is used as the evidence for erroneous psychological conclusions, will be discussed in the final section.

It was said earlier that extralinguistic voice features fall into two major divisions. The second division was described as the product of the way in which the speaker 'sets' his muscular vocal apparatus for speaking. *Voice settings* of this sort are habitual tendencies towards maintaining particular muscular adjustments (Abercrombie 1967: 92; Honikman 1964). Settings in this category include *voice quality settings* and *voice dynamic settings*. The acoustic parameters that characterize voice quality and voice dynamic settings are the same as those that reflect anatomically derived features of the voice, although voice settings necessarily exploit a more limited range of values on those parameters.

Voice quality settings include habitual adjustments of the vocal tract and of the larynx. Settings of the vocal tract involve habitual tendencies towards constricting (or expanding) the tract at some particular point along its length. Examples would be the tendency to keep the tongue raised towards the soft palate, in 'velarized voice'. Another would be the tendency to maintain the lips in a rounded posture throughout speech, in 'labialized voice'. Another would be a tendency to keep the soft palate lowered throughout speech, giving 'nasal voice'. Habitual laryngeal settings involve adjusting the phonatory muscle system in such a way that the vocal folds tend to vibrate in an auditorily characteristic mode. Examples would be 'whispery voice', 'harsh voice', 'harsh whispery voice', 'creaky voice', etc. Laver (1975) gives an extended account of all such voice quality settings and their acoustic correlates.

Voice dynamic settings include pitch settings and loudness settings, as habitual choices of a comfortable range within the anatomically limited extremes. Discussion of voice quality settings and voice dynamic settings will be limited here to a consideration of their marking function.

Because voice settings are under potential muscular control, they are learnable and imitable. The adoption of a particular voice setting often acts as an individuating marker, when its use is idiosyncratic to a particular speaker. But voice settings often form part of the typical vocal performance of particular regional accents, and can thus also act as social markers.

Habitual nasality is a frequent component of many accents: it characterizes speakers of Received Pronunciation (RP) in Britain, and many accents
of the United States and Australia (Laver 1968: 50). Velarized voice marks
the speech of speakers from some areas of New York, from Liverpool and
from Birmingham, England (Laver 1968: 50). Trudgill (1974) has shown,
in a sociolinguistic study of speech in Norwich, that the speech of
working-class speakers, compared with that of middle-class speakers, is
marked by the habitual use of a number of settings: a 'creaky' phonation,
a high pitch range, a loud loudness range, a fronted, lowered tongue
position, a raised larynx position, a particular type of nasality and a
relatively high overall degree of muscular tension throughout the vocal
tract (Trudgill 1974: 186–7). Esling (1978: 176) has shown, in a sociolinguistic study of speech in Edinburgh, that social class correlates with
laryngeal settings, in that greater social status corresponds to a greater
incidence of 'creaky' phonation and lower social status to a greater incidence of whisperiness and harshness.

The notion of voice settings has been developed in phonetic theory
mainly to account for general articulatory tendencies distinguishing the
pronunciation of different languages (Laver, 1978). In this application,
voice settings are usually called 'basis of articulation', or 'articulatory
setting'. Heffner (1950: 99), for example, describes French as being
spoken 'from a high and tense forward basis of articulation', and English
'from a comparatively low and relaxed basis of articulation'. Honikman
(1964: 73–84) describes the voice settings of many languages, including
English, French, German, Russian, Arabic, Italian, Polish, Danish and
Spanish. She points out, for example, that in many of the languages of
India and Pakistan the jaws are held 'rather inert and loosely apart',
which she says gives them a distinctive quality which 'is very noticeable
in the English spoken by Indians' (Honikman 1964: 80). Settings of this
sort can thus act as markers of linguistic group membership.

2.2. Paralinguistic features of tone of voice

Extralinguistic voice features involve relatively permanent vocal effects.
We move now to vocal effects with a medium-term temporal relevance, to
consider the paralinguistic communication of affect by manipulations of
'tone of voice'. Many of the same vocal phenomena are concerned, in that
a more temporary use is often made of settings. Anger in English is
frequently conventionally conveyed, for example, by a harsh phonatory
setting, with a raised pitch span and an increased loudness span ('span' is

a useful term taken from Brown (1977), to distinguish between the range of a quasi-permanent voice dynamic setting and the more temporary use of a particular span of the same parameter for paralinguistic uses). Other paralinguistic dynamic features are those of *rate* and *continuity*. Rate, sometimes called *tempo*, is self-explanatory; continuity refers to 'the incidence of pauses in the stream of speech – where they come, how frequent they are, and how long they are' (Abercrombie 1967: 96).

Affect in English, and probably in all languages, is signalled not only by paralinguistic settings, but also by various shorter-term segmental effects. Unfortunately, the field of affective markers in speech is still very much in the early stages of exploration. We still lack an adequate account of the paralinguistic conventions governing affective communication in spoken English – or in any other language. A number of scholars have made a start on this theoretically and methodologically very difficult area. One of the most comprehensive surveys is by Crystal (1969), who gives detailed coverage of paralinguistic dynamic settings involving pitch, loudness and rate. Others include Abercrombie (1968), Brown (1977), Crystal & Quirk (1964), Key (1975) and Scherer (1979). A satisfactory theory of paralinguistic communication is not likely to be available for some years, because of the complexity of the problem.

The experimental research that has been done in the area of paralinguistic communication has tended to focus less on the communication of affect, and more on markers of personality, particularly as conveyed by dynamic features. For example, Markel, Phillis, Vargas & Howard (1972) conducted an experiment where 104 male college students were rated both for personality factors and for loudness and rate of speaking. They identified four groups on the basis of these dynamic factors: 'loud-fast', 'loud-slow', 'soft-fast', and 'soft-slow'. In an analysis of variance they showed a significant difference between the four groups in personality traits. In experiments using synthetic speech, Brown, Strong & Rencher (1974) and Smith, Brown, Strong & Rencher (1975) showed that the attribution of 'competence' and 'benevolence' as personality factors was directly affected by manipulation of rate. Increased rate led to increased ratings of competence and decreased ratings of benevolence. Brown et al. (1974) also showed that ratings of competence and benevolence decreased with both decreased variance of pitch and increased mean pitch.

When attributions of personality are made on the basis of vocal settings, an interesting interaction is suggested between the personality feature concerned and the more ephemeral affective equivalent normally signalled by the use of that same setting in the paralinguistic code governing tone of voice. Since a harsh phonatory setting conventionally signals anger in the paralinguistic code of English, the habitual use of harshness can prompt listeners to conclude, linking anger and aggressiveness, that the speaker has an aggressive personality. A similar example would be the habitual use of a 'smiling' lip setting leading to judgements of a 'cheerful' personality. Further examples of personality markers in speech can be found in Scherer (this volume: ch. 5).

2.3. Features of phonetic realizations of linguistic units

We come now to the last entry in table 1, the short-term manipulation of vocal features for the signalling of linguistic units such as consonants and vowels, intonation, tone, rhythm, stress and length. The articulatory realizations of these units make up the phonetic basis of the speaker's accent. Accent is perhaps the outstanding example of a social marker in speech. It serves to indicate regional affiliation, and often social class as well. A number of linguistic concepts are available which can be directly helpful in the analysis of social markers in this area. The following comments on differences between accents are based partly on two very useful articles, by Wells (1970) and Abercrombie (1977). Discussion will be limited to a consideration of accent differences involving consonant and vowel phonemes.

There are four major ways in which the accents of two speakers may be different. The first two concern differences of phonological resources. The two accents can differ either in having different phonemic sound-systems, or in allowing different structural types of phonemic sequences. We can call the first type of difference a *systemic* difference, after Wells (1970: 232) and Abercrombie (1977: 22), and the second type a *structural* difference, after Abercrombie (1977: 21). A systemic difference between two accents is a matter of the number of word-differentiating distinctions that can be made by speakers of the two accents. One account might have a vowel system made up of ten different vowel phonemes, capable therefore of signalling ten word-differentiating distinctions by means of vowel quality alone. Another accent of the same language might have a vowel system made up of eleven different vowel phonemes, and speakers of that accent would thus be capable of making one more word-differentiating distinction by vowel quality alone than speakers of the first accent. A good example of systemic differences of this sort is offered by the accents of England and Scotland, where many differences exist between the vowel systems concerned. Scots accents often differ from English accents in allowing a smaller number of word-differentiating distinctions to be made. An example would be in the following situation: an English speaker of RP will differentiate *Sam* and *psalm* by using different vowel phonemes; many Scots speakers make no distinction between the two words, using the same vowel phoneme in both. Similarly, *tot* and *taut* are differentiated in RP but are indistinguishable in most Scots accents. *Pull* and *pool* would be another example. Conversely, the Scots consonant system allows more lexical distinctions to be made than that of RP. *Lock* and *loch* are pronounced identically in RP, with a final /k/, but in Scots accents, while *lock* is pronounced with a /k/, *loch* is pronounced with a final voiceless velar fricative consonant /x/.

A structural difference between two accents is a matter of the different rules governing the phonemic make-up of word shapes, in terms of the permissible sequences of phonemes. In some accents, /r/ is never pronounced before another consonant. In other accents, it is always pronounced in this position. The pronunciation of a word like *card* would have a different sequential structure in these accents. There are many examples of structural differences between accents involving /r/. All accents of Scotland, and all of the middle-west and west of the United States have the structural possibility of pronouncing an /r/ before a consonant or a pause; the accents of Australia, South Africa, many accents of England (including RP), and many accents of the east and south of the United States do not have this possibility (Abercrombie 1977: 22). Whether or not an accent is 'r-pronouncing' in this way thus marks regional affiliation, in a rather broad way.

There are other examples of structural differences between accents, involving other sounds than /r/, but generally structural differences are less varied than systemic differences. They are none the less perceptually striking when they do occur. Both systemic and structural differences are powerful markers of regional affiliation.

The third major type of difference between accents concerns the way in which otherwise systemically and structurally identical phonological resources are lexically distributed, by choosing different phonemes for the pronunciation of a given word. J. D. O'Connor has suggested the term *selectional* as a name for this kind of difference (Wells 1970: 244). Abercrombie gives the following example of a selectional difference (which, after Trubetzkoy, he calls a 'distributional' difference): 'two accents might have different vowel phonemes in *pat* and *past*, but one might have *photograph* with the *pat* vowel in the last syllable, while the other has the *past* vowel in the last syllable' (Abercrombie 1977: 22). A selectional difference involving the choice of different consonant phonemes is where two speakers both include /s/ and /z/ in their consonant systems, but where one pronounces the first *s* in *diagnosis* as /s/ (as speakers from England usually do) and the other pronounces it as /z/ (as speakers from Scotland often do).

The fourth major type of difference between accents is a phonetic matter, of how particular phonemes are actually pronounced. Both Wells (1970: 245) and Abercrombie (1977: 23) call this type a *realizational* difference. Thus two speakers may share the same vowel and consonant systems, have the same structural possibilities, choose the same lexical selection of phonemes, and yet have slightly different accents. The fine detail of how a given speaker pronounces his sounds can act as a marker of group membership, but it can also function as an individuating marker, distinguishing him from fellow members of his sociolinguistic group as we noted earlier. Realizational details can also be very influential as social markers allowing the attribution of gradations of particular social characteristics. As Wells states, 'Accent is still significantly linked to social class in England, and often constitutes an important index of class affiliation' (1970: 248). Because vowel quality is a continuum, small differences of vowel quality can be used, in England at least, as markers of small gradations of social class (cf. Giles, Scherer & Taylor, this volume: ch. 9, 3.2).

These comments about accent differences between speakers make the assumption that a speaker's accent is fixed and unchanging. It seldom is, of course, and a further area where linguistic concepts can help us to refine our analysis of social markers in speech concerns certain aspects of the notion of *linguistic variability*.

Work in the field of sociolinguistics has shown that social groups may differ not simply in terms of their phonological systems or what pronunciations they use but in *how often* they use certain pronunciations. In the pioneering work in this field, Labov (1966a) demonstrated that in New York City speech the pronunciation of /r/ in words such as *farm* (where the *r* occurs before another consonant) and *far* (where it occurs word-finally) is a *linguistic variable*. While very few New York City speakers actually pronounce the /r/ in these positions on every occasion, most pronounce it on some occasions. (In many other parts of the United States, of course, as mentioned earlier, the /r/ in *farm* is always pronounced, while in British RP it is never pronounced. In these varieties, then, /r/ is not a linguistic variable.) In New York City the frequency with which /r/ in *far*, *farm*, etc. is pronounced correlates very clearly with the age and social class of the speaker, and with the social context in which he is speaking. The methodology employed in this and other subsequent studies involved carrying out tape-recorded interviews with a random sample of informants and subjecting these recordings to analysis. In the New York City study, counts of how many /r/s were actually pronounced, and of how many could have been but were not, showed that middle-class speakers, on average, pronounced a higher percentage of /r/s than working-class speakers, that younger speakers had a higher percentage than older speakers, and that formal styles of speech produced more /r/s than informal styles. Interestingly enough, studies of English towns where /r/ is also a variable, such as Reading, show exactly the reverse pattern (see Trudgill 1975) – a good illustration of the arbitrary nature of linguistic markers of social categories.

This sort of technique can be applied to a large number of variable features of pronunciation in very many linguistic varieties. Obvious examples from British English would include the percentages of /h/s that are 'dropped', i.e. not present in words such as *hammer, house* for different groups of speakers; and the percentage of *t*s in words such as *butter, better* that are pronounced as glottal stops. Table 2 gives figures (from Trudgill 1974) for the percentage of *-ing* suffixes in words like *jumping, running* which were in fact pronounced as *-in'*, from tape-recordings of 60 speakers in Norwich. The correlation with social class and formality is clear.

Table 2. –in' suffixes (%) in Norwich (after Trudgill 1974)

	Formal speech	Casual speech
Middle class	3	28
Lower middle class	15	42
Upper working class	74	87
Middle working class	88	95
Lower working class	98	100

It is important to note that in all such cases correlations of this type apply to *averaged* scores for *groups* of speakers, and do not of course mean that any given individual will necessarily score at the same sort of level as those who have objectively the same social status characteristics. Indeed, it is clear that many other factors such as social mobility (Labov 1966b) and strength of social ambition (Douglas-Cowie 1978) can lead to differential behaviour. However, it is equally clear that individual speakers are not 'sociolinguistic automata' (Giles 1977), and there is much room for idiosyncratic and random variation. The correlations, nevertheless, are sufficiently strong that, other things being equal, speakers who use a high percentage of -*ing* (rather than -*in'*) suffixes will be perceived as middle class unless or until there is stronger evidence to the contrary, and that '*h*-dropping' and glottal stop realizations of *t*s are stereotyped as working-class characteristics. It is also interesting to note that, while speakers and groups of speakers often differ merely in terms of percentages and proportions, and we are thus in many cases presented with linguistic continua, it is often the case, it seems, that listeners *perceive* differences dichotomously (cf. Giles, Scherer & Taylor, this volume. ch. 9, 3.2). It may well be the case that there are thresholds such that speakers are heard as 'dropping their *h*s' only if they drop x per cent (rather than x−1 per cent) of all possible *h*s.

A relatively more recent and more refined type of analysis – and one that is more interesting to the theoretical linguist – has shown that the probability of occurrence of particular variants of a variable (e.g. /r/ or zero; [t] or glottal stop) may also be determined by *linguistic* context. For example, the occurrence of /r/, in those accents where it constitutes a linguistic variable, may be more likely after some vowels than after others. In the English of Reading, for example, /r/ is more likely in *bird, fur* than in *beard, beer*, and more likely here than in *far, farm*.

This finding is of relevance here, because it appears that the influence of different linguistic contexts may be relatively more or less important for different social groups. For instance, in most varieties of English, consonant clusters of the type /pt/, /kt/, /st/, as in *apt, act, mast*, are simplified, in certain circumstances, by the omission of the *t*. Most people, for example, will normally say *mos' people* rather than *most people*. The linguistic context in which the *t* appears, however, is very important in determining the probability of its omission. In some varieties of American Black English, where consonant cluster simplification of this type is more frequent than in many other English varieties, it has been demonstrated that, on average, simplification is (a) more likely before a following consonant, as in *past five, passed five*, than before a following vowel, as in *past eleven, passed eleven*, and (b) more likely where the *t* is not a marker of the past tense – *past five, past eleven* – than where it is – *passed five, passed eleven* (-*ed* is of course pronounced as [t] in these cases). However, closer examination of the relative importance of the two factors shows that, while for adults the grammatical constraint (past tense vs. nonpast tense) is the stronger of the two, for adolescents it is the phonological constraint (following vowel or consonant) which is the more powerful. This is illustrated in table 3. This also raises the interesting question, however, as to how far these social differences in language can legitimately be described as social *markers*. As we have seen, linguists were until recently not aware of these differences, and awareness came only as the result of detailed analyses. Speakers and hearers are certainly not consciously aware of them, and if, therefore, they do function in some way as social markers, it must be at a very low level of consciousness.

Table 3. Consonant cluster simplification in New York City Black English (after Labov 1972)

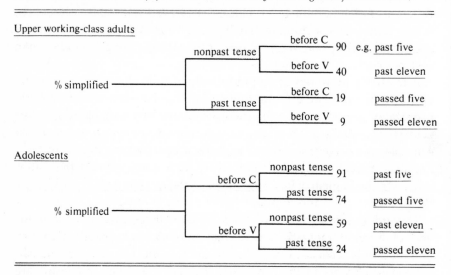

3. Grammatical aspects of markers

Linguistic variability is not confined to phonological phenomena. Grammatical features are also variable in many varieties, and can be subject to the same kind of analysis as phonological variability. In most areas of the English-speaking world, for example, use of multiple negation (*I don't want none* vs. *I don't want any*) correlates very closely with social class background, as does use of most other nonstandard grammatical forms. Again, moreover, we most often find that we are dealing with a social dialect continuum, with groups of speakers differing in terms of proportions of forms used rather than absolutely. However, unlike phonological variables, for which speakers most often are ranged along the continuum in such a way that more speakers are found in central ranges rather than at the ends, grammatical variables tend to stratify speakers more sharply with most speakers appearing at the 'top' or 'bottom'. Grammatical variables are also more difficult to investigate in that they occur less frequently than phonological variables in any given stretch of speech. They are also, like phonological variables, liable to be subject to linguistic constraints which may vary from social group to social group. In the nonstandard English of the town of Reading, for instance, present-tense verb forms variably add -s in persons other than the third-person singular, and the percentage of nonstandard ss that occur again correlates clearly with social-class membership and social context. For adolescent speakers, however, there is a constraint such that this nonstandard -s may not occur on the main verb if there is a following complement clause containing a finite verb (Cheshire 1978). That is, we find *I likes it* and *I wants to do it*, but not *I knows that it's true*. Older speakers do not have this particular constraint.

Sociolinguistic research on linguistic variation thus encourages us to be more sophisticated in a number of ways in our analysis of social markers in speech. It suggests, first of all, that linguistic differences are very often a matter of probabilities and tendencies: high percentages of *r* pronounced in New York City do not mean that a speaker is upper middle class but that he probably is. This also means that we have to be reasonably careful in our usage of labels for linguistic varieties. We can refer to 'Cockney' as if this label referred to a discrete linguistic variety, but we must be aware that this is not the case. We can also use terms such as 'Bristol accent', but here again we must be aware that it is a term which permits degrees of more or less (and linguistic analysis can of course help us to quantify exactly how 'Bristol' a particular variety is and give us some insights into what features of a Bristol accent listeners may and may not be reacting to in evaluating speakers in real life or experimental situations). Sociolinguistic research also indicates, as mentioned above, that while linguistic variation is often continuous, perception of it is often dichotomous: listeners may thus not be sufficiently consciously aware of linguistic differences to be able to report on them.

The differential realization of grammatical categories (e.g. /s/ vs. zero for present tense) may, we have seen, correlate with social categories. It has also been suggested, however, that social groups and individuals may also differ in their *usage* of different grammatical categories and constructions. Some workers have counted different parts of speech in texts and indicated that some speakers use a 'nominal style' (high proportion of nouns) while others use a 'verbal style' (high proportion of verbs) (cf. Brown & Fraser, this volume: ch. 2, 2.3). Bernstein's early work, too, produced counts of features such as adverbs, pronouns, passive verbs and subordinate clauses, and showed that use varied with social class membership (see Bernstein 1971; Robinson, this volume: ch. 6, 3.2). It is possible, although not certain, that more refined grammatical analyses than these would throw up more detailed grammatical markers of social features. It is possible that it is differential use of certain types of verb form, clause structures and so on that may lead listeners to characterize certain types of speech style as 'impressive', 'boring', 'tentative', 'blunt', etc. It might therefore be profitable to construct 'syntactic profiles' for speakers approximately after the manner in which language pathologists construct profiles for subjects who suffer from some form of syntactic disability. Crystal, Fletcher & Garman (1976) develop a methodology for carrying out work of this type involving the enumeration and measurement of sentence length, clause structures, etc., including details down to the level, for example, of how many phrases had the structure Determiner + Noun, Adjective + Noun, and so on; see also Crystal and Fletcher (in press).

4. Markers in discourse and conversational interaction

Work in the study of discourse and conversation also leads to a possibility similar to the one discussed immediately above. A project currently being led by Bent Preisler of the English Department of the University of Aarhus in Denmark seeks to investigate the linguistic correlates of Bales' (1970) communicative act categories by exploring the relationship between the role adopted by a speaker in a conversation and the characteristics of his speech in that conversation. For example, if a speaker taking part in a conversation makes relatively few suggestions, are those suggestions expressed differently (for example, more 'carefully') than those made by a speaker who makes many suggestions? And what exactly are the linguistic correlates of 'carefully'? Preliminary work has already produced some interesting results. Analyses of English conversations among groups of four people have shown that those speech acts which are categorizable, after Bales, as 'Gives Suggestion' constitute 8.1 per cent of the total number of speech acts for the male speakers but 2.8 per cent of the total for women. Even more interesting is the linguistic breakdown of the way in which these speech acts were performed. Table 4 shows that, when 'giving suggestions', men do so by means of imperative constructions more often and by means of interrogatives less often than women. The percentage of statements made is similar for the two groups, but further analysis indicates that 33.3 per cent of all statements functioning as 'giving suggestions' were accompanied by tag-questions in the case of the women, whereas this was true of only 3.7 per cent of cases for the men. These, it must be stressed, are preliminary findings only and can be no more than suggestive. They do suggest, however, that if there are sex-linked differences of this type in linguistic behaviour, then role is probably the primary factor at work here and that sex differences appear only because sex and role selection appear to be linked (cf. Smith, this volume: ch. 4, 1).

Table 4. Grammatical forms of speech acts 'Gives Suggestion' (after Preisler)

Speakers	Male	Female
% sentence type		
Interrogative	14.8	25.0
Statement	77.8	75.0
Imperative	3.7	0.0

Other work in conversational analysis (for a survey, see Coulthard 1977) demonstrates that conversation is a structured and rule-governed activity. There are norms and conventions for features of conversation such as turn-taking, silences, interruptions, speaker-selection, and topic-changing. It has also been shown that these norms and conventions may vary from culture to culture (see Bauman & Sherzer 1975). (In some cultures, for example, it is apparently possible for more than one speaker to speak at once for extended periods.) This opens up the possibility that variation may also occur from community to community and group to group, and that there may be reasonably rigorous methods for studying this. Since rules of this type are clearly also less firm, in some ways, than, say, syntactic rules, there is also the likelihood that they may be broken, and that the frequency and manner of their being broken may be socially significant.

5. Lexical aspects of markers

Finally, we can note that one of the most obvious areas where speech can act as a social marker is in the area of vocabulary. This, however, is probably one of the hardest and least profitable to study, and one where linguistic concepts and techniques have relatively little to offer. The

difficulty is that particular lexical items occur, generally speaking, relatively infrequently, and that they are also liable to conscious suppression
on the part of the speaker. Their function as social markers, nevertheless,
is undeniable. The bulk of the vocabulary of any language is shared by all
its speakers, but there are also usually certain sets of lexical items which
are restricted to, or more probable in, the speech of certain groups. This
may be a reflection of the qualifications, interests, experience or occupation of speakers: technical vocabulary, for instance, will normally be
confined to groups who specialize in the topic concerned. Very often,
though, group-typical vocabulary is social rather than, or as well as,
technical in function. Minority groups such as homosexuals, drug addicts
and criminals are well-known to have developed specialized vocabularies
which both reflect their particular interests and reinforce group solidarity,
as well as excluding outsiders who are not familiar with the words
involved (cf. Brown & Fraser, this volume: ch. 2, 2.4). And that area of
colloquial – and often fashionable and temporary – vocabulary known as
slang is also a very powerful social marker – particularly, it seems, of age.
Many speakers appear to keep abreast of changing patterns in slang
vocabulary for so long and then stop, so that usage of 'outdated' slang
words labels them as of a certain age. Stereotypes are also significant in
vocabulary use. Certain words, for example, are felt to be more common
in the speech of women than in the speech of men: *divine, sweet, adorable,
maddening*, might qualify for this category. We have, however, no empirical evidence to confirm that this is in fact the case, and it is clear that if
they are typical of women's speech, then they are typical only of certain
sorts of women. Probably more reliable are claims that women in many
societies use taboo words and swear generally less than men (see Thorne
& Henley 1975; Smith, this volume: ch. 4, 1.3).

6. Markers and the attribution process

A number of interesting questions arise from the discussion above of
phonetic and linguistic markers in speech, about the listener's process of
attribution.

It is possible to draw a distinction between *actual markers* and *apparent
markers*. Actual markers accurately indicate a true characteristic of the
speaker. Apparent markers fall into two classes: *misleading markers*, which
are deliberately projected by a speaker in order to lay claim to characteristics of identity which are not actually his; and *misinterpreted markers*,
which are mistakenly interpreted by the listener as signalling a particular

characteristic of the speaker when in fact the speaker is not actually thus characterizable.

An example of a misleading marker would be the consciously manipulated accent of a socially aspiring speaker. Using the terms 'informative' and 'communicative' as defined at the beginning of this chapter, we can say that the speaker in this situation manages to mislead the listener, if he is successful in his deception, by taking over communicative control of a factor normally understood by the listener to be of informative value only.

An example of a misinterpreted marker is illustrated by the following situation: a speaker with acute laryngitis has an extremely whispery voice; whispery voice is a type of phonation used paralinguistically in English as a conventional signal of a conspiratorially confidential interaction; the listener, in answering the speaker, himself adopts what he takes to be a situationally appropriate whispery voice, joining in the confidentiality he mistakenly believes the speaker initiated. Here the listener misinterprets the actual, symptomatic marker of the speaker's medical state as an apparent marker of the speaker's affective state. An actual physical marker has been misinterpreted as a psychological marker. In this case, the listener has mistakenly interpreted information that was in fact solely informative as if it were deliberately communicative.

The topic of misleading markers would be an interesting field of research. The concept of misinterpreted markers, or of misattribution, brings us closer to the heart of the attribution process, however. Two general research strategies are possible, in examining misattribution. One could explore the relations between the types of markers involved in cases of mistaken attribution. Or one could investigate discrepancies between listeners, which would give insight into the individual's process of attribution.

Beginning with the first possibility, we can ask whether mistaken attribution characteristically involves a mistake between major categories of markers, or more typically a mistake of degree within a marking category.

Certainly some categorial mistakes are made in the attribution process, as in the laryngitis example. It would be interesting to explore the question of whether intercategory mistakes between any two categories, say psychological and physical, or psychological and social, are equally common in both directions, or whether misattribution is usually biased in favour of a particular category. As a hypothesis, we might suggest that categorial mistakes tend to lead to psychological conclusions being drawn from physical and social evidence, more often than vice versa. For example, the fact that a given speaker has a long vocal tract, and that he speaks with a prestigious accent, might persuade a listener to attribute to him an authority that was in fact quite spurious. Such a hypothesis would imply that listeners sometimes use wider ranges of evidence to support conclusions about personality than is strictly legitimate.

It may be, more probably, that misattribution more often involves a misinterpretation of degree within a marking category. We saw earlier, in the case of linguistic variability, where percentage of use of a given linguistic form constituted a social marker, that listeners' perception of a continuum of this sort tended to be dichotomous. Such a phenomenon is one basis for the stereotyping process in attribution.

In considering the second avenue of research into misattribution, that of discrepancies between individual listeners, one obvious research area is the extent to which the judge's own personal physical, psychological or social characteristics lead him to minimize or maximize attributions on the particular marking parameter concerned.

Being a listener to speech is not unlike being a detective. The listener not only has to establish what it was that was said, but also has to construct, from an assortment of clues, the affective state of the speaker and a profile of his identity. Fortunately, the listener's task is made a little easier by the fact that the vocal clues marking the individual physical, psychological and social characteristics of the speaker are numerous. This chapter has attempted to show how phonetic and linguistic theory can help us to refine the analysis of markers of these characteristics in speech, by providing descriptions of the extralinguistic, paralinguistic and linguistic factors concerned.

References

Abercrombie, D. 1967. *Elements of General Phonetics*. Edinburgh.
    1968. Paralanguage. *British Journal of Disorders of Communication*, 3, 55–9.
    1977. The accents of Standard English in Scotland. *University of Edinburgh Department of Linguistics Work in Progress*, 10, 21–32.
Alpert, M. & Kurtzberg, R. L. 1963. Comparison of the spectra of the voices of twins. *Paper B9, 66th Meeting of Acoustical Society of America*.
Amado, J. M. 1953. Tableau général des problèmes posés pour l'action des hormones sur le développement du larynx, le classement d'une voix, la génèse des activités rythmogènes encéphaliques et l'excitabilité du sphincter laryngien. *Annales d'Otolaryngologie* (Paris), 70, 117–37.
Bales, B. F. 1970. *Personality and Interpersonal Behaviour*. London.
Bauman, R. & Sherzer, J. 1975. *Explorations in the Ethnography of Speaking*. Cambridge.
Bernstein, B. 1971. *Class, Codes and Control*, vol. I. London.

Bonaventura, M. 1935. Ausdruck der Persönlichkeit in der Sprechstimme und in Photogramm. *Archiv für die gesamte Psychologie, 94,* 501–70.

Braus, H. 1924. *Anatomie des Menschen.* Berlin.

Brown, B. L., Strong, W. J. & Rencher, A. C. 1974. Fifty four voices from two: the effects of simultaneous manipulations of rate, mean fundamental frequency, and variance of fundamental frequency on ratings of personality from speech. *Journal of the Acoustical Society of America, 55,* 313–18.

Brown, G. 1977. *Listening to Spoken English.* London.

Canter, G. J. 1963. Speech characteristics of patients with Parkinson's disease 1. Intensity, pitch and duration. *Journal of Speech and Hearing Disorders, 28,* 221–9.

Cheshire, J. 1978. Present tense verbs in Reading English. In P. Trudgill (ed.) *Sociolinguistic Patterns in British English.* London.

Coulthard, M. 1977. *An Introduction to Discourse Analysis.* London.

Crystal, D. 1969. *Prosodic Systems and Intonation in English.* Cambridge.

Crystal, D. & Fletcher, P. In press. Profile analysis of language disability. In C. Fillmore & W. Wang (eds.) *Individual Differences in Language Ability.* London.

Crystal, D. & Quirk, R. 1964. *Systems of Prosodic and Paralinguistic Features in English.* The Hague.

Crystal, D., Fletcher, P. & Garman, M. 1976. *The Grammatical Analysis of Linguistic Disability.* London.

Devine, K. D. 1960. Pathologic effects of smoking in the larynx and oral cavity. *Proceedings of Staff Meetings of the Mayo Clinic, 35,* 349–52.

Dordain, M., Chevrie-Muller, C. & Grémy, F. 1967. Etude clinique et instrumentale de la voix et de la parole des femmes agées. *Revue française de gerontologie, 13,* 163–70.

Douglas-Cowie, E. 1978. Linguistic code-switching in a Northern Irish village: social interaction and social ambition. In P. Trudgill (ed.) *Sociolinguistic Patterns in British English.* London.

Eco, U. 1976. *A Theory of Semiotics.* Bloomington, Ind.

Esling, J. K. 1978. Voice quality in Edinburgh: a sociolinguistic and phonetic study. PhD dissertation, University of Edinburgh.

Fant, G. 1953. Discussion of paper read by G. E. Peterson at the 1952 Symposium on the Application of Communication Theory. In W. Jackson (ed.) *Communication Theory.* London.

1960. *Acoustic Theory of Speech Production.* The Hague.

1966. A note on vocal tract size factors and non-uniform F-pattern scalings. *STL–QPSR, 4,* 22–30. Royal Institute of Technology, Stockholm.

Fay, P. J. & Middleton, W. C. 1940a. Judgement of Kretschmerian body types from the voice as transmitted over a public address system. *Journal of Social Psychology, 12,* 151–62.

1940b. The ability to judge the rested or tired condition of a speaker from his voice as transmitted over a public address system. *Journal of General Psychology, 24,* 211–15.

Feibleman, J. K. 1946. *An Introduction to Peirce's Philosophy.* New York.

Ferreri, G. 1959. Senescence of the larynx. *Ital. Gen. Rev. Oto-rhinolaryng., 1,* 640–709.

Fyfe, F. W. & Naylor, E. 1958. Calcification and ossification in the cricoid cartilage of the larynx with annotation on the mechanism of change of pitch. *Proceedings of the Canadian Otolaryngological Society*, pp. 67–9.

Giles, H. 1977. Social psychology and applied linguistics: towards an integrative approach. *ITL: Review of Applied Linguistics*, 33, 27–42.

Greene, M. C. L. 1964. *The Voice and its Disorders*. London.

Hardcastle, W. 1976. *Physiology of Speech Production*. New York.

Hartshorne, C. & Weiss, P. 1931–5. *C. S. Peirce: collected papers*. Cambridge, Mass.

Heffner, R.-M. S. 1950. *General Phonetics*. Madison.

Hildernisse, L. W. 1956. Voice diagnosis. *Acta Physiologia et Pharmacologica Neerlandica*, 5, 73ff.

Hollien, H. & Shipp, F. T. 1972. Speaking fundamental frequency and chronological age in males. *Journal of Speech and Hearing Research*, 15, 155–9.

Hollien, H., Dew, D. & Philips. P. 1971. Phonational frequency ranges of adults. *Journal of Speech and Hearing Research*, 14, 755–60.

Honikman, B. 1964. Articulatory settings. In D. Abercrombie *et al.* (eds.) *In Honour of Daniel Jones*. London.

Howie, T. O., Ladefoged, P. & Stark, R. E. 1961. Congenital sub-glottic bars found in 3 generations of one family. *Folia Phoniatrica*, 13, 56–61.

Jaffe, B. F. & de Blanc, G. B. 1970. Cleft palate, cleft lip, and cleft uvula in Navaho Indians: incidence and otorhinolaryngologic problems. *Cleft Palate Journal*, 7, 300–5.

Kaplan, H. M. 1960. *Anatomy and Physiology of Speech*. New York.

Key, M. R. 1975. *Paralanguage and Kinesics*. Metuchen, NJ.

Kiml, J. 1962. Trouble de la voix dans le sillon des cordes vocales. *Folia Phoniatrica*, 14, 272–9.

Kretschmer, E. 1925. *Physique and Character*. New York.

Labov, W. 1966a. *The Social Stratification of English in New York City*. Washington, DC.
  1966b. The effect of social mobility on linguistic behaviour. In S. Lieberson (ed.) *Explorations in Sociolinguistics*. The Hague.
  1972. *Sociolinguistic Patterns*. Oxford.

Ladefoged, P. 1962. *Elements of Acoustic Phonetics*. Chicago.
  1971. *Preliminaries to Linguistic Phonetics*. Chicago.
  1976. *A Course in Phonetics*. New York.

Lass, N. J., Beverly, A. S., Nicosia, D. K. & Simpson, L. A. 1978. An investigation of speaker height and weight identification by means of direct estimation. *Journal of Phonetics*, 6, 69–76.

Laver, J. 1968. Voice quality and indexical information. *British Journal of Disorders of Communication*, 3, 43–54.
  1975. Individual Features in Voice Quality. PhD dissertation, University of Edinburgh.
  1978. The concept of articulatory settings: an historical survey. *Historiographia Linguistica*, 5, 1–14.

Lawson, W. A. & Bond, E. K. 1968. Speech and its relation to dentistry II. The influence of oral structures on speech. *The Dental Practitioner*, 19, 113–18.
  1969. Speech and its relation to dentistry III. The effects on speech of variations in the designs of dentures. *The Dental Practitioner*, 19, 150–6.

Lowry, R. B. 1970. Sex-linked cleft palate in British Columbia Indian family. *Pediatrics*, 46, 123–8.

Luchsinger, R. & Arnold, G. E. 1965. *Voice–Speech–Language*. London.

Lyons, J. 1977. *Semantics*. 2 vols. Cambridge.

Markel, N. N., Phillis, J. A., Vargas, R. & Howard, K. 1972. Personality traits associated with voice types. *Journal of Psycholinguistic Research*, *1*, 249–55.

McCallum, J. R. 1954. Chronic laryngitis. *Speech*, *18*, 48–50.

Meader, C. L. & Muyskens, J. H. 1962. *Handbook of Biolinguistics*. Toledo, Ohio.

Morris, C. W. 1946. *Signs, Language and Behavior*. New York.

Moses, P. J. 1940. Is medical phonetics an essential part of otorhinolaryngology? *Archives of Otolaryngology* (Chicago), *31*, 444–51.

1941. Theories regarding the relation of constitution and character through the voice. *Psychological Bulletin*, *38*, 746.

Myerson, M. C. 1950. Smoker's Larynx – a clinical pathological entity? *Annals of Otology, Rhinology and Laryngology*, *59*, 541–6.

Mysak, E. D. 1959. Pitch and duration characteristics of older males. *Journal of Speech and Hearing Research*, *2*, 46–54.

O'Connor, J. D. 1973. *Phonetics*. Harmondsworth, Middx.

Palmer, J. M. 1956. Hoarseness in laryngeal pathology: a review of the literature. *Laryngoscope*, *66*, 500–16.

Perelló, J. 1962. La disfonia premenstrual. *Acta Oto-Rino-Larnygologica Ibero-Americana*, *23*, 561–3.

Peterson, G. E. & Barney, H. L. 1952. Control methods used in a study of vowels. *Journal of the Acoustical Society of America*, *24*, 175–84.

Pike, K. L. 1943. *Phonetics*. Ann Arbor, Mich.

Ptacek, P. H., Sander, E. K., Maloney, W. H. & Roe Jackson, C. C. 1966. Phonatory and related changes with advanced age. *Journal of Speech and Hearing Research*, *9*, 353–60.

Punt, N. A. 1959. Alteration in the voice. *The Medical Press*, 18 March, pp. 235–8.

Scherer, K. R. 1979. Non-linguistic vocal indicators of emotion and psychopathology. In C. E. Izard (ed.) *Emotions in Personality and Psychopathology*. New York.

Shipp, F. T. & Hollien, H. (1969). Perception of the aging male voice. *Journal of Speech and Hearing Research*, *12*, 703–10.

Smith, B. L., Brown, B. L., Strong, W. J. & Rencher, A. C. 1975. Effects of speech rate on personality perception. *Language and Speech*, *18*, 145–52.

Sonninen, A. 1960. Laryngeal signs and symptoms of goitre. *Folia Phoniatrica*, *12*, 41–7.

Tarneaud, J. 1941. *Traité pratique de phonologie et de phoniatrie, la voix – la parole – le chant*. Paris.

Terracol, J. & Azémar, R. 1949. *La senescence de la voix*. Paris.

Thorne, B. & Henley, N. (eds.) 1975. *Language and Sex: difference and dominance*. Rowley, Mass.

Trudgill, P. 1974. *The Social Differentiation of English in Norwich*. Cambridge.

1975. Sex, covert prestige, and linguistic change in the urban British English of Norwich. In B. Thorne & N. Henley (eds.) *Language and Sex: difference and dominance*. Rowley, Mass.

(ed.) 1978. *Sociolinguistic Patterns in British English*. London.

Vuorenkoski, V., Tjernlund, P. & Perheentupa, J. 1972. Auditory perception of voice qualities and speaking fundamental frequency in Mulibreynanism and in some other children with growth failure, *STL–QPSR*, 2–3, 64–74. Royal Institute of Technology, Stockholm.

Weinberg, B. & Zlatin, M. 1970. Speaking fundamental frequency characteristics of five- and six-year-old children with mongolism. *Journal of Speech and Hearing Research*, 13, 418–25.

Wells, J. C. 1970. Local accents in England and Wales. *Journal of Linguistics*, 6, 231–52.

2. Speech as a marker of situation[1]

PENELOPE BROWN and COLIN FRASER

A review of relations between speech markers and situations runs the danger of becoming a twenty-page summary of most of sociolinguistics. We trust, however, that though necessarily partial and superficial, such a broad review will act as a backdrop to other more specific contributions to this volume, in at least two ways. First, most of the other chapters deal primarily with speech variations associated with the nature of the participants in interaction, and our review should help to indicate what other sources of variation are being ignored and what confusions may result. Second, by pointing to the interrelations of different facets of the total situation and the frequent existence of multiple determinants of speech variations, we may be able to suggest hypotheses about possible determinants which will be alternatives to the emphases on participants *per se* which other contributors favour.

First, we shall propose a framework for analysing situations and discuss our view of the nature of markers. Then we shall briefly review more specific concepts and empirical evidence, ending with a discussion of relations between markers of participants and markers of other features of situations, and the possibility of resolving ambiguities between them by means of further work at both individual and social-structural levels of analysis.

1. Situations and markers

1.1. Situations

Although, as Goffman (1964) pointed out, the systematic analysis of 'situation' has been notoriously neglected by social scientists, it has come

[1] Preparation of this chapter was supported by SSRC Grant HR 3608. The authors are indebted to Stephen Levinson for numerous helpful comments and clarifications, and to Howard Giles and Klaus Scherer for their constructive suggestions.

to be invoked more and more in recent years, and by now many people interested in social aspects of language appear to have something like a shared view of what characteristics can be used to define a situation, even though there is no clear picture of how these identifiable bits and pieces really hang together.

The basic notion of situation as the context within which interaction or 'the speech event' occurs, has several components which can be distinguished. Everyone, we think, would invoke the notion of 'setting'. Thus, interaction in a bedroom as opposed to a church as opposed to a football stadium would be described as involving three different situations. Furthermore, differences in participants and their relationships, for example, bishops or barmen, clergymen or children, friends or strangers, would be sufficient to characterize differences in situations. And a third concept, or set of concepts, also seems common. This is what various writers call purposes, ends, or goals, which in turn are closely tied to notions of task and even of topic.

These three concepts – setting, participants, purpose – more than encompass Fishman's (1972) assertion that 'a situation is defined by the cooccurrence of two (or more) interlocutors related to each other in a particular way, communicating about a particular topic, in a particular setting' (48). And, as Fraser (1978) has noted, the first three major categories of Hymes' (1972) SPEAKING mnemonic are setting, participants, and ends. Unlike his other categories which are much more concerned with the nature of the message in communication, these three clearly deal with the situation, and 'ends' doubtless would have been 'purposes' if 'speaking' were spelled with two *p*s.

For us, purpose is the motor which sets the chassis of setting and participants going, and purpose is interlinked with the other two categories in very intricate ways. In particular, we find it necessary to consider at some length the intersection of setting and purpose in order to deal with a wide range of linguistic markers related to levels of formality. This amalgam of setting and purpose might have been dubbed 'context' had that not been such an imprecise and overused term. We shall call it 'scene'. Thus, situation involves scene (or context) plus participants. In addition, we make use of finer distinctions within our major categories. Figure 1 sets out all of our terms, and we hope this sketch of a taxonomy will help guide the reader through our review of markers of situation, as well as assist in relating discussions in other chapters to one general scheme.

But before that we must consider the nature of social markers in speech (cf. Giles, Scherer & Taylor, this volume: ch. 9, 3).

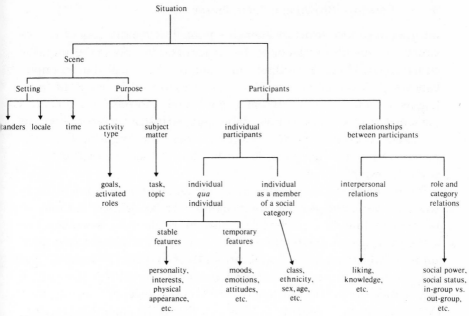

Figure 1. Components of situation

1.2. Social markers

The simplest definition of a marker would treat it as a member of an ordered pair <A,C>, where a (a member of A) is any definable feature of linguistic form and c (a member of C) is any definable aspect of social context. The a could be any phonological, syntactic, or lexical item whose presence correlates with some social category c, including those described above as components of the situation. A simple example of a marker in this sense would be an address term such as Dr, the use of which marks a particular speaker–addressee relationship.

By broadening the definition we can include in A paralinguistic, kinesic, or any other features of utterances produced in interaction. And we can treat the absence of a linguistic item (null elements) or the absence of any linguistic items (silence) as markers too. Thus, in languages with T/V pronoun systems (Brown & Gilman 1960; Brown 1965), the avoidance of a T or a V pronoun may be a marker of a particular state of change in the definition of the speaker–addressee relationship (Levinson 1977).

From the point of view of people, like Labov, who have worked empirically with social markers in speech, this definition of 'marker' requires amplification. In practice, the first member of the pair is restricted not to a category of surface structure elements alone, but to a category of surface structure elements in relation to their place of occurrence in the linguistic structure (cf. Laver & Trudgill, this volume: ch. 1, 2.3). For example, Labov's (1972a) well-known New York variable /r/ is restricted in its linguistic context; only postvocalic, word-final, and preconsonantal /r/s are sensitive to social categories of speakers. So instead of an ordered pair we need an ordered triple <A,B,C>, where the linguistic form *a* is matched up with a particular linguistic context *b* and correlated with a social context *c*.

But we must expand the definition yet again if we are not to exclude some relevant phenomena, for markers may be defined not only in relation to linguistic context but also in relation to meaning. The archetypal case of this is in fact T/V pronouns, for it is not any old V pronoun which marks the social categories of 'respect' or 'distance'; it is only Vs used to denote a singular referent (cf. Comrie 1975). Similarly, if one wanted to count lexical items as markers of register or formality, then *discipline* meaning 'academic field' is a marker of the academese register, but meaning 'stern child-rearing practices' it is not. And *bad* meaning 'good' can be a marker in Black English Vernacular of speaker–addressee relationship; *bad* meaning 'bad' is not (Halliday 1976). The point is, then, that surface form alone is not necessarily interestingly correlated with social categories; it is surface form in relation to a particular meaning that provides the relevant distribution.

We still need one further expansion. 'Can you play the piano? used as a request is more polite than 'Play the piano', but used as a question does not carry this implication about the speaker–hearer relation. To handle this, let us allow that some aspects of surface structure can be systematically aligned with social categories only when correlated with particular functions. Indirect speech acts or performative hedges as markers of politeness would be such pragmatically constrained markers; *sure* functioning as 'OK', as in 'Sure, I'll do it' (but not *sure* in 'John is sure to come'), might be a marker of certain kinds of speaker–addressee relationship, and *you know* in certain conversational functions might be a marker of a particular kind of speaking activity, chat (Goldberg 1976).

In sum, we can define a marker, *a priori*, in terms of relations amongst three kinds of categories (each of which contains subcategories). Specifically, we will understand a social marker to denote a relationship between A and C relative to B:

A	B	C
linguistic form	*internal context*	*external context*
phonological	phonological	social categories:
syntactic	environment	speaker
lexical	meaning	addressee
paralinguistic	function	setting
kinesic		purposes
etc.		etc.

But how do we actually identify markers in speech? When we attempt
to apply the concept empirically, certain difficulties arise. One is that the
relations between A and C may be either invariant or probabilistic (cf.
Giles, Scherer & Taylor, this volume: ch. 9, 3.2). An invariant marker
would be one where the presence of the linguistic item *a* is perfectly
correlated with the presence of the social context; an example would be a
language, such as Japanese, where speakers use different pronouns for
'I', depending on the sex of the speaker. Perhaps the majority of markers,
however, are probabilistic, that is, the probability of their occurrence
increases (or decreases) with the presence of the social category. In
addition, the influence of linguistic context can be invariant or probabilistic. Of course it may be the case that sometimes it appears to be probabilistic because the investigator has not isolated all the features of internal
contexts (*b*) which restrict the correlation of *a* and *c*. It is possible that
Labovian variable rules (Labov 1972a, b) in many cases would be less
variable if *a* were considered in relation to meaning and function and not
just to surface linguistic context. At the same time, it must be admitted
that the more one includes meaning and function in B, the more tricky it
becomes to quantify, to count up instances of a particular marker and
correlate it with *c*, and the more likely one is to consider it probabilistic.

A second major difficulty with markers resides in their tendency to
ambiguity regarding which aspect of a social context is being marked.
Perhaps the sociolinguist's dream (and the poet's nightmare) is a world
where each marker unambiguously correlates with a different aspect of
context; Marker 1 marks speaker's class, Marker 2 speaker's familiarity
with the addressee, Marker 3 a church setting, Marker 4 the presence of a
friendly bystander, and so on. But in reality a given marker is usually
multiply ambiguous, and even if strongly linked to one social variable will
be less strongly linked to others. Indeed, Labov's rather different definition of marker (1972a: 237) relies on this ambiguity; he restricts the term to
'more highly developed sociolinguistic variables' showing both social and
stylistic differentiation. So his markers, e.g. percentage of pronounced /r/
in New York English, are ambiguous between marking social status

(class) vs. marking levels of formality (attention to speech). More generally, the ambiguity between the expression of power and of solidarity first noted by Brown & Gilman (1960) appears to have widespread application; the idiom of 'speaker powerful over addressee' is the same as 'speaker and addressee intimate' in many linguistic respects (Brown & Levinson 1978). The cases where a particular marker is unambiguously correlated with only one aspect of social categories appear to be almost absent from some languages, though rich in others; Haas' (1964) report of features of women's speech in Koasati (where linguistic features unambiguously mark speaker sex) is one well-known case, but languages with elaborate honorifics provide many other examples.

Given the great variety of linguistic forms whose presence or absence may, usually probabilistically and ambiguously, mark some feature or other of the social context, how can the wood emerge from the trees? There are at least two ways in which we might restrict our attention. First, we could decide that it is not sufficient for us, as analysts, simply to correlate form with situation. Doubtless there are etic correlates, such as the rate of eye-blinks studied by psycholinguists, which are beyond the perception of members: as such, they are unlikely to be important in the process of interaction, and hence should be of limited interest to social psychologists and sociolinguists. We should insist that the markers we study do have some emic status, that interlocutors in a particular culture actually attend to the presence or absence of *a* in situated interaction and come to conclusions about the social categories operative in the interaction on the basis of the presence or absence of the markers. This is not to say that members of the culture are continually consciously aware of the markers being used, but only that they are potentially able to bring these markers to some level of awareness and to recognize that they play some part in the interaction. Labov, for example, has tested some, but not all, of his sociolinguistic variables for emic status (after Lambert's tests; see Lambert *et al*. 1960), and we should concentrate on variations which can not only be shown to occur but can also be shown to have specifiable consequences for participants[2] (cf. Robinson, this volume: ch. 6, 1.1; Giles, Scherer & Taylor: ch. 9, 3.4).

Second, as will become evident in section 2, it is often difficult, or indeed misleading, to concentrate on specific, isolated markers without

[2] The distinction between *emic* and *etic* levels of analysis was originally formulated by Pike (1964), on analogy with phonemic and phonetic levels in linguistics. Etic analyses are performed in terms of universal (or at least, precultural) grids or frameworks, while emic analyses are in terms of categories and frameworks that are meaningful to members of the society being studied.

taking into account systematic variations which involve the cooccurrence of sets of markers. A reasonable assumption is that socially significant linguistic variations normally occur as varieties or styles, not as individual markers, and it is on those varieties that we should focus. Furthermore, it is likely to be varieties and styles, rather than individual markers, which have the clearest emic status (see Brown & Levinson, this volume: ch. 8).

With regard to situational variations, the term normally used by linguists to describe them is 'register'. For Bolinger (1975: 358), 'a register is a variety . . . that is tied to the communicative occasion', rather than being identified with any geographically defined speech community. Similarly, Halliday, McIntosh & Stevens (1964) and Hasan (1973) relate registers to uses, not users (where user implies habitual user, e.g. a speaker of a dialect as opposed to an intermittent·user, such as a doctor, lawyer, parent, etc.). So our review might have been titled 'Situations and registers', which, interpreted liberally, covers a great deal of sociolinguistics.

2. A selective review

We shall start with purpose, go on, in turn, to setting, scene and participants, and as we go we shall try to point to those intersections where markers of one are confounded with markers of the others.

2.1 Purpose

The motive force in an analysis of situation comes from a notion like purpose. What are the participants trying to do; what is the interaction all about? For us, purpose is not unlike the concept of 'plan' (Miller, Galanter & Pribram 1960), and, like plans, purposes come in sets of different scope. That is, certain overarching purposes can continue to operate for considerable periods of time, but within such a purpose there are less sustained purposes, which in turn involve even more short-lived purposes. Whereas big fleas are held to have smaller fleas on their backs, which have smaller fleas on their backs . . . large purposes contain their smaller ones within them, as diverse means to overarching ends.

Let us briefly consider three levels of scopes of purpose, in order to discard two for the present. First, there are maxi-purposes, which may, in a rough and ready way, guide a participant through a whole series of distinguishably different situations. 'A visit to Paris' would be one such maxi-purpose. Even the apparently more limited 'visiting the doctor' would be too gross for an analysis of situation, for more than one situation is likely to be involved: talking to the receptionist, waiting in the waiting-room, and eventually seeing the doctor. At the other extreme, there are mini-purposes, which involve moment-by-moment changes in partici-pants' intentions. These mini-purposes might be analysed in terms of specific speech acts (requesting something, or soliciting information about something, or promising to do something); thus they are related to different 'topics', if topic is something that changes with every few utterances.[3] Within any one relatively stable situation there could be a large number of different mini-purposes.

The unprefixed purpose, which is of interest to us here, is of intermedi-ate scope. It directs the activities of participants throughout a situation or over the stretch of time that a social psychologist would expect to be necessary for someone to complete a 'task'. We shall discuss such pur-poses at two different levels of specificity: (i) in terms of a set of general activity types, (ii) in terms of the activity type plus specific subject matter.

Activity type. There appear to be a considerable number of quite general types of activities which are identifiable virtually irrespective of their specific content matter; for example: buying, selling, chatting, lecturing, conducting a meeting, negotiating, playing a game. Such 'activity types'[4] are culturally recognized units of interaction that are identifiable by constraints on (a) goals, (b) roles activated in the activity, (c) interactional structure, and (to some extent) (d) participants and setting. In the activity of teaching, for example, the purposes (goals) of imparting information (and/or ways of thinking, attitudes, etc.) and the roles of teacher/student are activated. It is because activity types define or constrain participants' purposes that we are interested in them here. And as 'activity types' we consider them at the generic level for which we have a folk concept labelled by a monolexeme – teaching, games, meetings – without refer-ence to specific content. But such purposes can be more specifically labelled – teaching physics, football games, business meetings – and that level of specific purpose we discuss subsequently under subject matter. It seems quite likely that there are speech markers of such generalized activity types, yet we know of little empirical study of such variations. In

---

[3] The notion of topic, like that of purpose, involves different scopes, e.g. the topic of politics, within which is the topic of current British government policy, within which is the topic of what the prime minister said yesterday, etc. (For formulations of the notion of topic in discourse, see Chafe (1972), Keenan & Schieffelin (1976).)

[4] This notion of 'activity type' was introduced by Levinson (1972) to label those larger-scale activities within which interaction takes place and which 'frame' the interaction (Goffman 1974). Levinson is currently developing an analysis of the role of activity types in structur-ing interaction (Levinson 1978b).

the ethnography of speaking, some of the work on analysing particular genres is suggestive, for example the studies of Black English 'rapping', 'marking', 'signifying' (e.g. Abrahams 1975; Kochman 1972; Labov 1972c; Mitchell-Kernan 1971), and Mitchell's (1957) study of the language of buying and selling in Cyrenaica. But such work tends to be about ritual speech activities, not about everyday transactional activities, and the aim is to write rules for conducting such an activity rather than to isolate linguistic markers which distinguish it from other activities.

From our own current work on stylistic variations (Fraser & Brown, n.d.), there appear to be very striking syntactic and lexical differences between the activities of lecturing and chatting, which can, in large part, be captured as 'nominal' and 'verbal' styles. Lecturing is nominal. Even when lectures are spontaneously composed from limited notes, there are lengthy syntactically complex utterances with many filled hesitations. There are very high frequencies of those word classes which are found in prepositional phrases and elaborate nominal groups: that is, nouns, adjectives and prepositions. The speech of the same participants chatting is, in comparison, verbal, being composed of much shorter utterances with a high frequency of finite verbs and personal pronouns. Such frequencies, then, provide markers of the activity type of lecturing as opposed to that of chatting.

Another illustration of an activity type marker comes from an experimental study of Moscovici (1967), who found that in interactions which were intended purely as discussions, without any need for agreement or decision, there was greater lexical variation (as measured by type–token ratios) than in interactions in which participants had the task of deciding something jointly. This would suggest comparable differences between planning sessions and seminars, for example.

A further set of materials from which markers of activity types may be drawn is the work on conversational structure by ethnomethodologists and conversational analysts (Sacks 1967, 1973; Schegloff 1972, 1976; Schegloff & Sacks 1973; Turner 1972). Certain distinguishable features of the structuring of different activities may constitute markers of those activities. Take, for example, different kinds of openings:

Let us begin.
Hello.
ringg
The meeting is called to order.
Well, we're all here now.
Benedictus benedicat.

Each of these initiating sequences is a marker of a different activity type.

In addition, the structure of the turn-taking system (Sacks, Schegloff & Jefferson 1974) is a marker of the kind of activity: local organization of turns, interruptions and finishing others' sentences characterize conversation, while monologue (one turn only, no interruptions) characterizes lectures and public speeches. There are also items within discourse which mark a change in activity type or goals – markers of asides (Jefferson 1972), of abrupt shifts in topic, etc. Over and above such general phenomena of interaction regulation, there are particular markers of particular types of activity – for example, markers of casual chat include repetition, exaggerated emphasis, expressions like *you know*, *I mean* (Brown & Levinson 1978; Goldberg 1976), as well as other markers that apply in general to highly verbal styles (Fraser & Brown, n.d.). Similarly, there are doubtless specific markers of the activity of auctioneering, or of presenting the news on radio or TV, or of sports reporting (cf. Crystal & Davy 1969).

It is reasonable to assume that activity types available to members of a society are not simply random lists of all possibilities, but are organized into clusters or groups of activities that seem to be of the same order. So we might suggest that public speaking activities, such as university lecturing, political speeches, barristers' arguments in court, are related activity types in members' conceptualizations, as opposed to business transactions, like auctioneering, buying and selling, negotiating a pay rise, and as opposed to casual chat, whether of dentist to patient, two pensioners on a park bench, or neighbours over the fence. Whether or not such plausible clusters of activity types would reveal similar clusters of markers in the speech they engender is a fascinating question for research.

Subject matter. But activity type alone does not give an adequate account of the purpose in a situation. An activity type specifies the range of possible purposes that participants will orient toward in the activity, but not which specific one will be involved. People do not set out to buy, or negotiate, or play; they intend to buy clothes or food, to negotiate a wage increase or a loan from a friend, to play football or golf. The notion of purpose requires the specification of content at a more detailed level than that of activity type. This we shall call 'subject matter', and we shall assume isomorphy between subject matter of the activity and topic of the speech, ignoring for the present situations where, for example, participants might be repairing a car while chatting about films.

A taxonomy of activity types would help to organize variations in associated linguistic markers. This is even more true of subject matter, whose range is enormous. One first thought, however, is that the type of linguistic variation associated with subject matter may be very limited, as well as obvious. Subject matter will, in large part, determine the lexical items encountered. We use different words to talk about different things, and it would require some unimaginable overextensions of metaphor if we were to be unable to distinguish a conversation about wine from one about rugby, or talk about politics from talk about child-care.

Giles & Powesland (1975) make some suggestions for the beginning of a taxonomy of topic by identifying a number of general dimensions of subject matter, such as salience, emotionality and technicality.[5] Thereby they are able to suggest, from a review of previous work, a limited number of markers other than lexical choice. The salience or importance of the subject matter is associated with increased productivity on the part of speakers. Anxiety-arousing subjects increase the rate of speech disfluencies, and Labov's work (1972a) fits with several other studies in demonstrating that emotionally arousing subjects lead to changes in stylistic level, moving toward the vernacular end of the stylistic continuum.

But perhaps the clearest demonstrations that subject matter has markers other than lexical choice come from the work of Linde and others (Linde, in press; Linde & Goguen, in press; Linde & Labov 1975). She shows that different activity types – describing, narrating, planning – have quite different discourse structures, with associated syntactic markers. From her work, it appears that such differences can also emerge in response to subject matter differences, when the activity type is constant. Thus the discourse structure and syntax of telling stories are quite different from those of telling jokes. From Linde's work on describing apartments, in which the overwhelming majority of respondents organized their descriptions as 'tours' of the apartment, it seems quite likely that changing the subject matter to larger houses rather than apartments would produce more map-like descriptions, with appropriately different syntactic organization.

An analysis of purpose in terms of activity type and subject matter seems central to an understanding of situation, but the identification and interpretation of markers of purpose has hardly begun.

---

[5] Unfortunately, they confound participants' knowledge of and attitude to a topic with the content of the topic itself. It is important to distinguish the two different things involved: knowledge and attitudes are attributes of participants, while topic content (our 'subject matter') is an attribute of purpose.

2.2. Setting

The physical setting in which interaction takes place generally has little determining power over linguistic characteristics of the speech used in that setting; it appears to be rare that speech choice is actually determined by the setting *per se*. But settings imbued with cultural import (what Hymes (1972), but not we, calls 'scenes') are associated with the activities which customarily take place in them: sermons in church, football on the playing field, buying and selling in the market place. The fact that such activities are not determined absolutely by the setting can be seen in the alternative activities which may occur in the same settings: builders repairing the sound system in the church, Sunday picnicking on the playing field, public protests in the market place. So we find it useful to distinguish between markers of setting *per se*, and markers of settings-associated-with-purpose, i.e. scenes.

Taking first the physical setting, we may note the hushed tone of voice that tends to be used for conversing in church as a marker of 'church (or sacred) setting'. Taboos on uttering certain words, or on using certain kinds of language, are often setting-specific; for example, the taboo on mentioning a king's name or anything that sounds like his name within his kingdom, reported for some Polynesian societies by Corbett (1976), would mean that the avoidance of his name and the presence of circumlocutions would be markers of the kingdom as a setting.

Another feature of physical setting for which there are markers in speech is the physical orientation of participants *vis-à-vis* each other. This is to some extent determined by the activity in which they are engaged; thus, in a lecture the speaker stands at a distance from and facing the addressees, whereas in a cocktail party participants are scattered in small, close face-to-face clusters, and at a dinner they may well be seated side by side. The effects of differing physical orientations have been studied experimentally by Moscovici & Plon (1966), who found linguistic correlates of face-to-face as opposed to side-by-side and back-to-back orientation, the latter two being more nominal. In addition, Fielding & Coope (1976) found that speech over an intercom was more nominal than speech in face-to-face communication. And, clearly, there are linguistic correlates of physical distance between speaker and addressee: whispering, talking to someone across the room and calling across distances are phonologically distinguishable in a number of ways.

Temporal setting is marked by variations in greeting and farewell formulae depending on the time of day (Good morning/day/afternoon/

evening/night) in many different languages, and in English it is also a marker of the temporal unfolding of an event. Differences in lexicon depending on temporal setting may go beyond such ritual formulae, however; Ferguson (reported in Fillmore 1975) claims that there are two different words in Moroccan Arabic for 'needle', one of which is used only in the morning, the other during the rest of the day. And in general, deictic forms in language (*here, there, this, that, now, then, today, tomorrow*) all mark aspects of the physical and temporal grounding of the speech, centred around the participants.

A third aspect of setting, the presence or absence of other persons in the environment who are not taking part in the interaction, may be marked in speech in various ways. A classic example is reported by Dixon (1970) for Dyirbal, an Australian aboriginal language, where there is a distinctive code which is used when a speaker is in the presence of his 'mother-in-law' or other taboo relatives, even if he is not speaking to them; the use then of this 'mother-in-law' language is an unambiguous categorical marker of the presence of a tabooed relative in the interactional setting. Such cases of 'bystander honorifics' (Comrie 1976) are one type of setting markers; another example, where not honour but secrecy is the motivation, is seen in the familiar phenomenon of adults spelling out parts of their message to one another when in the presence of children, as in *Let's get some C-A-K-E for tea but don't let you-know-who know*.

2.3. Scene and formality

When we consider setting and purpose together, as 'scene', we note a striking fact. In most, perhaps all, cultures, scenes may be arranged along dimensions of public–private, sacred–secular, serious–trivial, impersonal–personal, polite–casual, high culture–low culture, open network–closed network and many other value-scales. In large part, these diverse scales seem to be subsumed – for participants as well as analysts – under one bipolar dimension of formal vs. informal.[6] The kind of lan-

---

[6] Of course, to say that they are all subsumed under the single dimension of formality is an oversimplification, for it is clearly possible for some purposes to distinguish certain of these value-scales from the (culturally defined) scale of formality. Thus polite (as opposed to casual) scenes (such as tea parties, as opposed to picnics) are associated with the formal end of the scale, but there is not necessarily a one-to-one correspondence between polite behaviour and tea parties; it is possible to be formally rude or casually polite. The evidence for the cross-cultural generality of the formality dimension comes from work in the ethnography of speaking and in the anthropology of interaction, but questions concerning the precise nature of the distinction and why it should be so pervasive in societies remain unanswered (but see Irvine (1978) for an important discussion).

guage appropriate to scenes on the formal or 'high' end of the scale is then differentiated from that appropriate to those on the informal or 'low' end. From acquaintance with a number of very different languages, we can speculate that such differentiation follows universal principles, so that 'high' forms of language share certain properties, such as elaboration of syntax and lexicon, phonological precision and rhythmicity, whereas 'low' forms share other properties, including ellipsis, repetition, speed and slurring (see Levinson 1978a). If this is so, then we may expect such features to be markers of the scene, or at least of its position on the formal–informal scale, in all languages. Much research in sociolinguistics involves isolating features of language varieties aligned on this kind of formal–informal dimension. Here we shall briefly review work on diglossic codes, bilingual code-switching and stylistic variation.

The types of language appropriate to formal as opposed to informal scenes vary in the degree to which they are separate 'codes', separately identifiable, with cooccurrence restrictions constraining mixture of the two. Perhaps the most clear-cut case of scene-conditioned use of different codes can be found in certain diglossic communities (Ferguson 1959), where one form of the language ('High') is used in public, official, written, or formal contexts, and another form ('Low') in ordinary interaction. South Indian Tamil is a case in point (Herman 1976; Levinson, pers. comm.); literary (High) Tamil is used in writing (except for a few recent novels that have appeared in colloquial Tamil, and for conversations in some novels), on the radio (except for radio plays), by actors in certain roles (e.g. astrologists), for political speeches, lectures and any other formal public speaking from a rostrum (although off the rostrum, after the speech, the speaker may revert to colloquial Tamil). Some Tamil speakers also have another language, English, as a resource for particular scenes; the language of law courts, and most university lectures, is English. In this respect the Tamil situation appears to parallel another, reported by Trudgill (1974b): in Luxembourg, speakers use a Luxembourg dialect of German for ordinary conversation, Standard German for books, newspapers and letters, and another language altogether, French, as the language of parliament and of higher education. In both of these cases there is a specialization of function for the High and Low varieties, with well-defined situations of appropriateness. In speech communities of this sort there is a highly predictable one-to-one relationship between language usage and social context, and the choice of code – High vs. Low – is a straightforward marker of the formality or informality of the scene.

In other diglossic communities the basis for alternation between the two codes is more complex, with other aspects of the situation besides scene conditioning the use of High and Low forms. In Arabic-speaking countries, for example, where the dialect situation is complex, use of the High variety may be conditioned simply by speaker and addressee not understanding each other's colloquial dialect (Holes, pers. comm.), in which case the choice of the High variety would be a marker not only of scene, but of characteristics of the participants as well.

Diglossic switching is a particularly tidy case of a much more general phenomenon, code-switching, where members of multilingual or multi-dialectal communities switch between languages or dialects depending on various aspects of the communication situation, including the role relationship of participants as well as features of the scene (cf. Brown & Levinson, this volume: ch. 8, 2). This phenomenon has been reported in a variety of speech communities: Paraguay (Rubin 1962); New Guinea (Sankoff 1972); Mexican American communities (Fishman 1974; Gumperz 1970, 1975); North India (Gumperz 1975); Austria (Gumperz 1975); Norway (Blom & Gumperz 1972).

Code-switching, however, raises some difficulties for an overly simple notion of code choice as a marker of situation. For code-switching in some communities may be used metaphorically (Blom & Gumperz 1972; Gumperz 1975). That is, in such communities code-switching is a much more fluid phenomenon, occurring *within* a given situation and even within a single speech act. Speakers make use of their own and the audience's abstract understanding of situational norms to communicate metaphoric information about how they intend their words to be understood (cf. Blom & Gumperz 1972; Gumperz 1970; Gumperz 1975). Gumperz (1975) gives examples for three sets of languages, Hindi-English, Slovenian-German and Spanish-English, to illustrate how in each case the ethnically specific, minority language is regarded as a 'we'-code, associated with in-group and informal activities, while the majority language serves as the 'they'-code, and is associated with more formal, stiffer and less personal out-group relations (cf. Giles, this volume: ch. 7, 1.2; Brown & Levinson: ch. 8, 2.2). This is a symbolic association; it does not directly predict actual usage, but by switching between the we- and they-code, speakers can use the metaphorical associations of we-ness and they-ness to present nuances of attitude and belief towards what is being said. Metaphorical switches thus can call upon the normal associations between code and scene actually to change the definition of the current situation – for example to change from official to personal roles (Blom & Gumperz 1972). The fact that two codes, one associated with formal scenes and one with informal scenes, can be extracted from their appropriate scenes (externally defined) to change the definition of a scene for the moment, means that the codes are not simply passively marking but are in large part creating the situation.

If in bilingual communities choice of *code* marks formality, in monolingual, monodialectal speech communities the same kinds of information about formality of scene are conveyed by switching between levels of *style*. Here the switch is not between discrete, independently isolable codes, but between varieties of a single language; a great proportion of the codes overlap and the different styles may be signalled by a relatively few items which are loaded with social significance as markers of that particular style, as well as by discourse cues such as speed, rate of breathing, etc. In English, stylistic differences in speech, as opposed to writing, are only beginning to be systematically studied as a whole. But isolated chunks of styles – features on one linguistic level rather than clusters of cooccurring features – have been studied in some detail.

Perhaps most attention has been paid to a particular set of highly socially salient stylistic variables, forms of address and reference for persons. While much of this research deals with address forms as markers of characteristics of the participants and of their relationship (e.g. Brown & Gilman 1960; Brown & Levinson 1978; Ervin-Tripp 1972), we may observe here that address forms are sensitive to scene-based definitions of formality as well. So, in a meeting a speaker may well address or refer to someone as Dr Smith, even though the speaker is on first-name terms with Dr Smith and face-to-face in an informal context would always call him Joe. Ervin-Tripp (1972), in her formalization of the Russian T/V pronoun system reported by Friedrich, cites special status-marked settings as among the social factors conditioning the use of a T or a V pronoun. Similarly, Duranti (pers. comm.) claims that Italians choose pronouns of address in relation to setting; *egli* 'he' (literary or formal) rather than *lui* 'he' (informal) would be used in an examination setting, for example (cf. Brown & Levinson, this volume: ch. 8, 2).

Address forms are a subcase of a more general type of stylistic variation, lexical choice. And such variation in general may be conditioned by the formality of the scene. The choice of lexical items between alternates of pairs such as *dine/eat, reside/live, volume/book*, can be a marker of the formality of the occasion in English (Brown & Levinson 1978). An extreme case of such sets of lexical alternates is found in Javanese 'speech levels' (Geertz 1960), where whole sets of vocabulary with strict cooccurrence constraints covary with situational determinants such as activity type and setting (wedding vs. street), topic (religious vs. commercial), and presence vs. absence of bystanders, as well as with participant characteristics.

Phonological variation in style has been studied by Fischer (1958), and more extensively by Labov and others (Labov 1966, 1972a; Shuy, Wolfram & Riley 1967; Trudgill 1974a, b). Using 'style' in a particularly restricted sense to mean 'attention to speech', Labov and his associates have correlated the occurrence of particular phonological variables with aspects of the activity type – within an interview situation vs. outside, or as an aside vs. as part of an interview. Percentages of the crucial variables are correlated ambiguously with social class of speaker and with style.

We have already mentioned a third set of work on stylistic variation, which has directed attention to variations between nominal and verbal styles (Fielding & Fraser 1978; and our own ongoing work). Briefly, relationships between 'formal' style and extensive use of nominal constructions, nouns, adjectives and prepositions, vs. 'informal' style and elaboration of verbs, pronouns and adverbs have been found in data from a variety of sources – from both experimentally created and naturally occurring conversations, as well as transactions in public places of business and academic discussions in seminar or lecture settings. As mentioned above, the nouny material is associated with setting and activity type; academic lectures and seminars are considerably nounier than shopping transactions and casual conversation. Thus proliferation of nouns might be considered a marker of formal setting, and preponderance of verbs a marker of informal setting, although the emic status of such surface structure categories remains to be demonstrated. A further dimension of scene is also distinguished by the nominal/verbal difference: medium of communication (in this case whether written or spoken) proved to be significantly correlated with the nouniness of linguistic material. Academic journal articles were nounier than the spoken academic discourse, business letters nounier than spoken business interactions, and personal letters somewhat nounier than natural conversation.

A related line of research is being developed by E. O. Keenan (1978) in her investigation of differences between planned and unplanned discourse. The planned/unplanned dimension appears to us to be a major psychological correlate of the formal/informal dimension of a situational analysis. Keenan has suggested that a number of syntactic and discourse structure differences appear in samples of unplanned discourse (that which lacks forethought and organizational preparation) as opposed to planned discourse (that which has been thought out and organized prior to its expression). Among the differences she notes are that unplanned discourse more than planned relies on the immediate context, rather than on syntax, to express propositions; hence there is referent deletion and especially the deletion of pronouns, left dislocation, and avoidance of syntactic subordinators, e.g. *if*, *because*. She also finds greater reliance on deictic modifiers, avoidance of relative clauses, avoidance of the passive voice, reliance on the present tense, and repetition, both lexical and phonological. Keenan relates these differences to cognitive demands on participants which constrain discourse planning, but we would also note other demands. Formal scenes often demand planned discourse, and conversely, planned discourse may have some of the metaphorical connotations of formal scenes and may be used, in ways paralleling code-switching phenomena, to convey a shift to distancing or formality.

2.4 Participants

Speech varies with participants in numerous ways, as was indicated in figure 1. First, we can distinguish between speech as a marker of various characteristics of the individual speakers and speech as a marker of relationships between participants. Characteristics of individuals may be divided into those which appear to characterize the individual as an individual, and those which categorize the individual as a member of a significant social grouping. The individualistic characteristics, in turn, may be subdivided into relatively stable aspects of personal identity, as opposed to temporary states and attitudes.

These temporary features are not a primary focus for any of the chapters in this volume, but ways in which they can manifest themselves linguistically have been documented and discussed in some detail by Wiener & Mehrabian (1968) in their analyses of immediacy. Laver & Hutcheson (1972), Robinson (1972) and Scherer (1979) review paralinguistic markers of emotions and attitudes. Relatively stable markers of personal and of social identity appear to be the core of the other chapters in this volume. So let us turn our attention to social relationships.

Like characteristics of participants, social relationship can also be analysed at an individual (or interpersonal) level and at a social–institutional one. That is, social relationships may be described in terms of social or cultural roles or in terms of personally negotiated relations dependent on personal and interpersonal attitudes, or of course in terms of a mixture of the two. As Fielding & Fraser (1978) have pointed out, the work of Brown and his colleagues (Brown & Gilman 1960; Brown 1965) on address forms nicely illustrates the operation of both role and interpersonal relations. Thus a mutual Title + Last Name might mark the relationship between occupants of different and nonsolidary roles, and an asymmetrical pattern of address may mark, say, an employer–employee role relation of unequal power and status. But changes in forms of address probably reflect changes in personal relations. When the doorman becomes 'Jim' rather than 'Smith' this is because the manager feels he knows the doorman better, not because the role relation of employer–employee has changed. Fielding & Fraser's (1978) paper is a survey of markers of interpersonal relations in speech. Thus we may turn our attention to the one remaining gap regarding markers of participants – the marking of social roles.

The taking on of roles and role relations is commonly confounded with settings and purposes. When Dr Smith talks like a doctor, and not like a father or golfer, it is likely to be when he is in a surgery or hospital and is inquiring about the health of a patient or discussing new drugs with a colleague. Such confounding may well be more true of occupational roles, such as doctor or lawyer, than of kinship roles or nonoccupational roles such as stranger or friend. It is, however, about occupational roles that we have most information concerning registers, and indeed some writers (e.g. Trudgill 1974b) confine the term register to occupational registers.

There is at least suggestive evidence that distinguishable speech registers are part of the role performance of doctors (Candlin, Leather & Burton 1974), school-teachers (Sinclair & Coulthard 1975), university lecturers (Fraser & Brown, n.d.), radio commentators (Crystal & Davy 1969), stockbrokers (Turner 1973), professional gamblers (Maurer 1950), pickpockets (Maurer 1955), smugglers (Braddy 1956), drug addicts (Agar 1973) and other members of the underworld (Halliday 1976). And one imagines that the lawyer, the advertiser, the clergyman, various kinds of scientists and many other occupational roles have their associated registers. Another role-related register which has been described in some detail is 'motherese', i.e. the speech of mothers, and perhaps all adults and older children, when talking to young children (Fraser & Roberts 1975; Snow & Ferguson 1977).

What is most distinctive, and best described, about many of these registers is the nature of the lexicon. While performing their respective roles, doctors, stockbrokers and gamblers use different words. Since the topics of their talk are quite different this is hardly surprising, and if all that was being claimed was that different activities require different vocabularies, the term register might not be merited at all. But, of course, even as far as vocabulary is concerned there is more to it than that. For the professional groups are likely to be using technical terms for activities which would be discussed in different terms by the layman, and the underworld groups will use argots which the layman, and people in roles complementary to their own, are not expected to know at all.

Furthermore, registers are by no means confined to questions of individual word selection. They may involve complex, unusual semantic relations amongst perfectly commonplace words. As Turner (1973) notes, for the stockbroker animateness can appear where normally it would be least expected: tin can suffer, while oil soars but lead merely moves up hopefully. Also syntax may be distinctive. The speech of the university lecturer or seminar-giver is strikingly nominal for speech, though considerably less so than if the lecture is prepared for publication. In contrast, motherese involves the frequent use of short utterances with relatively simple syntax. Registers can also contain phonological markers. The radio commentator, for example, makes use of extra stress for loudness contrasts, and uses intonation both to connect segments into lengthy, apparently coherent sequences, and also to give clear indications of finality. And as Sinclair & Coulthard (1975) demonstrate with teacher talk, some of the most striking markers of a register may be revealed only by an analysis of chunks of discourse, such as question–answer sequences, particularly when it emerges that the questioner always knows the answers in advance.

It is conceivable that different registers are most obviously marked at different levels of linguistic analysis, but to some extent such impressions have probably been unduly strengthened by the linguistically selective nature of many of the studies. Thus, although we ourselves have done no phonological analyses of academic speech, it is most probable that the syntactic features of a nominal style are accompanied by the phonological markers that Labov attributed to high levels of 'attention to speech'. When investigators like Crystal & Davy (1969) have looked for markers at a variety of linguistic levels, they appear to have found them. The speech of the radio commentator, for example, is marked by the paralinguistic feature of absence of voiced hesitation, and phonologically by distinctive uses of stress and intonation. Given the repetitive nature of the events being described in, say, sports commentary, a certain amount of repetition of syntactic and semantic structures is likely, yet various devices are used to ensure that repetition is considerably less than might be the case. These include variations in tone unit length and variations in sentence

types, including the use of elliptical utterances. Despite content variations from one type of event to another, a basic vocabulary appears to be
used, with few scholarly words and with nouns signifying objects and
verbs signifying actions. Otherwise highly fluent and coherent units of
discourse have brief asides inserted into them.

It is not hard to see how such linguistic features achieve desired effects
by creating for listeners impressions of fluency, variety and interest,
spontaneity, specificity and detail. Most of the claims made by Crystal &
Davy about effects and attributions are very plausible, but like the other
studies of role registers, there is no independent evidence about the social
significance of the different linguistic varieties. We assume that, as a
minimum, the different roles could be readily identified from tape-
recordings alone (except that argot speakers might hope the precise role
could not be too closely identified by outsiders), in which case many
questions of stereotyping, attribution-making and expectations for
interaction could be posed. But, to the best of our knowledge, even our
minimal assumption remains to be demonstrated.

3. Concluding remarks

3.1. Relations between scene and participants

We do not wish to deny the importance of participant differences in
producing sociolinguistic variations. But we trust that our reviews of the
fragmented research efforts into markers of purpose, setting and scene
reveal some of the dangers of ignoring the wider situation.[7] Let us spell
these out more clearly.

One problem is that certain features which are generally attributed to
participants, such as social distance and social status or power, are in fact
not always stable attributes of individuals, or of relationships between
individuals, but are context-dependent assessments which may be
shifted depending on the setting and activity type (Brown & Levinson
1978). Two American strangers meeting on the streets of New York City
would consider each other to be socially distant; the same two if they were
to meet in a hotel in Singapore would be likely to consider one another
socially close, as compared with the even stranger strangers around
them. Hierarchical social status is also contextually relative in certain
respects, or at least the domains in which status expression are relevant

---

[7] The ramifications of situation have, of course, been elaborated over the last two decades by
  Goffman (1964, 1974) and Hymes (1972, 1974, 1975).

vary contextually, so that a doctor consulting a lawyer on a legal question might well express deference in formulating his query, whereas the lawyer when consulting the doctor about his heart condition would be the one to express deference. Even where the nature of the participants is crucial, as in the determination of address form usage, other situational factors can shift the assessment of participant characteristics toward greater or lesser social distance, status, etc. So an understanding of the nature of the scene, as viewed by participants, is essential in order to detect and interpret many of the markers that appear in their speech.

A second difficulty for analysts wishing to focus on markers of participants is the ambiguity of many social markers. As we noted above, address forms and Labovian phonological variables like the New York /r/ are ambiguous between marking class or socioeconomic status and marking formality of scene. Which marker one has in a given instance of usage must be determined by an examination of situational features. Examples of unambiguous markers are not always participant-related, as we have seen. And, anyway, unambiguous markers appear to be few and far between. A particular marker is more likely to be ambiguous than unambiguous, and if ambiguous, the chances are that it will be ambiguous between marking a feature of participants vs. a feature of scene. Thus tone of voice may mark mood or setting; the level of formality (a linguistically cross-cutting set of markers) may mark social class or activity type, and so on. Why there should be this fundamental ambiguity between participant-based and setting- or purpose-based markers is an important question. It may simply be that, given a set of markers, we may as well make them do as much work as possible. It is more likely, however, that there are good reasons for the particular ambiguities which appear, that they serve participants' purposes in specific ways. We might speculate that the New York /r/ is ambiguous because New Yorkers want to increase their social status, and address forms are ambiguous because interactors want to be able to keep their relationship obscured in front of bystanders; or more generally, interactants may not want to be held accountable regarding a particular attribute of their identity, rather they want to avoid being immediately and unambiguously classifiable on the various social dimensions which may be relevant.

A final, related reason for analysts to attend to scene is that there are relationships among the various components of situation which are likely to be sources of confusion if not carefully analysed. Some are necessary relationships; thus activity types and social roles are inextricably linked: one cannot imagine an activity type without imagining an associated set of roles to be activated. Others are contingent relationships; for example, it is empirically observable that activity types are correlated with social categories such as class, sex and age. So, the activity of playing darts is associated with the working class in England; register features of this activity will be more common among the working class. Similarly, the activities of mending cars, or of conducting executive business meetings, are associated (empirically, to date) with men; those of mothering, or of nursing, are associated with women. It may well be that certain features of 'women's speech' considered to be markers of sex are in fact markers of these sex-role-stereotyped activities, and the occasional male involved in a female-typed activity would probably show features of such 'women's speech' (cf. Smith, this volume: ch. 4, 2.3). This may be a reason for the cultural stereotype whereby male hairdressers in women's hair salons are assumed to be homosexual. In fact, we suspect that activity types (and even some superordinate purposes such as travelling in a foreign country, or trying to get a job) take priority over the stable features of participants in determining the linguistic characteristics of behaviour, so that a participant engaged in an activity not normally associated with the type of person he is would produce (or try to produce) linguistic behaviour associated with the activity type. Some support for this hypothesis comes not only from male hairdressers but also from other work on traditional male and female occupations that are practised by role-discrepant people (Aboud, Clément & Taylor 1974). If this is generally so, registers are inextricably linked with activity types, and the latter are contingently linked with stable personal characteristics such as age, sex and class.[8]

3.2. The situation, the individual and society

We might postulate, then, a model in which purposes are the crucial determiners of linguistic behaviour, a model in which we imagine settings as being associated with particular types of activity likely to occur in them, and activity types as determining the goals which actors will pursue in that setting and the roles actors will activate *vis-à-vis* one another. These in turn determine the mini-goals which participants try to

[8] This provides an alternative basis for explaining the phenomenon observed by Bernstein (1971), the relationship between class membership and what we would describe as nominal style (what he labels 'elaborated code'). Rather than imagining that this relationship is based in different cognitive capacities of the working and middle classes, a more plausible explanation is that working-class people do not as a rule take part in the activity types which call for nominal style, e.g. lecturing, conducting business meetings, writing scholarly articles. Hence they do not have as much need to use the features of a nominal style.

achieve, including tasks (such as coming to an agreement, or sharing information, or reinforcing a friendship) and topics (politics, the history of the chain, the weather). Such a model would contrast with the one which appears to be more current among social psychologists, where the cross-links between the situational factors (as charted in our figure 1) are seen as determined by participants' characteristics, so that a person's social identity determines the kinds of social roles he will take up, the kinds of activities he will indulge in and the kinds of settings he will frequent. But wherever one chooses to enter the causal chain, it is clear that situational factors, both participant and nonparticipant ones, are interlinked in highly complex ways: class is related to power and status at an interpersonal as well as institutional level, and mood, personality, social relationship, purpose and setting are all related, so that if a speaker uses a formal address term, for example, we do not know *a priori* whether it is because he is in a bad mood, has a standoffish personality, stands in a distant relationship with his addressee, is engaged in an activity with a serious purpose, or is in a formal setting. Granted that in a given instance a number of the possibilities may well be ruled out, still in many cases the potential ambiguity as to what is being marked remains to challenge the analyst.

For many social psychologists, the next step would be clear: ambiguities should be resolved by experimental manipulation. If formality of scene is naturally confounded with a nonsolidary relationship between participants, let us create experimental situations where the two can be separated and observe the outcomes. But as convinced 'situationalists' we are sceptical. The detailed dynamics of different situations are still poorly understood. As a result, for the naturalistic situation, the implications of findings from a stripped-down experiment are likely to remain problematic, particularly since an experiment is usually a distinctive type of situation in itself. (Something of its distinctive nature can be seen if the reader cares to apply the notions of setting, purpose and participants to a typical social psychological experiment.) If we study speech markers experimentally, we are as likely to learn about markers of experiments as about anything else. As social scientists studying language we should not devote all our energies to studying the register of one specific methodology.

Our preferred strategy for clarifying the operation of variables confounded within naturally occurring situations is the more ambitious one of expanding the scope of inquiry in two directions. On the one hand, we would do well to pursue lines of research that could get at the actor's-eye-view of the situation. What cues does an actor use to interpret markers in speech and to disambiguate the possible interpretations in a given instance? A speaker-based analysis of this sort is illustrated in the Geoghegan-style decision models for specifying the situational factors which enter into a speaker's choice of address form (Geoghegan 1971; Ervin-Tripp 1972; Levinson 1977). Such factors and their weighting in relation to each other are culturally, indeed subculturally, variable but can be specified (by means of elicitation and observation) for any individual and can presumably be expanded from address forms to other social markers in speech. One particular point of interest is that Geoghegan's distinction between marked and unmarked usages (Geoghegan 1973) suggests a promising way of distinguishing between stable bases for choice of an address form and shifts in temporary states such as mood or attitude to the addressee. Such speaker-based production models, however, are not necessarily applicable to how addressees actually interpret the production of a particular form, and for decoder-based models we must look elsewhere.

The work of Gumperz and others on conversational inference provides one framework for tackling such questions (Gumperz 1976, 1977, 1978). Work in this paradigm takes a passage of tape-recorded conversation and asks what inferences – for participants – are generated by the passage and what linguistic and extralinguistic cues provide the bases for these inferences. From this perspective it is possible to establish, for example, that members of different subcultures have different interpretive rules for formulating inferences from particular features of English. Thus Indian English and London English differ in intonation patterns, and inferences (or attributions) about speaker's intent, including inferences about intended meaning, speaker's attitude toward addressee, speaker's attitude toward the setting and activity, will differ systematically and predictably for speakers of the two dialects of English (Gumperz 1978; Gumperz, Agrawal & Aulakh, n.d.). Such work suggests that pragmatic principles can be described for attributing a reading to a given instance of a social marker, principles which are stable enough to be valid over time for speakers of a particular dialect.

These models provide ways into an individual participant's view of a particular situation; they thereby constrain some of the messiness or ambiguity of the elements which theoretically can enter into a situation. Any element which does not appear in a member's decision- or attribution-processes can be ignored. A second frame of reference for constraining the flux of theoretically possible elements in a situation, and ambiguities between elements, is one which takes a society-eye-view of the proceedings. Thus, for any society we are studying, we need an understanding of the kinds of social-structural considerations which help determine the features of a situation. It is simply not the case that all possible combinations of participants, roles, settings, activity types, topics and tasks do in fact occur, and if we understood why certain combinations do not occur, whereas others are unlikely or unusual, while yet others are common and expected, then we would have made a good start on eliminating some of the theoretically possible ambiguities in interpreting social markers in speech. If we start with the usual socio-logical categories – economic, political, legal, religious, military and edu-cational institutions, as well as kinship, friendship, class and role net-works – we may ask in what ways each of these institutions and networks constrains the types of situations which can occur and the definitions that members have of situations. As yet, no comprehensive taxonomy of situations has been constructed for any society, although ethnographers of speaking often have a partial stab at providing one for small-scale societies. Such a taxonomy would seem to be a necessary step in coming to grips with the social-structural constraints on situations. But, with regard to problems posed by multiple determinants and ambiguities in speech markers, some of the ways in which a social-structural perspective helps to resolve them are spelled out by Brown & Levinson (this volume: ch. 8).

In conclusion, two points emerge concerning the central position of situation in an analysis of speech markers. First, even if one's primary interest is in participant-linked markers, many of those are either linked in turn to situation, or, on closer examination, prove to be markers not of participant *per se* but of participant in a particular situation. Second, a situational analysis is particularly valuable strategically because, Janus-like, it encourages the social scientist to look both at the individuals who interact in the situation and at the structure of the society which encloses the interaction.

References

Aboud, F. E., Clément, R. & Taylor, D. M. 1974. Evaluational reactions to discrepancies between social class and language. *Sociometry*, 37, 239–50.

Abrahams, R. D. 1975. Black talking on the streets. In R. Bauman & J. Sherzer (eds.) *Explorations in the Ethnography of Speaking*. Cambridge.

Agar, M. 1973. *Ripping and Running: a formal ethnography of urban heroin addicts*. New York.

Bernstein, B. 1971. *Class, Codes and Control*, vol. I, London.

Blom, J.-P. & Gumperz, J. J. 1972. Social meaning in linguistic structures: code-switching in Norway. In J. J. Gumperz & D. Hymes (eds.) *Directions in Sociolinguistics: the ethnography of communication*. New York.

Bolinger, D. 1975. *Aspects of Language*. 2nd ed. New York.

Braddy, H. 1956. Smugglers' argot in the southwest. *American Speech, 31*, 96–101.

Brown, P. & Levinson, S. 1978. Universals in language usage: politeness phenomena. In E. Goody (ed.) *Questions and Politeness: strategies in social interaction*. Cambridge Papers in Social Anthropology, *8*. Cambridge.

Brown, R. 1965. *Social Psychology*. Glencoe, Ill.

Brown, R. & Gilman, A. 1960. The pronouns of power and solidarity. In T. Sebeok (ed.) *Style in Language*. Cambridge, Mass.

Candlin, C. N., Leather, J. H. & Burton, C. J. 1974. *English Language Skills for Overseas Doctors and Medical Staff*. Progress Reports 1, 2, 3 and 4, Department of English, University of Lancaster.

Chafe, W. L. 1972. Discourse structure and human knowledge. In R. O. Freedle & J. B. Carroll (eds.) *Language Comprehension and the Acquisition of Knowledge*, Washington, DC.

Comrie, B. 1975. Polite plurals and predicate agreement. *Language, 51*, 406–18.
  1976. Linguistic politeness axes: speaker–addressee, speaker–referent, speaker–bystander. *Pragmatics Microfiche* 1.7, A3–B1. Department of Linguistics, University of Cambridge.

Corbett, G. 1976. Syntactic destructors (problems with address, especially in Russian). *Pragmatics Microfiche* 2.3, A3. Department of Linguistics, University of Cambridge.

Crystal, D. & Davy, D. 1969. *Investigating English Style*. London.

Dixon, R. M. W. 1970. *The Dyirbal language of North Queensland*. Cambridge.

Ervin-Tripp, S. 1972. On sociolinguistic rules: alternation and co-occurrence. In J. J. Gumperz and D. Hymes (eds.) *Directions in Sociolinguistics: the ethnography of communication*. New York.

Ferguson, C. A. 1959. Diglossia. *Word, 15*, 325–40.
  1976. The structure and use of politeness formulas. *Language in Society, 5*, 137–51.

Fielding, G. & Coope, E. 1976. Medium of communication, orientation to interaction, and conversational style. Paper presented at the Social Psychology Section Conference of British Psychological Society.

Fielding, G. & Fraser, C. 1978. Language and interpersonal relations. In I. Markova (ed.) *Language and Social Context*. London.

Fillmore, C. J. 1975. Santa Cruz Lectures on deixis. *Indiana Linguistics Club Papers*, Bloomington, Ind.

Fischer, J. L. 1958. Social influences in the choice of a linguistic variant. *Word, 14*, 47–56.

Fishman, J. A. 1972. The sociology of language. In P. P. Giglioli (ed.) *Language and Social Context*. Harmondsworth, Middx.
  1974. The sociology of language: an interdisciplinary social science approach to language in society. In T. Sebeok (ed.) *Current Trends in Linguistics*, vol. XII. The Hague.

Fraser, C. 1978. Communication in interaction. In H. Tajfel and C. Fraser (eds.) *Introducing Social Psychology*. Harmondsworth, Middx.

60   Penelope Brown and Colin Fraser

Fraser, C. & Brown, P. n.d. Nominal and verbal language styles. MS, Social and Political Sciences Committee, University of Cambridge.
Fraser, C. & Roberts, N. 1975. Mothers' speech to children of four different ages. *Journal of Psycholinguistic Research*, 4, 9–16.
Geertz, C. 1960. *The religion of Java*. New York.
Geoghegan, W. 1971. Information processing systems in culture. In P. Kay (ed.) *Explorations in Mathematical Anthropology*. Cambridge, Mass.
 1973. A theory of marking rules. In K. Wexler & A. K. Romney (eds.) *Cognitive Organization and Psychological Processes*. Washington, DC.
Giles, H. & Powesland, P. 1975. *Speech Style and Social Evaluation*. London.
Goffman, E. 1964. The neglected situation. *American Anthropologist*, 66, no. 6, 133–6.
 1974. *Frame Analysis*. New York.
Goldberg, J. 1976. The syntax, semantics, pragmatics, and sociolinguistics of some conventionalised parenthetical clauses in English: *you know* and *I mean*. Diploma dissertation, Department of Linguistics, University of Cambridge.
Gumperz, J. J. 1970. Verbal strategies in multilingual communication. In *Monograph Series on Languages and Linguistics, 21st Annual Round Table*, no. 23. Georgetown University, Washington, DC.
 1975. Code-switching in conversation. *Pragmatics Microfiche* 1.4, A2. Department of Linguistics, University of Cambridge.
 1976. Language, communication and public negotiation. In P. R. Sanday (ed.) *Anthropology and the Public Interest: fieldwork and theory*. New York.
 1977. Sociocultural knowledge in conversational inference. In *Georgetown University 28th Round Table on Languages and Linguistics*. Washington, DC.
 1978. The conversational analysis of interethnic communication. In E. L. Ross (ed.) *Interethnic Communication*. Proceedings of the Southern Anthropological Society. Atlanta, Georgia.
Gumperz, J. J., Agrawal, A. & Aulakh, G. n.d. Prosody, paralinguistics, and contextualization in Indian English. MS (1977), Language Behavior Research Laboratory, University of California, Berkeley.
Haas, M. R. 1964. Men's and women's speech in Koasati. In D. Hymes (ed.) *Language in Culture and Society*. New York.
Halliday, M. A. K. 1976. Anti-languages. *American Anthropologist*, 78, 570–84.
Halliday, M. A. K., McIntosh, A. & Stevens, P. 1964. *The Linguistic Sciences and Language Teaching*. London.
Hasan, R. 1973. Code register, and social dialect. In B. Bernstein (ed.) *Class, Codes and Control*, vol. II. London.
Herman, V. 1976. Code switching in Tamil. Diploma dissertation, Department of Linguistics, University of Cambridge.
Hymes, D. 1972. Models of the interaction of language and social life. In J. J. Gumperz & D. Hymes (eds.) *Directions in Sociolinguistics: the ethnography of communication*. New York.
 1974. *Foundations in Sociolinguistics*. Philadelphia.
 1975. Ways of speaking. In R. Bauman & J. Sherzer (eds.) *Explorations in the Ethnography of Speaking*. Cambridge.
Irvine, J. 1978. Formality and informality in speech events. *Texas Working Papers in Sociolinguistics*, 52. Southwest Educational Development Laboratory, Austin, Texas.

Jefferson, G. 1972. Side sequences. In D. Sudnow (ed.) *Studies in Social Interaction*. New York.

Keenan, E. O. 1978. Unplanned and planned discourse. *Pragmatics Microfiche* 3.1, A3–D2. Department of Linguistics, University of Cambridge.

Keenan, E. O. & Schieffelin, B. B. 1976. Topic as a discourse notion: a study of topic in the conversations of children and adults. In C. Li (ed.) *Subject and Topic*. New York.

Kochman, T. 1972. *Rappin' and Stylin' Out: communication in Black urban America*. Urbana, Ill.

Labov. W. 1966. *The Social Stratification of English in New York City*. Center for Applied Linguistics, Washington, DC.

1972a. *Sociolinguistic Patterns*. Philadelphia.

1972b. Contraction, deletion, and inherent variability of the English copula. In *Language in the Inner City: studies in the Black English Vernacular*. Philadelphia.

1972c. Rules for ritual insults. In D. Sudnow (ed.) *Studies in Social Interaction*. New York.

Lambert, W. E. *et al.* 1960. Evaluation reactions to spoken languages. *Journal of Abnormal and Social Psychology*, 60, 44–51.

Laver, J. & Hutcheson, S. (eds.) 1972. *Communication in Face-to-Face Interaction*. Harmondsworth, Middx.

Levinson, S. C. 1972. The organisation of conversation: talk-exchange as a species of transaction. Field statement MS, Department of Anthropology, University of California, Berkeley.

1977. Social deixis in a Tamil village. PhD dissertation, University of California, Berkeley.

1978a. Universals in sociolinguistics. Working Papers in Linguistics, Department of Linguistics, University of Cambridge.

1978b. Activity types and language. *Pragmatics Microfiche* 3.3, D1. Department of Linguistics, University of Cambridge.

Linde, C. In press. The organisation of discourse. In T. Shopen, A. Zwicky & P. Griffin (eds.) *The English Language: English in its social and historical context*.

Linde, C. & Goguen, J. A. In press. Structure of planning discourse. *Journal of Social and Biological Structures*.

Linde, C. & Labov, W. 1975. Spatial networks as a site for the study of language and thought. *Language*, 51, 924–39.

Maurer, D. W. 1950. The argot of the dice gambler. *Annals of the American Dialect Society*, 269.

1955. Whiz mob: a correlation of the technical argot of pickpockets with their behaviour patterns. *Publications of the American Dialect Society*, 24.

Miller, G. A., Galanter, E. A. & Pribram, K. H. 1960. *Plans and the Structure of Behaviour*. New York.

Mitchell, T. F. 1957. The language of buying and selling in Cyrenaica: a situational statement. *Hesperis*, 26, 31–71.

Mitchell-Kernan, C. 1971. *Language Behaviour in a Black Urban Community*. Monographs of the Language Behavior Research Laboratory, Berkeley, California.

Moscovici, S. 1967. Communication processes and the properties of language. In L. Berkowitz (ed.) *Advances in Experimental Social Psychology*, vol. III. New York.

Moscovici, S. & Plon, M. 1966. Les situations colloques: observations théoriques et expérimentales. *Bulletin de psychologie*, 19, 702–22.

Pike, K. L. 1964. Towards a theory of the structure of human behavior. In D. Hymes (ed.) *Language in Culture and Society*. New York.

Robinson, W. P. 1972. *Language and Social Behaviour*. Harmondsworth, Middx.

Rubin, J. 1962. Bilingualism in Paraguay. *Anthropological Linguistics*, 4, no. 1, 52–8.

Sacks, H. 1967. Lecture notes. Dittoed MSS, University of California, Irvine.

1973. Lecture notes. Summer Institute of Linguistics, Ann Arbor, Michigan.

Sacks, H., Schegloff, E. & Jefferson, G. 1974. A simplest systematics for the organisation of turn-taking in conversation. *Language*, 50, 696–735.

Sankoff, G. 1972. Language use in multilingual societies: some alternative approaches. In J. B. Pride & J. Holmes (eds.) *Sociolinguistics*. Harmondsworth, Middx.

Schegloff, E. 1972. Sequencing in conversational openings. In J. J. Gumperz & D. Hymes (eds.) *Directions in Sociolinguistics: the ethnography of communication*. New York.

1976. On some questions and ambiguities in conversation. *Pragmatics Microfiche* 1.9. Department of Linguistics, University of Cambridge.

Schegloff, E. & Sacks, H. 1973. Opening up closings. *Semiotica*, 8, 289–327.

Scherer, K. R. 1979. Non-linguistic vocal indicators of emotion and psychopathology. In C. E. Izard (ed.) *Emotions in Personality and Psychopathology*. New York.

Sinclair, J. M. & Coulthard, R. M. 1975. *Towards an Analysis of Discourse*. London.

Shuy, R., Wolfram, W. & Riley, W. K. 1967. *A Study of Social Dialects in Detroit*. Final Report, Project 6–1347. Washington, DC.

Snow, C. E. and Ferguson, C. A. (eds.) 1977. *Talking to Children: language input and acquisition*. Cambridge.

Trudgill, P. 1974a. *The Social Differentiation of English in Norwich*. Cambridge.

1974b. *Sociolinguistics: an introduction*. Harmondsworth, Middx.

Turner, G. W. 1973. *Stylistics*. Harmondsworth, Middx.

Turner, R. 1972. Some formal properties of therapy talk. In D. Sudnow (ed.) *Studies in Social Interaction*. New York.

Wiener, M. & Mehrabian, A. 1968. *Language within Language: immediacy, a channel in verbal communication*. New York.

3. Age markers in speech[1]

HEDE HELFRICH

In most societies, age is an important category for social interaction and social organization. Among other things, age is associated with the role structure in the family and in social groups, with the assignment of authority and status, and with the attribution of different levels of competence. Since a large part of social interaction consists of verbal communication, it is highly likely that the social category age is also reflected in speech behaviour. Those speech cues which potentially differentiate between members of different age groups will be called 'age markers'. They include phonological, syntactic, semantic, extralinguistic and paralinguistic features. In some instances, a linguistic feature does not attain its marking character without reference to that which is signified, i.e. the referent. For example, while the word *dog* applied to a dachshund gives little information about the person using it, it may become an age marker when applied to all four-legged animals by a 2-year-old child. The speech behaviour of a person not only conveys information about his or her own age but also about the listener or the receiver of the verbal message. Thus, old people are spoken to in a different way from young people. Hence, a distinction will be made between 'sender age markers' and 'receiver age markers'. The same linguistic feature may be a sender age marker as well as a receiver age marker. For instance, if an elderly person usually speaks in a high-pitched voice, this will be a possible sender marker of age. If he or she speaks in a high-pitched voice only when speaking to young children, the high pitch will be a possible receiver marker of age.

Within the sender markers, a finer distinction must be drawn. On the one hand, there are sender markers with which the individual is endowed as a function of his age, while, on the other hand, there are sender markers which can be used by the individual according to specific

[1] The author gratefully acknowledges the contributions of K. R. Scherer, H. Giles, H. Balkenhol, H. Ophoff and H. Wallbott.

63

interaction situations. The first kind of sender markers will be referred to as 'static', since they occur relatively independent of interactional context. The second kind of sender markers will be called 'dynamic', since they may change according to the respective situation and since they are not interpretable without reference to a particular interaction situation. Static sender markers are often associated with linguistic competence, whereas dynamic sender markers are associated with communicative competence.

1. The nature of age marking

The kind of relationship between marker and age may be either invariant or probabilistic (see also Giles, Scherer & Taylor, this volume: ch. 9, 3.2; Brown & Fraser: ch. 2, 1.2). An invariant marker would be one which is perfectly correlated with the marked variable, i.e. with age in our case. It seems, however, that this perfect correlation is rarely to be found. For example, even the occurrence of first words in a child is not perfectly correlated with his chronological age. The relationship between most markers and what is marked must be assumed as being probabilistic, i.e. given the marker we may infer the presence of the marked age category with a certain probability, and conversely, given the age category we may expect to encounter the marker with a certain probability. A similar though not identical distinction is drawn by Bodine in terms of age-exclusive vs. age-preferential usage (Bodine 1975: 131; cf. Smith, this volume: ch. 4, 1.2). An age-exclusive marker would be a linguistic feature which is used only by members of a specific age class. If the marking is probabilistic, one would not necessarily find this feature for all members of a particular age class as would be the case for an invariant marker. Age-preferential usage, on the other hand, refers to differences in the relative frequency with which specific features occur in a certain age class.

Some further explanation concerning the relationship between marker and age is needed. There are many linguistic features which, once acquired, persist throughout life. Only the onset of those features, not their overall occurrence, is correlated with age. For example, when a child has learned to master syntactically complex sentence structures, he may use them throughout life. On the other hand, there are markers which are associated with a particular stage of life. Examples are the use of a specific vocabulary in adolescence and the use of one-word sentences by 1-year-old children.

The relationship between marker and age cannot be understood without taking into account the underlying mechanisms determining this relationship. What are these? In most instances, the occurrence of a particular feature in speech is not directly governed by chronological age, but rather by certain related factors, such as linguistic, cognitive or social competence. In some cases, a specific linguistic feature can be identified as an age marker only in a certain cultural or ethnic setting. We may then infer the relationship between marker and age to be determined by factors associated with a culture-dependent view of a particular life stage rather than associated with biological age (cf. the notion of conditional markers in Giles, Scherer & Taylor, this volume: ch. 9, 3.2).

The identification of a relationship between age and speech cues by an investigator does not imply that the naive human observer notices this relationship or even makes use of it in his social interaction. In terms of the Brunswikian lens model (cf. Scherer, this volume: ch. 5, 5.1) we have to distinguish between 'distal cues', which are defined as objectively measured externalizations of the particular social variable under consideration (i.e. age in our case), and 'proximal cues' which are defined in terms of the representations of distal cues in the decoder. The proximal cues may lead to decoder inferences about the encoder. These inferences may, but need not necessarily be adequate with respect to the externalized category. Research on the relationship between age and speech has been concerned almost exclusively with distal cues, whereas the communicative implications of age cues have been neglected.

One might assume that speech markers of age are not very important in most instances of face-to-face interactions, since there are other cues such as outward appearance which are more salient indicators of age. However, the significance of speech cues will increase in situations where the participants of an interaction cannot see each other, e.g. in telephone communication, and in situations where cues from other channels lead to attributions conflicting with that of the person's speech. An example of the latter situation is communication with children who on account of their size look older than they actually are. The adult initially infers the child's age from his physical appearance and consequently communication may be ineffective, but ongoing interaction and the decoding of the child's speech may lead to an alteration of the adult's speech so that it is better adapted to the child's cognitive and linguistic state of development.

The following selective review of studies on age markers in speech is organized according to the two aspects 'sender markers' and 'receiver markers'. Although the section on sender markers contains parts of what are usually referred to as developmental psycholinguistics, a review of this vast field is by no means intended. The primary focus in studying markers in speech is the question of what inferences can be drawn from features observed in speech for age-related categories or processes, whereas the primary focus of developmental psycholinguistics is the question of how language is acquired. Both objectives do not exclude, but rather complement each other. However, while the study of markers generally relies on speech production, the study of language acquisition is based on both production and comprehension of speech.

Speech can mark stages of age throughout the total life span – from infancy to old age. Unfortunately, the relevant literature reveals that there are many gaps in terms of the age ranges that have been studied. Studies of middle and old age are almost exclusively restricted to the investigation of extralinguistic components of speech such as voice and temporal phenomena, whereas speech components associated with linguistic competence tend to be investigated almost exclusively in the period of early language acquisition in children.

2. Static markers of sender age

Static markers of sender age are based on the relationship between the linguistic sign (in the sense of Morris (1939) or Bühler (1934)) and the sign encoder. This does not necessarily mean that the sign in its totality is a marker. Individual components or even a single component may enable us to draw inferences about the encoder. For example, incorrectly pronounced words may indicate young age irrespective of the actual meaning of the words used. The components may be related to the application of linguistic rules, and thus include phonological, syntactic and semantic features. In some instances, the components have no direct linguistic function and yet they are intrinsically linked to speech performance. These components include extralinguistic phenomena such as voice set as well as paralinguistic phenomena such as hesitation pauses, speech rate and tone of voice (cf. also Laver & Trudgill, this volume: ch. 1, 2).

The following review on static markers of sender age in speech is organized according to two main classes of speech cues: (a) linguistic features, (b) extra- and paralinguistic features. The section on linguistic markers will end with a brief discussion on the current controversies with regard to the underlying mechanisms concerning the marking of age in speech. Extra- and paralinguistic features will be divided into vocal and temporal aspects. Vocal aspects refer to variations of voice such as pitch and voice quality, while temporal aspects refer to variations of speech fluency such as speech rate and pauses.

2.1. Phonology

The earliest sounds a child produces include the birth cry and other cry vocalizations. The relationship of these cries to later development of speech production skills is not clear. No doubt parents may be able to relate different 'meanings' to different types of crying, e.g. hunger, pain, or boredom, but, as a study of Müller, Hollien & Murry (1974) showed, appropriate decoding of cries is not possible without knowledge of situational context, such as knowing the hour of previous feeding. Lenneberg (1967) suggests that the early cry vocalizations are quite divorced in their developmental history from speech-like sounds, the appearance of which being first represented in the 'cooing' sounds. Lenneberg suggests that these cooing sounds, phonetically often similar to back and rounded vowels, appear at the end of the second month, but according to the authors of a more recent study (Bullowa, Fidelholtz & Kessler 1976) it is as early as in the first days of life. The speech-like character of these cooing sounds is said to derive not only from the similar means of production but also from the fact that they may convey the beginnings of meaning. The observations of Bullowa *et al.* suggest that specific sound combinations may be related to specific behaviour patterns of the child as well as to specific external situations.

By the middle of the first year of life the child begins to babble. Although babble sequences often consist of consonant clusters or consonant–vowel combinations, many linguists (e.g. Jakobson 1968; Lenneberg 1967) see a marked discontinuity between the production of babbling sequences and the production of the first words. Babbling sounds seem to be independent of the specific linguistic community and of the environment. They are observed even in children born deaf (Oksaar 1977) and include sounds which do not occur in any known language (Jakobson 1968). Jakobson claims that the transition from the babbling stage to the production of the first words is characterized by a drastic restriction in the range of sounds, and that the discontinuity is often marked by a period of complete silence between the two stages. In contrast, other investigators emphasize the gradual addition of specific sounds, in addition to sound restrictions, before the true range of sounds of a language is fully acquired (Irwin & Chen 1946). Oller, Wieman, Doyle & Ross (1976) see a continuity between babbling and speech, since the preference for specific sound combinations is the same in both stages, and they conclude that 'phonological processes are the *output* of an innate phonological acquisition device' (1976: 10). However, continuity between the babbling stage and the stage of first words does not depend only on the sounds that are uttered being phonetically similar but on the ability symbolically to associate sounds with meanings. In order to demonstrate this ability, the child need not necessarily produce sound combinations similar to those of adult speech, but simply use similar sounds in similar situations as a means of successful communication. A number of observations (Halliday 1975; Leopold 1939; Lewis 1936; Lindner 1882; Oksaar 1977) suggest that children have already acquired this ability at the babbling stage, if not earlier.

Near the end of the first year of life, the child utters the first 'true' words. Though these words are recognizable as words of adult language, the child has by this time only mastered a small number of phonemes. Several hypotheses have been advanced concerning the principle governing the acquisition of the phonetic inventory of a language. The most elaborate of these is the structural theory of Roman Jakobson (Jakobson & Halle 1956; Jakobson 1968). According to Jakobson, the elements constituting the phonemic systems of a language are formed by twelve 'distinctive features' (Jakobson & Halle 1956) which describe consonants as well as vowels and have universal validity. The hierarchical structure of the distinctive features represents both the frequency of occurrence in the languages of the world and the order of acquisition of these phoneme classes in ontogenetic development. The most important principles gov-

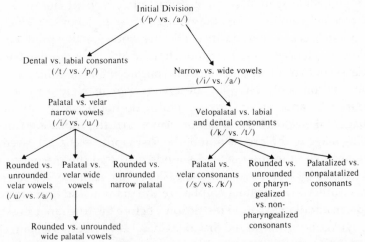

Figure 1. The order of feature acquisition according to Jakobson (1968). Adapted from Dale (1976:213)

erning the acquisition process are the principle of progression from maximal (i.e. occurring in all languages) to minimal contrast, and the principle of 'irreversible solidarity'. The latter states that certain phoneme classes presuppose others, this being true both for the different languages of the world and for the acquisition of phonemes. Figure 1 shows the hierarchical structure representing the order of acquisition of phonemes. However, Jakobson's system seems to be primarily of heuristic use. Empirical data available up to now do not allow us to decide if the process of phonological development described by him is the most frequent one (cf. Ferguson 1976; Oksaar 1977; Olmsted 1971).

2.2. Semantics

Empirical evidence available on semantic development is relatively small. Most work has been done on vocabulary growth (cf. McCarthy 1954; Templin 1957). While the number of words used in early childhood may be seen as a marker of state of general development, strong individual differences exist concerning the specific nature of words learned by a child. Nelson (1973), for example, found differences in the proportion of general nominal words to personal–social words at the early one-word stage and attributed these to birth order of the children and education of the parents. However, the difference in semantic usage between a child and an adult is not primarily a matter of number and kind of words but rather a matter of extension and structure of meaning of different words. Two questions arise here. The first one concerns the specific structure of a child's semantic space, and the second refers to the principles according to which a child generalizes the use of a specific word. An attempt to answer the first question is the so-called Semantic Feature Hypothesis proposed by Eve Clark (1973, 1974, 1975). This theory assumes that the meaning of a word is composed of features or components of meaning such as ± human, ± adult and ± long which the child acquires sequentially by adding more and more features to the word. Thus, early word meanings should be characterized by overextensions, since a word with few semantic features will be applied more widely than the same word with a lot of semantic features. In her earlier version of the theory, Clark argues that the acquisition of semantic features proceeds from more general to more specific features and that, within a feature pair, the positive member is learned before the negative. Thus, the correct use of *more, high, long* and *thick* precedes that of *less, low, short* and *thin*, because the child first acquires the positive quantity. Since the theory assumes that children at a certain stage have the full meaning of one of two opposite terms, Clark called it the Full Semantics Hypothesis (Clark 1973). In her more recent formulation, Clark argues that the same data which seemed to support the full semantics hypothesis could be explained in terms of the much weaker assumption that at a certain stage the full meanings of the two opposites are incomplete (the Partial Semantics Hypothesis). This hypothesis supposes both terms of the two opposites to be incomplete at a certain stage. For example, children might know only that both *more* and *less* refer to amount. As well as knowing this partial meaning, children are assumed to have a nonlinguistic preference for the more positive term. The children's responses, then, would be the output of combining their partial semantic knowledge with a non-linguistic strategy.

What conclusions can be drawn from this theory for the discussion of markers in speech? More specifically, what does a feature (e.g. the correct use of one of two opposite terms) mark in a child's speech? It is apparent that, given the particular feature, we cannot decide whether it is a marker of the child's semantic competence, a marker of a nonlinguistic strategy, or an interaction between both. Similarly, the reformulation of Clark's theory does not allow us to draw from the use of overextensions straightforward inferences about a child's semantic system. While the original version of Clark's theory holds that each overextension involves all the criterial properties constituting the meaning of a word for the child, the more recent version concedes the possibility of 'partial' overextensions. In such instances the child is assumed to pick out only some of the criterial properties he has identified with the meaning of a word when overextending it. The use of a 'false' concept (from the standpoint of adult speech) does not necessarily mark a false structure of a child's semantic space, but may simply mark the limited nature of his vocabulary. Hence, it is possible that a child overextends in production, but not in comprehension. We may conclude that, at least for the study of markers, we must examine a large number of overextensions produced in varying semantic settings in order to make reliable inferences about the degree of semantic competence.

While Clark's theory may provide a possible framework in which to analyse overextensions, cases of underextension cause more difficulty. Underextensions seem to be as common as overextensions (cf. Dale 1976); and, as early as 1949, Leopold characterized the process of meaning acquisition as an alternation between over- and underextension. A relatively common example of underextension is the restriction of action words to the self (Bowerman 1976). In terms of Clark's theory two explanations may be offered for underextensions. First, the theory may allow the acquisition of inappropriate or irrelevant features which are later eliminated. Second, the underextensions produced in a child's spontaneous speech may not be 'true' underextensions, but rather a result of the child's small repertoire. In this case, underextensions would not be expected to occur in comprehension tasks.

Bowerman (1975) has shown that there is at least one way in which the structure of the child's semantic space can be described which differs from that proposed by Clark. She suggests a structure which is consti- tuted by prototypes of meaning stored in memory together with the respective words. The probability of a specific word being actualized in a given situation increases according to the iconic similarity of the object to be named with the prototype. We may hypothesize that such a system represents an ontogenetic stage prior to that of semantic features. For the study of markers, it would be very important to investigate at which age the transition from the iconic processes described by Bowerman to the more abstract processes described by Clark takes place.

Concerning our second question, namely the principles governing the generalization of word meanings, Clark assumes that they are primarily determined by perceptual features such as size, shape, texture and movement (Clark 1973, 1975). Nelson (1973, 1974), however, claims a functional viewpoint (also claimed by John Dewey), holding that objects are classified as similar by the child when they have a similar function. An example for generalization according to functional principles would be the use of the word *toys* for a doll, a car, and a train (cf. Stemmer 1971). The difficulty often lies in distinguishing between the use of functional knowledge and the use of perceptual knowledge on the basis of words produced by a child, since there are many instances of concepts where function is highly correlated with form (cf. Clark 1975; Nelson 1973). It is most likely that the operating principles are themselves a function of age. There is evidence from studies using categorization tasks that children between the ages of 2 and 6 years tend to group pictures on the basis of colour, shape or size, while children of about 6 or 7 shift to symbolic representations (Bruner 1964). This view is compatible with Clark's notion holding that knowledge about function is acquired fairly late in some instances (Clark 1975). Moreover, it seems reasonable to take into account the labels a particular language offers to group specific words (cf. the theory of linguistic relativity proposed by Whorf (1965)). Thus, it will be more likely that a child uses the word *toys* to group a doll and a car if the language it learns provides this word than if it does not. More intercultural research would be needed to investigate this factor further.

Semantic competence consists of more than mastery of individual words. The meanings of individual words have to be integrated into sentence meaning. While there have been only a few empirical investigations of this aspect of semantic competence in later childhood and adulthood (mostly related to comprehension and not to production of speech), all of these suggest that semantic development is not completed during childhood, rather it seems to continue throughout life (Dale 1976).

2.3. Verbal styles

A lot of research has been conducted on age differences in the frequency of use of different parts of speech. These so-called 'verbal styles' refer to relatively consistent preferences for words or word classes and, hence, they have to be clearly distinguished from 'speech styles' which refer to speech patterns selected for specific situations. One of the first systematic studies on verbal styles was carried out in 1925 by Busemann, who was influenced by the observations of Clara and William Stern (Stern 1904, Stern & Stern 1907). Busemann analysed transcripts of both the oral and written speech of persons aged from 3 to 19, and distinguished between an 'actional' and a 'qualitative' verbal style. As a quantitative measure he suggested the 'action quotient' (generally referred to as 'verb–adjective ratio'; cf. Mahl & Schulze 1964) which means the number of action words (verbs) divided by the number of more qualifying descriptive words (adjectives). Moreover, the action style is characterized by a high proportion of one-syllable words. Analysing the speech samples of different ages, Busemann found a decrease of verb–adjective ratio with increasing age. This development does not proceed linearly however, but is interrupted rhythmically by phases of action occurring at the age of 12 or 13 and at 17 or 18. Busemann regards this verbal development as reflecting general psychophysical development, the action style revealing an 'emotional–subjective–motile attitude', corresponding to a slow-down of intellectual capacity, and the qualitative style representing an 'intellectual–objective attitude' combined with an increase of intellectual capacity (Busemann 1925). While other studies confirm the correlation of emotional excitement and verb–adjective ratio (Balken & Masserman 1940; cf. Mahl & Schulze 1964), Busemann's claim about the development rhythm has been challenged (cf. Bakker 1969). In contrast to Busemann and similar to the view of Stern, most empirical analyses of speech samples suggest that development is linear, proceeding from a more actional to a more qualitative style (Hetzer & Flakowski 1972; Klein 1978; Markey 1928; Storck & Looft 1973). As Markey points out, the course of development is accompanied by a marked decrease in the frequency of 'action' words and a decrease in first-person pronouns in speech, but also by an increase in nouns and their adjectival qualifiers (Markey 1928; quoted in Sanford 1942: 820). However, at least one study may support Busemann's claim for the existence of a discontinuity in late adolescence. Tooley (1967), who compared the writing style of late adolescence with that of adolescence and adults, found that the style of late adolescents was rated by judges as less 'flamboyant', which might mean that less adjectives and more verbs were used.

Extrapolating from the results of Busemann and more recent studies, old age should be characterized by a more qualitative speech style. However, in 1940 Boder carried out a longitudinal case study of Emerson's Journals, which begin in 1820 and continue until Emerson's death in 1876, the results of which showed a tendency for the verb–adjective ratio to increase with age (quoted in Miller 1951: 128).

We cannot therefore be sure whether the use of 'actional' or 'qualitative' style is intrinsically associated with age. As Brown & Fraser (this volume: ch. 2, 2.3) point out, 'verbal' and 'nominal' style (which roughly correspond to 'actional' and 'qualitative' style) may indicate different communication settings such as chatting and lecturing, the latter even when spontaneous. Bearing this in mind, we may assume that older people tend to define more situations as formal, and therefore prefer a more qualitative style. Boder's results on Emerson's Journals may be explained by the fact that Emerson became more and more familiar with the medium of the Journal. Moreover, it is likely that the historical trend or Zeitgeist has shifted from more formality to more informality.

2.4. Syntax

A widely held position has been that the onset of grammatically structured speech occurs at about 1 year. However, some current work tends to explore 'syntactic' structures inherent in certain forms of social interaction before the onset of patterned speech. Sugarman (1974) and Bates, Camaioni & Volterra (1973), for example, were able to identify nonverbal precursors of linguistic concepts such as 'agent' and 'instrument', and Bruner (1975) observed distinctive vocalizations for marking the giving and receipt of an object.

Beginning with the occurrence of the first real words, three stages can be distinguished in early syntactic development. A 'holophrastic' stage occurs at about 1 year, in which single-word utterances serve as functional equivalents to that of phrases in adult speech, and this is followed by a stage of two-word utterances at about 18 or 20 months (cf. Brown 1973; Leopold 1949; McNeill 1970a, 1970b; Menyuk 1969, Stern & Stern 1907). While there is agreement about these utterances not being unstructured combinations of lexical words, different frameworks are used to analyse these early phrases. Bowerman (1969), Braine (1963), McNeill (1970a, 1970b) and Slobin (1971) distinguish two classes of words generally referred to as 'pivot' and 'open'. Words of the pivot class are highly frequent in children's speech, have a fixed position within a phrase and cannot be combined together in a single phrase. The number of different pivots is very small. In contrast, open words are more numerous, have no fixed syntactic position, may be combined together within a single phrase, and' may function as single-word utterances. Bloom (1970), McNeill (1971) and Schlesinger (1971) have shown that pivot–open grammars cannot take full account of all sentences observed in a child of this age. They suggest an alternative framework which allows a description of children's utterances not primarily in terms of word classes and their combinations, but in terms of the functions the words serve in the sentence. They postulate deep structures underlying the two-word utterances and rules allowing the transformation from deep to surface structure. While, according to Bloom (1970) and McNeill (1971), the model of generative syntax developed by Chomsky yields the appropriate framework, Schlesinger (1971) suggests a model of interpretation which anticipates basic assumptions of generative semantics (see Leuninger, Miller & Müller 1972).

The third stage of syntactic development is formed by three-word phrases which are often combinations of the two-word structural meanings. By this time, single elements of structural meanings begin to be elaborated into noun phrases with a strong tendency to proceed right-to-left (Bloom 1970). Thus, in the earliest sentences, nouns frequently occur as objects of actions, but seldom as the agents performing the action. The syntactic structure discovered in the stage of early sentences is primarily one of word order (Braine 1963). At nearly the same time, though not as dominant a feature, inflections seem to appear in children's language (Slobin 1970), the acquisition of which is best described as an overregularization. This may be illustrated, for instance, for the past-tense forms of irregular verbs in English. The past-tense forms first used by a child are the correct ones – such as *came*, *went*, etc. Yet, after a few weeks, or months, the regular past-tense morpheme -*ed* suddenly appears on all verbs including the irregular ones. However, how the child returns to the irregular past-tense forms has not been studied in any detail (cf. Dale 1976).

Age is not a good predictor for syntactic development, since there are strong individual differences in rate of development (cf. Dale 1976; Oksaar 1977). However, some of the irregularities disappear when children are compared not on the basis of age but on the basis of a linguistic indicator of development. For this purpose, mean length of utterance (MLU) has been proposed (Brown 1973). MLU is defined as the average length of an utterance in morphemes. Typically, around MLU 1.5 the first more-word sentences and around MLU 2.0 the first inflections appear. The inflections begin to be mastered between MLU 2.0 and 2.5 (cf. Dale 1976). However, it has been doubted that MLU is a universal indicator. Since all inflections are counted as separate morphemes (Brown 1973: 54), MLU might be a misleading index in languages rich in inflections (e.g. German). In such languages, children may use inflections very early but inappropriately (cf. Oksaar 1977).

Research on later syntactic development is rare. After the age of 5 or 6, syntactic differences between children and adults are not obvious from observations of spontaneous speech. Among the difficulties that persist through late childhood are the mastery of subject–verb agreement and case endings of personal pronouns, the elimination of the double negative passive transformations, and causal patterns with *why* or *because* (Chomsky 1969; Dale 1976; Ervin & Miller 1963). However, syntactic markers in childhood are not restricted to syntactic mistakes (from an adult viewpoint) but include the 'elaborateness' of syntactic constructions used by children. In a systematic longitudinal study on the speech of children from 6 to 9, Lange & Neuhaus (1969), using picture descriptions, emphasize the increasing development of more and more differentiated structures, starting from primitive and proceeding to complete and extended affirmative clauses. Braun (1965), who studied essays of children from 5 to 10, found a significant increase in the availability of phrase patterns with a marked step at the age of about 8. Using a factor analytic approach, Hass & Wepman (1974), found five dimensions of syntactic usage in speech of children aged 5 to 13 years: general fluency, embeddedness, finite verb structure, noun phrase structure, and qualified speech. The embeddedness dimension was the only one with a sizeable relation to age. Results are interpreted by the authors in terms of developmental progression in the inclusion of transformationally processed content in the sentence.

2.5. Mechanisms underlying the acquisition of syntax and semantics

Theories which have been suggested in order to explain the mechanisms underlying language acquisition may be characterized in terms of two controversies, (i) empiricism vs. nativism and (ii) primacy of linguistic vs. primacy of cognitive structures. The first controversy arose, as psycholinguistics was being recognized as a discipline in its own right, between behaviourists on the one hand and those supporting generative transformational grammar on the other. From the viewpoint of a behaviourist, 'verbal behavior' (Skinner 1957) is seen as a special case of general behaviour and therefore described as the connection between stimulus and response, though in some models this connection is a very complicated one (Brown, Cazden & Bellugi 1969). On the other hand, transformational grammarians claim 'innate structures' (Chomsky 1968) or a 'language acquisition device' (McNeill 1966) which enables the child to produce and comprehend sentences. The nativistic position is not only challenged by behaviourists, but also by an approach in which individual language development is seen as strongly influenced by social interaction processes. The latter view is stressed particularly by investigators influenced by the so-called speech act theory. Theories of the latter school emphasize the performative or pragmatic element in meaning (Austin 1962; Searle 1969). The importance of social interaction processes is also stressed by work on speech differences related to social-class differences (Bernstein 1960, 1967; Oevermann 1972; Robinson, this volume: ch. 6, 3). The question as to whether 'restricted' and 'elaborated' codes reflect differences in general language development or only in social use of language has not yet been solved (e.g. cf. the results obtained by Robinson 1965). The second controversy concerns the specific nature of the structures which allow man to acquire and to use language. From the generative viewpoint, these structures are basically linguistic (Chomsky 1968; McNeill 1970a, 1970b). Chomsky (1967) argues for a genetic disposition independent of a specific language, underlying the acquisition of language. An even stronger view of linguistic primacy (though not in opposition to Chomsky's) is held by Whorf (1956) who claims that the thinking of an individual is 'calibrated' by the particular language to which he is exposed (the hypothesis of 'linguistic relativity'). As a consequence, the whole world view of an individual is assumed to be strongly influenced by his language. On the other hand, psycholinguists influenced by Piaget's ideas claim primacy for cognitive structures (Sinclair-de Zwart 1969, 1970). They attempt to account for the development of linguistic competence by a more general theory of cognitive development. Independently, the latter approach has been proposed by Bever (1970), Bloom (1970), Brown (1973) and Schlesinger (1971). Bloom points out that the emergence of syntactic structures in speech depends 'on the prior development of the cognitive organization of experience' (1970: 226). Perhaps the most explicit formulation of the 'cognition hypothesis' has been proposed by Cromer (1974). It consists of two parts. The first states that 'we are able to understand and productively to use particular linguistic structures only when our cognitive abilities enable us to do so' (Cromer 1974: 246). The second holds that when a child has cognitively grasped an idea he will be able to express it linguistically even though in a simple or indirect form. An example is given by Sachs (1976: 163) who reports that when her daughter first discovered the past tense she signalled it with the word *yesterday*. Thus, 'I go yesterday' meant 'I went'.

Although the discussion on linguistic vs. cognitive universals does not seem to have come to an end, a third viewpoint, influenced by speech act theory as well as by Piagetian ideas, has emerged. Representatives of this view (Bruner 1975; Dore 1975; Halliday 1975) not only stress the importance of the pragmatic element in speech but often seem to argue for the ontogenetic primacy of communicative structures (cf. Fraser, in press). According to this view, speech behaviour reflects interactional or functional structures such as requesting, denying, asserting and commanding, which are present even before linguistic development. Thus, Bates and her colleagues have claimed that communicative patterns such as 'declaring' and 'commanding' are apparent in prelinguistic gestures which later become subordinated in favour of grammaticalized forms of expressions (Bates *et al*. 1973). In this vein the one-word utterances of young children have been analysed in terms of speech act theory by Dore (1975). He postulates the single word of these utterances being the propositional element and the accompanying minimal prosodic pattern being the illocutionary act (cf. Searle 1969).

What is the relevance for the study of age markers of the discussion concerning the primacy of linguistic, cognitive or communicative structures? Each of these theoretical approaches would make different predictions as to the nature of age markers in speech. If there are linguistic universals (which are supposed to be syntactic in the Chomskian view), the appearance of specific linguistic features would allow us to draw inferences concerning the child's linguistic competence at a specific stage. From a Whorfian perspective, however, age markers would only exist with reference to the specific language the individual is going to acquire.

Speech markers within a specific culture or language group would allow us to assess the cognitive–linguistic competence of the speaker at a certain age.

In its strong form, the cognition hypothesis has two consequences for the study of age markers in speech. First, there is no specific linguistic feature which unequivocally allows us to draw inferences from it to a particular cognitive state. A specific feature cannot be interpreted without reference to the meaning being expressed. Second, when there are no related linguistic forms present we may infer the absence of the equivalent cognitive concept. However, such an extreme position seems unlikely considering the work of Brown & Fraser as well as of Bever, who suggest that the child's comprehension far outweighs his production (Brown & Fraser 1964: Bever 1970).

In terms of the speech act approach, the study of markers would not be restricted to linguistic forms of expression but would include gestures and other forms of nonlinguistic behaviour. The emergence of linguistic forms would allow us to assess the extent to which communicative forms have become grammaticalized as semantic and syntactic structures.

Summary. Most of the linguistic markers described in the preceding section are related to a particular stage of language acquisition which is associated with a particular age. Thus, the occurrence of first words, of first sentences and of first semantic generalizations mark highlights in the course of speech development. However, which aspect of the language acquisition process is marked, depends not only on the linguistic feature under consideration but also on the theoretical framework within which the feature is analysed. The marker may indicate linguistic universals, the occurrence of which at a particular age is viewed as a function of maturation. Examples are the occurrence of phonemes in terms of Jakobson's distinctive feature theory, and the occurrence of two-word sentences in the framework of generative grammar. On the other hand, there may be particular states of a cognitive or of a semantic–cognitive nature which are externalized in speech patterns. For instance, the mistakes a child makes in the naming of objects may indicate a structure of semantic representation typical of a particular age. A further possibility, which is derived from the Whorfian view of language, may be that both the markers and the cognitive–linguistic states being marked are the result of an interaction between the biological endowment of the individual and the specific language to which he is exposed.

There are only a few studies of verbal age markers which are not associated with linguistic competence, such as the speaker's preference for either a more action-orientated style (verbs dominating) or a more qualitative style (adjectives and nouns dominating). The preference for one of the two verbal styles is regarded as reflecting the emotional state associated with a particular age.

2.6. Extralinguistics and paralinguistics: vocal aspects

The voice of a person must be regarded as a prerequisite for the performance of any act of speech. This aspect of human speech is often referred to as the 'extralinguistic' (cf. Laver & Trudgill, this volume: ch. 1) or 'prelinguistic' component of speech or 'voice set' (Trager 1958). The quality of an individual voice is closely related to the physiologically determined state of the respiratory system, the vocal folds and the articulatory tract which most individuals cannot easily control (cf. Laver & Trudgill, this volume: ch. 1, 2.1). Thus, the voice of a person is one of the most important clues to the identity of that person and carries considerable information about long-term states such as personality, occupation, gender and age. It is not surprising, then, that judges succeed fairly well when asked to assess the age of other people by voice cues alone (Allport & Cantril 1934; Herzog 1933; Pear 1931; Ptacek & Sander 1966; Ryan & Capedano 1977). Some studies have attempted to explore the cues on which such judgements are based. In Ryan & Capedano (1977), for example, judges claimed to have paid particular attention to the pitch, tone and volume of the voice as well as to the clarity and speed of speech as cues of age. It should be noted that the cues reported are not necessarily the ones upon which judgements are really based, since judges may be influenced by 'vocal stereotypes' (Kramer 1963; Scherer 1972). Most of the studies in this area, however, concentrate on the investigation of the relationship between age and objectively measured or sometimes subjectively perceived differences in voice.

Voice characteristics in speech are not only significant as far as identifying the speaker is concerned. A number of studies (Dittmann 1972; Scherer 1979) suggest that most of the emotional components of meaning are conveyed by voice phenomena. This aspect of communication is often called 'paralinguistics', although the particular phenomena covered by this term have not been strictly defined. Most of the work in developmental psycholinguistics has concentrated on the structural properties of speech – especially syntax – and paralinguistics has been neglected. Given the fact that the meaning of an utterance may be modified and even reversed by paralinguistic cues (cf. Scherer 1977), paralinguistics ought to be an important area of concern in studies of linguistic development. It is intriguing to note that the paralinguistic transmission of meaning may be controlled by the right hemisphere (van Lancker 1975) and is thus assumed partly to operate independently of the linguistic functions of speech, which are controlled by the left hemisphere.

Most of the voice variables investigated are related to the control of voice production, or, physiologically speaking, to the control of the larynx. Acoustically, most of these variables are represented by measures derived from fundamental frequency (f_0), i.e. the lowest frequency occurring in the speech signal. Among these the following measures have been studied: mean f_0, f_0 range, f_0 perturbations and f_0 contour. Further measures are acoustically represented by the intensity of the speech signal and by the frequency spectrum, i.e. the intensity distribution over the single frequencies. In the following review on voice variables as a function of age, the labelling of the variables will follow the method used to identify the phenomena under consideration, i.e. when the results have been obtained primarily with acoustical methods, the acoustical term will be used, when the results rely on perceptual methods, the perceptual term will be used.

Mean fundamental frequency. In a number of studies fundamental frequency (f_0), which corresponds physiologically to the rate of vibration of the vocal folds and perceptually to pitch, has been investigated as a function of age. Mean f_0 is generally defined as the arithmetic mean (and sometimes median) of the f_0 of a whole utterance of a person. The mean fundamental frequency in babies has been found to be extremely high when crying (about 400–600 Hz) and somewhat lower when babbling (about 300–500 Hz; Keating & Buhr 1978; Ostwald 1963). Figures 2 and 3 illustrate a trend of general f_0 decrease with increasing age for both males and females – at least until adulthood is attained. The changes during adulthood and from middle to old age show a marked difference for the sexes. For women, no evidence for any systematic changes from young adulthood to advanced age has been found (see figure 2). On the other hand, average f_0 of men appears to decrease slightly from young adulthood until about 40 to 50 years and to shift upwards from about 65 years on (see figure 3).

There are several possible interpretations of the changes reported. The lowering of pitch may be attributed to an ossification of the larynx structure resulting in less elasticity in the cartilages and muscles. The rise in pitch reported for males of advanced years seems to be more difficult to interpret. It is possible to argue that the results obtained are merely a consequence of the data being based on cross-sectional analyses. The higher f_0 level found in old males may just reflect the fact that mean body size and, as a consequence, mean larynx size have increased during the last decades. Smaller larynxes are generally associated with higher voices. These histological facts may explain why, in the only longitudinal study (Endres *et al*. 1971), no f_0 increase could be shown. In this study, data from two older males (60 and 73 years old respectively at the beginning of the study) were collected over a period of 13–15 years and a lowering of mean pitch (defined by the maximum value of individual distribution curves) was found.

A second explanation would relate the rise in pitch in old age to a

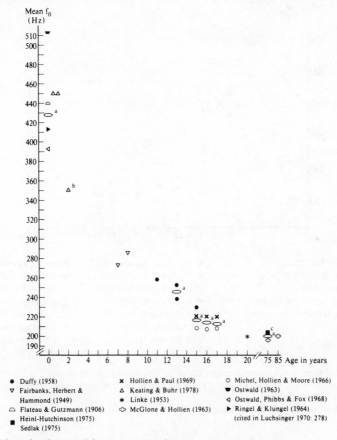

Figure 2. Mean fundamental frequency as a function of age in females
  a Mean of the respondent age group weighted according to the number of subjects included in each study.
  b Median fundamental frequency.
  c Age range from 65 to 93 with a mean of 80.5.

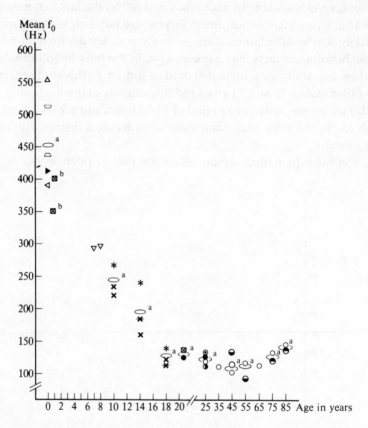

* Curry (1940)
⊖ Endres, Bambach & Flösser (1971)
△ Fairbanks (1942)
▽ Fairbanks, Wiley & Lassman (1949)
◺ Flateau & Gutzmann (1906)
◗ Hanley (1951)

● Hollien & Jackson (1967)
✕ Hollien & Malcik (1962)
○ Hollien & Shipp (1972)
✻ Hollien et al. (1965)
⊠ Keating & Buhr (1978)
□ Majewski, Hollien
  & Zalewki (1972)

⊖ Mysak (1959)
▼ Ostwald (1963)
◁ Ostwald et al. (1968)
◉ Philhour (1948)
  Pronovost (1942)
▶ Ringel & Klungel (1964)
  (cited in Luchsinger
  1970: 278)

Figure 3. Mean fundamental frequency as a function of age in males
  a Mean of the respondent age group weighted according to the number of subjects
    included in each study.
  b Median fundamental frequency.

weakening of the gonads in secreting hormones – a process comparable to puberty, a period in which one generally finds a marked decrease in f_0. However, it is also possible to explain this rise in pitch in old age without recourse to biology or histology. Fundamental frequency has been shown to be affected by both habitual and transitory emotional tension states (Scherer, this volume: ch. 5, 2.1; Scherer *et al.* 1977); most people tend to respond to stress with an increase in mean f_0. It thus seems reasonable to hypothesize that the upward shift reflects not only age-related physiological changes but also emotional tension caused by factors such as forced retirement, fewer social contacts, decreasing self-sufficiency and the low status associated with old age in western societies (cf. Siegman 1978). A study conducted with old women by Heinl-Hutchinson and Sedlak in our Giessen laboratory, in which average f_0 has been demonstrated to be related both to life satisfaction and to number of social contacts, partially supports this hypothesis. In this study, old women who were content with their lives and who had many social contacts tended to speak with significantly lower f_0 than old women who were unhappy and had few social contacts (Heinl-Hutchinson 1975; Sedlak 1975). The stress hypothesis would even be compatible with the fact that, in general, women do not show any changes in average f_0 with increasing age. Most of the female subjects studied had not worked outside the home during their lives, and were thus unlikely to suffer as much from anxiety upon reaching retirement age as their male age peers.

The lowering of pitch reported in the Endres *et al.* study may similarly also be influenced by emotional tension. Although most people respond to stress with an upward shift, some individuals shift in the opposite direction. Scherer (cf. this volume: ch. 5, 2.1) concludes from his results that the maintaining or lowering of f_0 may be a particular reaction to stress, due either to physiological differences in the central nervous system (Gellhorn & Kiely 1972) or to differences in coping strategies.

Intercultural studies on changes of voice with old age may well add a further dimension to the debate concerning the association of pitch shifts with the physiological aging process or with emotional state. We may assume, for example, that factors such as 'vitality' (Giles, this volume: ch. 7, 2.2), or the evaluation of old age (in terms of status and institutional support) in a particular ethnic community, play an important role in mediating voice changes.

Fundamental frequency range. An indicator of the flexibility of voicing is fundamental frequency range, i.e. the distance between the lowest and the highest tone a person is able to produce or habitually produces. F_0 range seems to remain constant during childhood (Hartlieb 1962) and to show an increase from adolescence to adulthood (cf. Luchsinger 1970). A reduction of total pitch range in old age, compared to young adulthood, has been reported for both males and females (Böhme & Hecker 1970; Endres *et al.* 1971; McGlone & Hollien 1963; Ptacek, Sander, Maloney & Jackson 1966), although Mysak (1959) found no changes in pitch range related to age. However, while Ptacek *et al.* (1966) and Yannoulis & Yannatos (1966) attribute the narrowing of range to the loss of high tones, Böhme & Hecker (1970) assume a loss of low tones. It seems reasonable to assume that factors operating on f_0 range are similar to those described for mean f_0, i.e. not only age-related physiological changes, but also socio-emotional and cultural factors.

Intonation. The term 'intonation' is used to denote the gross pitch movement throughout a sentence or part of a sentence. The intonation pattern of a sentence has a grammatical function (e.g. the distinction between a statement and a question can be signalled by a difference in intonation) as well as an emotional function (e.g. it may convey surprise or disgust; cf. Fry 1968). Studies on intonation as a function of age deal mostly with the acquisition of intonation contours in early childhood. Lenneberg (1967), Lewis (1936) and Lieberman (1967) point out that children acquire speech patterns not in terms of single sound segments but as pitch contours. According to Lewis, the imitation of adult intonation contours starts by 7 to 8 months (cf. Crystal 1975). Lieberman even hypothesizes that there is an innate physiological basis for the production of intonation patterns. Such a pattern is said to be realized in the so-called breath group, a speech or sound sequence which is uttered during a single expiration.

To test the biological basis of intonation contours, Tonkova-Yampol'skaya (1968) made f_0 recordings of 170 infants, including 30 newborn (1 to 6 months old), and compared the forms of infant intonation with the intonational structures of adults. Her results show that the intonation of 'discomfort' in adults coincides fully with that of infants from the immediate postnatal period onwards. Spectrographic recordings of baby cries made by Stark & Nathanson (1974) seem to provide some confirmation of this, as they show a rapid rise in pitch at the beginning and a rapid fall at the end of each cry unit. From the second to seventh month, Tonkova-Yampol'skaya discerned an 'indifferent' intonation pattern that was structurally comparable to the intonation of assertion, enumeration and comparison in adults. From the seventh month, an 'expressive calm cooing' appeared that resembled the intonation of 'affirmation' in adults. Up to the end of the second year, intonations structurally similar to 'emotional' requests were noted. A questioning intonation did not appear until the second year, but seemed from the outset similar in structure to an adult questioning intonation. Tonkova-Yampol'skaya concluded from her results that the first cry of an infant displays a biologically determined pattern which later acquires linguistic functions. Although it is not clear how the idealized adult intonation contours have been obtained, Tonkova-Yampol'skaya's results suggest an ontogenetic priority of intonation contours over segmental speech. Further evidence for this primacy is provided by the fact that processing of intonation contours (at least of those associated with emotion) is controlled by the right hemisphere (Blumstein & Cooper 1974; van Lancker 1975), the development of which phylogenetically precedes that of the left hemisphere. Observations of some aphasic patients, whose use of intonation patterns is less impaired than the performance in lexis and syntax, also supports the assumption of a priority of intonation over verbal control. Thus, intonation may be viewed as establishing a link between nonverbal and verbal modes of communication display.

There is little information about changes in intonation contours with advanced age, although Charlip (1968), who studied 25 subjects reading a standard text, found a significant increase in the number of downward inflections in women between 40 and 80.

Fundamental frequency perturbations. Rapidly varying f_0 differences (which are perceived by listeners as a trembling voice) are generally referred to as f_0 perturbations. They are shown on spectograms by a high variability of frequency lines, especially in the higher harmonics. It seems to be generally agreed that advancing age is accompanied by an increase in perturbations, which are said by Sedláčková, Vrticka & Supacek (1966) to be a consequence of impaired coordination in the central nervous system. A high pitch variability has also been found in early infancy (Stark, Rose & McLagen 1975) and in puberty (Depons & Pommez; cited by Luchsinger 1970: 287). While in old age these changes may be described as oscillations, the changes occurring in infancy and adolescence are rather abrupt shifts. It may be supposed that though both phenomena seem to reflect a lack of cortical control, the cortical centres involved are rather different.

Voice quality. Differences in phonatory and articulatory settings lead to different voice qualities which are subjectively perceived as timbre and acoustically measured by the energy distribution in the spectrum. Although voice quality is said to be one of the features which carry most information about individual characteristics such as sex and age (e.g. Fry 1968), virtually no research has been conducted in this area (see also Smith, this volume: ch. 4, 1.5). The stereotypes that exist with respect to changes of voice quality with age suggest that old age is accompanied by a 'hollow', 'weak', 'thin' and 'breathy' voice, but it seems difficult to define such labels acoustically. Scherer in ongoing studies on the verbal and vocal correlates of individual differences (cf. this volume: ch. 5) found an increase of breathiness, as judged by trained phoneticians, with increasing age, in German speakers ranging from 26 to 49 years of age. According to Sedláčková et al. (1966), the most common indicator of old age is the 'hollow' voice, due either to changes in chest resonance or to atrophy of vocal lips.

Intensity. Intensity of voice, the perceptual correlate of which is loudness, is physiologically determined mainly by the extent of subglottal pressure. Thus, we may expect a decrease in intensity with age due to diminishing vital capacities. Most results confirm this expectation (Luchsinger 1970; Ptacek & Sander 1966). Lefevre (1963; cited by Page 1966), however, found the voices of old persons to be either too loud or too soft. The loud voice may reflect a strategy to cope with the loss of hearing ability (Yannoulis & Yannatos 1966).

2.7. Paralinguistics: temporal aspects

Spontaneous speech is frequently interrupted by pauses, repetitions, mispronunciations, and nonlinguistic vocalizations. These and similar features are commonly referred to as hesitation phenomena and are seen (particularly silent pauses) to be strongly linked to the speaker's cognitive processes (Goldman-Eisler 1968; Lounsbury 1954). Goldman-Eisler distinguishes periods of long pauses and short speech time, indicating creative speech, and periods of short pauses and long speech time, indicating well-practised habitual sequences of words (Goldman-Eisler 1967). Two hypotheses may be derived from this. The first, assuming that the repertoire of well-practised word sequences increases with age, will state that fewer and shorter pauses should result. The second, assuming that with increasing age intellectual capacity declines and encoding processes require more time, will state that pauses should be longer in duration. A study by Kowal, O'Connell & Sabin (1975) using 5- to 18-year-olds supports the first hypothesis. When middle-aged subjects are investigated, the second hypothesis also seems to hold. Scherer (cf. this volume: ch. 5) found a positive relationship between mean length of computer-extracted pauses and age (r = 0.62 for German, r = 0.49 for American speakers). The results of Sabin, Clemmer, O'Connell & Kowal (in press), who noticed a tendency for length of silent pauses to increase from adolescence to adulthood (21 to 49 years), are also compatible with the second hypothesis. However, Sabin *et al.* suggest a different explanation. They argue that pause length increases as speech becomes more reflective. To decide whether encoding processes need more time or are more reflective as a function of age, the cognitive–semantic level of the speech output would have to be assessed independently of the occurrence of pauses. In advanced age (65 to 92 years), pauses tend to increase in duration and articulation time (phonation per time unit) tends to decrease (Mysak 1959). This may indicate that, in old age, the motor as well as the cognitive aspects of speech behaviour are impaired.

Results similar to those on pauses have been obtained with speech disturbances. In cases where studies are conducted with children and younger adults, a negative relationship between disturbances and age is found (cf. Yairi & Clifton 1972). When older people are included, a curvilinear relationship between age and disfluencies emerges. Thus, Yairi & Clifton (1972) report a mean disfluency rate (per 100 words) of 7.65 for children (mean age 5.5 years), 3.83 for younger adults, and 6.29 for older persons (69 to 87 years). According to these authors, similar factors are operating both in childhood and old age, the nature of these factors remaining unexplained.

Many problems have to be resolved before conclusions can be drawn from studies on hesitation phenomena. For example, the cognitive difficulty of the encoding processes required in a specific speech situation must be assessed independently of the occurrence of hesitation phenomena. Moreover, since the production of hesitation phenomena in speech has been shown to be strongly affected by emotional processes (see Mahl & Schulze 1964), the interaction of these processes with age has to be further investigated.

Summary of extralinguistic and paralinguistic features. In the preceding section, we saw that vocal and temporal aspects of speech can serve to differentiate between different categories of age. Intonation contours seem to provide information about the control of transmission of emotional meaning, while temporal phenomena in speech seem to reflect speed of cognitive encoding processes as well as the repertory of speech patterns in memory as a function of age. Most of these vocal and temporal markers are not directly linked to language acquisition but are likely to be independently determined by biological factors. For instance, fundamental frequency mean and range of voice seem to be primarily a function of biological factors, such as increasing body size (cf. Laver & Trudgill: this volume, ch. 1, 2.1). However, a closer inspection of the data available on f_0 suggests that there are factors operating which seem to reflect a culture-mediated view of biological changes.

3. Dynamic markers of sender age

Although speech behaviour may occur without reference to a listener, in most cases the sender intends to communicate his thoughts and feelings to a receiver, i.e. his speech has a communicative function. The purpose of this section is to discuss those sender markers in speech which reflect the state of the communicative ability of the speaker as related to his age and, more specifically, to examine the ways in which speakers of different ages adapt to the person they are addressing.

When a speaker varies his speech to cope with different communication settings or speech patterns, he selects different 'speech styles' (Giles & Powesland 1975), 'speech codes' (Berko Gleason 1973) or 'speech registers' (Halliday, McIntosh & Strevens 1964). While the term 'speech register' refers to individual morphological, phonetic, or paralinguistic features of an utterance, the terms 'speech style' and 'speech code' refer to a cluster of such features. The listener variables to which the speaker adapts may be of different kinds. For example, the speaker may talk to a foreigner, to a person of the other sex, to a familiar person or to a stranger. In empirical studies conducted in this field, the most salient feature of the person to which the speaker adapts is often age. Thus, it is not always easy to separate markers which indicate the communicative competence of the speaker from those which indicate the age of the receiver. Nevertheless, the specific manner in which a speaker adapts or fails to adapt to his audience can be a function of age and in this sense can be regarded as a sender age marker; the issue of receiver age markers will be discussed separately later.

Piaget, in describing the speech of children, makes a basic distinction between 'egocentric' and 'socialized' speech (Piaget 1955). In Piaget's view, egocentrism, indicated by a lack of awareness of any perspective other than one's own, is a salient characteristic of both cognition and speech in the preschool years. With development, 'socialized' speech takes the place of egocentric speech. In a critical reply to Piaget, Vygotsky (1962) claims that speech is socialized from the very beginning. He distinguishes 'egocentric' speech which has the function of self-guidance and later becomes 'inner speech' from 'communicative' speech (Piaget's socialized speech) which has the function of communication with others. It is difficult to decide at the present time which of these views is the more adequate, but they are not as incompatible as it may at first seem. Speech may be social in origin, and yet can be egocentric. As Kohlberg, Yaeger & Hjertholm (1968) point out, two factors may underlie egocentrism observed in communication: 'lack of social will', i.e. absence of desire to accommodate to a listener, and 'lack of cognitive skill', i.e. absence of competence to accommodate (cf. Dale 1976). There is considerable evidence that social will is present in the child very early, whereas cognitive skill sometimes lags behind.

A number of observations indicate a 'vocal empathy' – which might be interpreted as social will – at an early stage of life (cf. Crystal 1975). According to Lieberman, a child's fundamental frequency varies in height relative to that of his parent's voice (Lieberman 1967). For instance, the mean fundamental frequency of a 10-month-old boy reached 430 Hz when alone, 390 Hz when he was with his mother and 340 Hz when he was with his father. And the mean fundamental frequency of a 13-month-old girl's babbling was 390 Hz when she was with her mother and 290 Hz when she was with her father (the girl was not recorded alone). The fundamental frequency of the children's crying, however, did not change across situations. Wolff (1969), who states that a baby tends to follow adult pitch as early as 1 or 2 months, points out that the infant thus already has an active 'accommodation' of vocal patterns at his disposal. Using data from a two-year observational study of three children, aged 5, 3 and 2 years, Weeks (1971) concluded that children learn a number of different speech registers and begin to use them at approximately the same time as they begin to use language itself. She specifies the registers in terms of paralinguistic, phonological and morphological variations. Among the most frequently used registers are 'high pitch' and 'exaggerated intonation' which in one case occurred as early as 1 year 7 months; the least frequently used register is 'phonetic modification'. Weeks found clusters of registers correlating with specific behavioural situations, e.g. 'loudness' and 'clarification' (i.e. careful enunciation) are used in instruction-giving situations, 'high pitch' and 'exaggerated intonation' when talking to babies. According to Berko Gleason (1973),

4-year-old children may whine at their mothers, engage in verbal play with their peers, and reserve their narrative discursive tales for their grown-up friends (see Giles & Powesland 1975: 140). Shatz & Gelman (1973) observed strong syntactic differences in 4-year-old children depending on the age of the addressee. The children produced fewer, shorter and simpler sentences when speaking to 2-year-old children than when speaking to peers or adults. A case study by Bodine indicates that, at the age of 5, even a mongoloid baby had at least three styles of speech (cited by Giles & Powesland 1975: 139).

As regards the speech styles of older children, one might assume that speech with peers is composed of simpler structures than that with adults. However, just the opposite has been found in empirical investigations. Hahn (1948), studying 6-year-old children, and Houston (1969), studying 11-year-olds, showed that children use simplified syntax and foreshortened utterances when speaking to teachers and others in authority, while they construct a greater number of elaborated and compound sentences when speaking to other children. A possible explanation is that, when talking to adults to whom they ascribe status and power, children are afraid of failure and fall back into well-practised speech. This view is supported by the fact that such speech is characterized by hypercorrection of phonology (Houston 1969). When children are 6 or 7 years old, they have learned that language can provide different expressions according to the degree of familiarity they have with the person to whom speech is directed. For instance, children of this age use more casual words when speaking to their best friend than when speaking to a policeman, as shown by an experiment by Herrmann and Deutsch (cited in Herrmann 1978). At this age they have also adopted some of the politeness routines of formal adult speech (Berko Gleason 1973).

The studies reported so far suggest that children acquire communicative competence concurrently with linguistic competence. However, when such attempts at adaptation are also examined in terms of their efficiency, a considerable divergence between linguistic and communicative skills is revealed. To investigate efficiency of adaptation in terms of communication accuracy, Flavell and his colleagues used an experimental paradigm where children were instructed to explain the rules of a game either to a 'sighted' or to a 'blind-folded' listener (cf. Flavell et al. 1968). Results indicate that up to the age of 14, speakers' explanations do not differ markedly according to their listener. Only the 14-year-old-speakers provided the blind-folded listener with an appropriate amount of information. As Robinson and Robinson showed in several experiments, very young children are not even able to recognize when a message produced by a speaker is inadequate to a listener's requirements (cf. Robinson & Robinson 1977). Up to about 6 or 7 years, children tend to blame the listener for communication failure, but older children will attribute failure to the inadequacy of the speaker's message.

We cannot conclude from these experiments that young speakers are never able to meet the requirements of the listener. Studies conducted by Krauss & Glucksberg (1969, 1977) and by Shatz & Gelman (1973) have led to the specification of conditions under which young children's adaptation will or will not succeed. Krauss & Glucksberg (1969) used an experimental task in which pairs of visually separated subjects were required to communicate about unusual graphic forms. The designs were deliberately constructed so as not to have either short or familiar 'names'. Subjects were kindergarten children, first-grade, third-grade and fifth-grade children. Two kinds of measures were employed. The first kind reflected the speaker's success in transmitting the information, as measured by the receiver's ability to match the verbal report to the correct item in a set given to him. The second class of measures involved lexical characteristics of the speaker's message, such as type–token ratio (a measure of lexical diversity) and use of common words (classified according to the Thorndike–Lorge list). Initial performance in communication accuracy was roughly the same for all age groups, but the age groups differed markedly in the rates at which errors decreased when the experimenter commented on the mistakes the subjects had been making. While older children showed a rapid decrease in the number of errors over repetitive trials, the performance of kindergarten children showed no improvement. Of the lexical measures, none was related to the speaker's age. The results suggest that younger children, though they have acquired language skills, use an idiosyncratic rather than a shared code. The idiosyncrasy was further indicated by the fact that the young speakers could understand their own messages when presented with them after a three-week period. When older children were tested on the same problem, but without feedback from the experimenters, no marked improvement was observed over the course of successive trials before the ninth grade, and even children of this age did not attain the accuracy that adults displayed from the very first trial (Krauss & Glucksberg 1977). However, when the communication task was simplified (drawings of familiar objects instead of unusual graphic forms), the performance of even very young children began to approach the adult level. Shatz & Gelman's (1973) study, mentioned above, also suggests that children are not generally unable to take into account the age of the listener. Although performance of most of the 4-year-old children in tests of 'egocentrism' was poor (indicating that they were unable to take the perspective of another person), all children adjusted their speech to younger and older listeners in terms of syntactic complexity.

Given these empirical results, we may draw the following conclusions. Even very young children attempt to take into account the listener's requirements, and appear to be successful in terms of paralinguistic (e.g. Weeks 1971) and syntactic aspects (e.g. Shatz & Gelman 1973). However, the ability to reach full semantic adjustment (i.e. in relatively difficult semantic situations) is not acquired before the age of 14. The reason for the lack of semantic adjustment in younger children is probably, as Krauss & Glucksberg suggest, a limitation of processing capacity. Under conditions of cognitive overload (e.g. communication about unusual graphic forms) the child's linguistic–cognitive abilities are entirely self-directed, at the expense of the listener's requirements. Obviously, the individual aspects of communicative competence follow a similar pattern of development to those of general linguistic development. The ability to adapt syntactically is attained at about 6 years, but semantic development continues at least until adolescence.

Little information is available concerning the development of communicative competence in older people. From some results on interviewees' responses as a function of age (cf. Blake & Mouton 1961) which suggest that older people conform less to interviewers' opinions than younger people, we may hypothesize that the speech of older people is more 'egocentric' (i.e. takes the listener's requirements less into account). Actually, Labov (1970: 19) supposes that 'old men often show a narrow range in that their motivation for style shifting disappears along with their concern for power relationships . . .'. However, assuming that older people have available a wide variety of well-practised syntactic and semantic speech patterns, nonadjustment or egocentrism might be supposed to appear in gross semantic variations, such as choice of topic, rather than in syntactic or finer semantic features. Such stereotypes as older people who bore their listeners with tedious stories of former times and complaints about youth (Kogan 1961; Thomas 1972; Tuckman & Lorge 1953) would seem to support this prediction.

4. Markers of receiver age

A speaker's verbal and nonverbal behaviour is affected not only by his own age but also by that of his addressee (cf. Giles, Scherer & Taylor, this volume: ch. 9, 3.4) and specifically by those characteristics attributed to different ages. Thus, a speaker may talk in a loud voice and very slowly to older people, assuming that they are hard of hearing and have difficulties in comprehending. The best known phenomenon in this area is so-called baby-talk or 'Ammensprache'. Baby-talk is used by adults and even by older children when speaking to infants, and can be distinguished from normal speech by phonetic, morphological, syntactic and paralinguistic features. Most salient are the paralinguistic features. When speaking to young children, adults use a higher overall pitch, a greater rising intonation, more instances of emphatic stress (Sachs, Brown & Salerno 1976) and pause after each sentence (Dale 1974). Syntactically, the utterances directed to infants contain few or no complex clauses and few modifiers or optional constituents (cf. Newport 1977). While the phenomenon of baby-talk has been found in a variety of cultures (e.g. Nootka (Sapir 1915), Arab, English (Ferguson 1964), Marathi (Kelkar 1964), Comanche and Spanish (Casagrande 1964)) and may therefore assume the status of a language universal (cf. Rūķe-Draviņa 1976), there is no agreement upon the universality of its specific forms. A position of extreme universality is held by Lewis who claims that there are identical baby-talk words in all languages (Lewis 1936). Jakobson simply attempts to build up five possible phonomorphological models of universality (Jakobson 1960). On the other hand, Ferguson doubts whether there are any universal forms. According to him, 'baby-talk words are not universal, but are transmitted much like other language phenomena in the community' (Ferguson, 1964: 103). Nevertheless, some universal characteristics seem to exist, e.g. high pitch, reduplication, diminutive pet forms and the replacements of personal pronouns by names (see Rūķe-Draviņa 1976). Simplification of consonant clusters, general labialization and palatalization are found in some languages, but not in others (cf. Giles & Powesland 1975, Rūķe-Draviņa 1976). Moreover, the extent and duration of baby-talk varies from culture to culture. In most cultures, it is not restricted to mothers but is used by other adults as well as by older children (Weeks 1971). However, there are some cultures where men never use baby-talk (Crawford 1974). Rebelsky & Hanks (1971) found that in the American culture the overall verbal interaction of fathers with their infants is very rare during the first three months.

The exact age of the 'baby' addressed is not universally marked by baby-talk. For example, in Comanche, the upper limit for using baby-talk is about 3 to 4 years (Casagrande 1964). In Japan, it is up to kindergarten or nursery-school age; and in Cocopa (an American Indian language), baby-talk is used for boys up to 6 or 7 years, but for girls up to 10 years and even in the early and mid-teens when the mother wants to show affection (cf. Ferguson 1977).

The studies of baby-talk are mostly based on the judgements of informants, but there are also some studies where differences between speech directed to adults and speech directed to children of different ages have been experimentally investigated. Granowsky & Krossner (1970) compared the speech of kindergarten teachers talking to each other and talking to their children in the class-room, and found significant differences in measures of syntax and semantics. For instance, adult-to-children speech contained shorter and simpler sentences, and fewer compound and complex sentences, than was the case in teacher-to-teacher speech. Differences have also been found in vocabulary: adult-to-children speech showed a lower verbal diversification (measured by type–token ratio) and a greater number of the thousand most frequently used words. Snow (1972), investigating the speech of mothers to 2- and 10-year-olds found that the younger children were talked to in shorter and grammatically simpler utterances than older children. Fraser & Roberts (1975), comparing the speech of mothers to children of four different ages in terms of five different measures, clearly demonstrated significant effects of children's age on syntactic and semantic measures. The total amount of mothers' speech increases as the children progress through the ages of 1.5, 2.5 and 4, and then decreases slightly up to the age of 6. Mean utterance length, grammatical complexity and verbal diversification show a marked increase from 1.5 to 2.5, and small or even no changes thereafter. It would seem clear that marked changes in adults' speech to children occur only during early childhood, while no such fine discriminations are made when speaking to older children of different ages. This conclusion is supported by Kean's (1968) study which found no significant differences in verbal behaviour in the class-room between second-grade teachers and fifth-grade teachers, in both vocabulary and syntax. It is apparent from the findings reported that there are markers in adult speech which signal an adaptation or 'accommodation' (cf. Giles 1977) to the age of the child spoken to, but the question also arises of which aspects of age adult speech adapts to. A reasonable hypothesis would be that the speaker adapts to the linguistic competence of the child. This hypothesis would be compatible with the results of Fraser & Roberts (1975) and of Kean (1968), where adult speech behaviour was shown to correspond to children's development in terms of syntactic patterns. In early childhood, syntactic development shows marked improvements which seem to be reflected in mothers' speech. At the age of 6, when syntactic development is virtually complete, adaptation is no longer required. However, finer syntactic analysis may yield a somewhat different picture of adaptation to linguistically unsophisticated listeners. An approach in this direction has been attempted by Newport (1977), who compared the speech of adults directed to young children (from 1 to 2 years) with that directed to an adult experimenter. Newport found that, although surface sentence length is reduced in child-directed speech, this does not necessarily facilitate syntactic processing. Many utterances are shortened by the deletion of deep structure constituents, e.g. the auxiliary and *you* in yes–no questions, and the object in a variety of sentence types. The listener must therefore reconstruct the omitted constituents and, as Fodor, Bever & Garrett (1974) have argued, the processing of the sentence may thus become more complicated. Consequently the accommodations of adult speech to language learners may be counterproductive for the acquisition of linguistic competence. On the other hand, Newport argues that, by keeping an otherwise lengthy sentence within the limits of the child's short-term memory span, it serves rather to maintain the child's attention. Additional support for such a hypothesis may be drawn from studies of the paralinguistic modifications of adult speech directed to young children. Long pauses between sentences (Dale 1974), stressing of elements to which a response is desired (Garnica 1977), lengthening of content words (Garnica 1977) and repetition of short sentences (Newport 1977), all suggest that adult accommodation to child age is in terms of cognitive, rather than linguistic, competence.

However, adult accommodation to child age is not exclusively related to cognitive factors. It is, for instance, scarcely conceivable that the high overall pitch in baby-talk serves a cognitive function. We may suggest, rather that the adult is signalling affection by making his voice similar to that of the child. As we have seen above, this 'vocal empathy' has even been observed in infants, who adjust to their parents in terms of voice height (cf. Crystal 1975).

The speaker also adjusts to other aspects of age, and the authority ascribed to different age stages is an important one. This is perhaps best indicated in pronominal forms of address, which in many languages (including German, Russian and French) give information about the age of the addressee. In general, adults are addressed with the less familiar plural form of personal pronouns, while the more familiar singular form is addressed to children (cf. Lambert & Tucker 1976). In Japanese, thirty-one different forms of *you* and *I* have been noted (Balkenhol, pers. comm.). The age of both addressee and addressor influences the choice of form in a given situation. Three age classes are distinguished: young (adolescents and children excluding infants), middle and old. For example, the form *otaku* can only be used when a middle-aged person is speaking to an older person, or when an older person is speaking to a middle-aged person. It cannot be used when middle-aged people address their own age group or younger people. In many cases, the general age rules are modified by various other social factors, such as genealogical distance, sex, group membership, social situation and relative authority. Those speech communities employing the pronominal distinction differ with regard both to the ages at which changes occur and the relative influence of other social factors. For example, among the Russian gentry, a child would exchange *ty* (the singular form) with the mother until about school age, but older children and adolescents use the formal pronoun *vy* to their parents (Friedrich 1972). In Germany, a long-term trend raising the age at which the singular form *du* is exchanged for the plural form *Sie* can be observed.

Summary. The preceding section has shown that a speaker marks the age of the person he is addressing in his speech. Such age markers may be paralinguistic features, such as pitch, loudness and pauses, as well as syntactic patterns and semantic usage. Some studies have suggested that adult speakers adapt their speech to a child on the basis of sender age markers inferred from the child's speech. It had first been hypothesized that adult adaptation corresponds to the child's linguistic competence, but more recent investigations seem to suggest that it corresponds more closely to cognitive constraints, such as limitation of memory span. As the study of address forms in various cultures shows, there are markers which indicate both the age of the listener and the age of the speaker. Markers of this kind are primarily found in cultures where older age is associated with greater authority.

5. Concluding remarks

Any investigation of social markers in speech should be primarily concerned to describe *how* the social category under consideration is marked in speech. Thus, work on age markers should report results in observable speech differences between different ages. However, this task is complicated by the fact that the differences studied are mostly associated with developmental changes. Development consists not only of a continuous accumulation of behavioural elements but also of sudden shifts leading to a qualitatively different organization of these elements. Hence, in comparing speech phenomena at different age levels, we run the risk of comparing apples with pears, since we cannot be sure that we are using the descriptive concepts in an unequivocal manner. For example, there is no *a priori* reason for assuming it is justifiable to refer to sentences both for the utterances of a 1-year-old child and for adult speech. The theoretical viewpoint of the observer – more than is the case in investigations of sex, personality or ethnic background differences – will influence which phenomena are conceptualized by common terms and then compared through different ages. As we have seen, theoretical viewpoints influence even assumptions about the onset of speech-like behaviour. This chapter has therefore had to deal more extensively with underlying theoretical issues than other chapters in this volume.

The speech phenomena themselves as well as the functions they fulfil for the speaker change in the course of development, but unfortunately research into changes in speech functions has been neglected. At first all words or word-like formations a child utters appear to function as expressions of an affective state. For example, if a young child is hungry or afraid he may respond to that state with the word *mama*. From the age of 2 upwards the primary function of word utterances will be to express a thought linguistically. In adolescence, a further function may develop. Adolescents often use or even coin specific words to signal their membership of a specific group (similar to the use of Black English Vernacular to signal membership of that culture; cf. Labov 1972). In old age people may continue to use the language they learned when young irrespective of specific contexts (cf. Clyne 1977). As section 2 on static sender age markers has shown, a further problem in the study of age markers is that there is almost no case where changes in the variables under study can be said to occur only as a function of age. Even an apparently straightforward feature like voice is affected not only by biologically determined age-related processes, but also by social and emotional factors which may or may not be associated with age. Moreover, empirical evidence is often derived from cross-sectional studies which cannot take into account long-term changes in social standards or attitudes.

Section 3 on dynamic sender age markers has dealt with markers indicating the development of communicative competence involving social and role-taking skills, whereas section 4 on receiver age markers has focused on features reflecting the age of the addressee. Though both aspects are intrinsically linked they have been treated separately since most empirical studies have manipulated only one age variable, either age of speaker or age of addressee. However, it seems reasonable to assume, for instance, that a child talks to an old man in a different manner from a young adult speaking to the same old man, although both speakers' verbal behaviours are affected by the age of the old man. Both speakers adjust to age in a different way, and, presumably, to different aspects of age. More research than is presently available would be needed to disentangle the complicated relations between age of speaker and age of addressee.

Section 4 should have indicated that the concept of 'adjustment' or 'accommodation', which has elicited some promising ideas (see Giles 1977), needs further explication. The problem turns on the questions of what aspects of the addressee are adjusted to, and to what extent adjustment may be made without the information to be transmitted being lost. As we have seen, Newport (1977) has made a first attempt to specify the aspects of age to which adults adapt when speaking to young children. Two more points should be made concerning speech behaviour of adults when adjusting to children. The first one is that many of the studies are biased by the fact that they do not reflect adult-to-child speech in general, but rather mother-to-own-child speech (see Giles & Powesland 1975). The second point, related to the former, is that there are important variables other than age which exert a strong influence on adults' verbal behaviour to children. Among these variables are 'sex', 'birth order' (Rothbart 1971), 'retardedness' of the child (Spradlin & Rosenberg 1964), 'social class' of the mother (Bee et al. 1969) and 'topic' of speech (Fraser & Roberts 1975). Though investigation of the interaction of these variables with age has scarcely begun, it may be supposed that their influence sometimes overrides that of age. Ling & Ling (1974), who observed forty-eight male and female children of different ages (11 to 36 months) and birth order in communication with their mothers found that, while the amount of nonverbal vocalization was merely a function of age, the amount of verbal communication was affected neither by age nor by sex but only by position in family. Mothers of first-born babies communicated verbally to a significantly greater extent than did mothers of last-born children. However, this finding does not exclude the possibility of other age markers differentiating between the different ages of both first-

and last-born children. Further research ought to examine the combined effects of different variables within a single design to reveal the complicated interactions of these variables on speech behaviour.

References

Allport, G. W. & Cantril, H. 1934. Judging personality from voice. *Journal of Social Psychology*, 5, 37–54.

Austin, J. L. 1962. *How to Do Things with Words*. Oxford.

Bakker, F. J. 1969. Untersuchungen zur Entwicklung des Aktionsquotienten. In H. Helmers (ed.) *Zur Sprache des Kindes*. Darmstadt.

Balken, E. R. & Masserman, J. H. 1940. The language of phantasy: III: The language of the phantasies of patients with conversion hysteria, anxiety state, and obsessive-compulsive neuroses. *Journal of Psychology*, 10, 75–86.

Bates, E., Camaioni, L. & Volterra, V. 1973. *The Acquisition of Performatives Prior to Speech*. Technical Report no. 129. Consiglio Nationale delle Ricerche. Rome.

Bee, H. L., van Egeren, F., Streissguth, A. P., Nyman, B. A. & Leckie, M. S. 1969. Social class differences in maternal teaching strategies and speech patterns. *Developmental Psychology*, 1, 726–34.

Berko Gleason, J. 1973. Code switching in children's language. In T. E. Moore (ed.) *Cognitive Development and the Acquisition of Language*. New York.

Bernstein, B. 1960. Language and social class. *British Journal of Sociology*, 11, 271–6.

Bernstein, B. 1967. Soziokulturelle Determinanten des Lernens. In F. Weinert (ed.) *Pädagogische Psychologie*. Cologne.

Bever, T. G. 1970. The cognitive basis for linguistic structures. In J. R. Hayes (ed.) *Cognition and the Development of Language*. New York.

Blake, R. R. & Mouton, J. S. 1961. Conformity, resistance, and conversion. In I. A. Berg & B. M. Bass (eds.) *Conformity and Deviation*. New York.

Bloom, L. 1970. *Language Development: form and function in emerging grammars*. Cambridge, Mass.

Blumstein, S. & Cooper, W. E. 1974. Hemispheric processing of intonation contours. *Cortex*, 10, 146–58.

Bodine, A. 1975. Sex differences in language. In B. Thorne & N. Henley (eds.) *Language and Sex: difference and dominance*. Rowley, Mass.

Böhme, G. & Hecker, G. 1970. Gerontologische Untersuchungen über Stimmumfang und Sprechstimmlage. *Folia Phoniatrica*, 22, 176–84.

Bowerman, M. 1969. The pivot–open class distinction. Unpublished paper, Department of Social Relations, Harvard University.

1975. The acquisition of word meaning. An investigation of some current conflicts. Paper given at Third International Child Language Symposium, London.

1976. Semantic factors in the acquisition of rules for word use and sentence construction. In D. Morehead & A. E. Morehead (eds.) *Language Deficiency in Children: selected readings*. Baltimore, Md.

Braine, M. D. S. 1963. The ontogeny of English phrase structure: the first phase. *Language*, 39, 1–13.

Braun, P. 1965. Geläufige Satzbaupläne in Aufsätzen der Sieben- bis Zehnjährigen. *Westermanns Pädagogische Beiträge*, 1, 13–20.

Brown, R. 1973. *A First Language*. Cambridge, Mass.

Brown, R. & Fraser, C. 1964. The acquisition of syntax. In U. Bellugi & R. Brown (eds.) *First Language Acquisition*. Society for Research in Child Development Monographs, *29*.

Brown, R., Cazden, C. & Bellugi, U. 1969. The child's grammar from I to II. In a J. P. Hill (ed.) *Minnesota Symposium on Child Psychology, 19*, 1–15.

Bruner, J. S. 1964. The course of cognitive growth. *American Psychologist, 19*, 1–15.

1975. From communication to language – a psychological perspective. *Cognition 3*, 255–87.

Bühler, K. 1934. *Sprachtheorie*. Jena.

Bullowa, M., Fidelholtz, J. L. & Kessler, A. R. 1976. Infant vocalization: communication before speech. In W. C. McCormack & S. A. Wurm (eds.) *Language and Man: anthropological issues*. The Hague.

Busemann, A. 1925. *Die Sprache der Jugend als Ausdruck der Entwicklungsrhythmik*. Jena.

Casagrande, J. B. 1964 Comanche baby language. In D. Hymes (ed.) *Language in Culture and Society*. New York.

Charlip, W. S. 1968. The aging female voice: selected fundamental frequency characteristics and listener judgements. Dissertation, Purdue University. *Dissertation Abstracts*, 1968, *29 B*, 1198–B.

Chomsky, C. 1969. *The Acquisition of Syntax in Children from 5 to 10*. Cambridge, Mass.

Chomsky, N. 1967. The formal nature of language. Appendix A in E. H. Lenneberg, *Biological Foundations of Language*. New York.

1968. *Language and Mind*. New York.

Clark, E. V. 1973. What's in a word? On the child's acquisition of semantics in his first language. In T. E. Moore (ed.) *Cognitive Development and the Acquisition of Language*. New York.

1974. On opposites: studying the child's lexicon. In *Problèmes actuels en psycholinguistique*. Colloques internationaux du centre national de la recherche scientifique no. 206, Paris, December 1971. Paris.

1975. Knowledge, context, and strategy in the acquisition of meaning. In *Georgetown University Round Table on Languages and Linguistics 1975*. Washington, DC.

Clyne, M. G. 1977. Bilingualism of the elderly. *Talanya, 4*, 45–56.

Crawford, J. M. 1974. Baby talk in an American Indian language. Paper presented at the Conference on Language Input and Acquisition, Boston.

Cromer, R. F. 1974. The development of language and cognition: the cognition hypothesis. In B. Foss (ed.) *New Perspectives in Child Development*. London.

Crystal, D. 1975. *The English Tone of Voice: essays in intonation, prosody and paralanguage*. London.

Curry, E. T. 1940. The pitch characteristics of the adolescent male voice. *Speech Monographs, 7*, 48–62.

Dale, P. S. 1974. Hesitations in maternal speech. *Language and Speech, 17*, 174–81.

1976. *Language Development: structure and function*. 2nd ed. New York.

Dittmann, A. T. 1972. *Interpersonal Messages of Emotion*. New York.

Dore, J. 1975. Holophrases, speech acts, and linguistic universals. *Journal of Child Language, 2*, 21–40.

Duffy, R. J. 1958. The vocal pitch characteristics of eleven-, thirteen-, and fifteen-year-old female speakers. Dissertation, State University of Iowa. *Dissertation Abstracts*, *18*, 599.

Endres, W., Bambach, W. & Flösser, G. 1971. Voice spectrograms as a function of age, voice disguise, and voice imitation. *Journal of the Acoustical Society of America*, *49*, 1842–8.

Ervin, S. M. & Miller, W. 1963. Language development. In H. W. Stevenson (ed.) *Child Psychology*. Chicago.

Fairbanks, G. 1942. An acoustical study of the pitch of infant hunger wails. *Child Development*, *13*, 227–32.

Fairbanks, G., Herbert, E. S. & Hammond, J. M. 1949. An acoustical study of vocal pitch in seven and eight-year-old girls. *Child Development*, *20*, 71–8.

Fairbanks, G., Wiley, J. H. & Lassman, F. M. 1949. An acoustical study of vocal pitch in seven and eight-year-old boys. *Child Development*, *20*, 63–9.

Ferguson, C. A. 1964. Baby talk in six languages. *American Anthropologist*, *66* (Supplement no. 6), 103–14.

　1976. Learning to pronounce: the earliest stages of phonological development in the child. Paper presented at the Conference on the Early Behavioral Assessment of the Communicative and Cognitive Abilities of the Developmentally Disabled, Orcas Island.

　1977. Baby talk as a simplified register. In C. E. Snow & C. A. Ferguson (eds.) *Talking to Children: language input and acquisition*. Cambridge.

Flateau, T. S. & Gutzmann, H. 1906. Die Stimme des Säuglings. *Archiv für Laryngologie und Rhinologie*, *18*, 139–51.

Flavell, J. H., Botkin, P. T., Fry, C. L. Jr, Wright, J. W. & Jarvis, P. E. 1968. *The Development of Role-taking and Communication Skills in Children*. New York.

Fodor, J. A., Bever, T. G. & Garrett, M. 1974. *The Psychology of Language: an introduction to psycholinguistics and grammar*. New York.

Fraser, C. In press. The ontogenesis of syntax and semantics: a review of some recent developments. *International Journal of Psycholinguistics*.

Fraser, C. & Roberts, N. 1975. Mothers' speech to children of four different ages. *Journal of Psycholinguistic Research*, *4*, 9–16.

Friedrich, P. 1972. Social context and semantic feature: the Russian pronominal usage. In J. J. Gumperz & D. Hymes (eds.) *Directions in Sociolinguistics: the ethnography of communication*. New York.

Fry, D. B. 1968. Prosodic phenomena. In B. Malmberg (ed.) *Manual of Phonetics*. Amsterdam.

Garnica, L. K. 1977. Some prosodic and paralinguistic features of speech to young children. In C. E. Snow & C. A. Ferguson (eds.) *Talking to Children: language input and acquisition*. Cambridge.

Gellhorn, E. & Kiely, W. F. 1972. Autonomic nervous system in psychiatric disorder. In J. Mendels (ed.) *Biological Psychiatry*. New York.

Giles, H. 1977. Social psychology and applied linguistics: towards an integrative approach. *ITL: Review of Applied Linguistics*, *331*, 27–42.

Giles, H. & Powesland, P. F. 1975. *Speech Style and Social Evaluation*. London.

Goldman-Eisler, F. 1967. Sequential temporal patterns and cognitive processes in speech. *Language and Speech*, *10*, 122–32.

　1968. *Psycholinguistics*. London.

Granowsky, S. & Krossner, W. J. 1970. Kindergarten teachers as models for children's speech. *Journal of Experimental Education*, *38*, 23–8.

Hahn, E. 1948. An analysis of the content and form of the speech of first grade children. *Quarterly Journal of Speech, 34*, 361–6.

Halliday, M. A. K. 1975. *Learning How to Mean*. London.

Halliday, M. A. K., McIntosh, A. & Strevens, P. D. 1964. *The Linguistic Sciences and Language Teaching*. London.

Hanley, T. D. 1951. An analysis of vocal frequency and duration characteristics of selected dialect regions. *Speech Monographs, 18*, 78–93.

Hartlieb, K. 1962. Erbliche Merkmale der menschlichen Stimme. *Zeitschrift für menschliche Vererbung und Konstitutionslehre, 36*, 413.

Hass, W. A. & Wepman, J. M. 1974. Dimensions of individual difference in the spoken syntax of school children. *Journal of Speech and Hearing Research, 17*, 455–69.

Heinl-Hutchinson, M. 1975. Untersuchung zur Sprechweise und deren Beziehung zur Lebenszufriedenheit bei älteren Menschen. Master's thesis, University of Giessen.

Herrmann, R. 1978. Zur Entwicklung der Sprachschichtrepräsentation in der späteren Kindheit. In G. Augst (ed.) *Spracherwerb von 6–16*. Düsseldorf.

Herzog, H. 1933. Stimme und Personlichkeit. *Zeitschrift für Psychologie, 130*, 300–79.

Hetzer, H. & Flakowski, H. 1972. *Die entwicklungsbedingten Stilformen von kindlichen und jugendlichen Schreibern*. 4th ed. Munich.

Hollien, H. & Jackson, B. 1967. Normative SSF data on southern male university students. Progress Report to NIH, Grant NB-OX397.

1973. Normative data on the speaking fundamental frequency characteristics of young adult males. *Journal of Phonetics, 1*, 177–200.

Hollien, H. & Malcik, E. 1962. Adolescent voice change in southern Negro males. *Speech Monographs, 24*, 53–8.

Hollien, H. & Paul, P. 1969. A second evaluation of the speaking fundamental frequency characteristics of post-adolescent girls. *Language and Speech, 12*, 119–24.

Hollien, H. & Shipp, F. T. 1972. Speaking fundamental frequency and chronological age in males. *Journal of Speech and Hearing Research, 15*, 155–9.

Hollien, H., Malcik, E. & Hollien, B. 1965. Adolescent voice changes in southern White males. *Speech Monographs, 32*, 87–90.

Houston, S. H. 1969. Child Black English: the school register. Paper read at the 44th Annual Meeting of the Linguistic Society of America, San Francisco.

Irwin, O. C. & Chen, H. P. 1946. Development of speech during infancy. *Journal of Experimental Psychology, 36*, 431–6.

Jakobson, R. 1960. Why 'mamma' and 'papa'? In B. Kaplan (ed.) *Perspectives in Psychological Theory*. New York.

1968. *Child Language, Aphasia, and Phonological Universals*. The Hague.

Jakobson, R. & Halle, M. 1956. *Fundamentals of Language*. The Hague.

Kean, J. M. 1968. Linguistic structure of second and fifth grade teachers' oral classroom language. *American Educational Research Journal, 5*, 599–615.

Keating, P. & Buhr, R. 1978. Fundamental frequency in the speech of infants and children. *Journal of the Acoustical Society of America, 63*, 567–71.

Kelkar, A. 1964. Marathi baby-talk. *Word, 20*, 40–54.

Klein, W. H. 1978. Kindersprache–Erwachsenensprache. Texte im Vergleich. In G. Augst (ed.) *Spracherwerb von 6–16*. Düsseldorf.

Kogan, N. 1961. Attitudes toward old people: the development of a scale and an examination of correlates. *Journal of Abnormal and Social Psychology*, *62*, 44–54.

Kohlberg, L., Yaeger, J. & Hjertholm, E. 1968. Private speech: four studies and a review of theories. *Child Development*, *39*, 691–736.

Kowal, S., O'Connell, D. C. & Sabin, E. J. 1975. Development of temporal patterning and vocal hesitations in spontaneous narratives. *Journal of Psycholinguistic Research*, *4*, 195–207.

Kramer, E. 1963. Judgement of personal characteristics and emotions from non-verbal properties of speech. *Psychological Bulletin*, *60*, 408–20.

Krauss, R. M. & Glucksberg, S. 1969. The development of communication competence as a function of age. *Child Development*, *40*, 255–66.

1977. Social and nonsocial speech. *Scientific American*, *236*, 100–5.

Labov, W. 1970. *The Study of Nonstandard English*, 19–21. National Council, of Teachers of English, Urbana, Ill.

1972. *Language in the Inner City: studies in Black English Vernacular*. Conduct and Communication, *3*. Philadelphia.

Lambert, W. & Tucker, G. R. 1976. *Tu, Vous, Usted: a social-psychological study of address patterns*. Rowley, Mass.

Lancker, D. van 1975. *Heterogeneity in Language and Speech: neurolinguistic studies*. UCLA Working Papers in Phonetics, *29*.

Lange, G. & Neuhaus, W. 1969. Der Strukturwandel der Kindersprache während der Zeit vom 6. bis 9. Lebensjahr (first published 1934). In H. Helmers (ed.) *Zur Sprache des Kindes*. Darmstadt.

Lenneberg, E. H. 1967. *Biological Foundations of Language*. New York.

Leopold, W. F. 1939. *Speech Development in a Bilingual Child: a linguist's record*, vol. I, *Vocabulary Growth in the First Two Years*. Evanston, Ill.

1949. *Speech development in a Bilingual Child: a linguist's record*, vol. III. *Grammar and General Problems in the First Two Years*. Evanston, Ill.

Leuninger, H., Miller, H. & Müller, F. 1972. *Psycholinguistik. Ein Forschungsbericht*. Frankfurt.

Lewis, A. 1936. *Infant speech: a study of the beginnings of language*. New York.

Liebermann, P. 1967. *Intonation, Perception and Language*. Cambridge, Mass.

Lindner, G. 1882. Beobachtungen und Bemerkungen über die Entwicklung der Sprache des Kindes. *Kosmos*, *6*, 321–42, 430–41.

Ling, D. & Ling, A. H. 1974. Communication development in the first three years of life. *Journal of Speech and Hearing Research*, *17*, 146–59.

Linke, E. 1953. A study of pitch characteristics of female voices and their relationship to vocal effectiveness. PhD dissertation, State University of Iowa.

Lounsbury, F. G. 1954. Transitional probability, linguistic structure, and systems of habit-family hierarchies. In C. E. Osgood & T. A. Sebeok (eds.) *Psycholinguistics*. 1st ed. Baltimore, Md. 2nd ed. 1965, Bloomington, Ind.

Luchsinger, R. 1970. *Die Stimme und ihre Störungen*. 3rd ed. Vienna. (1st ed. 1959.)

McCarthy, D. 1954. Language development in children. In L. Carmichael (ed.) *Manual of Child Psychology*. New York.

McGlone, R. E. & Hollien, H. 1963. Vocal pitch characteristics of aged women. *Journal of Speech and Hearing Research*, *6*, 164–70.

McNeill, D. 1966. Developmental psycholinguistics. In F. Smith & G. A. Miller (eds.) *The Genesis of Language: a psycholinguistic approach*. Cambridge, Mass.

1970a. *The Acquisition of Language: the study of developmental psycholinguistics.* New York.

1970b. The development of language. In P. H. Mussen (ed.) *Carmichael's Manual of Child Psychology*, vol. I. 3rd ed. New York.

1971. The capacity for the ontogenesis of grammar. In D. I. Slobin (ed.) *The Ontogenesis of Grammar.* New York.

Mahl, G. F. & Schulze, G. 1964. Psychological research in the extralinguistic area. In T. A. Sebeok, A. S. Hayes & M. C. Bateson (eds.) *Approaches to semiotics.* The Hague.

Majewski, W., Hollien, H. & Zalewki, J. 1972. Speaking fundamental frequency of Polish adult males. *Phonetica, 25,* 119–25.

Markey, J. F. 1928. *The Symbolic Process and its Integration in Children.* New York.

Menyuk, P. 1969. *Sentences Children Use.* Cambridge, Mass.

Michel, J. F., Hollien, H. & Moore, P. 1966. Speaking fundamental frequency characteristics of 15, 16 and 17 year-old girls. *Language and Speech, 9,* 46–51.

Miller, G. A. 1951. *Language and Communication.* New York.

Mitchell, J. 1958. Speech and language impairment in the older patient. *Geriatrics, 13,* 467–76.

Morris, C. W. 1939. Foundations of the theory of signs. In O. Neurath, R. Carnap & C. Morris (eds.) *International Encyclopedia of Unified Science*, vol. I. Chicago.

Müller, E., Hollien, H. & Murray, T. 1974. Perceptual responses to infant crying: identification of cry tapes. *Journal of Child Language, 1,* 89–95.

Mysak, E. D. 1959. Pitch and duration characteristics of older males. *Journal of Speech and Hearing Research, 2,* 46–54.

Mysak, E. D. & Hanley, T. D. 1958. Vocal aging. *Journal of Gerontology, 13,* 309.

Nelson, K. 1973. *Structure and Strategy in Learning to Talk.* Society for Research in Child Development Monographs, *38,* no. 149.

1974. Concept, word, and sentence: interrelations in acquisition and development. *Psychological Review, 81,* 267–85.

Newport, E. L. 1977. Motherese: the speech of mothers to young children. In N. J. Castellan, Jr, D. B. Pisoni & G. R. Potts (eds.) *Cognitive Theory,* vol. II. Hillsdale, NJ.

Oevermann, U. 1972. *Sprache und soziale Herkunft.* Frankfurt/M.

Oksaar, E. 1977. *Spracherwerb im Vorschulalter: Einführung in die Pädolinguistik.* Stuttgart.

Oller, D. K., Wieman, L. A., Doyle, W. J. & Ross, C. 1976. Infant babbling and speech. *Journal of Child Language, 3,* 1–11.

Olmsted, D. L. 1971. *Out of the Mouth of Babes: earliest stages in language learning.* The Hague.

Ostwald, P. F. 1963. *Soundmaking: the acoustic communication of emotion.* Springfield, Ill.

Ostwald, P. F., Phibbs, R. & Fox, S. 1968. Diagnostic use of infant cry. *Biology of Neonates, 13,* 68–82.

Page, E. R. 1966. Speech and language characteristics of institutionalized geriatric patients. In *7th International Congress of Gerontology, Vienna, Austria, 1966, Proceedings, Clinical Medicine,* vol. IV: 7.

Pear, T. H. 1931. *Voice and Personality.* London.

Philhour, C. W. 1948. An experimental study of the relationships between perception of vocal pitch in connected speech and certain measures of vocal frequency. Doctoral dissertation, University of Iowa.

Piaget, J. 1955. *The Language and Thought of the Child*. Cleveland, Ohio.

Pronovost, W. 1942. An experimental study of methods for determining natural and habitual pitch. *Speech Monographs, 9*, 111–23.

Ptacek, P. H. & Sander, E. K. 1966. Age recognition from the voice. *Journal of Speech and Hearing Research, 9*, 273–7.

Ptacek, P. H., Sander, E. K., Maloney, W. H. & Jackson, C. C. R. 1966. Phonatory and related changes with advanced age. *Journal of Speech and Hearing Research, 9*, 353–60.

Rebelsky, F. & Hanks, C. 1971. Fathers' verbal interaction with infants in the first three months of life. *Child Development, 42*, 63–8.

Robinson, E. J. & Robinson, W. P. 1977. Development in the understanding of causes of success and failure in verbal communication. *Cognition, 5*, 363–78.

Robinson, W. P. 1965. The elaborated code in working-class language. *Language and Speech, 8*, 243–52.

Rothbart, M. 1971. Birth order and mother–child interaction in an achievement situation. *Journal of Personality and Social Psychology, 17*, 113–20.

Rūke-Draviņa, V. 1976. Gibt es Universalien in der Ammensprache? In G. Drachmann (ed.) *Akten des 1. Salzburger Kolloquiums über Kindersprache*. Tübingen.

Ryan, E. B. & Capedano, H. L. 1977. Stereotyping speakers on the basis of their perceived age. Mimeo, Department of Psychology, University of Notre Dame.

Sabin, E. J., Clemmer, E. J., O'Connell, D. C. & Kowal, S. In press. A pausological approach to speech development. In A. W. Siegman (ed.) *Of Time and Speech*. Hillsdale, NJ.

Sachs, J. 1976. The development of speech. In E. C. Carterette & M. P. Friedman (eds.) *Handbook of Perception*, vol. vii, *Language and Speech*. New York.

Sachs, J., Brown, R. & Salerno, R. A. 1976. Adults' speech to children. In W. von Raffler-Engel & Y. Lebron (eds.) *Baby Talk and Infant Speech*. Lisse.

Sanford, F. H. 1942. Speech and personality. *Psychological Bulletin, 39*, 811–45.

Sapir, E. 1915. *Abnormal Types of Speech in Nootka. Memoir 62*. Anthropological Studies, 5. Biological Survey of Canada, Ottawa.

Scherer, K. R. 1972. Judging personality from voice: a cross-cultural approach to an old issue in interpersonal perception. *Journal of Personality, 40*, 191–210.

1977. Die Funktionen des nonverbalen Verhaltens im Gespräch. In D. Wegner (ed.) *Gesprächsanalyse*. Hamburg.

1979. Non-linguistic vocal indicators of emotion and psychopathology. In C. E. Izard (ed.) *Emotions in Personality and Psychopathology*. New York.

Scherer, K. R., Haltof, H., Helfrich, H., Standke, R. & Wallbott, H. 1977. Psychoakustische und kinesische Verhaltensanalyse zur Bestimmung distaler Indikatoren affektiver Erregungszustände. In W. Tack (ed.) *Bericht über den 30. Kongress der Deutschen Gesellschaft für Psychologie*. Göttingen.

Schlesinger, I. M. 1971. Production of utterances and language acquisition. In D. I. Slobin (ed.) *The Ontogenesis of Grammar*. New York.

Searle, J. R. 1969. *Speech Acts: an essay in the philosophy of language*. Cambridge.

Sedláčková, E., Vrticka, K. & Supacek, I. 1966. Das Altern der Stimme. In *7th*

International Congress of Gerontology, Vienna, Austria, 1966, Proceedings, Clinical Medicine, vol. IV: 7, 469–72.

Sedlak, L. 1975. Gerontologische Studie zur Psycholinguistik – soziale und emotionale Aspekte. Master's thesis, University of Giessen.

Shatz, M. & Gelman, R. 1973. *The Development of Communication Skills: modifications in the speech of young children as a function of listener*. Society for Research in Child Development Monographs, *38*, no. 152.

Siegman, A. W. 1978. The tell-tale voice: nonverbal messages of verbal communication. In A. W. Siegman & S. Feldstein (eds.) *Nonverbal Behavior and Communications*. Hillsdale, NJ.

Sinclair-de Zwart, H. 1969. Psychologie der Sprachentwicklung. Reprinted in H. Leuninger, M. H. Miller & F. Müller (eds.) *Linguistik und Psychologie: ein Reader*, vol. II, *Zur Psychologie der Sprachentwicklung*. Frankfurt/M., 1974.

   1970. Der Übergang vom sensumotorischen Verhalten zur symbolischen Tätigkeit. Reprinted in H. Leuninger, M. H. Miller & F. Müller (eds.) *Linguistik und Psychologie*, vol. II, *Zur Psychologie der Sprachentwicklung*. Frankfurt/M., 1974.

Skinner, B. F. 1957. *Verbal Behavior*. New York.

Slobin, D. I. 1970. Universals of grammatical development in children. In G. B. Flores d'Arcais & W. J. M. Levelt (eds.) *Advances in Psycholinguistics*. New York.

   1971. Early grammatical development in several languages with special attention to Soviet research. In R. G. Bever & W. Weksel (eds.) *The Structure and Psychology of Language*. New York.

Snow, C. E. 1972. Mothers' speech to children learning language. *Child Development*, *43*, 549–65.

Spradlin, J. & Rosenberg, S. 1964. Complexity of adult verbal behavior in a dyadic situation with retarded children. *Journal of Abnormal and Social Psychology*, *68*, 694–8.

Stark, R. E. & Nathanson, S. N. 1974. Spontaneous cry in the newborn infant; sounds and facial gestures. In J. F. Bosma (ed.) *Fourth Symposium on Oral Sensation and Perception: development in the fetus and infant*. Bethesda, Md.

Stark, R. E., Rose, S. N. & McLagen, M. 1975. Features of infant sounds: the first eight weeks of life. *Journal of Child Language*, *2*, 205–21.

Stemmer, N. 1971. Some aspects of language acquisition. In Y. Bar-Hillel (ed.) *Pragmatics of Natural Languages*. Dordrecht.

Stern, C. & Stern, W. 1907. *Die Kindersprache*. Leipzig.

Stern, W. 1904. Die Sprachentwicklung eines Kindes, insb. in grammatischer und logischer Hinsicht. In F. Schelmann (ed.) *Bericht über den I. Kongress für experimentelle Psychologie*. Leipzig.

Storck, P. A. & Looft, W. R. 1973. Qualitative analysis of vocabulary responses from persons aged six to sixty-six plus. *Journal of Educational Psychology*, *65*, 192–7.

Sugarman, S. 1974. A sequence for communicative development in the prelanguage child. Unpublished paper.

Templin, M. C. 1957. *Certain Language Skills in Children: their development and interrelationships*. Minneapolis.

Thomas, W. 1972. Untersuchungen über Altersstereotypien anhand der modifizierten Skala 'Attitude toward old people' von Tuckman und Lorge. Dissertation, University of Düsseldorf.

Tonkova-Yampol'skaya, R. V. 1968. Razvitiye rechevoy intonatsii u detey pervykh dvukh let zhizni. *Voprosy psikhologii, 14,* 94–101. Translation in *Soviet Psychology,* 1969, 7, 48–54.

Tooley, K. 1967. Expressive style as a developmental index in late adolescence. *Journal of Projective Techniques and Personality Assessment, 31,* 51–9.

Trager, G. L. 1958. Paralanguage: a first approximation. *Studies in Linguistics, 13,* 1–12.

Tuckman, J. & Lorge, I. 1953. Attitude toward old people. *Journal of Social Psychology, 37,* 249–60.

Vygotsky, L. S. 1962. *Thought and Language.* Cambridge, Mass.

Weeks, R. 1971. Speech registers in young children. *Child Development, 62,* 1119–31.

Weir, R. 1966. Some questions on the child's learning of phonology. In F. Smith & G. A. Miller (eds.) *The Genesis of Language: a psycholinguistic approach.* Cambridge, Mass.

Whorf, B. L. 1956. *Language, Thought, and Reality.* New York and Cambridge, Mass.

Wolff, P. H. 1969. The natural history of crying and other vocalizations in early infancy. In B. Foss (ed.) *Determinants of Infant Behavior 4.* London.

Yairi, E. & Clifton, N. F. Jr. 1972. Disfluent speech behavior of preschool children, high school seniors and geriatric persons. *Journal of Speech and Hearing Research, 15,* 714–19.

Yannoulis, D. P. & Yannatos, G. 1966. Der heutige Stand und unsere Ansichten otorhinolaryngologischer Geschehen im Alter. In *7th International Congress of Gerontology, Vienna, Austria, 1966, Supplement,* vol. VII: 7.

4. Sex markers in speech[1]

PHILIP M. SMITH

Within the past decade, several volumes and an annotated bibliography have appeared on the topic of language and sex (cf. Dubois & Crouch 1976a; Eakins & Eakins 1978; Henley & Thorne 1975; Key 1975; Lakoff 1975; Miller & Swift 1976; Nilsen, Bosmajian, Gershuny & Stanley 1977; Thorne & Henley 1975a). These can be regarded as part of a widespread resurgence of interest in relations between the sexes on one hand (cf. e.g. Ruble, Frieze & Parsons 1976), and with the role of spoken language in society on the other (witness the chapters in this volume). At the intersection of these fields of interest arise two of the questions of concern in this chapter: do women and men speak differently, and what are the societal implications of these differences? Yet a study of speech differences alone will tell us little about which of these are recognized as salient markers of sex and why. Furthermore, many features that do not in fact differentiate the sexes are nevertheless typically associated with one sex or the other. Clearly, by focusing exclusively on the processes of men's and women's speech production, we would be neglecting important issues in the understanding of speech markers and sex. Therefore, another major task of this chapter is to examine evidence that relates to processes which affect the recognition and interpretation of sex-associated speech, whether differences or stereotypes.

Section 1 of this chapter is primarily a review of the evidence for sex-based differences at several levels of linguistic analysis. These differences, many of which have been discovered and corroborated by professional and sometimes highly specialized techniques, we will call *speech markers*. We will reserve the term, *speech stereotypes*, to refer to the features

[1] The preparation of this chapter was supported by Canada Council Awards nos. W762117 and 453-774478, and by an award from the Linguistic Society of America to attend the 1977 LSA Summer Institute. I should also like to thank Howard Giles, Klaus Scherer and Donald M. Taylor for their comments on earlier drafts of this chapter.

which have, for many different reasons, become associated with and expected of men and women, regardless of their diagnostic efficiency.

Under the definitions of marker and stereotype used in this chapter, there is no necessary relationship between the two. That is, the degree to which stereotypes about men's and women's speech, and actual differences between them overlap, is a matter for empirical research. Furthermore, the heuristic value of sex as an explanatory variable in sociolinguistics is also an empirical issue, which involves a close examination of the processes whereby our ideas about social groups originate, stabilize and evolve. These are topics with which section 2 of the chapter is concerned.

1. Speech differences between women and men

The picture of male and female speech that emerges from this review is necessarily coloured by an uneven concentration of research attention at some levels of analysis, and hardly any data at others. There is also an uneven distribution of English and non-English language data at the different levels. Nevertheless, the data base as it exists points clearly to several specific research questions, even if it does not lend itself easily to generalizations.

We begin by looking at differences in pronunciation and grammatical form, then move on to vocabulary and speech style differences, and to differences in the use of codes and dialects by women and men from the same speech community. Following this, we turn to examine some data on the nonsegmental (that is, prosodic and paralinguistic) correlates of speaker sex, (cf. Crystal 1969). Finally, considering that speech most often occurs in person-related and/or goal-related situations, we devote section 1.6 to a few studies of sex differences in dyadic and small-group verbal interaction.

1.1. Differences in pronunciation

Anthropological linguists have been reporting data on pronunciation and grammatical form intermittently since the beginning of the twentieth century (Bodine 1975), and more recently contributions have come from several urban linguistic surveys (cf. Labov 1970; Shuy 1970; Trudgill 1975, 1978). Differences in pronunciation between men and women are much more numerous than differences in grammatical form, and we will look at these first.

Nonvowel sounds. Bodine (1975), in an excellent review, enumerates three general types of pronunciation differences and three types for form, into which most of the existing data can be categorized. The first type of pronunciation difference is that wherein members of one sex group omit one or more sounds realized by the other sex. For example, Bogoras (cited in Bodine 1975) reported that male speakers of Chukchi, a Siberian language, often dropped consonants such as /n/ and /t/ when they occurred between vowels, and in some native American Muskogean languages (Haas 1944), men often add a final /s/ to words.

More recent studies show a consistent tendency for women to produce more standard, or rhetorically correct pronunciations, which generally correspond to the realization, as opposed to the omission, of certain speech sounds. In Montreal, Canada, Sankoff & Cedergren (1971) found that French Canadian women pronounced the liquid /l/ in pronouns and articles such as *il, elle, la* and *les* more often than men. Romaine & Reid (1976) found that among a group of Scottish school children, girls pronounced the dental /t/ in the middle and at the end of words (e.g. *water, got*) about 10 per cent more frequently than did boys, who more often replaced the dental with a glottal stop (*wa'er, go'*). In the United States, women pronounce the postvocalic /r/ in words like *car* and *bare*, which is the standard variant, more often than men do (Anshen 1969; Levine & Crockett 1966; Wolfram 1969; cf. Cheshire 1978 for contrasting British data).

Bodine's second and third types of pronunciation difference can be combined into one, thus yielding a category characterized by differences in either (i) the manner of articulation or (ii) the articulatory position of one or more speech sounds, with the number of sounds remaining the same for men and women. Two examples cited by Bodine are Bengali, where men often pronounce initial /n/ as /l/ (Chatterji, cited in Bodine 1975), and the American Indian Gros Ventre language, where women pronounce the male /tc/, /dj/ and /ty/, as /k/ and /ky/ (Flannery, cited in Bodine 1975). Numerous examples from English language studies, which can only be summarized here, add to the list of cases where women realize more correct pronunciations. Fischer (1958), in an early study, demonstrated that girls pronounced the standard realization of the verb ending, /ing/ (*reading, visiting, interesting*), more frequently than boys, who realize /in/ (*punchin', chewin', swimmin'*) more often. Later studies of adults, both Black (Anshen 1969; Wolfram 1969) and White speakers (Fasold 1968; Shuy, Wolfram & Riley 1967) in the United States, and White speakers in Norwich, England (Trudgill 1975) have corroborated this tendency. In the same vein, men tend to reduce or otherwise alter the interdental voiced fricative /th/ in words like *these* and *brother* (a popular substitute for /th/ is /dh/) while women more often realize the standard sound (Anshen 1969; Labov 1966; Milroy 1976; Wolfram 1969).

Vowel sounds. With respect to vowel sounds, also instances of Bodine's second and third categories, the standard pattern for women is repeated for the vowels studied in New York City (Labov 1966), Detroit (Fasold 1968; Shuy *et al*. 1967), London, England (Hudson & Holloway 1977), Belfast (Milroy & Milroy 1978), Glasgow (Macaulay 1978) and among English-speaking South Africans (reported in Trudgill 1974), especially in formal situations. In vernacular or casual speech, members of both sexes use less standard pronunciations, and often innovate with the use of newly emerging sounds. For example, Labov (1966) reports that women in New York City constitute the leading edge of a sound change characterized by raised pronunciation of the vowels /eh/ and /oh/ in casual speech, but that they shift to an even more standard low pronunciation than men in the formal task of reading a word list. Similar patterns have been observed for the vowels /æ/ and /a/ in Detroit speech (Fasold 1968; Shuy *et al*. 1967). In Labov's study of speech on the island of Martha's Vineyard off the New England coast (reported in Labov 1972) however, it was men who led the way in some vernacular sound changes, as it was in Trudgill's study of speech in Norwich (1975). Preliminary data from three working-class communities in Belfast, Northern Ireland (Maclaren 1976; Milroy & Margrain 1978; Milroy & Milroy 1978) show that here innovative usage probably depends more on community structure and employment patterns than upon sex as such (see also Cheshire 1978). In this light, Labov (1972) notes that, while 'the sexual differentiation of speech often plays a major role in the mechanism of linguistic evolution', it would be wrong to generalize about the relative innovative tendencies of women and men.

Standard pronunciation and prestige speech. Is it any more accurate then to say, as we have been doing, that women are relatively more *standard* speakers than men? To the extent that the standard pronunciation, grammar and vocabulary are relatively explicit and invariant, we are warranted in drawing conclusions about the tendency of one sex to use more standard speech than the other. This is because the criteria are linguistic, and exist independently of the speakers' perceptions and evaluations, at least in theory.

However, much of the foregoing data has been summarized by the comment that women regularly employ the use of more *socially prestigious* speech than men (Labov 1970; Trudgill 1975). Sociolinguists usually use the term prestige in one of two ways, to mean either (i) the value of a way of speaking for upward social mobility (Weinreich 1963), or (ii) the avoidance of stigmatized speech variables. It may be that the use of standard speech accomplishes both of these conditions at once, but this begs the crucial question of how the standard, defined on linguistic grounds, acquires its *evaluative* connotations. It certainly poses problems for the traditional sociolinguistic view that speech simply reflects underlying social reality, for women, despite their more standard speech, do not enjoy a prestigious position in society compared to men. In short, *prestige* cannot be used interchangeably with *standard* in sociolinguistics, for the linguistic varieties that are socially advantageous (or stigmatized) for one group, may not be for another. That is, the evaluative connotations of speech cannot be assessed independently of the people that use them.

At least three questions must be addressed before we can conclude that either men or women use more prestigious speech: (a) are the social advantages that the use of a certain speech style presumably results in, equally applicable to both sexes; (b) are the speech variables seen as prestigious when used by one sex, similarly valued in the other sex; and (c) do men and women apply the same evaluative criteria in judging what is prestigious? We will examine data relevant to these issues in the second part of the chapter, but here it is appropriate to note that Labov (1966) and Trudgill (1975) present data pertaining to the third question above. Both of these researchers asked their informants to choose between a standard and a nonstandard variant of several linguistic variables, in order to pick the sound which they thought characterized their speech. In Labov's study, both men and women reported that they used more of the standard variants than they were actually observed to do, suggesting that men and women here shared similar evaluative standards. But the men in Trudgill's study reported that they used more of the nonstandard variants of some vowel sounds, while women continued to over-report their use of the standard sounds. The standards of evaluation for men and women clearly differed in certain fundamental respects in this work, and Trudgill chose the term *covert prestige* to characterize the men's unexpected behaviour. Just how covert the esteem attached to nonstandard speech by men in Norwich is, remains to be investigated, as does the question of whether it applies to women as well as themselves.

1.2. Differences in grammatical form[2]

Returning to the data, we find that form differences have not been found frequently. The first of Bodine's three types is that where one sex-based version omits an affix used by the other sex. Bodine cites the native Californian language, Yana, as an instance. Here women drop the final vowel of several forms. Another example is Japanese (Jorden 1974) where the appearance of the sentence-final particle *ne* typically indicates a female speaker.

The second type of form difference corresponds to the occurrence of different, though analagously patterned affixes in women's and men's speech. In Thai, for example, women tend to emphasize the action of a verb by reduplicating it (an approximate example in English might be, *He beat and beat the rug until it was clean!*), while men usually place a descriptive verb, *mak*, after the verb instead (Warotamasikkhadit 1967). In the Dravidian language of Kŭṛux, only women pronounce the conjugation of verbs for the feminine gender, and then only when speaking with other women (Ekka 1972). In several European languages, adjectives and descriptive nouns take affixes so as to agree in gender with the subject of the sentence. When the subject is also the speaker, this acts as a clue to speaker sex (e.g. the sentence, *I am an actress*, would be considered incorrect if spoken by a man).

The final grammatical form difference category suggested by Bodine is that where one to several dozen words used by one sex have a different stem from those used by the other sex, but the words are handled the same syntactically. The extinct Carib language of the Lesser Antilles is probably the best example of this (Trudgill 1974). At one time, it was thought that men and women here spoke different languages altogether, so numerous were the apparent differences. Several languages also have different pronouns, depending upon the sex of the speaker. Faust (cited in Key 1975) discusses this occurrence among the speakers of Cocama in South America. In Japanese, the self-referents *wasi* or *ore* indicate a male speaker, and in informal conversation, the occurrence of *watasi* or *atasi* are clues that the speaker is a woman (Jorden 1974).

[2] The term *grammatical form* is used in this chapter as an heuristic device, and should not be read as indicative of a theoretical affinity for generative or transformational theories of linguistic competence. Differences in grammatical form are to be distinguished from pronunciation differences on the one hand, and differences in vocabulary choice on the other. Differences in grammatical form appear to be more sex-exclusive than differences in vocabulary choice, and their misuse in a speech community to cause more consternation than either pronunciation or vocabulary differences. A fuller treatment of these issues is not possible here.

Having reviewed the data available on sex differences in pronunciation and form, there are several points that we should make in order to place them in context and to set the frame of reference for the differences that we shall discuss in the sections to follow. The first thing we might note is that the differences are subtle and few. Indeed, differences have sometimes not been found where expected. Labov (1966), for example, did not find significant differences between women and men in the pronunciation of postvocalic /r/ in his New York City study. Fasold (1972), in a study of tense-marking among Black speakers in the United States, found that men and women did not differ in their use of several grammatical forms that differentiate between standard and nonstandard speech. Nevertheless, to the extent that the differences that have been found are recurrently and consistently used (as in e.g. Japanese), they serve as constant reminders of sex.

However, the second point is that almost all the examples that we have cited are instances of *sex-preferential tendencies* rather than *sex-exclusive*, all-or-none differences (Bodine 1975). It is doubtful whether many examples of isolated sex-exclusive features could be found today. In most of the early studies, where we might be led to believe that they had been found (e.g. Haas; Furfey; Flannery; all cited in Bodine 1975), the authors were probably not sensitive to the distinction between sex-exclusive and sex-preferential speech (cf. Giles, Scherer & Taylor, this volume: ch. 9, 3.2).

The distinction is an important one, for only if the correlation between a speech feature and sex is perfect, is the inferential link between speech and sex a direct one. Otherwise the observed covariation may be the result of a coincidental correlation of sex with another social division (e.g. occupation) which has stronger implications for speech than does sex. The authors of more recent urban linguistic surveys have pointed out that the speech variables they were interested in were usually better predicted by ethnicity, age and socioeconomic status than by sex (e.g. Labov 1970). The third point then is that differences between female and male speech are not necessarily primarily markers of sex.

The fourth point relates closely to the second and third, and concerns a distinction between saturated and unsaturated usage. Even though some forms and/or features may be used only by members of one sex (let us take women's high-pitched 'baby-talk' as an example), they may be used only by some members (mothers caring for young children). Thus an apparently sex-exclusive feature may not be an indicator of sex as such, but rather of something that is itself a consequence of sex (in our example, social divisions of labour), but does not saturate the sex group nor cross the sex boundary.

Bearing in mind these distinctions, we can depict an idealized scheme within which the use of any speech feature, or features in combination, could be located in terms of both the proportion of members within each sex who use it, and in terms of the relative proportion of women and men who use it. In figure 1, points A and C represent sex-exclusive, saturated usage (possible examples are the different pronoun series used by women and men in Cocama, and the male–female forms in Kŭṛux, both cited above). A feature that can be placed anywhere else in the scheme except on the diagonal BD (which represents equal usage by women and men), is technically an example of sex-preferential usage. Examples are variants of postvocalic /r/, verb ending /ing/, and initial /th/, discussed above.

Finally, figure 1 is not meant to be cross-situationally applicable. It is probable that the position of a given feature in the scheme would vary depending on the purpose of the interaction and the characteristics (sex, status, age, etc.) of the listener. To illustrate this, we need only consider languages in which the use of some forms depends on the sex of the listener, such as in Kŭṛux. Bodine (1975) gives several other examples, where the sex of the listener influences the men's as well as the women's forms.

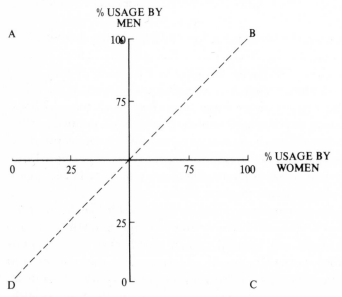

Figure 1. An idealized scheme for representing the relative use of a feature by women and men, and the proportion of members of each sex who use it

The question that arises from this final point is, what effect has the sex of the interviewer had on the results of the urban linguistic surveys, where most of our English language data come from (Conklin 1974). With a couple of exceptions (Sankoff & Cedergren 1971; Cheshire 1978), these interviews have been carried out by men. Giles (1973) has drawn attention to the importance of the interviewer's social characteristics and speech style for the kind of speech that will emerge in linguistic surveys. His theory of *interpersonal speech style accommodation* (1977) would lead us to suspect that speech might differ depending on the sex of the listener. It is most important that the findings reported in the sections above can be repeated controlling for interviewer sex before generalizations are made about the standard or nonstandard usage of women and men.

1.3. Differences in vocabulary choice and speech style

Vocabulary choice. Our speech, besides having a propositional content, also has a 'scene-setting' or stylistic significance, which helps to create a common set of assumptions and expectations between speakers. The analysis of the linguistic indices and conversational functions of speech styles usually proceeds on the basis of ideas about the correlation between the surface structure of an utterance and its capacity to evoke situational norms related to both the personal (e.g. status relationships) and the impersonal (e.g. the technicality of the topic) aspects of the interaction.

Inasmuch as the same proposition can be expressed in many different ways, vocabulary choice is an important index of style. Flannery (cited in Cappell 1966) reports that women and men of the native North American Gros Ventre tribe use different interjections in discourse, and cites findings of similar phenomena among the Chaco of Paraguay and the Cuna of Panama. While we do not know what social significance, if any, attached to the use of these different items by men and women, there are other examples for which such data are available. Trudgill (1974), for instance, discusses the case of Zulu women, for whom there is a taboo against uttering the name of their father-in-law, and even words that sound similar.

The notion of strict social sanction, akin to taboo, may also be invoked to help explain why women in Sweden (Oftedal 1973), the United States (Bailey & Timm 1976) and Brazil (Head 1977) use fewer profane and obscene expletives than men do in these countries. There is a general sanction against the use of rude language, which applies unequally strongly to women. However, in Brazil, Head (1977) found that women reported that they spoke rudely as often in front of men as in front of women, while men attenuated their use of profanity and obscenity in the presence of women. This suggests that there is a belief that women are harsher judges of improper language than are men.

Key (1975) mentions informal studies by students which show that women use more reduplicated adjectival forms like *itsy-bitsy* and *teeny-weeny*, as well as more 'feminine' adjectives where men use more adjectives with masculine connotations. Swacker (1975) found that women often prefaced definite numerical terms by adjectives of approximation (*about* six books; *around* five or six books) in a picture describing task, while men did not. Barron (1971) recorded samples of teachers' and pupils' class-room discussions, and analysed noun phrases according to grammatical case, which gives roughly the semantic domain and use of the noun. Women, she found, produced more participative and purposive cases, ostensibly indicating a more internally oriented and functional approach to conversation, while men produced cases (instrumental, source and objective) showing orientation towards objects and actions.

Other approaches to style. The connotations and functions of such style differences as these undoubtedly derive from many sources, including their differential use by men and women. Thus it would only be partially correct to conclude that men typically use more forceful or decisive speech on the bases of these differences, since the connotations of these styles may to some extent derive from their asymmetrical use by women and men.

Brown (1977) illustrates the ways in which a class of modifiers, particles in this case, are employed to strengthen or weaken the force of assertions and demands among Tzeltal-speaking Mayans of Tenejapa, Mexico. Her data indicate that women use more of these particles among themselves than men do, appearing consequently more aware of the possibly threatening tone of bald, unelaborated speech. On the other hand, Maher (1976) suggests, on impressionistic grounds, that in Morocco the use of exaggerated and formal speech is more characteristic of men amongst themselves, than among women. Unfortunately, in neither case are we presented with a description of mixed-sex encounters.

Jayawardena (1977) reports that among the villagers of Acheh Besar, Northern Sumatra, women are the hereditary guardians of old-fashioned sayings and the meaning of proverbs. In contrast, Keenan (1975) studied a Malagasy community where only men possessed the skills of a speech style characterized by indirectness, metaphor and proverb. Women here were perceived as informal and direct speakers, as usurpers of a conversational norm prohibiting confrontation.

These examples, from a wide variety of societies, illustrate the ways in which the question of style differences between the sexes has been approached, yet the findings are not suggestive of any obvious classificatory heuristic. Brown (1977) relates her findings to a theory of politeness, wherein speech styles characterized by surface structural features are indicative of underlying strategic motives concerned with maintaining face in interactions. Keenan (1975) invokes the concept of a community-wide conversational norm that men defend and women break. However, in neither of these studies is it clear, with respect to the particular aspects of speech that they discuss, that the normative and strategic implications of their use are the same for both men and women; whether or not they are community-wide is open to examination. Also, it is likely that the symbolic significance of these styles is in part due to the fact that they are used unequally by men and women. Thus, the connotations of 'politeness' and 'indirectness' communicated by the speech styles may partially derive from the male–female relations themselves. If we attempt to avoid these problems by anchoring the notion of speech style in a set of descriptive linguistic definitions, as for the concept of standard pronunciation, we beg the central questions of how speech styles come to be recognized and labelled, and how they acquire significance as social symbols, questions which are presumably at the root of professional interest in style. The same questions that we proposed to ask of 'prestige' speech are apropos here; are the implications of using a particular surface structure the same for women as for men speakers, and the same for female and male listeners? There are many fewer data pertaining to style than to the significance of pronunciation differences, yet the approaches to be outlined in section 2 of this chapter are equally applicable in principle.

1.4. Code and dialect differences

Bilingualism and language change. In an early book, Jespersen (1922: ch. 13) relates anecdotal evidence that Basque-, Livonian-, and Albanian-speaking women tended to conserve the use of their mother tongues longer than men of these groups, who adopted encroaching tongues more readily. In Oaxaca, Mexico, Diebold (1961) found that 80 per cent of the few people who learned Spanish in addition to their native Huave were men, citing as a primary reason for this fact that it was the men of the village who most often had mobility out of the community. Similarly, Lieberson (1965) discerned from Canadian census data that male French Canadians in Montreal consistently showed a higher rate of French–English bilingualism, and a higher rate of increase in the proportion of bilingual speakers, than women between the 1920s and the 1960s. In Montreal during this period, English was the language necessary for occupational mobility, while French was the language of the home and most other, nonoccupational, domains.

Code-switching and dialect. The women in these studies, apparently by virtue of their domestic role, did not have access to, nor much reason to learn, a second language. They thus appear to be linguistically conservative, retaining traditional behaviour in preference to innovation. However, among women competent in more than one language or dialect, exactly the opposite tendency has been observed. Oftedal (1973) cites Steinsholt as finding that it is women in rural Norway who first adopt the use of terms new to the dialect of the region, especially those referring to feminine interests and materials. Gal (1975) illustrates the way in which young women along the Austro-Hungarian border are mobilizing out of their peasant networks by refusing to speak the local Hungarian dialect, which is the language of the peasant network in general, and opting instead for the local German, associated with the industrial workers.

Trudgill & Tzavaras (1977) report somewhat similar trends amongst young Greeks of Albanian descent (Arvanites). Arvanite women report that they use the Attican variety of Albanian, Arvanitika, less often, and have less favourable attitudes towards its use, than men do. The shift away from Arvanitika, and the discrepancies between men and women are greatest for those under 25 years of age.

Bilingual Mexican–American college women in Texas report that they use English in more situations than do men of the same social and demographic background (Solé 1976). Solé explained this in terms of the different cultural experiences and expectations of the women, who, she says, perceive more rewards for assimilating to the dominant (English-speaking) culture than the men do. Hartford (1976), moreover, found that Mexican–American women used more standard pronunciation and grammatical forms when they spoke English. These were also the features that correlated significantly with her informants' scores on a measure of occupational aspiration, even though this measure did not in itself differentiate the sexes. Unlike the Arvanites, the Mexican–Americans' attitudes towards their mother tongue do not parallel their reported usage of it. Politzer and Ramirez (cited in Ryan & Carranza 1977) report that women evaluate the use of Spanish more favourably in the south-west United States than men do.

Factors to consider in interpreting these data. These data serve as a reminder that both language use and language attitudes must be sampled in order to gain a complete picture of the processes of linguistic and social change within a group, a point frequently made in the context of studies of language and ethnicity (e.g. Smith, Tucker & Taylor 1977). We should also be wary of the validity of self-reported language use data, which are the basis of most of the studies cited here. Over- and under-reporting are likely to be an important source of information about the value that men and women attach to different languages, just as they were in the studies of pronunciation by Labov (1966) and Trudgill (1975).

Note that all the cases we have so far discussed involve ethnolinguistic minorities. This is partially a consequence of the fact that language-shifting on a large scale is commonly a facet of minority assimilation to a majority culture (cf. Giles, this volume: ch. 7, 1.2). Yet the post-1948 resurgence of ethnic and linguistic nationalism, and the consequent reversal of many assimilative trends, have provided forums for inquiry which have not yet been tapped for information on sex and language change. In these cases, innovation would involve a trend against linguistic assimilation, and the role that women and men might play is by no means easy to predict. In addition, there are many instances in recent history of a majority assimilation to a dominant minority language, especially on the African continent, from which information could be gleaned. The diversity of factors likely to influence the role of sex, including indigenous community structures, opportunities for mobility into the dominant culture, the structure of the labour market, subjective affinity for one's ethnic group, etc., are beyond the range of the present review. However, they certainly fall within the scope of the broader sociolinguistic endeavour to be outlined in section 2.

A good small-scale illustration of the sensitivity of innovative tendencies to nonlinguistic factors is Nichols' (1976) study of an all Black river island community in South Carolina. She compared the use of archaic Gullah dialect forms by men and women on the island, with their use by less upwardly mobile inhabitants of part of the mainland. In the relatively prosperous island community, where women had access to educational and occupational opportunities not available to the mainland community, women used less dialect than men. The opposite pattern was found on the mainland, where women tended to conserve the use of Gullah forms.

Women again appear to be the main exponents of linguistic change in a study by Feinberg (1977). She examined popular response to the official introduction of twenty-five neologisms into the Hebrew language of Israel, and found that women claimed to know and use more of the terms, and had a more favourable attitude towards their propagation.

A final, original and provocative study confirms the innovative tendencies of bilingual women, this time on a semantic level. Hill (1975) studied the responses of 346 bilingual (French and either Hausa or Djerma) school students in Niger, on a test of spatial relations between people and objects. She asked the students to indicate the front and back of a ball in relation to a stick figure in a series of simple illustrations. Amongst the population from which the students came, the front of objects lacking an intrinsic front (such as balls and ameboid forms) is the surface facing *away* from the stick figure, whereas among native French speakers, the front is the surface *facing towards* the figure. Hill found that female students made consistently more nonindigenous (French semantic) indications for front and back than the boys did, although more indigenous responses were made overall (the test language was either Hausa or Djerma). This illustration of semantic innovation indicates a neglected area worthy of further attention.

This concludes our review of differences between the speech of women and men at levels of analysis bounded by, or defined in terms of, morphophonemic units; that is, *segmental* differences. Nonsegmental variables associated with pitch and intonation, and paralinguistic features of speech such as loudness, pausing and voice quality, have only recently begun to get the attention they deserve in sociolinguistics (Crystal 1971). Their study promises to find enthusiastic support from those interested in sex and language, for many argue that nonsegmental features are the most recognizable and informative clues to speaker sex within a given language.

1.5. Nonsegmental differences

Even in languages like English, where tone is not integral to the meaning of speech segments (in contrast to languages like Chinese, for example), nonsegmental features are more than peripheral adjuncts to strings of syllables and words.[3] In English, pauses and intonation mark the intended start and finish of utterances, and disambiguate otherwise unclear utterances by locating segments to be stressed or contrasted in emphasis. Furthermore, nonsegmentals are considered to be a most important source of information about a speaker's affective state, and attitudes towards the listener.

Pitch and the identification of speaker sex. Pitch and intonation phenomena figure prominently in impressionistic accounts of male–female speech differences from the earliest writings. At the empirical level, acoustical analysis of adult speakers in the United States and Germany has demonstrated that women have both a higher fundamental frequency (roughly equivalent to perceived pitch), and greater pitch variability, than men (Herbst 1969; Takefuta, Jancosek & Brunt 1971).

Pitch itself is often cited as the most salient male–female speech difference. For instance, Schwartz & Rine (1968) discuss evidence that speaker sex can be identified on the basis of isolated voiceless fricatives (/s/, /sh/) and whispered vowels (/i/ and /a/) alone, at close to 100 per cent accuracy. This is due to the fact that the male sounds were displaced downwards in frequency by about 1 kHz, while retaining the same shape as the women's. Similarly, Coleman (1971) finds that sex identification from laryngeal speech (voiceless speech driving an electronic larynx) is more than 80 per cent accurate, and correlates highly (r + 0.70) with average formant frequency. In adults, the relatively greater size of men, and their thicker vocal folds are, in part, responsible for these frequency differences. But anatomy alone does not account for all of this difference (McConnell-Ginet 1974; Mattingly 1966). Meditch (1975) found that, amongst a group of 3- to 5-year-olds, boys were better identified by listeners than were girls, and more incorrect judgements were made for older girls than for any other speakers. Thus listeners were picking up something in boys' speech that distinguished it from undifferentiated children's speech. The sex of girl speakers, on the other hand, was more often guessed at, and the guesses were skewed towards incorrect 'masculine' identification the older the girls were. If we can safely assume that there were no differences between the vocal apparatus of boys and girls at this age, then whatever it is that distinguishes 'masculine' children's speech is learned by boys earlier than by girls. Presumably, listeners alter their criteria for the identification of speaker sex once they perceive some

---

[3] For a fuller treatment of the nonsegmental features of speech, cf. Crystal (1971) and Lehiste (1976).

influence due to anatomical modification of the vocal tract with maturation. A rating-scale type speaker evaluation study (Sachs, 1975) has suggested that there are sentential clues such as 'fluency' and 'activity' (perhaps intonational?) that add to listeners' discriminative capabilities, which are generally as good as 70–80 per cent accurate, with children as speakers (but cf. Lass & Davis 1976; Lass *et al*. 1976; Lass, Mertz & Kimmel 1978; Murray, Amundsen & Hollien 1977).

Some recent data from Britain complicate the picture somewhat, for Local (in preparation) has found that girl speakers between 5 and 9 years old were correctly identified by adult listeners 67 per cent of the time, and boys only 59 per cent of the time. There is no apparent correlation between the age of the speaker and the accuracy of identification, and there is a distinct tendency for judges to express greater confidence in their identifications of female speakers. The reasons for the discrepancies from Meditch's (1975) results await clarification, but a few important differences between the studies should be noted. The first and perhaps most crucial is demographic; Meditch's work was done in Texas, Local's in northeastern England. Meditch's samples were culled from spontaneous interactions with a female interviewer, while Local's were the result of rather more structured interactions with a man. With respect to these points, Lieberman (1967) has noted that mothers and fathers speak differently to children, and that children may react to this by shifting their pitch in an attempt to match that of the parent. Furthermore, parents speak differently to male and female children in terms both of the purpose of the interaction (Cherry & Lewis 1975) and the situations when interaction will be initiated (Woll, Ferrier & Wells 1975). Taken together, these findings strongly suggest that it is possible to account for at least some of the results of studies like Meditch's and Local's in terms of the sex of the interviewer interacting with that of the informant, just as in studies of adults (cf. also Harris 1977).

Finally, we should take note of a study which demonstrates that speaker sex identification is influenced by factors outside the immediate interaction, as well as those within. Edwards (in press) recorded twenty working-class and twenty middle-class 10-year-olds, balanced for sex, reading the same short passage. Fourteen student teachers judged the sex of each speaker, achieving an overall accuracy of 83.6 per cent. However, significantly more errors were made in the identification of working-class girls and middle-class boys than for the other speaker groups. Something about working-class speech skewed the judgements towards *male*, while the opposite effect operated for middle-class speakers. The voices were further rated by five listeners on some impressionistically speech-related scales, where working-class speakers were rated as having lower, rougher and more masculine voices overall.

Patterns of intonation. The suggestion that intonation patterns might serve as consistent indicators of sex in English has received some empirical attention. Brend (1975) has reported on informal observations which indicate that female speakers use a 'polite' pattern of assertive intonation (*Yés Yés/Í kǹow*)[4] while men use a more 'deliberate' pattern (*Yes Yes/I knǫw*), and that women further use certain patterns that men usually do not (notably 'surprise' patterns of high fall-rises, and others; cf. Brend 1975). She hypothesizes that men hardly ever use the highest tone level that women do and that women therefore have a more varied range of tone changes to draw upon. McConnell-Ginet (1974) reviews other evidence which confirms both the greater pitch range and intonational variability of White, middle-class women in the United States.

In England, Pellowe and Jones' (1978) survey of Tyneside speech indicates that men use a much greater proportion of falling tones than rising tones, while women generally realize more rising tones. Furthermore, women displayed a greater variety of intonational patterns than men did. Elyan's (1978) analysis of twenty female and twenty male students in Bristol confirms these results.

Loudness and speech fluency. Loudness and speech fluency (the absence of pauses and hesitations) are the only two paralinguistic features for which there is even a modicum of data. Markel, Prebor & Brandt (1972) found that men spoke with a greater average intensity than women in interpersonal communication, although both sexes speak with greater intensity to a member of the opposite sex than to a same-sex listener. Women, however, apparently compensate for the occurrence of external noise by raising their vocal intensity more than men do (an average of 17dB for women, and only 10 dB for men), perhaps to the point of unpleasant distortion (von Raffler-Engel & Buckner 1976).

With regard to verbal fluency, Garai & Scheinfeld (1968) report that women display greater grammatical competence and sentence complex-

---

[4] The prosodic symbols used here are different from Brend's. Following Gumperz (1977), the / indicates the boundary between two minor tone groupings. The markers of nucleus placement within a tone group are ' for rising intonation and ` for falling intonation. Two contrastive levels of intonation, high and low, are distinguished, with changes on the high level being indicated by placing the markers above the segment, and changes on the lower level marked below the line.

ity, and fewer speech disabilities of all types, from an early age. Cherry (1975), however, found no differences between the fluency of instructor–male and instructor–female dyads in a class-room of preschoolers, in terms of either utterances per turn or words per utterance. Similarly, Silverman & Zimmer (1976) find few differences in the conversational fluency of adult men and women.

The majority of studies that we have reviewed so far in this chapter have been concerned with the performance of idealized, isolated speakers even though speech almost always occurs, in these studies as elsewhere in life, in actual interactions with other speakers. From a social psychological point of view, it is less interesting and informative to inquire about male–female speech differences apart from their realization and interpretation *in situ* (cf. Ervin-Tripp 1976; McConnell-Ginet 1974; Thorne & Henley 1975b, for articulation of this plea from sociolinguistic and feminist perspectives). To this end, we review several studies of dyadic and small-group verbal interaction where the focus has been on women and men.

1.6. Differences that emerge in situated interaction

Output variables: verbosity and speaking time. Although the data here again are far too piecemeal and English language centred to make any reliable generalizations, it appears, tentatively, as though women contribute quantitatively less, and exert less control over, male–female conversations than men do. Several studies show that men speak for a disproportionate amount of time in mixed sex dyads (Argyle, Lalljee & Cook 1968; Hilpert, Kramer & Clark 1975; Strodtbeck 1951; Wood 1966). This pattern is repeated in small-group contexts such as faculty meetings (Eakins & Eakins 1976) and mock-jury deliberations (Strodtbeck & Mann 1956). This finding of male verbosity is not necessarily repeated in studies of isolated speakers. For example, while Swacker (1975) found that men spoke for far longer than women when asked to describe a picture (an average of 13.0 minutes for men vs. 3.17 minutes for women), women produced a higher average word count than men in a similar study by Gall, Hobby & Craik (1969).[5] Then again, some workers have not found differences in the output of women and men in dyads (Hirschman 1973, 1974), or alone (Brotherton & Penman 1977).

[5] The correlation between word counts and speaking time is generally low, and the two results cited here are mentioned together only for contrastive purposes. It would be difficult to believe that the men in Swacker's study did not have a higher word count than the women.

The sensitivity of output variables to other factors is highlighted by a study of marital decision-making in twenty-eight husband–wife pairs, in half of which the wife was active in the Women's Liberation Movement. The couples discussed differences between them that arose earlier in the study. Hershey & Werner (1975) found that while feminist wives spoke longer than their husbands, the opposite was true of couples where the wife was not a feminist. Furthermore, feminist wives had the last word ('speaks last') significantly more often than their husbands, while it was the husbands of non-feminist wives that did.

Content and style. Turning to the content and style of same- and mixed-sex conversations, three early studies of sidewalk conversations in New York, Columbus, Ohio, and London, England, showed that men talk to each other about money, business, amusement and other men, while female conversations were about men, clothes and other women (Landis 1927; Landis & Burtt 1924; Moore 1922). In mixed-sex conversations in the United States, the women appeared more often to accommodate to masculine topics, while in England, the men adapted to the women somewhat (Landis 1927).

Aries (1976) made a detailed study of the conversations of small mixed- and same-sex groups who met over five one-and-a-half hour sessions to 'get to know each other'. Not only the content, but the whole style of the same-sex and mixed-sex groups differed. The male groups were characterized by stable dominance hierarchies wherein a few men did most of the talking, which centred around the content categories of *competition and teasing*, *sports*, *physical aggression* and *doing things*. In the female groups, dominance hierarchies were not so prominent a feature, and members directed much of their comment to the group as a whole instead of to a single listener. Their talk was distinguished by the categories of *self*, *feelings*, *affiliation with others*, *home* and *family*. In mixed-sex groups, men both initiated and received more communication, although the sexes seemed to compromise in terms of topics somewhat; the men spoke less of competition and physical aggression, the women less of home and family, and more discussion was about the group itself.

Frost (1977) discusses the significance of some of the style differences implicit in Aries' study for the kinds of verbal conflict strategies adopted by men and women. She asked college students to list and describe the methods that they used in arguments and disputes, and found that women prefer to avoid confrontation, whereas men assert themselves in conflict by talking and interrupting. These suggestions, based on self-report, are corroborated by the repeated finding that men do interrupt more, especially in mixed-sex encounters (Eakins & Eakins 1976; Zimmerman & West 1975).

Conversational control. Finally, in another demonstration of the sensitivity of interaction variables to factors other than sex, Feldstein (1977) has shown that the pause following a White male's turn in a mixed-sex White dyad is likely to be longer than that following the female's turn, but exactly the opposite tendency is found in dyads composed of Black speakers. Longer *switching pauses*, as these are termed, may be the result either of the speaker failing to signal the end of the turn, or of the listener's hesitancy to respond. Clearly, the factors influencing turn-taking, and hence conversational control in male–female dyads merit further research attention.

2. The social significance of speech in female–male relations

In this section, we turn our attention away from speech production *per se*, and focus on the recognition and evaluation of male and female speakers, and sex-associated speech. Some of the work that has been done in this connection has examined the initial impression elicited by male and female speakers. Work at this level is of value in helping us to determine if men and women share common schemes for speaker evaluation, and whether or not the same features are salient markers of both men's and women's speech. However, the recognition of speaker sex is not a problem, for there is obviously some little understood combination of elementary speech features that cues our recognition of sex before almost anything else about the speaker's social identity, except perhaps age (cf. Ryan & Capedano 1977). The impressions offered on the basis of speaker sex alone could presumably be elicited by any other, nonspeech stereotype method, such as a questionnaire.

2.1. The importance of speech

Speech as a basis for speaker evaluation. The question of more importance then is whether or not the mere recognition of speaker sex precludes a reassessment of the speaker on the basis of the way he/she speaks subsequently. If it does, then further inquiries into the evaluation of sex-associated speech are academic, for the connotations of speech are the connotations of sex itself, not a topic within the domain of this chapter. There are good reasons for not viewing the relationship between sex and speech as such a one-way process, however. On an interpersonal level, Erickson, Lind, Johnson & O'Barr (1977) have shown that sex-associated speech style was a more important determinant of how a court-room witness was evaluated than was the sex of the witness. On the basis of stereotypical accounts of men's and women's speech, they constructed two versions of a witness' key testimony, controlled for content, where one version included instances of several stereotypically feminine constructions and expressions (called the *Powerless* version since it corresponded to Lakoff's (1975) description of non-authoritative, inde-cisive speech) and the other did not (the *Power* version). They trained a male and female actor to read the testimonies keeping as many of the non-experimental features as possible constant, and then had listeners rate one of the versions on ten personality trait scales, and several other items about the credibility of the witness. In brief, both male and female speakers were rated as more competent and credible when reading the Power script. The male and female Powerless versions were not strictly comparable (due to slight differences in the scripts), but the only scale on which the male and female actor were rated differently for the Power version was the *Masculine* item. The male witness was rated as more masculine than the female witness.

Speech as a basis for broader social attributions. On the broader societal level, while speech does not function with sex, as it may with ethnicity, as a primary arbiter of group membership, it nevertheless features promi-nently in itself as a justification for the attribution of different traits to the sexes. McConnell-Ginet (1974), for example, argues that women's higher pitch and more variable intonation are among the most important sources of the idea that women are emotional and unsuited for responsible positions. Williams & Giles (1978) reported that some of their colleagues had made unwarranted inferences about biologically based cognitive deficits of women, after reading evidence of an increase in women's speech disfluencies during menstruation (i.e. Silverman & Zimmer 1975). In addition to the possibility of being a primary source of our ideas about men and women, beliefs about sex-associated speech may act as guides to where we seek confirming and disconfirming evidence for other sex differences. As an hypothetical example, suppose that someone asserts that men are discourteous speakers, but we are sceptical and desire confirmation. Supposing that we already believe that men speak with deep voices, we may confine our search to men with deep voices as the best exemplars of the sex, even though they may not be at all typical (Smith 1978).

In addition to knowing about the evaluation of *speakers* according to sex, we must therefore also inquire about the recognition and evaluation of *sex-associated speech*. In sections 2.2 and 2.3 we shall address these two issues. Finally, in the concluding section, we shall present a brief outline of the range of factors that have to be taken into account in further theorizing about the role of speech in the male–female context.

2.2. The social evaluation of women and men as speakers

Vocal markers of female and male personality. The results of studies on the perception and evaluation of speakers' personality reveal that female speakers are evaluated very differently from males, and on the basis of different speech cues. For example, Aronovitch (1976) had university students rate the tape-recorded voice of twenty-five adult men and thirty-two women on ten personality trait scales. He also measured six objective parameters of each voice (measures of speech rate, vocal intensity, sound–silence ratio and fundamental frequency), and intercorrelated the results of the vocal and personality analyses. While the raters of both sexes relied on the same voice cues to rate the speakers, the cues that correlated with variation in the personalities of male speakers were different from those that correlated with variation among female speakers. Thus, the vocal cues that were salient markers of male personality were variance in vocal intensity, variance in fundamental frequency, and speech rate. For females, the salient markers were average intensity, average fundamental frequency, speech rate and sound–silence ratio.

In a study of the effects of altering selected vocal parameters on personality perception, Addington (1968) recorded two male and two female speakers reading a short passage again and again, each time simulating one of seven voice qualities, and one of three speech rates, and pitch varieties. He obtained two sets of ratings for each speech sample; one set of judgements from trained listeners on nine vocal characteristics, and another set of personality ratings on forty scales. The results, similar to those of Aronovitch (1976), indicate that men and women judges rated personality according to the same vocal parameters, but changes in female voices were rated differently from similar changes in male voices (cf. Scherer, this volume: ch. 5, 3.1).

Standard and nonstandard accented speech in Britain. Research in Britain and elsewhere has shown that male speakers of standard varieties of English are upgraded in terms of social competence (intelligence, industriousness, etc.), and nonstandard-sounding men are rated higher on traits related to social attractiveness (friendliness, sincerity, etc.; cf. Giles & Powesland 1975 for a detailed review). Elyan, Smith, Giles & Bourhis (1978) compared the ratings given to RP (received pronunciation) and regional accented women speakers in a matched-guise study, and found a very similar pattern for the evaluation of females. The RP guises were rated higher in competence and occupational prestige, while the nonstandard (in this case, Northern) guises received higher ratings on the scales, likeable and sincere, and lower ratings for aggressiveness and egotism. Interestingly, the RP guises were definitely associated by the raters with masculine traits (adventurous, independent, egotistical, aggressive), yet at the same time were rated as more feminine. Here, the overall pattern of ratings attributed to male and female standard and nonstandard speech in Britain were similar, but with important differences; the standard pronunciation of women carries with it the connotation of social competence and occupational status that accrues to male standard speech, while eliciting perceptions of femininity as well.[6]

In a follow-up study, Giles & Marsh (in press) included two male guises with two female guises of RP and South Welsh accents. They replicated the usual finding that RP guises are upgraded in terms of competence and status, but they were also rated higher on masculine traits, egalitarianism and profeminism. Regional guises were not rated as more socially attractive, nor were RP guises perceived as more feminine. Female speakers, irrespective of accent, were seen as more feminine and profeminist, and men were rated as more masculine and statusful. Here, the prestige related ratings all went to men, and on two of the scales, intelligent and job status, the relative upgrading of the RP guises was attenuated for female speakers of RP, who were rated closer to the South Welsh speakers. In this study the relative salience of the prestige connotations of speech were overshadowed by effects due to speaker sex *per se*. Whether this was due to the different connotations of Northern English and South Welsh accents relative to RP, or to the fact that male and female speakers were explicitly compared on tape in this study, is a matter for further research.

---

[6] These surprising results were discussed by the authors in terms of the concept of *psychological androgyny* (cf. Kelley & Worrel 1977; Smith 1978) i.e. that some people can display aspect of both a masculine and a feminine personality together. Elyan *et al*. (1978) speculate that, in Britain, women speaking with RP accents are perceived as somewhat androgynous. For a full discussion, cf. the original citation.

Standard accent as a dependent variable. In these studies, accent was manipulated as an independent variable. In two further studies, concerned with speech as a basis for making judgements about a speaker's concern for feminist issues (Giles *et al.* in press), listener-judges were asked to rate female speakers on a scale for standard accent–nonstandard accent, among others. In both cases, nonfeminist women were rated as speaking with more standard pronunciation than feminists. However, in one study, based on spontaneous, topic-controlled speech, feminist speakers were upgraded on prestige related scales, while in the other, based on a prose reading, feminist speakers were downgraded compared to nonfeminists. Of course, it is an empirical question whether the speakers rated as more standard in these two studies would be so considered on the basis of linguistic analysis. Taking these two studies together, it appears that, for female speakers at least, the vicissitudes of speaker evaluation are not strongly tied to the use of standard variants. It must be noted, though, that such a conclusion depends upon a linguistic corroboration of the naive listeners' judgements about standard accent.

The similarity of women's and men's evaluative standards. In three of the above-mentioned social psychological studies, there were no differences between the ratings given by men and by women; they were applying the same standards, as in the Addington (1968) and the Aronovitch (1976) studies. Similar findings have been reported with respect to the attribution of stereotypical speech markers to men and women (Edelsky 1976b). Kramer (1978a) found that students rated typical male and female speakers differently on 36 out of 51 speech-related characteristics, in a questionnaire study. On 13 of these, raters of one sex discriminated when the other sex did not, but there were no cases of actually opposing ratings being given.

These findings of the similarity of men's and women's judgemental standards militate against the hypothesis that 'prestige' speech may be different for listeners of opposite sex. Nevertheless, the pronunciation variables influencing naive listeners' judgements of men and women have yet to be brought under phonological scrutiny, and it is the isolated variables of the phonetician which are the basis of sociolinguistic arguments about prestige usage. We recall that Trudgill (1975a) found clear evidence that some phonological variables were evaluated differently by men and women. These linguistic variables could be systematically incorporated into the design of social psychological studies like those described above. Hints that this might prove valuable are provided by

Elyan *et al*. (1978) who found that female raters were more discriminating between standard and nonstandard speech than were men, giving RP speakers even higher ratings, and regional speakers even lower ones, on six scales where RP was already higher (egotistical, intelligent, independent, has own job, occupational status, occupational salary). Evidence from other sources leads us to believe that women are in fact more attentive and accurate observers of verbal style than men are. In several studies, Mazanec, McCall and colleagues (Mazanec & McCall 1975; Mazanec & McCall 1976; McCall, Mazanec, Erickson & Smith 1974) have found that women recall actions and features of style with greater accuracy and in more detail than men, who are better at recalling people's appearance and the content of what they say.

Furthermore, the notion of prestige extends beyond pronunciation to the levels of dialect and even language use. A fruitful place for inquiry about the extent to which men and women share the same speech-related norms would be in communities where they were in flux, due either to internal influences such as the changing status of women within a community, or to external factors such as employment opportunities. For example, would the mobile male of Oaxaca, Mexico, regard Huave or Spanish as the more prestigious alternative? Would the Oaxacan woman, more or less bound to her community all her life, agree with him. Recalling Lieberson's (1965) finding that French Canadian (FC) men had a consistently higher rate of bilingualism, and a higher rate of increase in the proportion of bilinguals than FC women, we might not be surprised that FC men rated English Canadian (EC) speakers, regardless of sex, more favourably than representatives of their own language group (Preston, cited in Giles & Powesland 1975). FC women however, traditional guardians of the *langue maternelle*, found the FC men most attractive and competent. While FC women might have agreed that English was the language of occupational mobility for men, their own mobility and prestige in the feminine sector depended more on French.

We can see that both the judgemental standards applied by men and women, and the value they attach to the rewards that accrue from the use of certain features, will probably depend on many factors only secondarily associated with sex, as in the case of apparent markers of sex in speech. This applies even more obviously to the processes by which speech acquires evaluative connotations, the topic to which we now turn.

2.3. The recognition and evaluation of sex-associated speech

The discrepancy between markers and stereotypes. Speech can, by virtue of its real or imagined association with sex, acquire masculine or feminine connotations. But a given feature serves as a marker of a speaker's location along many dimensions of social identity at once, and we have seen that sex is probably not the primary determinant of any feature in isolation. Thus, even though the masculine or feminine connotations of aspects of speech may reflect the actual distribution of markers between the sexes, the attribution of this distribution to sex is not apt. Furthermore, many features and patterns stereotypically associated with sex are not reliable markers even in a statistical sense. While the precise points of discrepancy between speech markers and speech stereotypes of sex have yet to be discovered for any language, there are enough data to conclude that our preconceptions about men's and women's speech are significantly at odds with male–female speech differences, at least in English-speaking America.

An example: the tag question. We can illustrate this with the example of the *tag question*, a favourite feature of stereotypical women's speech. Tag questions modify assertions into implicit pleas for confirmation (e.g. *That would be a good idea, wouldn't it?*). Their use carries connotations of powerlessness and indecisiveness, as well as of lack of intelligence, and sentences of this type are consistently attributed to women by experimental subjects who are asked to identify the author of anonymous transcripts (Edelsky 1976a, 1976b; Siegler & Siegler 1976). But observational studies of men and women have not found any consistent differences between the sexes in the actual use of tags (Baumann 1976; Dubois & Crouch 1976b; Hartman 1976). Other impressionistic accounts of pronunciation, grammatical and vocabulary markers abound, some of which are consistent with controlled observations, some of which are not. But virtually all of these accounts have been offered as examples of speech *differences*. This confusion has led some writers to base arguments about the implications of, for example, women's speech, on patterns that have not been linguistically corroborated (e.g. Lakoff 1973, 1975).

Nevertheless, these sex-associated speech stereotypes merit study in their own right for the insight they give into what is assumed by listeners, and will tend to be expected until disconfirmed. More than idle caricatures, these expectations may define listeners' predispositions towards conversation with women and men, and confirmation of them may be actively sought.

Other common stereotypes. Many of the more common and frequently mentioned speech stereotypes appeared in Jespersen (1922: ch. 13), for example that women are more euphemistic in expression, and that they tend to use more hyperbolic and circumlocutive turns of phrase. These impressions have since been reiterated in several places, along with notes about women using more adverbs ending in *ly*, and being enthusiastic but largely trivial speakers (Bernard 1972; Farb 1973; Key 1972; Pei 1973).

Several of Lakoff's (1975) suggestions about male–female speech differences have been the focus of subsequent research, virtually none of which has supported her assertions. For example, Erickson *et al*. (1977) observed that men used some features characteristic of their Powerless script more than women did. Similar patterns have been reported by Crouch & Dubois (1977) with respect to tag questions, broken fluencies and garbled sentence structures, all supposedly more characteristic of women. Brotherton & Penman (1977) found no differences between male and female students in Australia in terms of verbosity, the proportion of incomplete ideas expressed, or on a global rating of 'abstractness' of the ideas presented in response to Thematic Apperception Test pictures. These studies of young people in university environments should not tempt us to new generalizations. Their value lies in their empirical approach, which makes the results susceptible to controlled replication and systematic extension in other situations.

Speech stereotypes per se: *Kramer's work.* One of the few researchers to inquire about the prevalence of male and female speech stereotypes *per se* is Kramer (1978a, 1978b) who asked students to rate the extent to which each of fifty-one speech-related characteristics (e.g. loud speech, smooth speech, deep voice, good grammar) typified the average male and female speaker. On thirty-six of the scales, men were rated different from women speakers. Male speech was characterized as more attention-seeking (demanding, boastful, loud, forceful), dominating, authoritarian, aggressive and frank. On the other side, 'Female speech can be summarized as friendly, gentle, enthusiastic, grammatically correct, but containing jibberish on trivial topics. *Kind, correct, but unimportant*' (Kramer 1978a; author's italics).

Besides inquiring about the tendency to ascribe certain speech characteristics to men and women, we can also ask whether if given speech or speech-related samples (transcripts, masked or altered tape-recordings), there are cues that lead to them being consistently attributed to one sex or the other. We have seen that this is so with tag questions, and Edelsky

(1976a, 1976b) included a number of other features in her studies which are sex-typed regularly. Kramer (1974) had students assign sex to the speakers of isolated cartoon captions taken from magazines. The assigned sex was the same as that depicted in the unseen cartoons for more than 75 per cent of the captions. When asked how they had decided which sex to attribute, the students mentioned the logical, concise, business-like and controlling nature of the male captions, and the stupidity, vagueness, emotional, confused and wordy features of the female.

Alternative approaches to speech stereotypes and their theoretical importance. These examples serve mainly as illustrations of approaches that could be applied to investigate the degree of match–mismatch between markers and stereotypes of speaker sex, and their evaluative implications (cf. Giles, Scherer & Taylor, this volume: ch. 9, 3.4). As theories of speech functions in conversation develop (e.g. Gumperz, 1977) it is to be hoped that behavioural and interpretive correlates of the paper-and-pencil measures now used can be subjected to study as well. Role-playing and imitation suggest themselves as candidates for exploitation here, where the performance of the person-in-role (e.g. a theatre performer, for example) can be empirically contrasted to that of the model, and to the role player's normal performance (cf. Ginsberg 1977; and especially Sloan & Feldstein 1977).

Another approach, this time a radical departure from any sociolinguistic methods now in practice, would consist of allowing the speech stereotypes to govern the explanations that we construct for how speech features become associated with sex. We have already remarked that sex alone is probably not the best determinant of any isolated feature, either marker or stereotype. By discovering the social divisions and contexts that *do* primarily determine the distribution of a speech marker of sex, we would arrive at a better understanding of the source of sex stereotypes, and how to change them. For example, we may find that the use of tag questions is confined primarily to informal interactions between people of different social status, regardless of their sex. The idea being proposed is that speech stereotyping might, in some cases, provide a mechanism for the transposition of metaphors and evaluations derived from one domain of social life (power and dominance relationships, in the tag question example) to another domain (e.g. male–female relations). Of course, it is not necessary to postulate such a process in the presumably many instances where speech stereotypes and speech markers overlap, i.e. where the stereotypes accurately reflect actual usage by women and men. Nor is this meant to imply that the evaluative and stylistic connotations of speech features can simply be reduced to an analysis of who uses them and when. We have already had occasion to remark that speech can acquire connotations independent of its users. Rather, this last approach is intended only to indicate another alternative in the attempt to understand the dynamics of speech in society.

3. Concluding remarks

The relation between markers and stereotypes of sex in speech is not yet well understood, and it is towards this understanding that future research on sex and language should be directed. In the broadest terms, the tasks that this chapter sets for researchers are the discovery of (i) processes in society which result in the association of speech features with sex, and attributions and evaluations based on them; (ii) the sources from which these impressions derive; and (iii) their relation to male–female speech differences. Barely an outline of how we might proceed has been presented here, yet it would be well to broaden the scope of the inquiry somewhat before concluding, to indicate the range of factors that are relevant to the endeavour.

In the first place, we have avoided an explicit discussion of sociostructural factors, such as status and dependency relationships, and demographic variables, that will probably be a major source of variation between communities in male–female relations and the role of speech. A very useful set of such factors has been outlined by Giles, Bourhis & Taylor (1977) in their consideration of language and ethnic group relations, where they discuss the salience and 'vitality' of speech as a group marker (cf. Giles, this volume: ch. 7, 2.2). Certainly, a straight transposition of their framework to the area of sex and language is not implied, but they do offer a starting-point that has been taken up by at least one worker in this field (Kramer, in preparation).

Giles, Bourhis & Taylor (1977) point out that social structure cannot be assigned a position of causal priority, however. Equally important will be the factors associated with the subjective identity of members of the group; the extent to which they perceive common problems and goals; the existence of relevant groups to which to compare themselves; the apparent legitimacy of the status quo; the possibility for organized action; etc. The relevance of these notions, adapted from Tajfel's theory of intergroup relations (Tajfel 1978; Tajfel & Turner 1978), for theories of speech in society at all levels has been taken up by Giles and others (Giles, forthcoming; Giles & Smith 1979).

This same framework of intergroup relations has been adopted by Williams & Giles (1978) in a discussion of the changing status of women in society. They consider both the objective and the subjective factors that might contribute to women, either as individuals or as members of a common group, wanting to change aspects of their social positions. While speech changes might be a strategy that individual women employ for individual mobility or assimilation into male society, it seems unlikely that speech would ever become the focal point of popular concern over relations between the sexes, as it has for some ethnic and nationalist movements (cf. Giles, this volume: ch. 7). Nevertheless, changes in relations between men and women are bound to result in changes in the salience and evaluation of speech markers of sex.

Once again, though, we must beware of relegating speech to the role of the 'symptom' of social relations. Speech and language use itself may play an active role in the development of the subjective aspects of gender identity and hence in the development and use of language itself. At the crudest level, synonyms for the semantic markers, *male* and *female*, may be chosen with specific connotations in mind, as referred to by Schulz (1975).

In English, the use of the generic *he* has been cited as one mechanism whereby women's roles may be obscured or minimized in importance, by the implicit overgeneralization of the domain of masculine influence, and the simultaneous underplay of the responsibility of the female agent. This feature has become a prime target for critics of sexist bias in language, and change of it has been advocated as one element in a programme of equalization of opportunities for the sexes (Bate 1977; Martyna 1977, in press; Rubin 1977; see Miller & Swift 1976, for a comprehensive review of how such mechanisms operate in English). Similar mechanisms exist in other languages, yet we know little about how they are employed and interpreted. Turning to consider possible roles played by other features of language, Beit-Halahmi *et al.* (1974) have suggested that there might be a relationship between the degree of gender-loading of a language, and the age at which children are able to categorize themselves as male or female. In a language like Arabic or Hebrew, where grammatical concord according to the gender of the object, and even of the audience, is pervasive, children perhaps become aware of the relevance of the male–female distinction earlier than in, for example, Hungary, where the main language is not at all gender-loaded. As it stands, this hypothesis is in need of much elaboration before it is testable, for there are many extralinguistic factors that could override the importance of linguistic gender-loading, such as the range of domains where sex divisions mattered in a given society. Social invisibility (few sex-based distinctions) might cancel the effect of linguistic visibility, and vice versa.

The need for continued research has been highlighted at several points in the chapter. Two specific sites stand out as deserving immediate attention by those interested in sex and speech. First, there is a startling lack of non-English data at the level of nonsegmental analysis. While this may be understandable, given the combination of changing relations between the sexes and a concentration of language-oriented students in English-speaking countries, it is time to submit the hypotheses that have grown from this work to the test of different environments. Second, we need a better understanding of how speech is realized and interpreted in social contexts before we can generalize about the speech of members of any social categories, including men and women. Here we have been restricted to discussing aspects of vocal–auditory communication, yet it is clear that many of the most significant markers of sex in daily encounters are visual in nature, such as physical appearance, dress and movement. Nevertheless, it is unlikely that speech is always, or ever, just a secondary source of information about a speaker's social category membership, even in the apparently clear-cut case of sex. The cultural and physical characteristics that serve as a basis for social divisions vary greatly, both within and between cultures, and the role of speech in these discriminations is open to empirical investigation.

References

Addington, D. W. 1968. The relationship of selected vocal characteristics to personality perception. *Oklahoma State University Monographs* (Social Science Series), no. 15.

Anshen, F. 1969. Speech variation among Negroes in a small southern community. PhD dissertation, New York University.

Argyle, M., Lalljee, M. & Cook, M. 1968. The effect of visibility on interaction in a dyad. *Human Relations*, *21*, 3–17.

Aries, E. 1976. Interaction patterns and themes of male, female, and mixed groups. *Small Group Behavior*, *7*, 7–18.

Aronovitch, C. D. 1976. The voice of personality: stereotyped judgements and their relation to voice quality and sex of speaker. *Journal of Social Psychology*, *99*, 207–20.

Bailey, L. A. & Timm, L. A. 1976. More on women's – and men's – expletives. *Anthropological Linguistics*, *18*, no. 9, 438–49.

Barron, N. 1971. Sex-typed language: the production of grammatical cases. *Acta Sociologica, 14, 24–72.*

Bate, B. A. 1977. Generic man, invisible woman: language, thought, and social change. *Michigan Papers in Women's Studies, 2,* no. 1.

Baumann, M. 1976. Two features of 'Women's Speech?' In B. Dubois & I. Crouch (eds.) *The Sociology of the Languages of American Women.* San Antonio, Texas.

Beit-Halahmi, B., Catford, J. C., Cooley, R. E., Dull, C. Y., Guiora, A. Z. & Raluszny, M. 1974. Grammatical gender and gender identity development: cross cultural and cross lingual implications. *American Journal of Orthopsychiatry, 44,* no. 3, 424–31.

Bernard, J. 1972. *The Sex Game.* New York.

Bodine, A. 1975. Sex differences in language. In B. Thorne & N. Henley (eds.) *Language and Sex: difference and dominance.* Rowley, Mass.

Brend, R. 1975. Male–female intonation patterns in American English. In B. Thorne & N. Henley (eds.) *Language and Sex: difference and dominance.* Rowley, Mass.

Brotherton, P. L. & Penman, R. A. 1977. A comparison of some characteristics of male and female speech. *Journal of Social Psychology, 103,* 161–2.

Brown, P. 1977. How and why are women more polite: some evidence from a Mayan community. Mimeo, Cambridge University.

Cappell, A. 1966. Studies in sociolinguistics. *Janua Linguarium, 46.* The Hague.

Cherry, L. 1975. Teacher–child verbal interaction: an approach to the study of sex differences. In B. Thorne & N. Henley (eds.) *Language and Sex: difference and dominance.* Rowley, Mass.

Cherry, L. & Lewis, M. 1975. *Mothers and Two-Year Olds: a study of sex differentiated aspects of verbal interaction.* Research Bulletin of the Educational Testing Service. Princeton, NJ.

Cheshire, J. 1978. Present tense verbs in Reading English. In P. Trudgill (ed.) *Sociolinguistic Patterns in British English.* London.

Coleman, R. O. 1971. Male and female voice quality and its relationship to vowel formant frequencies. *Journal of Speech and Hearing Research, 14,* no. 3, 565–77.

Conklin, N. F. 1974. Toward a feminist analysis of linguistic behavior. *Michigan Papers in Women's Studies, 1,* no. 1, 51–73.

Crouch, I. & Dubois, B. L. 1977. Interpersonal communication in the classroom: Whose speech is inferior? Paper presented at a Conference on Language and Style, Queen's College, City University of New York.

Crystal, D. 1969. *Prosodic Systems and Intonation in English.* Cambridge.

1971. Prosodic and paralinguistic correlates of social categories. In E. Ardener (ed.) *Social Anthropology and Language.* London.

Diebold, A. R. 1961. Incipient bilingualism. *Language, 37,* 97–112.

Dubois, B. & Crouch, I. (eds.) 1976a. *The Sociology of the Languages of American Women. Papers in Southwest English IV.* Proceedings of the Conference on the Sociology of the Languages of American Women. San Antonio, Texas.

1976b. The question of tag questions in women's speech: They don't really use them, do they? *Language in Society, 4,* 289–94.

Eakins, B. W. & Eakins, C. 1976. Verbal turn-taking and exchanges in faculty dialogue. In B. Dubois & I. Crouch (eds.) *The Sociology of the Languages of American Women.* San Antonio, Texas.

Eakins, B. W. & Eakins, R. G. 1978. *Sex Differences in Human Communication*. Boston.

Edelsky, C. 1976a. Subjective reactions to sex-linked language. *The Journal of Social Psychology, 99*, 97–104.

1976b. The acquisition of communicative competence: recognition of linguistic correlates of sex roles. *Merrill-Palmer Quarterly, 22*, no. 1, 47–59.

Edwards, J. R. In press. Social class and the identification of sex in children's speech. *Child Language*.

Ekka, F. 1972. Men's and women's speech in Kŭṛux. *Linguistics, 81*, 25–31.

Elyan. O. 1978. Sex differences in speech style. *Women Speaking, 4*, April.

Elyan, O., Smith, P., Giles, H. & Bourhis, R. Y. 1978. RP-accented female speech: The voice of perceived androgyny? In P. Trudgill (ed.) *Sociolinguistic Patterns in British English*. London.

Erickson, B., Lind. E. A., Johnson, B. C. & O'Barr, W. M. 1977. *Speech Style and Impression Formation in a Court Setting: the effects of 'Power' and 'Powerless' speech*. Law and Language Project Research Report, *13*. Duke University.

Ervin-Tripp, S. 1976. What do women sociolinguists want? Prospects for a research field. In B. Dubois & I. Crouch (eds.) *The Sociology of the Languages of American Women*. San Antonio, Texas.

Farb, P. 1973. *Word Play: What happens when people talk?* New York.

Fasold, R. W. 1968. *A Sociolinguistic Study of the Pronunciation of Three Vowels in Detroit Speech*. Washington, DC.

1972. *Tense Marking in Black English: a linguistic and social analysis*. Washington, DC.

Feinberg, Y. 1977. Linguistic and socio-demographic factors influencing the acceptance of Hebrew neologisms. PhD dissertation, Hebrew University, Yeshiva. Israel.

Feldstein, S. 1977. Race and gender effects on conversational time patterns. Paper presented at the American Psychological Association Annual Meeting, San Francisco.

Fischer, J. L. 1958. Social influences on the choice of a linguistic variant. *Word, 14*, 47–56.

Frost, J. H. 1977. The influence of female and male communication styles on conflict strategies: problem areas. Paper presented at the International Communication Association Convention, Berlin, West Germany.

Gal, S. 1975. Peasant women can't get wives: changing sex roles and language choice in a European community. Paper presented to the American Anthropological Association Annual Meeting, San Francisco.

Gall, M. D., Hobby, A. K., & Craik, K. H. 1969. Non-linguistic factors in oral language productivity. *Perceptual and Motor Skills, 29*, 871–4.

Garai, J. E. & Scheinfeld, A. 1968. Sex differences in mental and behavioral traits. *Genetic Psychology Monographs, 77*, 169–299.

Giles, H. 1973. Accent mobility: a model and some data. *Anthropological Linguistics, 15*, 87–105.

1977. Social psychology and applied linguistics: towards an integrative approach. *ITL: Review of Applied Linguistics, 33*, 27–42.

Giles, H. Forthcoming. Accommodation theory: some new directions. In S. DeSilva (ed.) *Aspects of Linguistic Behavior*.

Giles, H. & Marsh, P. In press. Perceived masculinity and accented speech. *Language Sciences*.

Giles, H. & Powesland, P. F. 1975. *Speech Style and Social Evaluation*. London.

Giles, H. & Smith, P. M. 1979. Accommodation theory: optimal levels of convergence. In H. Giles & R. St Clair (eds.) *Language and Social Psychology*. Oxford.

Giles, H., Bourhis, R. Y. & Taylor, D. M. 1977. Towards a theory of language in ethnic group relations. In H. Giles (ed.) *Language, Ethnicity and Intergroup Relations*. London.

Giles, H., Smith, P. M., Browne, C., Whiteman, S. & Williams, J. A. In press. Women speaking: the voices of perceived androgyny and feminism. In R. Borker, N. Furman & S. McConnell-Ginet (eds.) *Language and Women's Lives: a feminist perspective*. Ithaca, NY.

Ginsberg, G. P. 1977. Role playing and role performance in social psychological research. In *The Social Contexts of Method: readings in the sociology of methodology*. London.

Gumperz, J. 1977. Sociocultural knowledge in conversational inference. In *Georgetown University 28th Round Table on Languages and Linguistics*. Washington, DC.

Haas, M. R. 1944. Men's and women's speech in Koasati. *Language*, 20 no. 3, 142–9.

Harris, L. J. 1977. Sex differences in the growth and use of language. In E. Donelson & J. E. Gullahorn (eds.) *Women: a psychological perspective*. New York.

Hartford, B. S. 1976. Phonological differences in the English of adolescent Chicanas and Chicanos. In B. Dubois & I. Crouch (eds.) *The Sociology of the Languages of American Women*. San Antonio, Texas.

Hartman, M. 1976. A descriptive study of the language of men and women born in Maine around 1900 as it reflects the Lakoff hypothesis in 'Language and Woman's Place'. In B. Dubois & I. Crouch (eds.) *The Sociology of the Languages of American Women*. San Antonio, Texas.

Head, B. 1977. Sex as a factor in the use of obscenity. Paper presented at the Linguistic Society of America Summer Meeting, Honolulu.

Henley, N. & Thorne, B. 1975. Sex differences in language, speech, and nonverbal communication: an annotated bibliography. In B. Thorne & N. Henley (eds.) *Language and Sex: difference and dominance*. Rowley, Mass.

Herbst, L. 1969. Die Umfänge der physiologischen Hauptsprechtonbereiche von Frauen und Männern. *Zeitschrift für Phonetik*, 22, 426–38.

Hershey, S. & Werner, E. 1975. Dominance in marital decision making in women's liberation and non-women's liberation families. *Family Process*, 14, 223–33.

Hill, C. A. 1975. Sex based differences in cognitive processing of spatial relations in bilingual students in Niger. In R. K. Herbert (ed.) *Patterns in Language, Culture and Society: Sub-Saharan Africa*. Ohio State University.

Hilpert, F., Kramer, C. & Clark, R. A. 1975. Participants' perceptions of self and partner in mixed sex dyads. *Central States Speech Journal*, Spring, 52–6.

Hirschman, L. 1973. Female–male differences in conversational interaction. Paper presented at the Linguistic Society of America Annual Meeting, San Diego.
  1974. Analysis of supportive and assertive behavior in conversation. Paper presented at the Linguistic Society of America Summer Meeting, Amherst.

Hudson, R. A. & Holloway, A. F. 1977. Variation in London English. Final Report to the Social Science Research Council of Great Britain on Grant 4595.

Jayawardena, C. 1977. Woman and kinship in Acheh Besar, Northern Sumatra. *Ethnology, 16*, no. 1, 21–38.

Jespersen, O. 1922. *Language: its nature, development and origin*. London.

Jorden, E. 1974. Language – female and feminine. In B. Hoffer (ed.) *Proceedings of a U.S.–Japanese Sociolinguistics Meeting*. San Antonio, Texas.

Keenan, E. O. 1975. Norm-makers, norm-breakers: uses of speech by men and women in a Malagasy community. In R. Bauman & J. Sherzer (eds.) *Explorations in the Ethnography of Speaking*. Cambridge.

Kelley, J. A. & Worrell, J. 1977. New formulations of sex roles and psychological androgyny: a critical review. *Journal of Consulting and Clinical Psychology, 45*, no. 6, 1101–15.

Key, M. R. 1972. Linguistic behavior of male and female. *Linguistics, 88*, 15–31.

1975. *Male/Female Language*. Metuchen, NJ.

Kramer, C. 1974. Folklinguistics. *Psychology Today, 8*, 82–5.

1978a. Female and male perceptions of female and male speech. *Language and Speech, 20*, no. 2, 151–61.

1978b. Women's and men's ratings of their own ideal speech. *Communication Quarterly, 26*, no. 2, 2–11.

In preparation. Women and men speaking: frameworks for analysis (working title). Newbury House.

Labov, W. 1966. *The Social Stratification of English in New York City*. Center for Applied Linguistics, Washington, DC.

1970. The study of language in its social context. *Studium Generale, 23*, 66–84.

1972. *Sociolinguistic Patterns*. Philadelphia.

Lakoff, R. 1973. Language and woman's place. *Language in Society, 2*, 45–80.

1975. *Language and Woman's Place*. New York.

Landis, C. 1927. National differences in conversation. *Journal of Abnormal and Social Psychology, 21*, 354–75.

Landis, M. H. & Burtt, H. E. 1924. A study of conversation. *Journal of Comparative Psychology, 4*, 81–9.

Lass, N. J. & Davis, M. 1976. An investigation of speaker height and weight identification. Paper presented at the Accoustical Society of America Annual Meeting, Washington.

Lass, N. J., Hughes, K. R., Bowyer, M. D., Waters, L. T. & Bourne, V. T. 1976. Speaker sex identification from voices, whispered and filtered isolated vowels. *Journal of the Accoustical Society of America, 59*, no. 3, 675–8.

Lass, N. J., Mertz, P. J. & Kimmel, K. L. 1978. The effect of temporal speech alterations on speaker race and sex identifications. Language and Speech, *21*, no. 3, 279–90.

Lehiste, I. 1976. Suprasegmental features of Speech. In N. J. Lass (ed.) *Contemporary Issues in Experimental Phonetics*. New York.

Levine, L. & Crockett, H. R. Jr. 1966. Speech variation in a Piedmont community: postvocalic r. In S. Lieberson (ed.) *Explorations in Sociolinguistics*. The Hague.

Lieberman, P. 1967. *Intonation, Perception and Language*. Cambridge.

Lieberson, S. 1965. Bilingualism in Montreal: a demographic analysis. *American Journal of Sociology, 71*, 10–25.

Local, J. In preparation. Studies towards a description of the development and functioning of children's awareness of linguistic variability. Working title, PhD dissertation, Newcastle University.

Macaulay, R. K. S. 1978. Variation and consistency in Glaswegian English. In P. Trudgill (ed.) *Sociolinguistic Patterns in British English*. London.

McCall, G. J., Mazanec, N., Erickson, W. I. & Smith, H. W. 1974. Same-sex recall effects in tests of observational accuracy. *Perceptual and Motor Skills*, *38*, 830.

McConnell-Ginet, S. 1974. Intonation in a man's world. Paper presented at the American Anthropological Association Annual Meeting, Mexico City.

Maclaren, R. 1976. The variable (ʌ), a relic form with social correlates. In *Belfast Working Papers in Language and Linguistics*, *1*, no. 2, 45–68.

Maher, V. 1976. Kin, clients and accomplices: Relationships among women in Morocco. in D. L. Barker & S. Allen (eds.) *Sexual Divisions in Society: process and change*. Cambridge.

Markel, N. N., Prebor, L. D. & Brandt, J. F. 1972. Biosocial factors in dyadic communication: sex and speaking intensity. *Journal of Personality and Social Psychology*, *23*, no. 1, 11–13.

Martyna, W. 1977. Comprehension of the generic masculine: inferring 'She' from 'He'. Paper presented at the American Psychological Association Annual Convention, San Francisco.

In press. What can 'He' mean? – Exploring our use of the generic masculine. *Journal of Communication*.

Mattingly, I. M. 1966. Speaker variation and vocal tract size. *Journal of the Acoustical Society of America*, *39*, 1219 (Abstract).

Mazanec, N. & McCall, G. J. 1975. Sex, cognitive categories and observational accuracy. *Psychological Reports*, *37*, 987–90.

1976. Sex factors in allocation of attention in observing persons. *The Journal of Psychology*, *93*, 175–80.

Meditch, A. 1975. The development of sex-specific speech patterns in young children. *Anthropological Linguistics*, *17*, no. 9, 421–33.

Miller, C. & Swift, K. 1976. *Words and Women*. Garden City, NY.

Milroy, J. & Milroy, L. 1978. Belfast: change and variation in an urban vernacular. In P. Trudgill (ed.) *Sociolinguistic Patterns in British English*. London.

Milroy, L. 1976. Phonological correlates to community structure in Belfast. In *Belfast Working Papers on Language and Linguistics*, *1*, no. 1, 1–44.

Milroy, L. & Margrain, S. 1978. Vernacular language loyalty and social network. *Belfast Working Papers on Language and Linguistics*, *3*, no. 1, 1–58.

Moore, H. T. 1922. Further data concerning sex differences. *Journal of Abnormal and Social Psychology*, *4*, 81–9.

Murray, T., Amundsen, P. & Hollien, H. 1977. Acoustical characteristics of infant cries: fundamental frequency. *Journal of Child Language*, *4*, 321–8.

Nichols, P. C. 1976. Black women in the rural south: conservative and innovative. In B. Dubois & I. Crouch (eds.) *The Sociology of the Languages of American Women*. San Antonio, Texas.

Nilsen, A. P., Bosmajian, H., Gershuny, H. L. & Stanley, J. P. 1977. *Sexism and Language*. National Council of Teachers of English; Urbana, Ill.

Oftedal, M. 1973. Notes on language and sex. *Norwegian Journal of Linguistics* (NTS), *27*, 67–75.

Pei, M. 1973. *Double-Speak in America*. New York.

Pellowe, J. & Jones, V. 1978. On intonational variability in Tyneside speech. In P. Trudgill (ed.) *Sociolinguistic Patterns in British English*. London.

Romaine, S. & Reid, E. 1976. Glottal sloppiness? A sociolinguistic view of urban speech in Scotland. *CITE Journal 'Teaching English'*, *9*, no. 3, 12–16.

Rubin, J. 1977. Why change language? In *Women, Men and the New Language*. Task Force for Equal Treatment of the Sexes in Media, Washington, DC.

Ruble, D., Frieze, I. H. & Parsons, J. E. (eds.) 1976. Sex roles: persistence and change. *Journal of Social Issues*, *32* (entire issue).

Ryan, E. B. & Capedano, H. L. 1977. Stereotyping speakers on the basis of their perceived age. Mimeo, Department of Psychology, University of Notre Dame.

Ryan, E. B. & Carranza, M. A. 1977. Ingroup and outgroup reactions to Mexican American language varieties. In H. Giles (ed.) *Language, Ethnicity and Intergroup Relations*. London.

Sachs, J. 1975. Cues to the identification of sex in children's speech. In B. Thorne & N. Henley (eds.) *Language and Sex: difference and dominance*. Rowley, Mass.

Sankoff, G. & Cedergren, H. 1971. Some results of a sociolinguistic study of Montreal French. In R. Darnell (ed.) *Linguistic Diversity in Canadian Society*. Edmonton and Champaign.

Schulz, M. 1975. The semantic derogation of women. In B. Thorne & N. Henley (eds.) *Language and Sex: difference and dominance*. Rowley, Mass.

Schwartz, M. F. & Rine, H. E. 1968. Identification of speakers from whispered vowels. *Journal of the Acoustical Society of America*, *44*, 1736–7.

Shuy, R. W. 1970. Sociolinguistic research at the Center for Applied Linguistics: the correlation of language and sex. In *International Days of Sociolinguistics*. Rome.

Shuy, R. W., Wolfram, W. A. & Riley, W. K. 1967. *Linguistic Correlates of Social Stratification in Detroit Speech*. Final Report, Project 6-1347. US Office of Education, Washington, DC.

Siegler, D. M. & Siegler, R. S. 1976. Stereotypes of males' and females' speech. *Psychological Reports*, *39*, 167–70.

Silverman, E. M. & Zimmer, C. H. 1975. Speech fluency fluctuations during the menstrual cycle. *Journal of Speech and Hearing Research*, *18*, 202–6.

1976. The fluency of women's speech. In B. Dubois & I. Crouch (eds.) *The Sociology of the Languages of American Women*. San Antonio, Texas.

Sloan, B. & Feldstein, S. 1977. Speech tempo in introversion and extraversion. Mimeo, University of Maryland.

Smith, P. M. 1978. Talking about androgyny: getting there is half the fun. *Resources in Education*, August, ERIC document 151686.

Smith, P. M., Tucker, G. R. & Taylor, D. M. 1977. Language, ethnic identity and intergroup relations: one immigrant group's reaction to language planning in Québec. In H. Giles (ed.) *Language, Ethnicity and Intergroup Relations*. London.

Solé, Y. R. 1976. Sociocultural and sociopsychological factors in differential language retentiveness by sex. In B. Dubois & I. Crouch (eds.) *The Sociology of the Languages of American Women*. San Antonio, Texas.

Strodtbeck, F. L. 1951. Husband–wife interaction over revealed differences. *American Sociological Review*, *16*, 468–73.

Strodtbeck, F. L. & Mann, R. D. 1956. Sex role differentiation in jury deliberations. *Sociometry*, *19*, 3–11.

Swacker, M. 1975. The sex of the speaker as a sociolinguistic variable. In B. Thorne & N. Henley (eds.) *Language and Sex: difference and dominance*. Rowley, Mass.

Tajfel, H. (ed.) 1978. *Differentiation Between Social Groups*. London.

Tajfel, H. & Turner, J. 1978. An integrative theory of intergroup conflict. In W. G. Austin & S. Worchel (eds.) *The Social Psychology of Intergroup Relations*. Monterey, Calif.

Takefuta, Y., Jancosek, E. G. & Brunt, M. 1971. A statistical analysis of melody curves in the intonation of American-English. In *Proceedings of the 7th International Congress of Phonetic Sciences*. The Hague.

Thorne, B. & Henley, N. (eds.) 1975a. *Language and Sex: difference and dominance*. Rowley, Mass.

1975b. Difference and dominance: An overview of language, gender and society. In B. Thorne & N. Henley (eds.) *Language and Sex: difference and dominance*. Rowley, Mass.

Trudgill, P. 1974. *Sociolinguistics*. London.

1975. Sex, covert prestige, and linguistic change in the urban British English of Norwich. In B. Thorne & N. Henley (eds.) *Language and Sex: difference and dominance*. Rowley, Mass.

(ed.) 1978. *Sociolinguistic Patterns in British English*. London.

Trudgill, P. & Tzavaras, G. A. 1977. Why Albanian-Greeks are not Albanians: language shift in Attica and Biotia. In H. Giles (ed.) *Language, Ethnicity and Intergroup Relations*. London.

von Raffler-Engel, W. & Buckner, J. 1976. A difference beyond inherent pitch? In B. Dubois & I. Crouch (eds.) *The Sociology of the Languages of American Women*. San Antonio, Texas.

Warotamasikkhadit, U. 1967. Some phonological rules in Thai. *Journal of the American Oriental Society*, *87*, no. 4.

Weinreich, U. 1963. *Languages in Contact*. The Hague.

Williams, J. A. & Giles, H. 1978. The changing status of women in society: an intergroup perspective. In H. Tajfel (ed.) *Studies in Intergroup Behavior*. London and New York.

Wolfram, W. 1969. *A Sociolinguistic Description of Detroit Negro Speech*. Center for Applied Linguistics, Washington, DC.

Wolfram, W. & Fasold, R. W. 1974. *The Study of Social Dialects in American English*. Englewood Cliffs, NJ.

Woll, B., Ferrier, L. & Wells, C. G. 1975. Children and their parents – who starts talking – why and when? Paper presented at the Conference on Language and Social Context, Stirling, Scotland.

Wood, M. 1966. The influence of sex and knowledge of communication effectiveness on spontaneous speech. *Word*, *22*, nos. 1, 2 and 3, 112–37.

Zimmerman, D. H. & West, C. 1975. Sex roles, interruptions, and silences in conversation. In B. Thorne & N. Henley (eds.) *Language and Sex: difference and dominance*. Rowley, Mass.

5. Personality markers in speech[1]

KLAUS R. SCHERER

There is little controversy about the existence and the social and psychological significance of such categories as sex, age, or ethnic background and the strong likelihood that members of these different categories may be discernible on the basis of specific speech markers. The existence of personality markers in speech seems to be much less self-evident. This is not only due to the fact that little is known about the way in which personality affects speech but also due to the controversy that surrounds the concept of personality itself. While most people seem quite convinced that they 'have' personality and that other people with whom they interact have different personalities, social and behavioural scientists hotly debate the nature of personality and its impact on behaviour (cf. Endler & Magnusson 1976; Mischel 1968).

One of the central issues is the question to what extent the psychological categories implied by personality trait labels used in naive person perception correspond to actual trans-situationally stable differences in psychological states and behaviour patterns. For example, while the psychological categories male/female correspond directly to the biological categories of sex, it is difficult to specify objectively the psychological and/or behavioural categories which correspond to trait labels of 'conscientiousness' used in naive personality attribution.

[1] This chapter has benefited from the work, the expertise, and the advice of so many collaborators and colleagues that a minor acknowledgement paper would be required to do justice to everybody. The only reasonable alternative is an alphabetical list of all those to whom the author feels indebted for their contribution: Sylvia von Borstel, Janis Flint, Colin Fraser, Howard Giles, Hede Helfrich, Gudrun Herpel, Stephanie Kühnen, Peter Ostwald, Ursula Scherer, Peter Schönbach, Philip Smith, Rainer Standke and Harald Wallbott.

As usual, the author assumes full responsibility for any errors or shortcomings which may have found their way into the final version of this chapter despite the excellent advice received in the course of the many revisions of the manuscript.

1. Personality dispositions and personality attributions

In order to discuss speech markers of personality we shall have to distinguish actual, enduring individual differences between actors, which we will call personality dispositions, and the inferences observers make concerning such personality dispositions, which we will call personality attributions. Speech markers of personality will be defined as speech cues serving as the basis for personality attributions of listeners which correspond to the respective personality dispositions of the speaker.

For the purposes of the present chapter we will define personality dispositions as enduring individual differences in the nature of the cognitive processes, the relative dominance of specific motivational states, the degree of emotional reactivity and the preference for certain behaviour patterns. These personality dispositions can be (and sometimes are) measured by physiological recording procedures, perceptual and reasoning tests, projective tests, assessment of emotional expressiveness and behaviour analysis. However, the most frequently used technique consists in obtaining self-reports of relevant cognitive and motivational states and behaviour preferences via personality inventories and rating forms.

While scientific analyses of individual differences in personality dispositions tend to be oriented towards differences in isolated determinants of behaviour, the lay conception of personality which is operative in personality attribution seems more oriented towards capturing the significance of recurring cognitive/motivational states and stable behaviour patterns for social interaction. This is accomplished by assigning *trait labels* to clusters of behaviour dispositions and behaviour patterns that are seen to cooccur frequently enough to warrant classing them together and to be relevant to rendering intelligible a person's interactive behaviour. By labelling perceived determinants of behaviour in terms of personality traits, actors obtain a sense of stability and predictability of behaviour which is required for the strategic planning of interaction sequences (cf. Jones & Nisbet 1971).

Consequently, an analysis of the semantic structure of personality labels used in everyday attribution should reveal the underlying factors or dimensions commonly regarded as essential determinants of social interactive behaviour. Careful analyses of the factor structure of frequently used personality trait adjectives (cf. Wiggins 1973: 342–57) have yielded a fairly stable set of dimensions. Some of these dimensions refer to interpersonal behaviour dispositions (extroversion, assertiveness and, to some extent, agreeableness), others refer to intrapersonal dispositions (conscientiousness and emotional stability).

In this chapter we are concerned with the processes whereby observers arrive at such personality attributions on the basis of speech markers of personality dispositions. While it is abundantly clear that observers rely heavily on speech style to attribute personality traits to the speaker (Giles & Powesland 1975), it is at present much less clear to what extent these inferences accurately reflect actual differences in personality disposition and to what extent they reflect 'vocal stereotypes' without any basis in fact (Kramer 1963; Scherer 1972). Thus, the investigation of personality markers in speech is strongly linked to the question concerning the possibility of 'accurate' personality inferences from speech.

Scherer (1974b, 1978) has suggested using a modified version of Brunswik's (1956) lens model to allow a systematic assessment of the various components of the 'accuracy' of personality judgements from voice and speech. This model, shown in figure 1, will serve to structure the survey of the evidence concerning personality markers in speech. The model simply suggests that personality dispositions are 'externalized' or expressed via indicator cues, i.e. objectively measured speech variables ('distal cues'), which are in turn perceived by listener–observers and represented as subjective percepts (which can be assessed by lay ratings of speech). These perceptual representations of speech cues ('proximal cues') are the basis for the cognitive inference processes which lead to a particular personality attribution to the speaker. Personality 'markers' in speech, then, are defined as those distal speech cues that are definitely, although possibly probabilistically (cf. Scherer 1977a, c; Giles, Scherer & Taylor, this volume: ch. 9, 3.2), associated with particular personality dispositions, and which can be accurately perceived and correctly interpreted by untrained listeners to result in veridical personality attribution; cf. the distinction between 'emic' and 'etic' markers in Brown & Fraser (this volume: ch. 2, 1.2) and Giles, Scherer & Taylor (this volume: ch. 9, 3.4).

Of course, the notion of accuracy in this model implies that there is conceptual congruence or at least overlap between a personality disposition and respective personality attributions which can be entered into the model. This need not be the case. It is possible that there are individual differences in terms of personality dispositions for which there are no equivalent concepts or categories in personality attribution. For example, field dependence (cf. Witkin & Goodenough 1977) may not be very adequately reflected in any category normally used in naive personality

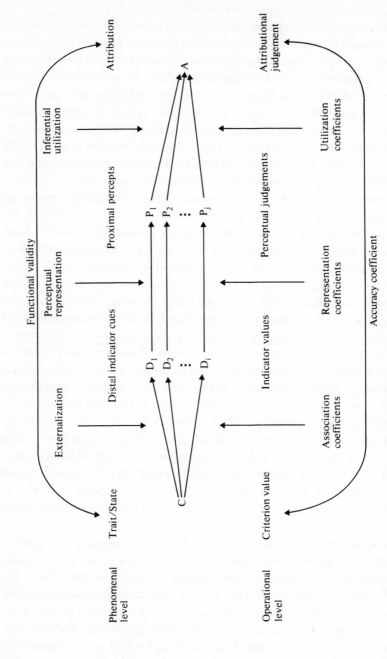

Figure 1. A modified version of the Brunswikian lens model

attribution even though it seems to affect interpersonal behaviour. In such a case, it does not seem useful to talk about markers of this personality disposition even if it does affect speech style.

Unfortunately, the present state of the art in personality research does not allow us to specify (and then to concentrate on) those dispositions for which there seem to be matching attributional categories or vice versa. Most studies in this area have been concerned *either* with the correlation between personality dispositions and distal speech cues *or* with the correlation between distal speech cues (or sometimes their proximal representation in lay judges) and personality attributions by listener–judges; very few studies have examined both sides of the 'lens' (cf. Scherer 1974b, 1978) as would be required to establish the existence of personality markers in the sense defined above. Given this shortcoming of the available research literature, this review will deal separately with (i) studies concerned with externalization, i.e. the association between personality dispositions of speakers and objectively measured distal speech cues, and (ii) studies concerned with personality attributions based on specific distal speech cues.

2. Externalization of personality in speech

Although the history of scientific interest in relationships between speech and personality can probably be dated back further than most behavioural science questions (cf. Laver 1975; Sanford 1942), the present state of the art is bleak and the amount of hard data negligible. This state of affairs is certainly not due to a lack of publications in this field – Görlitz (1972) lists more than 1,500 references in his 600 page review. A sizeable number of (mostly German) voice and speech experts have written lengthy books or book chapters on the relationship of virtually every aspect of voice and speech style to virtually every imaginable personality trait (cf. Fährmann 1967; Moses 1954; Rudert 1965; Trojan 1975). While these workers have doubtless engaged in extensive and careful case observations, their conclusions must be treated as hypotheses rather than hard data.

While making occasional references to these phenomenologically oriented writings, this review will focus on empirical studies in which an attempt was made to measure one of several aspects of voice and speech style – by expert ratings, systematic coding, or electro-acoustic analyses –and to relate it to standardized personality measures. This research has been generally beset by a large number of difficulties including, among many others, the problem of defining appropriate voice and speech variables and their units and methods of measurement, finding reliable and valid instruments of personality measurement, and developing research strategies for speech sample selection that violate neither linguistic, social, psychological or ethical demands (cf. Crystal 1969: 62–82; Kramer 1963; Scherer 1972). Coverage will be restricted to aspects of 'normal personality'; research dealing with pathological personality development (cf. Moses 1954; Ostwald 1973; Vetter 1969) and emotion (for a recent review cf. Scherer 1979a) will be referred to only in a few exceptional cases.

The attempt at comparative evaluation of research findings in this area will have to be somewhat speculative given the nature of the field. The studies in this area are not only separated by many years, there is also a wide range of methodological and procedural differences. One of the most problematic aspects is the wide diversity of types of speakers and speech situations used. Findings could be sex- or age-specific and a large amount of the variance could be due to the nature of the speech sample ranging from reciting numbers or nonsense syllables to group discussions. Given the notoriously low intercorrelations between personality assessment methods measuring the same trait, comparability of results across studies is difficult to achieve even if the same trait names are used. While most studies have used self-report techniques (via personality inventories or self-ratings), some workers have also used peer ratings in their studies which frequently requires differentiating between relationships of self- vs. peer ratings of personality since these two are not always very strongly correlated. Clearly, chances for finding replications across studies are extremely slim and thus the lack of stable patterns of results should not at present be interpreted as evidence for the absence of speech–personality relationships.

The picture becomes even more blurred by introducing cross-cultural differences. One must rather suspect that the happy consistency of findings and interpretations across studies which one sometimes finds in American textbooks or review chapters is a consequence of a culture-blind approach (which cannot always be blamed on the lack of appropriate research in other cultures). Since there seem to be rather strong intercultural differences, the reader will have to be frequently bothered by qualifications concerning the validity of findings for a particular culture. In the light of the scarcity of published research results, the author will refer to his own cross-cultural work somewhat more frequently than decorum normally allows. This is particularly true for what will be called the 'juror study' hereafter (Scherer 1970, 1972, 1974b, 1978, in preparation).[2]

We will begin the following review of the literature bearing on the questions of *possible* personality markers in speech by discussing the evidence on the externalization of personality dispositions in speech style. In this section, both extra- and paralinguistic speech cues (cf. Laver & Trudgill, this volume: ch. 1, 2.1–2), subdivided into vocal aspects (fundamental frequency, vocal intensity and voice quality) and fluency aspects (pauses and speech rate, speech discontinuities) of speech style, as well as linguistic cues (morphological and syntactical aspects of speech style) will be discussed. In addition, personality differences in conversational behaviour (number and length of turns, total verbal output) will be reviewed. The externalization section is followed by a review of the literature on personality inferences from speech style and the chapter will be concluded by a summary of the evidence on personality markers in speech and a discussion of the origins of these markers.

2.1. Vocal aspects of speech style

Vocal aspects of speech style comprise those speech cues that are determined by the respiratory, phonatory and articulatory processes of human sound production. If the acoustic speech signal is chosen as the basis for analysis, three major parameters can be investigated: fundamental frequency (level and variability), vocal energy or intensity (level and variability) and energy distribution in the voice spectrum. Each of these acoustic parameters, which can be objectively assessed by electro-acoustic equipment or digital computer analyses, has its counterpart in perception – pitch, loudness, and voice quality respectively – but there is no one-to-one relationship between the acoustic parameters and their perceptual

[2] Since the 'juror study' is frequently referred to in this chapter a short description of the procedures used seems appropriate. Twenty-eight American and twenty-nine German adult males betwen 25 and 50 years of age were recruited from adult education centre files under the guise of taking part in a study on personality influences on jury decision-making. Groups of six jurors each discussed a criminal case in order to reach a verdict for about an hour, after having filled out a battery of personality tests and rating forms. In addition, three acquaintances of the same age, sex and social class of each subject were asked to return peer ratings of personality directly to the investigator. The contributions of the jurors to the discussion were subsequently analysed for a large variety of speech style cues, and speech samples, treated with content masking techniques, were played to various groups of judges. Details of the procedures used can be found in published reports (cf. Scherer, 1970, 1972, 1974b, 1974c, 1978). However, most of the data reported in this chapter stem from recently completed voice and speech analyses by trained coders and computerized digital speech processing (see von Borstel 1977; Herpel 1977, Kühnen 1977; Scherer 1979b, in preparation).

analogues. Thus, perceived pitch seems to be determined not only by fundamental frequency (f_0), which corresponds to the rate of vibration of the vocal cords, but also by the energy distribution in the frequency domain (Laver 1975: 258). Consequently, one would not expect a perfect correlation between f_0 and subjectively rated pitch. Scherer (1974c, in preparation) found that lay judges and phoneticians agree quite well on their ratings of pitch (correlations around 0.80) but that both sets of subjective pitch ratings correlate only moderately with computer-assessed f_0 for equivalent speech samples of the same speakers (correlations around 0.50). Similarly, judgements of loudness of the voice may be influenced by other acoustic factors in addition to acoustic energy (Lehiste 1970: 113–20). For example, Scherer (1974c) found that phoneticians' ratings of vocal effort or loudness tended to correlate with their ratings of pitch. The relationships between subjectively perceived voice quality such as harshness, hoarseness, breathiness, or resonance – to name but a few of a large number of descriptive voice quality terms – and objective measures of spectral composition are not very well known at present (cf. Laver 1975). Since both objective acoustic measures and subjective ratings of these vocal aspects of speech style have been used in the studies reported below, it is often difficult to compare the findings. Inconsistencies may at least partly be due to the fact that acoustic measures of distal cues and subjective ratings of their proximal representation may measure somewhat different things. Given the scarcity of published research reports, studies on the relationship of personality measures to both acoustic measures of distal cues and subjective ratings of proximal cues will be reviewed for each of the three major vocal aspects of speech style in the sections to follow.

Fundamental frequency (f_0). Most results to be reported in this section stem from the juror study (cf. n. 2 above; Scherer, in preparation), since there are only very few studies in which the relationship of f_0 to normal personality traits has been investigated. For the male American speakers in the juror study fairly strong positive correlations of f_0 with self-attributions (on inventories and rating scales) of achievement, task ability, sociability, dominance and aggressiveness, and peer attributions of dominance and assertiveness are found. The notion that competent and dominant speakers have higher f_0 than non-taskoriented, submissive speakers does not violate popular expectations since these voices may not *sound* particularly high-pitched to an observer as long as they remain within the normal range of f_0 for male adult American speakers (which they do in this case), and as long as the general muscular tension of the vocal system remains at a normal level and there is no energy concentration in the upper part of the spectrum (cf. Laver 1975: 258; and the discussion in the preceding paragraph). This interpretation is supported by the fact that phoneticians' ratings of pitch height of the same voices, representing the subjective impression of voice pitch, do not correlate nearly as strongly with the competence/dominance cluster as f_0 although the correlation coefficients point in the same direction.

To account for these results, the following hypothesis can be advanced: Competence and dominance in males may be accompanied by a habitually high degree of arousal or state of readiness of the organism. Since arousal seems to lead to an increase in muscle tension (Gellhorn 1967; Malmo 1975), competence and dominance may be reflected in a heightened degree of habitual muscle tone, which in turn may lead to a level of f_0 which is comparatively higher than that of speakers with lower levels of habitual arousal. This hypothesis is admittedly highly speculative; the only evidence at present can be adduced from a relationship between transitory states of arousal under stress and increase in f_0.

Scherer (1979a) has argued that the anatomical structure of the larynx and the physiological aspects of voice production qualify f_0 as a major vocal indicator of psychological arousal and has hypothesized a close relationship between degree of muscle tension and mean f_0 for transitory states of arousal. Using f_0 extraction via digital computer-processing, Scherer and his associates have been able to show that stress induction (nurses lying about a gory film) leads to a significant rise of f_0 compared to baseline (Ekman, Friesen & Scherer 1976; Scherer 1977b; Scherer, Helfrich, Standke & Wallbott 1976), and that the presumably stress-reducing effects of therapy significantly lower f_0 in the voices of depressives from admission to discharge from the hospital (Scherer *et al*. 1976). A review of the literature (Scherer 1979a) reports findings from other laboratories consistent with the notion that f_0 may be a powerful indicator of stress even though there are individual differences in f_0 responses to stress.

Since all of these studies are concerned with either transitory stress or psychopathology, further research concerning a hypothetical relationship between competence/dominance, level of arousal and f_0 is needed. Clearly, this hypothesis will be difficult to test. An earlier result, however, may bolster the assumption of a link between muscle tension as a competence/dominance concomitant and f_0 as a biophysical indicator. Scherer, London & Wolf (1973) found that an actor used an f_0 rise of almost 20 Hz to render a linguistically doubtful text in a confident manner and succeeded in being seen by naive judges as only insignificantly less forceful, active and competent compared to the judgements of his rendering of a confident text. Thus, he may have raised his level of arousal in delivering the message to overcome the drawback of a rather defeatist text.

In the juror study, the German speakers' f_0 in the discussion does not correlate with a competence/dominance pattern, contrary to the American results. Here we find a relationship between f_0 and a pattern of self-ratings of adjustment, orderliness and lack of autonomy as well as peer ratings of dependability and likeability (Kühnen 1977; Scherer, in preparation). It can be hypothesized that this pattern of discipline, responsibility and social conformity may also be associated with a somewhat elevated pattern of muscular tension.

Lomax (1974), relating cultural complexity, sexual repression and other structural aspects of societies to various phonatory and articulatory patterns in song style, has claimed that 'back, loosely enunciated and lax sounds decrease and front, narrow, sharply enunciated sounds generally increase as culture grows more complex and laden with rules' (204–5). This notion seems entirely compatible with the assumption of a higher level of muscular tension in societies where conformity to rules and general discipline and self-control are highly valued. Similarly, individuals who have, by internalization or external pressure, developed particularly strong dispositions in this respect may very well show higher muscular tension than somewhat more easy-going and less disciplined persons. Both everyday observation and learned theoretical accounts point to a reflection of such physiological patterns in various aspects of voice and speech style (cf. Fährmann 1967; Trojan 1975).

A similar relationship between higher f_0 and a personality syndrome suggesting discipline, dependability and self-control has been found in a sample of very different subjects in a different culture. In the stress film study with American student nurses mentioned above (cf. Ekman et al. 1976), f_0 was significantly correlated with the following personality scales in the California Psychological Inventory (CPI): positively with femininity and socialization and negatively with capacity for status, sociability, social presence and self-acceptance (Scherer 1977b). According to the CPI scale descriptions, girls with higher f_0 can be described as patient, helpful, persevering, sincere, steady, conscientious, responsible, methodical, conservative, self-restrained but also as dull, simple, slow and awkward. Again, the notion of self-control and discipline with just a touch of rigidity which pervades these descriptions is not incompatible with the presence of a habitually higher level of muscular tension which may be the somatic concomitant of comparative higher levels of f_0. These findings partially confirm earlier results reported by Mallory & Miller (1958), who found a weak negative correlation between subjectively rated pitch and dominance and extroversion for 372 female American students.

At this point, the reader may be confused to find that muscle tension is invoked as an explanation for higher f_0 for both competence/dominance and discipline/dependability. However, in both cases a relatively higher level of activation or arousal and thus a preponderance of the ergotropic (activation) system could prevail. It is possible that there is an imbalance in the reciprocal relationship between the ergotropic (activation) and the trophotropic (rest) systems favouring ergotropic activation (cf. Gellhorn 1967) for both of these personality types. In the competence/dominance syndrome this energy may be directed outward and made to serve achievement and self-enhancement, whereas in the discipline/dependability syndrome this energy may serve to maintain self-control and strict adherence to rules and obligations. It is not inconceivable that both syndromes may be mixed in some persons with high habitual muscle tone. It should be stressed that this hypothesis does not contain any causal implications as to whether muscle tension determines personality or vice versa. It is most likely that biophysical factors, individual response tendencies and sociocultural factors interact in the course of the socialization process to produce somewhat more stable behaviour dispositions in the adult.

To summarize: Higher f_0 seems to be associated with a personality syndrome of competence and dominance in male American and – to some extent – male German speakers as well as with a syndrome of discipline/dependability in male German and female American speakers. An explanation in terms of habitually elevated level of arousal is suggested in both cases.

A final note on cultural differences: There is a very significant difference in mean f_0 for the 28 American (128 Hz) and the 29 German speakers (161 Hz, difference significant at $p < 0.001$) in the juror study (Scherer, in preparation). Although the samples are obviously too small to draw any conclusions about stable cultural differences in terms of f_0, this result supports Laver's (1975: 268) impression of a very low pitch range in American males, which he attributes to cultural stereotypes. If one were to find stable intercultural differences of f_0 it would be a challenging task for social psychologists to determine whether the difference is due to physiological factors – possibly related to national character or modal personality – or to differential expectations or evaluations concerning desirable pitch levels – strongly influenced by historical tradition or mass media portrayals – or the interaction of both of these factors.

Vocal intensity. A second major voice dimension is amplitude or intensity of the speech signal, subjectively perceived as loudness. In one of the earliest judgement studies in the field, Allport & Cantril (1934) point out that all their extroverts who had 'properly' spoken in a loud and bois- terous voice had been reliably recognized. While further evidence is needed, an actual covariation of vocal intensity and extroversion is indi- cated. Mallory & Miller (1958) reported a low positive correlation between introversion and 'inadequate' loudness. Trimboli (1973) found a signifi- cant correlation between extroversion and electro-acoustically assessed vocal intensity. In the juror study, Scherer (1974c, in preparation) found significant correlations between phoneticians' ratings of vocal effort and self- and peer ratings of extroversion, sociability and emotional stability for American speakers.

Objectively measured loudness does *not* seem to correlate with *domi- nance* in spite of Mallory & Miller's (1958) finding of a negative correlation between dominance and subjectively rated 'inadequate' loudness. In the juror study no such correlations were found. The findings of Markel, Phillis, Vargas & Harvard (1972) on 'peak-loudness' are difficult to relate to other approaches since they simply report actuarial descriptions of Minnesota Multiphasic Personality Inventory (MMPI) profiles, without attempting an interpretation in terms of the trait labels generally used in this literature.

Voice quality. The role of voice quality or timbre, i.e. the energy distribu- tion in the voice spectrum, as a personality marker is most promising but quite unresearched. This may be due in part to the difficulty of defining voice quality characteristics objectively. There is an enormous number of voice quality adjectives which are used freely and somewhat inconsis- tently by fiction writers and voice quality experts alike, but only recently have attempts been made to specify the articulatory–phonetic bases of voice quality rigorously (Laver 1975). Serious research in this area will most surely be hampered until there is reliable evidence on the acous- tic–phonetic nature of voice quality as assessed by spectral voice analysis.

Early research, using expert rater assessment (cf. review in Diehl 1960), has shown that breathy voices may be indicative of introversion, neurotic tendency and anxiety (Diehl, White & Burk 1959; Moore 1939). In the juror study, German speakers with breathy voices were seen as neurotic and dominant but not sociable by their peers and tended to describe themselves as emotionally unstable; for American speakers there was not sufficient variability in the breathiness ratings to compute correlations (Scherer, in preparation). Harsh, metallic and resonant voices may be indicative of emotional stability, extroversion and dominance (Mallory & Miller 1958; Moore 1939). Laver (1975), in a very careful review of studies dealing with resonant, metallic, strident etc. (tense voice) vs. muffled, mellow, etc. voice quality characteristics (lax voice), hypothesized that these voice qualities may be the result of variations in overall level of muscular tension throughout the vocal system. Obviously, this notion is a welcome ally for the hypothesis that vocal style may mark personality-related dimensions of physiological response tendencies, particularly habitual muscle tone. One would assume active and dominant as well as disciplined and controlled speakers to have rather tense voices and more passive, submissive and relaxed speakers to have rather lax voices. Some support for this notion can be derived from the findings on resonant and metallic sounding voices quoted above. There may be an optimal level of tension setting of the vocal system resulting in a 'clear' and 'resonant' voice which is neither 'muffled' or 'gloomy' (too lax) nor 'shrill' or 'strident' (too tense).

It has been stated before that there may be excessively high muscular tension in extreme emotional states and for some psychopathological syndromes which may be associated with abnormally tense vocal systems. In such cases, reduction of tension should result in a change towards lax voice. Laver (1975) has argued that for lax voices a relatively greater proportion of total energy would be expected in the frequency range below 500 Hz, whereas tense voices may show an energy concentration between 500 and 1,000 Hz. In the study of depressives mentioned above, Scherer and his associates found some evidence that tension reduction after therapy is associated with a change in energy concentration indicating a laxer setting of the vocal system (Scherer 1979a). In a recent psychopharmacological study we found that antidepressant drugs may produce similar but weaker effects in normal subjects (Helfrich & Scherer 1977).

Emotional reactivity would seem to play a major part in the mediation of vocal style markers of personality. There is little doubt that discrete emotions are accompanied by strong and fairly consistent vocal concomitants including voice quality. Thus, individual differences in stable personality dispositions may also consist in particular emotional reaction patterns coupled with specific vocal style in certain situational contexts without showing persistent and continuous states in physiological and vocal patterning. If this is the case, one-shot studies dealing with a single speech situation, usually devoid of any emotional content (such as reading a standard text), are not likely to demonstrate strong relationships between voice and personality. It is a major task for future research to determine to what extent vocal personality markers are continuously present across situations (which could be due to generalization from frequently and dominantly recurring emotional reaction patterns) and to what extent they may be situation- or emotion-specific.

There are a large number of other paralinguistic features which may be important markers of personality such as rhythm, intonation, accentuation, shape of the vowel sound, etc. (cf. Fährmann 1967; Ostwald 1964; Trojan 1975). Unfortunately, as yet there are very few empirical studies dealing with such features. In the juror study a correlation between precision of articulation and peer attributions of dominance and task ability were found for German speakers (Scherer 1974b, in preparation).

2.2. Fluency aspects of speech style

Compared to voice, the research landscape for fluency aspects of speech is much less barren (cf. Feldstein & Welkowitz 1978; Mahl & Schulze 1964; Murray 1971; Rochester 1973; Siegman 1978). Since these reviews provide a representative overview of the relevant issues in this research area, our survey will focus on the relationship of pausing and speech rate to extroversion and anxiety (trait or predispositional anxiety) in normal subject populations.

A short review of the fluency speech cues that have been studied in this area will precede the survey of the literature. Contrary to the assumption that fluency cues are easy to define and to measure, researchers have found it remarkably difficult to break the stream of sound and silences in speech into meaningful units. One of the most difficult problems has been the definition of various types of pauses according to formal or functional criteria. Since the controversy surrounding the definition and measurement of different types of pauses is well summarized in Rochester (1973), only some of the more fundamental distinctions will be discussed below. The distinction between 'filled' pauses, i.e. interruption of the speech flow by sounds such as *ehm*, *ah*, *mhmm*, and 'silent' pauses between periods of vocalizations is fairly straightforward from the measurement point of view, although the differences in the functions of the respective type of pause are less clear. There seems to be little doubt that silent pauses do not constitute a unitary class but need to be differentiated according to function as 'juncture' pauses, i.e. short interruptions of the speech flow between syntactic units which may serve cognitive planning purposes, and 'nonjuncture' or hesitation pauses which do not occur at syntactically predictable breaking-points but may indicate encoding difficulties or psychological arousal. While juncture pauses tend to be somewhat shorter than hesitation pauses, duration alone does not seem to be a satisfactory criterion. This difficulty constitutes one of the major problems for automatic computer analyses of speech sounds and silences (cf. Feldstein & Welkowitz 1978; Jaffe & Feldstein 1970; Matarazzo 1965). In this chapter we will distinguish computer-extracted *silent periods*, which are usually defined as nonvocalization periods longer than 200 or 250 msec., from silent hesitation pauses as assessed by coders trying to identify silent periods which are not necessary for articulation, i.e. the very short silence between stops, and which are not juncture pauses. It may be necessary to make further distinctions within the class of silent hesitation pauses: Siegman (1978) argues on the basis of a review of the literature that pauses below 2 sec. and longer than 2 sec. may be determined by different cognitive and/or emotional processes and may serve different functions.

In most studies, the number and duration of silent pauses and silent periods are related to the length of utterances or total speaking time by forming ratios, such as average number of silent pauses per utterance, average duration of pauses, or pausing time over total speaking time. One frequently used variable is the sound–silence ratio which measures total vocalization time (without pauses) over total duration of silent periods.

The tempo or rate of speech can be assessed in two ways. Either by dividing the total speaking time including silent periods by the number of words, or syllables, which is usually called speech rate, or by dividing vocalization time exclusive of silent periods by some index for the number of linguistic units produced. The latter is called rate of articulation. Needless to say, most of these parameters of pausing and speech rate are not independent of each other since often the same data base is used for different ratios. These interrelationships are very complex, however (cf. Goldman-Eisler 1968).

Table 1 shows the intercorrelations for some of the variables described in the speech samples of the speakers in the juror study (Scherer, in preparation). The size of the correlations shows that while there is some

Table 1. Intercorrelations between fluency variables, emotional stability, and extroversion for 28 American (A) and 29 German (G) speakers in the juror study[a]

		Filled pauses A/G	Silent pauses A/G	Av. dur. sil. per. A/G	Speech rate A/G	Artic. rate A/G	Sound–sil. ratio A/G
No. filled pauses/total words		–					
No. silent pauses/total words		-06/ 26	–				
Average duration of silent periods		-13/-19	44/-03	–			
Speech rate		27/ 09	40/ 17	30/ 26	–		
Articulation rate		27/ 13	-32/ 14	-28/-08	28/ 86	–	
Sound–silence ratio		20/-14	-38/ 05	-46/-49	-43/-28	57/ 01	–
Emotional stability	Self-rating	-40/-37	30/-24	16/ 14	29/-31	-17/-31	-62/ 08
	Peer rating	08/-31	-36/-20	03/ 10	03/ 08	-01/ 20	-28/-05
Extroversion	Self-rating	-11/-08	-39/ 38	-04/ 10	04/ 30	15/ 20	-23/-17
	Peer rating	03/ 48	-65/ 24	-46/ 20	-11/-14	13/-26	-01/-28

[a]Pearson rs; coefficients in italics are significant at p < 0.05 or lower.

degree of overlap the variables cannot be used interchangeably. It seems entirely possible that the individual variables measure specific fluency cues which may indicate or mark different psychological traits or states. Particularly, relative number and average duration of silent periods and/or pauses may differ in significance in terms of indication of personality, as we shall see below.

By speech discontinuities we mean disruptions of the continuity of the speech flow such as filled pauses (*ahm, hm*), speech intrusions, false starts, tongue slips, sentence correction or change, omissions, repetitions, etc. (cf. Mahl 1956).

Pauses and speech rate. Since researchers have often used several of these variables in the same study and since their interrelationships need to be discussed, the following review of the literature is organized by personality traits rather than speech cues. We will discuss extroversion and anxiety, in this order.

Siegman & Pope (1965) found *extroversion* to be associated with shorter latency, fewer 'filled' brief pauses and fewer silent pauses (2 sec. and over). Ramsay (1966, 1968), using automatic pause analysis with 0.01 sec. intervals, found shorter periods of silence between sound bursts for extroverts than introverts. Siegman (1978) concludes that these studies, which both used the Eysenck E-scale (Eysenck 1967), show that there is a correlation between extroversion and speech tempo. If one defines speech tempo by speech rate (number of words or syllables/utterance duration), this conclusion does not seem to be supported by the existing evidence since Siegman & Pope (1965) and Ramsay (1966, 1968) apparently did not compute speech *rate* as defined above. Ramsay fails to find a significant extroversion effect for sound–silence ratio (which normally correlates with speech rate) in his 1968 experiment with Dutch subjects and suggests that the length of silence between sound bursts may be the critical variable which distinguishes introverts and extroverts; he links this finding to higher cognitive activity in introverts ('thoughtful types', p. 61).

Neither the tempo nor the pause *duration* assumption are supported by comparable results in the juror study. The pattern of results for American speakers shown in table 1 shows that *extroversion* (self- *and* peer ratings) seems to be negatively related to the *number* of silent hesitation pauses rather than to the duration of silent periods between sound bursts longer than 0.25 sec. or to speech or articulation rate. Consequently, in the juror study, extroverts seem to produce fewer pauses that are identified as hesitation pauses by listeners. However, the silent pauses were not differentiated according to length (above or below 2 sec. as suggested by Siegman 1978) in the juror study. It is possible that such a distinction would increase the correlation between extroversion and *number of longer silent pauses*. The issue of number vs. duration of silent pauses may be important for a better understanding of the psychological processes underlying the relationship between pausing and extroversion.

Siegman (1978) has stated that the relationship between extroversion and pausing could be due to individual differences in cognitive activity or impulsivity (which is one component of extroversion as defined by Eysenck 1967: 220). If a biophysical factor of this sort affects pausing behaviour we would expect similar results for the German speakers in the juror study. This is not the case. On the contrary, there is a positive correlation between self-ratings of extroversion and number of silent pauses (cf. table 1). This suggests a need to look for alternative explanations of the phenomenon that could take intercultural differences into account. One possibility is that Americans attribute introversion and other unfavourable (in the context of personality trait evaluation within a particular culture) traits to speakers who show many hesitation pauses in their speech. Results by Addington (1968b) and Lay & Burron (1968), to be reviewed later, point in this direction. In this case, the need for self-presentation may result in the extroverted speakers' attempting to avoid hesitation pauses to parade their sociability. Alternatively, extroverts may avoid hesitation pauses in speech communities where such breaks in the speech flow are frequently used for turn claiming attempts.

The nature and measurement of *anxiety* has become one of the major preoccupations of psychological research (cf. Spielberger 1972). We cannot attempt to cope with the complexities of the distinctions between the different types of anxiety such as situational anxiety, test anxiety, predispositional anxiety and their differential ramifications for normal and clinical populations within the confines of this chapter. Referring to the specialized reviews of this topic (Mahl & Schulze 1964; Murray 1971; Rochester 1973; Siegman 1978), we concentrate on a general concept of trait anxiety implying emotional instability.

There seems to be general agreement that, contrary to earlier expectations (Mahl 1956), the proportion of silence in the speech of highly anxious speakers is lower than in the speech of low anxious speakers (Murray 1971; Rochester 1973). As shown in table 1 this seems to be supported by the results for American speakers in the juror study: The relationship between silent periods and sound bursts (sound–silence ratio) seems to be related to the emotional stability (self-ratings) of the speaker, with neurotic, impulsive, anxious and generally unstable speakers showing a higher sound–silence ratio but more filled pauses. This pattern becomes even more pronounced if one controls for the intercorrelations between speech variables in table 1 by partial correlation. However, the respective correlations for the German speakers are close to zero and do not point in the same direction.

On the other hand, some studies have found *more* frequent *longer* pauses for anxious speakers (cf. Siegman 1978). Trying to reconcile the conflicting evidence, Siegman proposes a drive-activation explanation of the relationship between anxiety and pausing, assuming that an increase in arousal affects pausing according to a U-shaped function: pausing may decrease with an increase of anxiety-induced arousal. As far as trait anxiety is concerned, Siegman suggests that it may be associated with a decrease in the frequency of short pauses and with an increase in the frequency and/or duration of long pauses. He argues that highly anxious speakers may compensate for their generally faster speech rate by using more frequent longer silent pauses for cognitive planning to ensure fluent speech.

While there is some evidence for more frequent longer pauses in the speech of highly anxious speakers, the correlations are generally quite low. In an experiment using the repression-sensitization concept (repressors denying threat, sensitizers emphasizing threatening stimuli; cf. Byrne 1964) Helfrich & Dahme (1974), attempt to explain why these correlations are generally low. Linking high anxiety to sensitization and low anxiety to repression, they are able to show that highly anxious subjects show an increase in the number of long silent pauses (> 1.2 sec.) only in threatening situations, whereas there is no difference to low anxiety subjects in a positively valued situation. This is another case where response tendencies to specific situations rather than continuously present dispositions may be at the heart of individual differences in terms of vocal style and the underlying physiological or psychological processes. Helfrich & Dahme (1974) propose a self-presentation explanation assuming that sensitizers use the rather noticeable long pauses to appeal for support to their environment, and repressors avoid such pauses to demonstrate their equanimity in the face of adverse circumstances. The data reported by Helfrich & Dahme (1974) seem to support their explanation since high anxiety subjects should have equal need for cognitive planning pauses in positively valued situations (in which there is no difference in the number of pauses as a function of anxiety level) and in threatening situations. On the other hand, worrying induced by sensitization or greater concern for self-presentation in unpleasant situations may reduce the cognitive capacity for the planning of fluent speech sequences (which would support Siegman's hypothesis).

In all of these explanations cognitive and motivational factors are emphasized and social psychological factors are somewhat neglected. Since speech is a social phenomenon, pausing might be as well. For example, one reason for the faster speech rate in highly anxious speakers may be their greater sensitivity to listener response and/or greater need for social approval. Experimental research on observers' reactions to manipulated hesitancy and speech rate (cf. section 3 below) show quite conclusively that absence of hesitation pauses and a generally faster speech rate yield more speaker evaluations in terms of extroversion, competence and likeability. Similar results are found in the juror study where subjects rated each other in each group of six participants (Scherer, in preparation). American speakers with frequent long silent pauses are judged as significantly less extroverted, less emotionally stable, less dominant and less likeable. There was a similar but rather weak tendency for slow speech rate in the same direction (the stronger findings in the manipulation studies are probably due to the fact that a much wider range of rate was used than would occur in the naturalistic setting of the juror study).

Highly anxious speakers may be very sensitive to these inference rules and may try to attain a speech rate which will avoid negative personality attributions by the listener. In this attempt, speakers may 'overshoot' the target as is often seen in situations of linguistic overcompensation. Alternatively, or additionally, anxious subjects may have fairly low self-esteem and may be afraid to bore their listeners or fear interruptions which should also speed up their speech rate (cf. the notion of over-accommodation suggested by Giles & Smith 1979). If these assumptions are correct, anxious speakers should also try to avoid long silent pauses. It may be that they are unsuccessful in this attempt because of cognitive overload as outlined above. Alternatively, one could assume that their self-presentation concerns have sensitized them to signals of listener reaction which they attempt to monitor closely. If so, unexpected listener signals such as a frown of doubt or disapproval should severely interfere with their ongoing thought and speech processes, requiring longer silent pauses to reorient and restructure their cognitive planning. A test of this hypothesis requires a much more interaction-oriented research design than is customary in research on the fluency aspects of speech.

In addition, speakers with high social anxiety and/or lack of essential social skills may find it stressful, and may have to invest a disproportionate amount of cognitive effort, to decode the meaning of the verbal message and the nonverbal signals of their interaction partners (and to evaluate the possibility of hidden meanings or strategies) which should require more frequent pausing in ongoing speech activity. This problem will be aggravated by the anxious person's tendency to show greater physiological arousal to stress, slower habituation to repeated stresses and slower recovery from stress (Martin 1971: 34). The socially anxious person's need for positive self-presentation may also explain the significantly shorter latency times for their responses which have been found in six studies (Murray 1971). They may again overcompensate in trying to avoid giving the impression of untrustworthiness which seems to be inferred from lengthy latency periods (Baskett & Freedle 1974).

Speech discontinuities. While the Ah-Ratio (filled pauses) and the Non-Ah-Ratio (remaining speech disturbances) looked very promising in the early days of paralinguistic interest in vocal style as a function of affect and personality (cf. Cook 1969; Mahl & Schulze 1964), the empirical results have been controversial, inconsistent and generally disappointing. As far as trait anxiety is concerned, Rochester (1973) concluded that when differences *are* found between high and low anxiety speakers they are usually in the direction of fewer unfilled *and* fewer filled pauses for high anxiety speakers. This assumption is not supported by the results in the juror study if one assumes that speakers rating themselves as emotionally stable are low on anxiety. For both American and German speakers self-ratings of emotional stability correlate significantly with *fewer* filled pauses.

As in pause research generally, the possible effects of sociolinguistic factors on the frequency of filled pauses have been somewhat neglected. It is not unlikely that some of the variance could be traced to non-psychological factors. In the juror study (Scherer, in preparation), we found a negative correlation between speech disturbances (Non-Ah-Ratio) and the speakers' ranking on a socioeconomic index for American speakers (for German speakers the SES index has not yet been determined).

Also, there is a very strong, significant difference in the frequency of speech disturbances between the German and the American sample, the Germans producing 2.6, the Americans 4.3 disturbances per 100 words. Many intriguing explanations are possible, ranging from the degree of syntactic complexity or structuredness of a language and the respective cognitive processing capacity to differences in terms of cultural expectations or sanctions concerning speech fluency. Contrary to the expectation that Americans use *ahs*, *uhms* and *ehrs* much more freely than people of other nations, there is no significant difference for the Ah-Ratio (Germans have a mean of 3.3, Americans a mean of 2.7 filled pauses per 100 words). However, the American speakers spend a much higher proportion of their turn time with silent periods – their average pause duration is longer (767 msec. for Americans, 426 msec. for Germans, $p < 0.0001$) and their sound–silence ratio is only about a fourth of that of Germans ($p < 0.001$).

2.3. Morphological and syntactical aspects of speech style

'Style is the man himself' (Cuvier, cited after Busemann 1948: 76). Statements like this, asserting a strong link between linguistic style and the individuality or personality of a speaker are not difficult to find. At a time when quantitative, statistical analyses of linguistic style started to mushroom and 'speech and personality' was still a hot area within psychology, Sanford (1942: 814) wrote: 'If we set up the hypothesis that a study of the individual's verbal behaviour will disclose a facet of his personality, it appears unlikely that we are weaving a rope entirely of sand.' Today, more than thirty-five years later, we seem to have just quicksand and no rope. Not only has there been a lamentable lack of research on the relationship between linguistic style and normal personality – no more than fifteen to twenty relevant studies have appeared in the literature since Sanford's 1942 review – but research that has been reported has also been beset by methodological shortcomings and an almost total lack of cumulativeness.

One of the major problems in this area is the lack of a conceptual scheme or even an agreed-upon terminology for stylistic variables. This is partly due to the fact that no one seems to know what 'style' really is (cf. Sandell 1977) and partly due to the babylonic terminological confusion and the vicious fights about the significance of particular conceptual distinctions within linguistics – to say nothing about the feud between the adherents of 'old grammars' and 'new grammars' (cf. Lyons 1970). This situation has led to the point where investigators seem to be more concerned with the quantity of the stylistic variables they are assessing (cf. Cope 1969; Moerk 1972) than with their conceptual clarity or potential significance.

While this is not the place to develop a new terminology, a conceptual scheme is offered as framework to guide the reader through the confusing proliferation of stylistic variables and as a pointer to unexplored variables and areas of research. This scheme starts from the assumption that various linguistic units in speech like morphemes, morpheme strings (words or expressions), clauses, clause strings (sentences), speech acts or arguments, and turns can be classified in terms of different criteria and analysed according to individual differences in terms of the relative frequency, the variability and the periodicity of their occurrence. Among the criteria that can be used for the classification of various types of such units are formal characteristics (i.e. the length of words or sentences), semantic functions (i.e. categorizing units by specific types of reference such as self-reference, action, or quantification), syntactical functions (i.e. parts of speech like nouns, verbs, adjectives, etc., or type of transformation) or pragmatic functions (i.e. categorizing units by the sender states they are expressing, e.g. 'avoidant verbalization' (cf. Nelson & Groman 1975); hostility (cf. Gottschalk & Gleser 1969); expressions of 'immediacy' (cf. Wiener & Mehrabian 1968)).

For each type of linguistic unit in each of these categories one can compute, for both spoken and written material, frequency, variability and periodicity measures. Frequency measures are obtained by assessing the frequency of the occurrence of a particular type of linguistic unit in relation to either the total number of equivalent units which indicate the length of the utterance (i.e. percentage of verbs among total number of words) or in relation to the frequency of a different type (i.e. verb–adjective ratio). The diversity or variability of the units used can be determined by assessing the number of different units in relation to the total number of units; for words or parts of speech as units this yields the familiar type–token ratio (TTR). Periodicity measures consist of an assessment of the length of intervals between the recurrence of the same token of a linguistic unit or between the same class of units (cf. Moerk's (1972) perseveration measures). We will use the structure provided by this conceptual scheme to review the scarce literature in this area, following the criteria that have been used to classify linguistic units for stylistic analysis. Since the distinction between morphemes and morpheme strings and between clauses and clause strings is rarely made in the literature, these categories will be combined to 'words' and 'sentences' respectively in the following review.

While this review is primarily concerned with spoken language, the scarcity of relevant studies on morphological and syntactical aspects of speech style led to the inclusion of studies on stylistic features of written material in relation to personality. Since we know very little about the correspondence between speech style and writing style, it is difficult to assess the relevance of these studies for an examination of *speech* markers of personality. However, the respective results may be useful in the process of developing hypotheses concerning potential personality markers in speech.

Formal characteristics. While the length of words in terms of number of letters has been one of the favourite variables for lexicostatisticians for centuries (cf. Miller 1951: 88), there is as yet no empirical evidence on personality differences in the use of long or short words. Moerk (1972) analysed this variable in 300-word samples from essays written by thirty students and found that use of words with four letters correlates significantly with personality traits more frequently than other word lengths. Unfortunately, he does not interpret these correlations. In a factor analysis of his data, Moerk finds that words with ten letters or more load negatively on a factor 'precise vs. lengthy style' for which there are also positive loadings for Rorschach form responses, the MMPI hysteria scale and interest in art. However, given the methodological shortcomings of his factor analysis (115 style variables and 30 subjects) these results are difficult to interpret.

Considering the well-known inverse relationship between the length of a word and the frequency of its occurrence (Miller 1951; Zipf 1935), we can assume that the processing of longer words requires greater cognitive effort and possibly also greater cognitive capacity in terms of memory and processing speed. If this is the case we would expect individual differences in the use of words of different length to the extent that there are personality differences in cognitive structure and processing. It is not unlikely that there are important differences between writing style and speech style in this respect since longer words may require more effort both in terms of the demands made on cognitive processing and on the precision of articulation in speaking.

Given the strong preoccupation of cognitive psychology with transformational linguistics and vice versa, it is surprising that there is no systematic research on personality differences in cognitive processing and the complexity of syntactical structure. Number of words per sentence is one index of syntactical complexity, although the relationship is less than perfect due to the existence of deletion rules (cf. Thorne 1970: 189). Two recent studies support the notion of a relationship between cognitive organization and syntactical complexity and/or sentence length.

Lazarus-Mainka (1973) asked twenty-one students to describe and interpret a series of cartoon drawings and measured the speaker's susceptibility to interference by using the Stroop colour-word test (which requires the subject to read out loud colour names which are printed in colours that are different from the colour referred to by the respective word). She analysed the number of words and the frequencies of different parts of speech in these speech samples and found that Ss scoring high on susceptibility to interference spoke significantly more words (nouns and verbs in particular) than Ss low in susceptibility to interference. Since the number of sentences was not different for the two groups, Lazarus-Mainka concludes that Ss high in susceptibility to interference construct longer and syntactically more complex sentences. She interprets this as an attempt to include more details in their descriptions on the part of the high susceptibility to interference Ss who have been shown in past research to pay more attention to marginal or irrelevant aspects of the stimulus situation (cf. Lazarus-Mainka 1973).

Steingart, Freedman, Grand & Buchwald (1975) analysed the average number of words per sentence in the speech of nineteen female students in three communication situations – dialogue, 'warm' (visually supportive) monologue and 'cold' (visually nonsupportive and stressful) monologue – in which Ss talked about various aspects of their personal lives. Individual differences in cognitive organization were assessed by a measure of field dependence/independence (rod-and-frame test). While there were no differences in the dialogue situation, average number of words per sentence correlated negatively with field independence (controlling for verbal fluency) in the monologue situation. Sentence length increases from the dialogue to the monologue situation for the field-dependent Ss while there is no change for field-independent Ss. Steingart *et al.* interpret this to mean that the latter 'continue to "package" their language as if they are in dialogue' (1975: 253).

The results of both of these studies seem to be consistent with the assumption that persons whose cognitive information processing is highly affected by the nature of the stimulus configurations in the respective perceptual field pay more attention to detail, process more information and also attempt to communicate more detailed information in speech communication. In terms of linguistic behaviour, specification of detail in the information conveyed in a sentence is likely to be achieved by adding subordinate clauses rather than starting a new, additional sentence. This should lead to an increase in the number of noun phrases and verb phrases (cf. findings by Lazarus-Mainka 1973) and generally to an increase in the length and syntactical complexity of sentences. It should be noted that it is entirely possible that personality differences in cognitive organization become evident only in monologue speech style (as suggested by the results of Steingart *et al*. 1975) since dialogue requires greater cognitive effort for both speaker and hearer – among other things for the regulation of turn-taking – which would require less complex syntactical structure to ease the cognitive burden on encoding and decoding.

Semantic functions. Linguistic styles can differ according to the relative frequency of linguistic units belonging to different semantic classes such as abstract vs. concrete words, words for animate or inanimate referents, etc. Until now this criterion for the grouping of linguistic units has been rarely used in research on linguistic style.

One of the variables relevant in this context is the index of self-reference and related ratios in which the frequency of use of first-person pronouns to total number of words or other parts of speech are computed. Sanford (1942: 821) hypothesized that the use of personal pronouns is an index of egocentrism. While this hypothesis has received some support in studies with clinical populations (cf. Balken & Masserman 1940; Fairbanks 1944), there is at present no clear evidence for a relationship with normal personality. In the juror study no correlations exceeding chance expectations were found, for either American or German speakers. Gaines, Fretz & Helweg (1975) asked fifty-two male students to write a sentence in response to stimulus words. They found no differences in the number of sentences beginning with *I* for Ss high or low on social desirability. In a summary of an Indian study by Sinha & Sinha (1968), who studied free verbalizations of twenty Ss, a positive correlation between high test anxiety and negative self-references is reported. Given the scarcity of research results, more empirical work is needed to test the egocentrism hypothesis.

Syntactical functions. A classification of linguistic units by syntactical function has been frequently used, mostly with words as units, to study individual differences in style. Often the syntactical criterion has been paired with the semantic criterion as in the case of distinguishing abstract vs. concrete nouns, or verbs of action vs. verbs of locomotion. A clear distinction between purely syntactic and purely semantic functions is difficult to maintain. If one uses clauses or clause strings as linguistic units the syntactical aspect concerns the types of transformations contained in the clause or sentence, such as transitive–intransitive, active–passive, negation, question, etc. Obviously, these are not devoid of semantic functions. Consequently, the grouping of studies in terms of the classification criteria given above is somewhat arbitrary since in most cases several of these criteria have been used to define the linguistic variable under study.

As with many of the other potential variables of linguistic style, one is surprised by the scarcity of relevant research as far as relationships to personality are concerned. Zatzkis (1949, cited after McClelland, Atkinson, Clark & Lowell 1953) analysed different morpheme classes in essays of twenty-five Ss who had been assessed in terms of the strength of their need for achievement (nAch). It was found that Ss high on nAch used significantly more abstract nouns and made more use of anticipatory tense whereas low nAch Ss used more negations and more dependent clauses. McClelland *et al*. (1953: 253–4) interpret this to mean that highly achievement-motivated people think more often in anticipatory and generalized terms and are concerned with general and vague life goals whereas people with low need for achievement think less often in generalized terms and are more often concerned with the difficulties in the way of achievement.

Doob (1958) also used essay-writing to study the relationship between Rorschach scores, authoritarianism and field independence and linguistic style for forty-nine male students. No clear-cut relationships emerged; there was a tendency for Ss with an 'active, analytical cognitive style' to use more adverbs, noun qualifiers, pronouns and verbs indicating action, possession and internal relation.

Busemann (1925) suggested an 'action quotient' consisting of the ratio of 'actional statements' (mostly verbs) to 'qualitative statements' (mostly adjectives, participles and nouns) as an important index of individual differences in cognitive and emotional development. While he himself was mostly concerned with changes of this action quotient in child development (Busemann 1925, 1926), various versions of verb–adjective ratios have been used in later studies on personality differences and emotional disturbance. As for most other variables in this review, the large majority of these studies have been conducted with clinical populations (Balken & Masserman 1940; Lorenz & Cobb 1953) and are thus of little relevance for our present purpose. Osgood & Walker (1959) successfully used a modified noun–verb/adjective–adverb ratio to assess state of arousal in trying to distinguish real from faked suicide notes.

As far as normal personality is concerned, an early observation by Busemann (1925: 25) might be relevant. He had asked the teachers of the thirty-one children whose verbalizations he had been analysing to rate these in terms of their liveliness, or vivacity and talkativeness. He found that the children rated as very lively and talkative, difficult to keep quiet in class, had a significantly higher verb–adjective ratio than the quiet children. He was able to replicate this result with twenty-six of the same children a year later (Busemann 1926: 418), indicating that the relationship seems to be a stable one (cf. Helfrich, this volume: ch. 3, 2.3).

In the juror study we found strong and consistent personality differences for the verb–adjective ratio for the German speakers but no differences whatsoever for American speakers. For the former, the verb–adjective ratio correlates with both self- and peer ratings of agreeableness and sociability (see von Borstel 1977; Scherer, in preparation). Thus, German males who are outgoing and sociable as well as likeable and agreeable, and are similarly perceived by their peers, tend to speak with a more actional style. If we had found similar results for the American speakers, a number of interesting hypotheses concerning the relationship between extroversion, agreeableness and speech behaviour would have suggested themselves. Given that the present findings are restricted to the German sample, it remains to be seen to what extent the nature of the language or the cultural setting determines the relationship between personality and actional style, and whether the present findings can be replicated. Given the lack of intercultural stability, it is unlikely that biophysical factors, such as emotional reactivity (which is implied by Busemann 1925, 1948), are at the root of this relationship.

Pragmatic functions. The nature of pragmatic functions in classifying linguistic units for the study of stylistic differences is difficult to define exactly. In line with received definitions of pragmatics we imply the relationship between states of the sender or speaker and the linguistic sign used. For example, Dollard & Mowrer (1953) suggested the Discomfort-Relief-Quotient to measure tension in written documents by counting words that 'identified by the common sense of intelligent people' (240), indicated discomfort or reward or relief of the author of the text. Consequently, the relationship between the sign user and the sign, rather than between sign and referent (as for semantic functions) or between sign and other signs (as for syntactic functions), is the basis for the classification used. Similarly, the content analysis system proposed by Gottschalk & Gleser (1969) seems to classify linguistic units on the basis of pragmatic functions of linguistic units, for example, by scoring expressions of 'hostility'.

Nelson & Groman (1975) classified linguistic units on the basis of the pragmatic criterion of 'avoidant or neurotic verbalization' consisting of avoidance of silence (e.g. mannerisms, etc.) and avoidance of responsibility (e.g. qualifying statements, etc.). The hypothesis that high neuroticism as measured by the Eysenck Personality Scale should correlate with the frequency of avoidant verbalizations in thirty students' answers to stressful questions was not supported.

Alban & Groman (1976) studied 'pronoun distantiation' (avoiding the use of the proper personal pronoun) in the answers of forty-five students to stressful questions. They found that Ss with medium neurotic anxiety distantiate more in answers to questions involving negative stress. They argue that the results are due to differential thresholds for stress induction in Ss with different degrees of neurotic anxiety and that distantiation occurs when the threshold is exceeded.

Based on Busemann (1948) and Ertel (1973) we used a certainty–uncertainty ratio in the juror study. This index measures the ratio of certainty expressions such as *obviously, naturally, without any doubt, certainly* to expressions of uncertainty such as *it is possible, perhaps, maybe, I am not sure*. Ertel (1973) assumes that frequent use of expressions of certainty in relation to expressions of doubt is an index for dogmatism. In the juror study we found significant correlations of the certainty–uncertainty ratio with self-ratings of aggressiveness and dominance for American speakers. However, these relationships are not very pervasive, i.e. there are no correlations with similar traits. There were no significant correlations for the German speakers (see von Borstel 1977; Scherer, in preparation).

Another pragmatically defined style variable that has been used in clinical studies is the frequency of mannerisms such as *you know, well*, etc. In the juror study we found negative correlations with the American speakers' self-ratings of endurance, order, conscientiousness and dependability. For the German speakers, mannerisms correlated with self-ratings of lack of neuroticism, lack of agreeableness and lack of autonomy. While the pattern of results for the German speakers is difficult to interpret, it seems likely that conscientious American speakers avoid mannerisms (see von Borstel 1977; Scherer, in preparation).

2.4. Conversational behaviour

Until now we have dealt with fairly molecular aspects of speech style up to the sentence level. One may extend the units studied to speech acts, turns and total verbal output, and it is not unreasonable to expect that there are personality-related individual differences. Since conversational analysis is just at the point of getting established (cf. Laver & Trudgill, this volume: ch. 1, 4), there is even more of the usual amount of terminological and methodological muddle and controversy. In this section, we can do little more than point to some areas of research which look promising judging from some exploratory studies.

Since there are not yet any empirical studies on personality-related differences in the use of specific speech acts (or types of arguments or rhetorical devices), this review is restricted to turns, i.e. the period during which a speaker holds the floor before relinquishing the speaker role, and to total verbal output. The latter refers to the total amount of time an individual holds the floor in a conversation or discussion. The total verbal output of a speaker relative to the length of a conversation is referred to very differently in different studies – productivity, verbosity, interaction or participation rate, to name but a few. Many of these concepts are clearly not equivalent since sometimes number of words or syllables produced are used as a dependent variable, whereas in other studies temporal measures such as the total time during which the speaker held the floor are used. Obviously, one may expect very different results if number of words spoken or number of minutes of floor-holding are used to measure the contribution or participation of a speaker to a discussion, since speech rate is an important determinant of the temporal measurement. Unfortunately, the number of relevant studies is not yet sufficiently large to attempt to evaluate possible differences in relation to their psychological significance. Thus, both word counts and temporal measurements are reported jointly and without detailed discussion in the following review.

Number and length of turns. The intricate regulation of turn-taking in social interaction has become one of the most intensively studied aspects of face-to-face interaction. Yet we do not have much in terms of empirical data concerning personality differences in the frequency of turn-claiming and length of turn-holding, even though one might expect interpersonal traits such as extroversion, dominance and aggressiveness to be related to turn behaviour.

Duncan & Fiske (1977) asked eighty-eight male and female graduate students to engage in two seven-minute conversations, one with a same-sex and one with an opposite-sex partner, to 'get to know each other'. Among many other nonverbal behaviour types, the authors assessed total turn time, number of turns and average length of turn (in time units) for these Ss in both dyadic interactions, and correlated these measures with three personality tests. No stable pattern of relationships was found. Duncan & Fiske attribute this partly to the fact that these turn variables were not very stable across the two interactions, arguing that they seem to depend very much on the respective interaction partner. Feldstein & Welkowitz (1978) report in the context of research with the Automatic Vocal Transaction Analyzer that while average duration of vocalization within turns remained stable over conversations with different interaction partners, *length of turn* seems to be less influenced by the speakers' personalities than by their respective partners' personalities.

For the group discussion material in the juror study we found some significant correlations between personality ratings and turn variables. Although the relationship does not seem to be very strong, number of turns correlated significantly with peer ratings (but not self-ratings) of dominance for both German and American speakers (Herpel 1977; Scherer, in preparation). It is not impossible that these correlations result from the peers' basing their ratings of a speaker's dominance in part on the frequency with which they have seen the latter claim turns in conversations.

Length of turn, as measured by the average number of words per turn, correlates positively with peer ratings of conscientious and emotional stability for American speakers and with self-ratings of low nurturance, low personal adjustment, and low likeability for German speakers (Herpel 1977; Scherer, in preparation). Both the results themselves and the cross-cultural differences are difficult to interpret. It would be most important to know more about standard lengths of turns in different speech communities and about the nature of the reaction to deviations from such norms, if one were to draw up specific hypotheses about personality differences in turn-taking behaviour. The present results for American speakers, and Cope's (1969) finding that there is a tendency for students rated as zestful or optimally psychologically healthy to have somewhat longer turns in group discussions, could give rise to the very tentative suggestion that longer turns are seen as an indicator of emotional stability in the American culture.

Length of total verbal output. The total number of words spoken or the productivity of a speaker in a particular speech situation has been frequently assessed in studies of verbal behaviour. Often, this variable was more reliably associated with personality traits than many of the other variables studied. For example, Cope (1969) found that out of seventy-five variables assessed, total words spoken in the group discussions was basically the only variable on which 'zestful' and 'normal' students differed. Her students rated as zestful or optimally psychologically healthy by university staff generally spoke more than the normal students. A somewhat similar result was found for the American speakers in the juror study. Speakers who generally spoke more in the discussion (total number of words spoken) were rated by their peers as more extroverted, more emotionally stable and more likeable (Scherer, in preparation), a pattern of traits which seems quite close to 'zestfulness'. Similarly, Weinstein & Hanson (1975) found that subjects with a high level of interaction rate scored higher on dominance, self-confidence and exhibitionism. The relationship between extroversion and greater length of verbal output is confirmed by a number of English studies which found that extroverts tended to speak a greater proportion of the time (Campbell & Rushton 1978; Carment, Miles & Cervin 1965; Patterson & Holmes 1966; Rutter, Morley & Graham 1972).

Some isolated results on the influence of cognitive styles do not yet allow us to make any predictions concerning these personality dispositions. Axtell & Cole (1971) found that repressors, as determined by the repression–sensitization scale, spoke less. In Lazarus-Mainka's (1973) study persons high on susceptibility to interference tended generally to speak more, whereas Steingart *et al.* (1975) found that field-independent Ss spoke more. Although these two dimensions of cognitive organization are not identical one might have expected field-dependent Ss to behave more like Ss high on susceptibility to interference. On the other hand, the verbal tasks were quite different in these two studies, quite apart from the cultural and linguistic differences between the Ss, which may explain the differences in results. Clearly, the possible interaction of demand characteristics of different tasks or speech situations with specific personality traits will have to be assessed, before one can compare results on total verbal output across different speech situations.

In summary, extroversion seems to be the only trait which is consistently found to be associated with a greater amount of verbal output or longer total speaking time.

3. Inference of personality from speech style

We now turn to the examination of the inference processes that determine the nature of the personality attributions from speech style. In terms of the lens model which structures our discussion we will deal mostly with correlations between distal indicator cues of speech style and personality attributions. The intervening class of variables, the proximal representations of these speech style variables in lay perception and judgement, has been rarely studied and will have to be somewhat neglected except for occasional references.

3.1. Review of relevant studies by research technique used

If there is one clearly established finding in this field, it is the fact that people tend to agree strongly on their inferences of personality from speech. The existence of 'vocal stereotypes', i.e. the consensual agreement of judges on personality attributions which are often not accurate in the sense that they do not correlate with external criteria of personality, has been a frequent finding ever since the beginning of empirical research on voice and personality (cf. Pear 1931; Allport & Cantril 1934; Kramer 1963; Scherer 1972). Since most researchers in this field have been concerned with the accuracy of personality inference from speech style, vocal stereotypes were something of a nuisance and there was consequently little concern with the origin and nature of such inference processes.

Recent social psychological interest in the process characteristics of person perception and cognitive inferences independent of the validity or accuracy of the resulting attributions has led to a number of studies concerned with the utilization of specific cues of speech style in personality inference. In order to assess the role of specific cues in the inference process, new experimental paradigms had to be developed, since the usual technique, confronting judges with standard speech samples, does not allow us to separate out the effects of different cues of speech style variables on the personality attribution of the judges. The relevant studies in this area will shortly be reviewed according to the type of technique adopted. This organization of the section suggests itself, since, as we shall see, an attempt to integrate the various findings has to take the effects of the special research techniques used into account.

Correlational techniques. The simplest technique is to assess a number of relevant voice and speech parameters in the standard speech samples used and to correlate these with personality attributions. This procedure was used by Aronovitch (1976), who measured six vocal characteristics in speech samples of twenty-five male and thirty-two female students and correlated personality ratings for the speakers with these vocal characteristics. He found that different cues seem to be used to infer the personality traits of male and female speakers. Whereas males are judged as more extroverted, confident, dominant and bold when their speech shows higher variance of intensity, higher variance of fundamental frequency and faster speech rate, women are rated as more extroverted, confident, dominant and bold when their speech shows higher mean intensity, fewer silent pauses and a faster speech rate. For women, higher mean fundamental frequency leads to ratings of being more kind, humorous, immature and emotional.

Correlating personality attributions with many different vocal characteristics in the speech sample is somewhat inconclusive, since one cannot be sure which of the many cues available have been utilized by the judges, and to what extent the cues measured correlate with important cues that went unmeasured.

Masking techniques. One possible means of reducing the size of this problem is the use of various masking techniques that remove specific types of cues from the speech samples before they are played to the judges. One potential technique is electronic filtering (cf. Rogers, Scherer & Rosenthal 1971) which removes content cues as well as many voice quality cues. Another possibility is 'randomized splicing' (Scherer 1971) which removes content cues as well as pauses, sequence and many rhythm cues while preserving voice quality. Of course, both techniques can be combined to reduce still further the number of cues available for the judges (cf. Scherer, Koivumaki & Rosenthal 1972).[3]

Scherer (1978) has used randomized splicing as a cue reduction technique for speech samples of twenty-four American speakers from the juror study. The resulting voice samples were rated by six expert phoneticians to obtain a number of distal voice quality indicator cues (cf. Scherer 1974c), by ten lay judges rating voice quality to obtain proximal percepts, and by nine lay judges rating personality to obtain attribution judgements (cf. Scherer 1978). This procedure allows us to assess both the perceptual

[3] The use of such masking techniques has the additional advantage that natural speech can be used rather than requiring speakers to read a standard text in a somewhat artificial speech situation. Selective cue reduction by various types of masking techniques can be used in experimental designs to study the impact of different types of cues on personality impression formation (cf. Scherer, Scherer, Hall & Rosenthal 1977).

representation of the relevant voice cues as well as the inferential utilization of these cues. Figure 2 (modified from Scherer (1978) and sup-
plemented by data not contained in this report) shows the results for
emotional stability and a cluster of personality traits consisting of
extroversion, assertiveness and lack of agreeableness which were highly
correlated for these ratings (mean correlation coefficients for these three
traits are given in figure 2).

The figure shows that voices with high pitch and strong vocal effort are
perceived as sharp and not gloomy or warm. Voices perceived as warm
and not sharp lead to the attribution of emotional stability whereas voices
perceived as sharp and not gloomy lead to the attribution of extroversion,
assertiveness and lack of agreeableness. From the correlations between
the distal cue ratings and the attributions, which are comparable to the
data reported in the other studies reviewed in this section, one finds that
high pitch[4] and strong vocal effort seem to encourage the attribution of
extroversion, assertiveness, lack of agreeableness on the one hand and
absence of emotional stability on the other hand – at least for American
speakers.

Manipulation techniques. Another technique for studying the importance
of specific vocal cues for personality inferences is cue manipulation by
asking actors or other speakers to vary systematically specific voice and
speech parameters. Compared to the cue reduction technique which is
restricted to the cues that happen to be present in the respective speech
samples, cue manipulation provides the experimenter with much more
systematic control of vocal parameters. On the other hand, it is not clear
to what extent speakers can independently vary specific vocal parameters
without affecting others at the same time. One of the most comprehensive studies of this kind has been conducted by Addington (1968a, b). He
obtained 252 standard text speech samples from two male and two female
trained speakers who had been instructed to simulate seven voice qualities as well as different degrees of speaking rate and pitch variety. These
speech samples were subsequently rated by a large of number of judges
using a semantic differential type rating scheme with personality relevant
adjectives. A short summary of Addington's most important results is
reproduced in table 2.

---

[4] It should be noted that the expert phoneticians' ratings of pitch height are not equivalent to
an assessment of fundamental frequency of the voice – computer-assessment f_0 correlates
only $r = 0.37$ for American speakers and $r = 0.56$ for German speakers with phoneticians'
pitch ratings of equivalent but not the same voice samples (Scherer, in preparation).

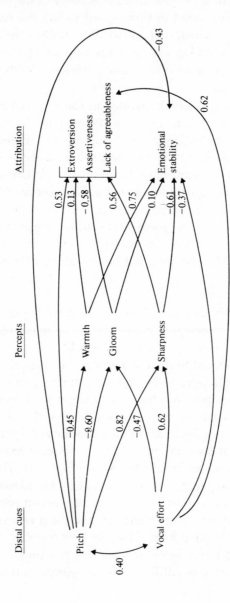

Figure 2. Partial lens model for personality inference from speech (adapted from Scherer 1978) Curvilinear arrows indicate hypothetically assumed causal relationships. Strength of the relationships are indicated by Pearson rs. Intercorrelations among variables for each type of measurement have been omitted to simplify the figure. (N = 24 speakers; significance levels: p_c (0.10) r = 0.34, p_c (0.05) r = 0.40, two-tailed.)

Scherer *et al*. (1973) used a more indirect cue manipulation technique. They asked one actor to read a standard text in either a confident or doubtful manner. In the confidence condition, the actor spoke significantly faster, louder and with higher pitch. When judges (forty-seven female students) were asked to rate the personality attributes of the speaker, they found him significantly more enthusiastic, forceful, active, competent, dominant, self-confident and self-assured on the basis of the confident speech style.

Table 2. *Effects of voice quality manipulation on personality attribution (from Addington, 1968a: 70)* [a]

Male speakers

Increased	Means tendency to be perceived as more:
Breathy	youthful and artistic
Flat	sluggish, cold, withdrawn
Nasal	unattractive, lethargic, foolish, self-effacing, neurotic
Tense	cantankerous
Throaty	stable
Orotund	vigorous and aesthetic or perhaps suave
Rate	animated and extroverted
Pitch variety	dynamic and extroverted

Female speakers

Breathy	feminine, pretty, callow, highly strung, petite, effervescent
Thin	immature, mentally and physically disorganized, interested in others
Flat	sluggish, cold, masculine
Nasal	crude, unattractive, foolish, lethargic, unemotional, self-effacing
Tense	highly strung, pliable
Throaty	oafish, or like a 'clod'
Orotund	aggressive and aesthetic or urbane
Rate	extroverted, highly strung, inartistic, un-cooperative
Pitch variety	dynamic and extroverted

[a]Reproduced by permission of the Board of Regents for Oklahoma State University.

To avoid the problem of uncontrollable side-effects in cue manipulation studies it has been attempted to edit cues in or out of speech samples by tape-splicing or other procedures. Lay & Burron (1968), in one of the few studies on the impression value of hesitation pauses, took a speech sample with hesitancies and prepared a nonhesitant version by splicing out all filled pauses and repetitions and shortening all silent pauses by 1 sec. They found that judges rated the speaker significantly more favourable in the nonhesitant condition. Obviously, this cue manipulation technique can only be used with a small number of cues amenable to this type of operation.

Synthesis techniques. The advent of speech-processing on fast digital computers and advances in speech synthesis techniques have allowed the development of cue synthesis techniques. This technique allows the researcher to vary independently a number of vocal parameters and to assess both main and interaction effects on subjective ratings of the source. For example, in a study on cue utilization in emotion attribution, Scherer (1974a; Scherer & Oshinsky 1977) used a MOOG synthesizer to vary independently a large number of acoustic parameters on different levels, in a factorial design which allowed the strength of the utilization of each cue in the inference process to be directly assessed.

Although Uldall used speech synthesis to study the effect of intonation contours as early as 1960 (Uldall 1960, 1964), systematic studies on personality inferences using synthesized speech cues are fairly recent. Brown and his collaborators have conducted a series of studies (summarized by Brown, Strong & Rencher 1975) in which they synthesized, for the same speech sample, widely varying levels of fundamental frequency, variability of fundamental frequency and speech rate, respectively, of several speakers. Using the 'competence' and 'benevolence' personality dimensions which can be frequently found in speech effectiveness or persuasion studies (cf. Scherer 1979b), they found that increase in fundamental frequency generally leads to a decrease in both competence and benevolence ratings. An increase in the variability of fundamental frequency leads to an increase in benevolence ratings whereas a decrease in variability results in a decrease of both competence and benevolence attributions. Speech rate was found in these studies to have the strongest impact on subjective impressions (confirming earlier results by Scherer 1974a; Scherer & Oshinsky 1977, for emotion ratings). Speech rate seems to be monotonically related to competence attributions – increases and decreases in rate are accompanied by a corresponding change in competence attribution in the same direction. Ratings of benevolence have an inverted 'U' relationship with speech rate with the highest benevolence ratings coinciding with middle values of rate (Brown et al. 1975: 26).

Using somewhat less dramatic changes of f_0 and speech rate to ensure naturalness of the synthetic speech samples,[5] Apple, Streeter & Krauss (1977) found, in a series of three experiments, that speakers with raised f_0

---

[5] One of the major problems with the cue synthesis technique is the naturalness or realism of the resulting speech samples. Brown et al. (1975: 24) report that voices with changed f_0 were judged as normal 50 to 58 per cent of the time, whereas rate changed voices were judged as normal 78 per cent of the time. Apple, Streeter & Krauss (1977) have pointed out that pitch changes of the extent used by Brown and his colleagues (up to 80 per cent raise) may have the effect of raising a male voice into the female register and that speech rate change may also have been too high to expect natural-sounding speech. These experimenters have used a pitch change of 20 per cent and a rate change of 30 per cent above or below normal in 27 male speakers' answers to two interview questions.

voices were judged less truthful, less empathic, weaker and more nervous. Decreased rate had the effect of the speakers being rated as less truthful, less fluent and less persuasive as well as more passive and weaker.

Comparability of results. These studies have been organized according to the technique used in order to highlight the problem of comparability of results. For example, while voices with synthetically raised f_0 led to attributions of lower potency (Apple *et al.* 1977) and less competence (Brown *et al.* 1975), Scherer (1978) found in a cue masking study with natural speech samples that higher f_0 and particularly higher perceived pitch correlate positively with extroversion and assertiveness. Since these personality traits generally imply potency and competence, the results are not easily reconciled. Attempts to explain these discrepancies are hampered by the fact that relevant details are often not reported. For example, in the studies by Brown *et al.* (1975) normal f_0 of the speakers whose voices are synthetically changed are not reported. It can be argued that the relationship of f_0 to perceived competence and assertiveness is curvilinear and that a mean pitch level above a certain threshold of normal range results in attributions of submissiveness and incompetence. It is not unlikely that the high f_0 condition in Brown *et al.*'s experiments lies way beyond this threshold (cf. n. 5 above). Even the more modest raise in the Apple *et al.* study may fall close to or actually beyond this threshold. Terango (1966) found that voices judged to be effeminate had a median f_0 of 127 Hz compared to 100 Hz for voices judged to be masculine. Terango argues that male voices judged to be effeminate are considerably lower than the typical female pitch. If one assumes (on the basis of available research findings) that the median pitch of unselected American males is about 130 Hz, clearly a 20 per cent or more synthetic rise (cf. n. 5 above) is most likely to produce impressions of effeminacy with possible negative ramifications for the potency and competence attributions to the speaker.

A further problem in trying to interpret the results from cue synthesis studies derives from the fact that the interaction of the synthesized parameters with other parameters – both acoustically and perceptually – is not at all well understood at the present time. Natural changes in f_0 seem to be accompanied by changes in pitch range and pitch variability as well as the energy distribution in the spectrum (cf. Laver 1975). It is quite possible that synthetic changes of f_0 have different effects on the acoustic spectrum and that listeners perceive such changes differently due to well-established auditory information-processing patterns. We urgently need more information about the patterns of covariation between different vocal parameters, the effects of changes in isolated parameters and the perceptual representation of these parameters in the listener.

3.2. Summary of inference patterns by speech cues

In this section we try to take stock of the emerging features of personality inference patterns from various vocal parameters.

Fundamental frequency. As far as f_0 is concerned one can venture the hypothesis, based on the discussion above, that for male speakers, up to a certain threshold well within the male pitch range, a higher mean f_0 will be perceived as indicative of greater extroversion, assertiveness, confidence and competence (Scherer, in preparation; Scherer *et al.* 1973). This might well reflect generally higher muscle tone and control which may accompany these and similar personality traits (cf. discussion in section 2.1 above). If this threshold is passed and f_0 gets close to the female pitch range, personality inferences may radically change and lead to attributions of weakness, effeminacy and lack of competence (Apple *et al.* 1977; Brown *et al.* 1975; Terango 1966). Unfortunately, the lack of relevant data does not allow us to speculate on comparable effects for female voices.

However, high f_0 seems to have yet another and quite different effect on personality attributions. Both male and female speakers with higher, or heightened, f_0 were judged to be more immature and emotional (Aronovitch 1976), more nervous and less truthful (Apple *et al.* 1977), less emotionally stable (Scherer, in preparation) and more withdrawn, tense and agitated (Ekman *et al.* 1976). Consequently, higher pitch seems to lead to an attribution of emotional instability and psychological tension. How can this be reconciled with the apparent inference rule linking competence/assertiveness and higher f_0 (within a normal range)? One possibility would be to argue that observers interpret high f_0 resulting from heightened arousal state as indicative of a stable disposition. F_0 rise seems to be a definite indicator of a state variable – psychological arousal or stress, at least for the majority of speakers for whom f_0 seems to increase between 3 and 10 Hz under stress (cf. section 2.1 above; Scherer 1979a). The studies by Ekman *et al.* (1976), Streeter *et al.* (1977) and Apple *et al.* (1977) show that judges seem to recognize the changed state in the speaker. In addition, they may generalize their attribution to the disposition of emotional stability. Such a generalization from state to disposition may underlie the results in which higher base f_0 was seen as indicative of emotionality (Aronovitch 1976).

In spite of the possibility of such generalizations in observer judgement, it seems reasonable to assume that the type of f_0 rise due to psychological arousal and stress may manifest itself acoustically differently from higher f_0 due to heightened muscle tone accompanying discipline, competence or assertiveness. Since the physiological substrata may be different in the two cases, acoustic manifestations may be different also. For example, f_0 rise under stress may be accompanied by increased f_0 perturbation (cf. Hecker, Stevens, von Bismarck & Williams 1968) or greater proportion of the total energy in the upper part of the voice spectrum (cf. Scherer 1979a). In addition there might be a different relation of f_0 to the formant frequencies or to the extent of f_0 variability in intonation contours. Judges may well be able to pick up these cues which differentiate between higher pitch due to control and due to stress, and attribute state and traits of speakers accordingly. Obviously, it will be one of the most important tasks for future research in this area to assess to what extent f_0 changes are accompanied by changes in other acoustic parameters, and to what extent listeners utilize the resulting cue configurations to infer whether pitch is habitually at the observed level or whether this level is due to a change in psychological or physiological state.

The results on the variability of f_0 are rather consistent in all studies where this parameter has been assessed (Addington 1968b; Aronovitch 1976; Brown et al. 1975; Scherer, in preparation): High variability is seen as indicative of a dynamic, extroverted and outgoing and benevolent person, and seems to connote potency in terms of the semantic differential. Unfortunately, the consistency of findings may yet turn out to be spurious since f_0 variability seems to have been defined and measured rather differently in the various studies.[6]

[6] Apart from the usual differences in terms of electro-acoustic measurement or synthesis vs. subjective perception and actor–speaker manipulation, it is rarely clear what kind of variability – in statistical terms – is used. It is important to distinguish pitch range (the difference between the highest and lowest f_0 value used by the speaker, either habitually or in a specific speech situation) from pitch variation (which one might define by the standard deviation of f_0 values for a particular utterance which represents a summary measure of both regular and irregular, as well as small and large, changes in f_0 in the flow of speech) and to distinguish both of these from parameters concerning intonation contours (i.e. regular changes in f_0 following definite trends of gradients and integrated with syntactic and pragmatic functions of speech), which might consist of measures of steepness, periodicity and extensiveness of the f_0 contour, to name but a few relevant aspects. Unfortunately, the role of intonation contours on personality inferences is virtually unexplored. The pioneering studies by Uldall (1960, 1964) and a study by Keating (1974) are mostly concerned with emotion or attitude inferences from intonation.

Speech rate. Among all of the acoustic parameters studied to date, speech rate is obviously the most powerful in terms of its effect on listener evaluation of the speaker. Compared to other acoustic variables listeners seem to agree better both on the degree of distinctiveness of this speech parameter (cf. McGehee cited by Diehl 1960) as well as on the nature of the respective personality inferences. In all of the relevent studies (Addington 1968b; Apple *et al*. 1977; Aronovitch 1976; Brown *et al*. 1975; Scherer 1974a; Scherer & Oshinsky 1977) fast rate is judged to indicate high activity, dynamism and potency, as well as extroversion and competence. However, as for all other acoustic parameters, we know very little about the exact nature of the function that links speech rate to these personality inferences. One of the few attempts to measure this function has been made by Brown *et al*. (1975: 27) who find a 'monotonic, if not linear' relationship between competence and rate as well as an inverted U relationship between benevolence and rate. However, since Brown *et al*. do not give exact parameters for rate (in terms of syllables per second or a related measure), it is difficult to know in which part of the range of speech rate normally encountered they have been working, and whether there are thresholds at the upper and lower end of this range at which inference patterns change sharply – as has been argued for pitch.

Other features of speech style. Studies on inferences from other parameters of speech style are very rare and scattered. Given the large number of studies on psychological correlates of pausing and speech rate, it is rather surprising that there are very few studies on the personality inferences listeners derive from these fluency cues. Similarly difficult to explain is the virtual absence of research on personality inferences from variations in linguistic style in spoken speech and written text. Some studies on the formal characteristics of length of utterances and participation rate in group discussions point to the potential fruitfulness of such attempts. Schönbach and his collaborators (1977) manipulated the length of utterances with content kept constant, and found that speakers with longer utterances are seen as more polite under certain conditions, depending on situational context and speaker as well as listener status. However, it is not impossible that the manipulation of utterance length in these experiments is accompanied by changes in linguistic style.

Another major formal parameter affecting personality inferences seems to be the total volume of a speaker's participation in a dyadic interaction or a group interaction. Although it is not quite clear whether the number or the length of turns is a more important determinant of the inferences drawn from total contribution or total length of utterances to a discussion, a rather large number of studies (Morris & Hackman 1969; Stang 1973; Stein, Geis & Damarin 1973; Scherer 1979b) leave little doubt that speakers who speak more are perceived as possessing higher leadership ability. While this relationship may be a linear one, the relationship between total verbal output and the favourableness of impressions in terms of sympathy or liking seems to be curvilinear, with medium-length utterances yielding the most positive attributions (Hayes & Meltzer 1972; Stang 1973).

Another aspect of speech style yielding powerful cues for personality inferences is accent or dialect. The extensive literature on personality attributions based on accented speech has been ably summarized by Giles & Powesland (1975). In general, speakers with accented speech are seen as more friendly, likeable and sociable whereas speakers using standard or 'high' pronunciation, such as RP in English, are seen as more dominant and competent as well as more intelligent (cf. Smith, this volume: ch. 4, 2.2). In spite of the strength and pervasiveness of such personality inferences from accented speech, this literature will not be reviewed in depth since it is not clear to what extent accented speech is a personality marker in the sense that this term has been used. It is not inconceivable, however, that the *use* of accented speech in particular situations may be related to personality dispositions and may thus assume marker status.

4. Summarizing the evidence of personality markers in speech

In this section the evidence on the existence of personality markers in speech will be reviewed. Consequently, in line with the definition of personality marker offered in section 1, we have to ascertain whether the literature reviewed in this chapter reveals speech style cues that are not only empirically associated with specific personality traits (in the sense of externalization) but can also be appropriately interpreted by listeners (in terms of inference processes), assuming that the distal cues are appropriately represented as proximal cues in the listener's perception. There are two ways to assess the evidence for the existence of personality markers. One possibility is to check for studies in which *accurate* judgement of personality from speech style has been demonstrated, since accuracy can result only when the conditions described above are fulfilled – unless accuracy is the result of chance or other mediating factors. The second, and more cumbersome, procedure is to locate studies demonstrating significant correlations between specific personality traits and specific speech cues as well as complementary studies on different material which show inference patterns that correspond to the externalization patterns.

Accuracy studies. Using accuracy studies to establish the existence of personality markers is a difficult enterprise. In most accuracy studies on voice and personality, for example, only personality criteria (personality test scores) and personality attributions (lay personality judgements) have been assessed and correlated to check accuracy of inference (cf. Kramer 1963; Scherer 1972, 1978). Even if there is a significant correlation between criteria and attributions, it remains unclear which speech style cues have 'marked' the personality trait in question, particularly since most studies have not used a cue reduction and isolation strategy (cf. Scherer 1972; Scherer *et al.* 1977). Furthermore, in addition to a large number of methodological problems in many of these studies (cf. Kramer 1963; Scherer 1972), tests of significance of accuracy have often been faulty.[7]

If one eliminates studies of this kind in which the claim for accurate judgement is subject to doubt, little remains in terms of accurate personality inference from speech style. Of all the studies on the accuracy of judging extroversion and dominance from speech (summarized in Diehl 1960; Kramer 1963), none has demonstrated evidence for accurate judgement of these two most frequently studied traits. However, in more controlled cue masking studies using self- and peer ratings, Scherer (1972, 1978) has been able to show that both self- and peer ratings of extroversion can be accurately (in terms of a significant correlation between criteria and attributions) inferred from voice quality only for American speakers. For German speakers, peer ratings of dominance and assertiveness correlate significantly with respective attributions made on the basis of voice quality samples. It is not clear whether the partial success, compared with many earlier studies, in finding accuracy of inference is due to the cue reduction via random splicing of the speech samples (which may have helped the listeners to concentrate on important cues and may have eliminated irrelevant cues), to the differences in

---

[7] For example, Hunt & Lin (1967) asked judges to rate two speakers on 18 bipolar scales and assessed the accuracy of judgement by performing t-tests to check whether subjects rated more than 9 scales per speaker (which would be expected by chance) in the same way as the speaker himself. Since the scales used in the study are probably highly intercorrelated, they cannot be used as independent observations for a t-test. If a listener gets one scale right by chance, the intercorrelations between the scales (due to implicit personality theories) would result in his getting a large number of other scales right too.

obtaining personality criteria, or to other factors such as the use of interactive speech, the nature of the judgement procedure, etc.

However, the use of the Brunswikian lens model as a research paradigm has allowed the isolation of cues which may serve as markers of extroversion in the speech of American speakers and of dominance in the speech of German speakers (cf. Scherer 1974b, 1978). The lens model version for the attribution of extroversion shown in figure 3 (from Scherer 1978) shows that vocal effort perceived as loudness of the voice seems to be an essential marker of extroversion. The evidence for the markers of dominance for German speakers is less clear – precision of articulation seems to be a possible candidate (Scherer 1974b). The lens model paradigm also allows those speech cues which do not qualify as markers of personality to be specified, even though listeners may use them as such in their inference processes. For example, f_0 is *not* a marker of emotional stability as a stable personality disposition even though listeners utilize this cue in this way (cf. figure 2; also pp. 186–7), since there is no empirical covariation between f_0 and emotional stability.

Externalization/attribution compatibility. At present, there is no other work using the lens model paradigm which could be used to assess the likelihood of the existence of personality markers in speech in a similarly stringent way. Consequently, we have to use the second method described above, i.e. searching for complementary externalization and attribution studies, to derive at least some hypotheses about the existence of further personality markers in speech. A possible candidate for marker status for some personality dispositions (except emotional stability) may be f_0. The results of the juror study show that extroversion and assertiveness may be externalized in higher f_0 and that judges seem to interpret higher pitch within normal range as a sign of extroversion and assertiveness.

Another, although less clear-cut marking relationship seems to exist for hesitation pauses and extroversion. While there is some evidence that, for English speakers at least, extroversion may be associated with fewer hesitation pauses and fewer long pauses in particular (cf. section 2.2 above), the inference patterns are less clear. All the studies investigating the role of rate of speech have found powerful effects on the attribution of extroversion. Unfortunately, it is not clear to what extent these speech rate differences or manipulated changes involve hesitation pauses. Since articulation rate does not seem to covary with extroversion, one could not assume this cue to be a marker of extroversion even though judges

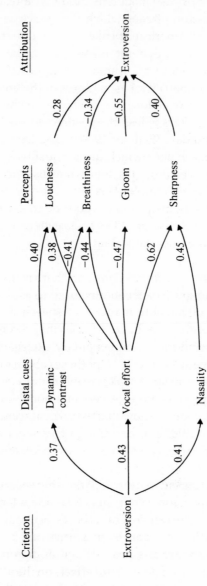

Figure 3. Full lens model demonstrating the accuracy of extroversion inference (from Scherer 1978a)
Curvilinear arrows indicate hypothetically assumed causal relationships. Strength of the relationships are indicated
by Pearson rs. Intercorrelations among variables for each type of measurement have been omitted to simplify the
figure. (N = 24 speakers; significance levels: p_c (0.10) r = 0.34, p_c (0.05) r = 0.40, two-tailed.)

perceive it in this way. Clearly, the relationship between pausing, articulation rate and rate of speech generally will have to be explored much more thoroughly before the marking status of any of these cues can be properly assessed.

Length of total verbal output in conversations seems to be a rather safe bet. In quite a number of studies, extroverted and dominant speakers talked more – both in terms of number of words and in terms of total speaking time. As far as the inference side is concerned, there can be very little doubt that attributions of extroversion, competence and dominance are based on greater verbal output. This resumé has shown that extroversion seems to be virtually the only personality trait which is likely to be definitely marked by speech cues. However, while extroversion, as one of the personality dispositions most important for social interaction, may be a prime candidate for marking – particularly in the United States where most of the studies reported have been done (cf. Scherer (1972) on the importance of personality traits in a particular social structure) – there are still possibilities for alternative explanations. Extroversion may easily stand out in terms of speech marking since this trait has been studied much more frequently than any other personality trait. Consequently, further research using more personality traits and, it is to be hoped, more satisfactory assessment methods, may yet find that many more personality dispositions are marked in speech.

Marker power. Until now we have been concerned with the question of whether a specific speech cue is or is not a personality marker. To discuss the marker status in terms of a binary all-or-nothing status does not do justice to the fact that most nonverbal signals are probabilistically rather than invariantly coded (cf. Giles, Scherer & Taylor, this volume: ch. 9, 3.2; Scherer 1977a, c), i.e. the presence of a specific cue implies with a certain probability that the trait marked is present in the actor. Consequently, personality markers in speech may differ according to the strength of the probabilistic associations between the respective cue, the trait marked and the trait attribution. The strength of these associations can be referred to as the power of a marker – the more likely a particular cue is to lead to the correct attribution of a particular personality trait, the more powerful a marker it is.

This notion of power is independent of the fact that the degree or extent of a continuously graded speech style variable can mark different levels of strength or distinctiveness of a personality disposition (cf. discussion of discrete vs. continuous coding in Giles, Scherer & Taylor (this volume:

ch. 9, 3.2)). Using the lens model paradigm, the power of a marker can be operationalized quantitatively as the product of the association, representation and utilization correlation coefficients for a particular cue in the model (cf. figure 1 above; Scherer 1974b, 1978). If a 'power' of a marker is quantitatively assessed in this manner, it becomes possible directly to compare the results of different studies, in order to arrive at a population estimate of the power of personality markers, as well as an assessment of the effects of speaker and listener characteristics and linguistic and situational contexts on the power of a marker.

5. Origins of personality markers in speech

We have seen that the quantity of verbal output, or the amount of participation in conversation, loudness of voice and possibly voice pitch and hesitation pauses, seem to be markers of extroversion – at least for American speakers. In order to understand the nature of personality marking in speech we obviously need to know more about the biological, psychological and cultural factors, and about the mechanism underlying the production and utilization of personality markers. However, it is not sheer scientific curiosity which stimulates further inquiry into the origins, functions and mechanisms of personality marking. It has become painfully clear in the course of this review that most of the research done in this area has been carried out in the spirit of dragnet fishing expeditions – including some of the author's own work. In order to develop a theoretical framework and to generate hypotheses which could guide further research efforts, it seems necessary to speculate about the possible origins and mechanisms of personality marking in speech. We will conclude this chapter with some considerations relevant to this concern.

In the terminology of the lens model paradigm, the personality marking characteristics of speech cues can be classified as externalization based or inferential utilization based. In the first case, the basis of the marking is an association between a personality disposition and a particular speech cue. The appropriate inferential utilization of the respective cue is established when observers become aware of this association and use it for personality attribution. In the second case, the basis of marking is the existence of a specific inference rule pattern linking a specific speech cue to the attribution of a specific personality trait. The appropriate externalization may develop when speakers with the respective personality dispositions produce the speech cues which are seen as indices of these dispositions in the particular culture. These two possible bases of personality marking will be discussed in turn, using the example of loudness as an extroversion marker.

5.1. Externalization based marking

Loudness of voice would be an externalization based marker of extroversion if there were a lawful relationship between being extroverted and speaking relatively loudly, and if listeners discovered this lawful relationship and used it in inferring and attributing extroversion (or sociability). In order to render this assumption more transparent, we will discuss possible bases for an association (or lawful relationship) between personality dispositions and speech cues as well as for the acquisition of appropriate inference rules. Among the factors that could account for a lawful relationship between personality dispositions and speech, are (i) biophysical or psychological factors, in which case the respective speech cues would be *concomitants* of these factors, and (ii) the functional efficiency of certain speech cues in producing certain interaction outcomes or attaining goals that serve important functions for the respective personality disposition, in which case it is the *effect* of the speech cues that explains the association.

Biophysical and psychological factors. Speech production like any other kind of human behaviour is determined by biophysical and psychological characteristics of the organism (cf. Laver & Trudgill, this volume: ch. 1, 2). Unfortunately, our knowledge about the degree of this determination is rather limited. Among the variables that are likely to affect speech cues, the following seem to be the most promising: body type, cognitive structure and emotional reactivity. It is evident that some structural properties of the human body, particularly of the vocal apparatus (e.g. size of the larynx) affect speech characteristics. The extent to which constitutional body type, in the sense of Kretschmer and Sheldon, affects speech remains unclear (Fährmann 1967; Görlitz 1972). Since speech production is to a large extent controlled by cognitive processes, there can be little doubt that cognitive structure exerts a strong influence on language and speech. While this influence is fairly obvious in those cases where cognitive processes are disturbed by pathological factors such as brain damage leading to aphasia and other speech disturbances (cf. Lenneberg 1967; Whitaker 1976), the role of factors such as cognitive complexity or cognitive differentiation is less clear (cf. Witkin & Goodenough 1977). Emotional reactivity which might be reflected in individual differences in habitual muscle tone (Gellhorn 1967; Goldstein 1964), as well as in other physiological parameters and processes, is also likely to affect speech production, particularly phonation and articulation.

Earlier in this review we have invoked the biophysical factor of heightened habitual muscle tone as a tentative explanation of the correlation between f_0 and extroversion/assertiveness (cf. section 2.1 above). While several physiological parameters are involved in the regulation of vocal effort (Harris 1974: 2284–5), it is not inconceivable that a relatively loud voice could also be due to high habitual muscle tone. While this biophysical factor may explain the occurrence of specific speech cues, it is less clear why extroversion should be accompanied by heightened habitual muscle tone. Eysenck (1967) postulates a biological basis for extroversion, but since he assumes extroverts to be generally less aroused or excited than introverts we would expect lower muscle tone for extroverts (unless one assumes complex rebound patterns; cf. Gellhorn 1967). Obviously, we need to know much more about the physiological bases of personality (cf. Fahrenberg 1967) before we can pursue the question of biophysical factors in speech–personality association.

Research on the effects of biophysical differences in voice and speech is difficult, since some differences in physiological processes may occur only in certain situations. For example, the physiological response to stress may vary quite markedly from individual to individual depending on differences in coping strategies. Depending on the particular physiological response, fundamental frequency of the voice can go up or down in stressful situations, with some evidence that these coping strategies may be related to self-attributions of personality (cf. section 2.1 above; Scherer 1977b).

Functional efficiency. Some speech–personality covariation seems to be due to the functional efficiency of the respective voice or speech characteristics in facilitating the attainment of interaction goals congruent with certain personality dispositions. Thus, dominant persons should be interested in not losing their turn to interrupting interlocutors and in winning turns at strategic points in the interaction. Consequently, it is functionally efficient habitually to use voice and speech characteristics serving as continuation or turn-claiming signals in conversation (cf. Duncan 1974). It has been experimentally demonstrated, for example, that to increase vocal amplitude is a very efficient mechanism in claiming or defending turns (Meltzer, Morris & Hayes 1971). This effect could lead to a long-term rise in vocal amplitude for speakers whose personality dispositions encourage more frequent and longer speaking turns, since we can assume that speakers quickly learn effective communication strategies.

Functional efficiency could nicely explain most of the extroversion markers described in this chapter. If we take for granted that extroverts tend to speak more, i.e. take turns more frequently and/or for longer periods of time (possibly because of 'arousal seeking'; cf. Eysenck 1967: 110), it would be functionally efficient to speak with a relatively loud voice, to raise pitch frequently (which would result in higher mean f_0 when measured and averaged across utterances in a conversation) and to avoid lengthy hesitation pauses.

5.2. Development of inference rules

Given that there is an externalization of a personality disposition in speech style, how do receivers develop the appropriate inference rules? Since the processing of social information via categorization seems to be one of the most important organizing principles of human cognitive systems, one would expect speech markers of personality categories to play an important role in the categorization of people according to personality (cf. the discussion of the cognitive organization function of speech markers in Giles, Scherer & Taylor, this volume: ch. 9, 2.1). Considering the remarkable proficiency of the human cognitive system for the discovery of lawful or rule-governed relationships in the environment (cf. Carroll & Payne 1976; Kaplan & Schwartz 1975), it is not surprising that existing speech–personality relationships should be reflected in appropriate cognitive inference rules.

While a discussion of the mechanisms whereby these inference rules could develop would be beyond the scope of this chapter, since it would require a review of a sizeable part of the literature on cognitive psychology, person perception and attribution processes, it might be useful to discuss briefly one important aspect of speech–personality inference rules – the tendency towards overestimation of actual speech–personality associations in personality attribution from speech.

The following example may illustrate this tendency: Scherer (1970) converted simple paper-and-pencil ratings of speech–personality relationships (obtained by asking subjects to answer questions like 'How likely is it that a dominant speaker will speak in a loud voice?' on a 9-point scale representing different probability levels) to prediction coefficients. These can be used to predict personality ratings made on the basis of actual voice samples by different subjects with a high degree of success. This analysis showed that these prediction coefficients (which represent the utilization coefficients of figure 1) are much higher than the correlation coefficients representing the actual speech–personality association. While the methodology used may account in part for these results, the study does point to the possibility that human information-processing systems assume a much stronger relationship between speech and personality than may actually exist. It would be a fascinating and highly profitable task to explore the nature of this phenomenon, which we will call 'tendency towards overestimation'. It may be due either to lack of sufficient distributional evidence in the process of inference rule acquisition or to a general tendency of the cognitive system to ensure that categorization is always possible even when the relationships between underlying dispositions or states and distal cues are rather weak.

This tendency towards overestimation may thus lead to an overgeneralization of very weak relationships, or even to the development of inference rules which do not correspond to any actually existing speech–personality association. Examples for the development of such invalid or 'stereotypical' inference rules are the overgeneralization of speech–personality relationships which may have existed only during a certain historical period or for a certain group or class of people. For example, in many societies members of a particular social class or elite have been obliged to exhibit both certain modal personality traits and a group-specific speech style (cf. the nasal burr of the dependable – and rigid – Prussian officer). Similarly, many followers of specific trades or occupants of ceremonial roles are supposed to possess certain types of personality traits, and can also often be observed to adhere to a speech style which seems particularly suited to the pursuit of their role obligations (e.g. parsons, military officers, common criminals). The fact that such role-specific speech–personality correspondences are frequently used in a stereotypical fashion by the media may not only be a result of the respective inference rules but may also provide additional support for the continuance of the tradition. Another interesting indicator for the ubiquity of, and the high degree of cultural consensus on, speech–personality inference rules is the frequency with which verbal descriptions of voice and speech characteristics are used in fiction to portray indirectly a character's personality or affective state.

While many of these inference rules are culturally shared, there may be important subcultural variations according to social class or ethnic groups. For example, although no hard empirical data can be cited, loudness of the voice seems to lead to opposing inferences according to social class, being a sign of friendliness and sociability for lower-class people, and an indicator of boorishness and aggressiveness for upper-class persons – at least for some situations in some cultures. Thus 'stereotypical' speech–personality inference rules may also be based on the correspondence between desirable personality dispositions for certain social groups and the speech style seen as proper for members of these groups.

5.3. Inferential utilization based marking

Given the existence of strong stereotypical speech–personality inference rules, it is not impossible that the appropriate externalization will develop. This could happen either by speakers with the respective speech style developing the personality dispositions which are seen to correspond to it in the particular group or culture, or by speakers with the respective personality dispositions adopting the appropriate speech style. The former case we could call self-fulfilling prophecy, the latter self-presentation.

Self-fulfilling prophecy. While it may sound improbable, it is not impossible for people to acquire certain personality dispositions simply because others expect them to possess these dispositions on the basis of their speech style. While one would not expect biologically based personality dispositions to be acquired in this way, personality dispositions subject to learning experiences (Mischel 1968), and dispositions strongly related to the self concept or the ego processes of a speaker, may well be amenable to the influence of interpersonal expectations. There can be little doubt that interpersonal expectations can affect the behaviour of actors (Rosenthal 1973; Rosenthal & Rubin 1978), and it seems feasible that long-term changes in behaviour may result in changes in some personality dispositions.

In many cases, the effects of interpersonal expectations may be part of the socialization process. Symbolic interaction theory (cf. Cooley 1956; Mead 1934) assumes that the self, including personality dispositions, is acquired in part by taking the role of the 'generalized other', which involves adapting to interpersonal expectations. Thus, the moulding of a speaker's personality dispositions according to the inferences listeners draw from his voice and speech style may occur over a longer period of time and in a rather subtle way in the course of the socialization process.

However, since the behaviour of co-actors towards a speaker also changes in line with their personality inferences from his behavioural cues, such self-fulfilling prophecies might well occur in much shorter periods of time later in life. For example, if a pupil moves to a school with a different ethnic or regional student body, certain aspects of the speech style of his region of origin might be interpreted as signs of weakness or submissiveness by his new schoolmates. If they all behave in a very domineering fashion towards this speaker on the basis of these inferences, he might well develop a more submissive personality disposition than he might otherwise have had.

Self-presentation. Goffman's (1959) claim that actors present and often stage a desirable self-identity for inspection and acceptance by their co-actors in social interactions has been widely accepted in social psychology. Clearly, actors often use behavioural cues for the presentation of self and, given the importance of speech in social interaction, it is not surprising that speech cues are prime candidates for self-presentation purposes. Of course, actors can use speech–personality inference patterns to present personality dispositions that they do not really possess. Such fraudulent self-presentations via speech cues cannot serve as the basis for personality marking with inferential utilization origin, given the definition of markers offered above. Self-presentation can be the origin of true personality markers in those cases where speakers – with or without awareness – produce those speech cues which listeners take as indicators of the personality tendencies that the speakers actually possess.

Given the pervasiveness of personality attributions on the basis of voice and speech, it is obviously an important aspect of one's social skill to provide observers with voice and speech cues which lead to accurate inferences. Consequently, self-presentation in vocal behaviour may not just be a strategic device in certain situations but a matter of necessity in everyday interactions. Of course, this does not mean that we constantly monitor and manipulate all our voice and speech characteristics. As in the case of functional efficiency, we may assume that a speech style is formed as a result of a particular mode of self-presentation in many different situations and then becomes a habit.

How, then, do the functional efficiency and the self-presentation explanation for speech marking differ? In the case of functional efficiency, a speaker produces certain speech cues because they result in *interaction outcomes* (e.g. allowing him frequently to take speaking turns) which are desirable in terms of his personality dispositions. Appropriate inference rules develop *on the basis* of this speech–personality association. In the case of self-presentation strong speech–personality inference rules exist *independently* of an actual speech–personality association, and speakers may later start to model parts of their speech style according to these inference rules to produce a certain *personality attribution* in receivers. As mentioned above, speakers may not necessarily be aware of their self-presentation strategies or of the functional efficiency of specific speech cues. As soon as the majority of speakers with a certain personality disposition self-present themselves by using the appropriate speech style, an actual speech–personality association exists and the inference rules are no longer stereotypical.

The extroversion markers discussed above could well be inferential utilization based with the association component provided by self-presentation strategies. As we have seen in section 3 above, there are rather strong and pervasive inference rules linking loudness of voice and quantity of verbal output to extroversion (and assertiveness). Since extroversion seems to be a socially desirable personality disposition (at least in the United States), it seems feasible that extroverted speakers advertise their sought-after personality dispositions by displaying a speech style which is generally assumed to be indicative of extroversion.

6. Concluding remarks

Since a case could be made for virtually all the bases for marking described in the preceding section being explanations of extroversion markers, it will be a difficult task to decide on the relative merit of each of these explanations. It may even be impossible to select one of the explanations as the correct one, since it is highly likely that many or even all of the mechanisms described are operative at the same time and may even mutually reinforce each other.

For example, if there is an association between loudness of voice and extroversion in terms of externalization (due to either biophysical factors or functional efficiency or both), the inferential utilization of this cue may exaggerate the strength of this relationship due to the tendency toward overestimation described above. The resulting importance of the loudness cue for extroversion attributions in social interactions may in turn lead to an increase in loudness of speech in those extroverted speakers motivated to project their extroversion in a highly visible way.

We assume the tendency toward overestimation to be a rather pervasive phenomenon in personality attribution, since observers seem to be prone to search for person variables which may account for the behaviour of an actor (cf. Jones & Nisbet 1971), and may thus overestimate the significance of certain speech cues as indicators of personality dispositions. Consequently, we should expect rather frequent interaction effects between externalization based and inferential utilization based marking.

In spite of the high probability of a strong interlocking of these two bases of personality marking in speech, there is some value in trying to trace the origin of existing personality marking to either one of these bases. An assessment of the origins of marking relationships may help to explain differences between cultures, social classes, specific groups of speakers and listeners, and situational contexts, and may help to explain changes over time. One would expect less diversity and context dependence in marking relationships if these are externally based, particularly if the externalization is due to an association between biophysical factors and speech cues (i.e. the association between larynx size and voice pitch), than if it is based on inferential utilization patterns which may be highly variable across cultures, social groups and time periods (cf. Brown & Fraser, this volume ch. 2, 3.2; Brown & Levinson: ch. 8).

Clearly, significant advances of our knowledge on personality marking in speech cannot be obtained by one-shot, single-culture studies with small groups of college undergraduates in rigged 'waiting-room' encounters. In order to assess *both* the existence and power *and* the origins and functions of personality markers in speech, we have to embark on long-term intercultural research programmes utilizing natural speech samples from different social situations. As mentioned before, such research programmes should be guided by hypotheses based on theoretical considerations concerning both the externalization of personality dispositions as well as the inferential utilization of speech cues within an integrative model of marking (such as the lens model proposed in this chapter).

Furthermore, research on personality markers in speech must be interdisciplinary in nature. As we have seen, an understanding of the phenomenon requires much further knowledge concerning biophysical concomitants of personality dispositions; the degree of correspondence between personality dispositions and personality attributions; the effects of cognitive and emotional processes on speech production; the role of specific speech cues on interaction processes and outcomes; the interaction between personality, social structural factors and situational demands; the social structural importance and desirability of specific personality dispositions; the ability to monitor and manipulate speech cues for self-presentation purposes – to name but a few of the areas involved. Consequently, expertise from the disciplines of physiology, psychology, social psychology, sociology, anthropology, as well as phonetics and linguistics, must be sought in order properly to study personality marking in speech.

The large number of factors that have been shown to be potentially involved in the issues discussed in this chapter seem to demonstrate rather convincingly that the type of piece-meal research conducted in this area can no longer be justified. In order to render research on speech and personality scientifically reputable we have to make an attempt at integrating and cumulating research evidence. It is therefore proposed to researchers who feel a calling to continue to work in this fascinating but frequently frustrating and even infuriating area to agree on some common baselines for research. There is an urgent need to concentrate on a few variables and to agree on definitions and methods that will allow a comparison of research findings. It is suggested that two or three major personality clusters such as extroversion/sociability, dominance/assertiveness and emotional stability should be chosen for study and that agreements should be reached about a minimal set of measures which will always be used. It is to be hoped that the results of such research efforts will serve to alleviate the controversy about the existence and the social and psychological significance of personality as an important category in social interaction, and about the likelihood that personality differences are marked in speech.

References

Addington, D. W. 1968a. Voice and the perception of personality: an experimental study. *Oklahoma State University Monographs* (Social Science Series), no. 15.

1968b. The relationship of selected vocal characteristics to personality perception. *Speech Monographs, 35*, 492–503.

Alban, L. S. & Groman, W. D. 1976. Neurotic anxiety, pronoun usage and stress. *Journal of Clinical Psychology, 32*, 393–9.

Allport, G. W. & Cantril, H. 1934. Judging personality from voice. *Journal of Social Psychology, 5*, 37–54.

Apple, W., Streeter, L. A. & Krauss, R. M. 1977. The effects of pitch and speech rate on personal attributions. MS, Columbia University.

Aronovitch, C. D. 1976. The voice of personality: stereotyped judgements and their relation to voice quality and sex of speaker. *Journal of Social Psychology, 99*, 207–20.

Axtell, B. & Cole, C. W. 1971. Repression–sensitization response mode and verbal avoidance. *Journal of Personality and Social Psychology, 18*, 133–7.

Balken, E. R. & Masserman, J. H. 1940. The language of phantasy: III. The language of the phantasies of patients with conversion hysteria, anxiety state, and obsessive-compulsive neuroses. *Journal of Psychology*, *10*, 75–86.

Baskett, G. D. & Freedle, R. O. 1974. Aspects of language and the social perception of lying. *Journal of Psycholinguistic Research*, *3*, 117–30.

Borstel, S. von 1977. Sprachstil und Persönlichkeit: Analyse des Zusammenhangs von Variablen des Sprachstils und der Persönlichkeit. Diploma thesis, University of Giessen.

Brown, B. L., Strong, W. J. & Rencher, A. C. 1975. Acoustic determinants of the perceptions of personality from speech. *International Journal of the Sociology of Language*, *6*, 11–32.

Brunswik, E. 1956. *Perception and the Representative Design of Psychological Experiments*. Berkeley and Los Angeles, Cal.

Busemann, A. 1925. *Die Sprache der Jugend als Ausdruck der Entwicklungsrhythmik*. Jena.

1926. Über typische und phasische Unterschiede der kategorialen Sprachform. *Zeitschrift für pädagogische Psychologie*, *27*, 415–19.

1948. *Stil und Charakter*. Meisenheim/Glan.

Byrne, D. 1964. Repression–sensitization as a dimension of personality. In B. A. Maher (ed.) *Progress in Experimental Personality Research*, vol. I. New York.

Campbell, A. & Rushton, J. R. 1978. Bodily communication and personality. *British Journal of Social and Clinical Psychology*, *17*, 31–6.

Carment, D. W., Miles, C. S. & Cervin, V. B. 1965. Persuasiveness and persuasibility as related to intelligence and extroversion. *British Journal of Social and Clinical Psychology*, *4*, 1–7.

Carroll, J. S. & Payne, J. W. (eds.) 1976. *Cognition and Social Behaviour*. Hillsdale, NJ.

Cook, M. 1969. Anxiety, speech disturbances and speech rate. *British Journal of Social and Clinical Psychology*, *8*, 13–21.

Cooley, C. H. 1956. *Human Nature and the Social Order*. Glencoe, Ill. (1st ed. 1902).

Cope, C. S. 1969. Linguistic structure and personality development. *Journal of Counseling Psychology*, *16*, 1–19.

Crystal, D. 1969. *Prosodic Systems and Intonation in English*. Cambridge.

Diehl, C. F. 1960. Voice and personality: an evaluation. In D. A. Barbara (ed.) *Psychological and Psychiatric Aspects of Speech and Hearing*. Springfield, Ill.

Diehl, C. F., White, R. & Burk, K. W. 1959. Voice quality and anxiety. *Journal of Speech and Hearing Research*, *2*, 282–5.

Dollard, J. & Mowrer, O. H. 1953. A method of measuring tension in written documents. In O. H. Mowrer (ed.) *Psychotherapy: theory and research*. New York.

Doob, L. W. 1958. Behavior and grammatical style. *Journal of Abnormal and Social Psychology*, *56*, 398–401.

Duncan, S. 1974. On the structure of speaker–auditor interaction during speaking turns. *Language in Society*, *3*, 161–80.

Duncan, S. & Fiske, D. 1977. *Face-to-Face Interaction: research, methods, and theory*. New York.

Ekman, P. Friesen, W. V. & Scherer, K. R. 1976. Body movement and voice pitch in deceptive interaction. *Semiotica*, *16*, 23–7.

Endler, N. S. & Magnusson, D. 1976. *Interactional Psychology and Personality*. Washington, DC.

Ertel, S. 1973. Erkenntnis und Dogmatismus. *Psychologische Rundschau, 23,* 241–69.

Eysenck, H. J. 1967. *The Biological Basis of Personality.* Springfield, Ill. (3rd ed. 1977.)

Fahrenberg, J. 1967. *Psychophysiologische Persönlichkeitsforschung.* Göttingen.

Fährmann, R. 1967. *Die Deutung des Sprechausdrucks: Studien zur Einführung in die Praxis der charakterologischen Stimm- und Sprechanalyse.* 2nd ed. Bonn. (1st ed. 1960.)

Fairbanks, H. 1944. The quantitative differentiation of samples of spoken language. *Psychological Monographs, 56,* no. 255, 17–38.

Feldstein, S. & Welkowitz, J. 1978. A chronography of conversation: in defense of an objective approach. In A. W. Siegman & S. Feldstein (eds.) *Nonverbal Behavior and Communication.* Hillsdale, NJ.

Gaines, L. S., Fretz, B. R. & Helweg, G. C. 1975. Self-referent language and need for approval. *Psychological Reports, 37,* 107–11.

Gellhorn, E. 1967. *Principles of Autonomic Somatic Integrations: physiological basis and psychological and clinical implications.* Minneapolis.

Giles, H. & Powesland, P. F. 1975. *Speech Style and Social Evaluation.* New York.

Giles, H. & Smith, P. M. 1979. Accommodation theory: optimal levels of convergence. In H. Giles & R. St Clair (eds.) *Language and Social Psychology.* Oxford.

Goffman, E. 1959. *The Presentation of Self in Everyday Life.* Garden City, NY.

Goldman-Eisler, F. 1968. *Psycholinguistics: experiments in spontaneous speech.* New York.

Goldstein, I. B. 1964. Role of muscle tension in personality theory. *Psychological Bulletin, 61,* 413–25.

Görlitz, D. 1972. *Ergebnisse und Probleme der ausdruckspsychologischen Sprechstimmforschung.* Meisenheim/Glan.

Gottschalk, L. A. & Gleser, G. C. 1969. *The Measurement of Psychological States through the Content Analysis of Verbal Behavior.* Berkeley, Cal.

Harris, K. S. 1974. Physiological aspects of articulatory behavior. In T. A. Sebeok (ed.) *Current Trends in Linguistics,* vol. xii, *Linguistics and Adjacent Arts and Sciences.* The Hague.

Hayes, D. P. & Meltzer, L. 1972. Interpersonal judgements based on talkativeness: I. Fact or artifact, *Sociometry, 35,* 538–61.

Hecker, M. H. L., Stevens, K. N., von Bismarck, G. & Williams, C. E. 1968. Manifestations of task-induced stress in the acoustic speech signal. *Journal of the Acoustical Society of America, 44,* 993–1001.

Helfrich, H. & Dahme, G. 1974. Sind Verzögerungsphänomene beim spontanen Sprechen Indikatoren persönlichkeitsspezifischer Angstverarbeitung. *Zeitschrift für Sozialpsychologie, 5,* 55–65.

Helfrich, H. & Scherer, K. R. 1977. Experimental assessment of antidepressant drug effects using spectral analysis of voice. Acoustical Society of America Meeting, Miami 1977. *Journal of the Acoustical Society of America, 62,* Supplement no. 1, 26 (Abstract).

Herpel, G. 1977. Sprechweise und Persönlichkeit: Analyse des Zusammenhangs zwischen Sprechweise-Variablen und Persönlichkeitsvariablen. Diploma thesis, University of Giessen.

Hunt, R. G. & Lin, T. K. 1967. Accuracy of judgements of personal attributes from speech. *Journal of Personality and Social Psychology*, 6, 450–3.

Jaffe, J. & Feldstein, S. 1970. *Rhythms of Dialogue*. New York.

Jones, E. E. & Nisbet, R. E. 1971. The actor and the observer: divergent perceptions of the causes of behavior. In E. E. Jones *et al.* (eds.) *Attribution: perceiving the causes of behavior*. Morristown, NJ.

Kaplan, M. F. & Schwartz, S. (eds.) 1975. *Human Judgement and Decision Processes*. New York.

Keating, L. 1974. An experimental study of the effect of intonation pattern on listener response. *Dissertation Abstracts International*, 34 (11–A), 7366–7.

Kramer, E. 1963. Judgement of personal characteristics and emotions from non-verbal properties of speech. *Psychological Bulletin*, 60, 408–20.

Kühnen, S. 1977. Stimme und Persönlichkeit: Analyse des Zusammenhangs von Stimmqualitätsvariablen und Persönlichkeitsvariablen. Diploma thesis, University of Giessen.

Laver, J. D. M. 1975. Individual features in voice quality. PhD thesis, University of Edinburgh.

Lay, C. H. & Burron, B. F. 1968. Perception of the personality of the hesitant speaker. *Perceptual and motor skills*, 26, 951–6.

Lazarus-Mainka, G. 1973. Persönlichkeitsspezifisches im Sprachverhalten. *Zeitschrift für experimentelle und angewandte Psychologie*, 20, 68–91.

Lehiste, I. 1970. *Suprasegmentals*. Cambridge, Mass.

Lenneberg, E. H. 1967. *Biological Foundations of Language*. New York.

Lomax, R. 1974. Social structure and sound change. In R. W. Westcott (ed.) *Language Origins*. Silver Springs, Md.

Lorenz, M. & Cobb, S. 1953. Language behavior in psychoneurotic patients. *Archives of Neurology and Psychiatry*, 69, 684–94.

Lyons, J. (ed.) 1970. *New Horizons in Linguistics*. Harmondsworth, Middx.

McClelland, D. L., Atkinson, J. W., Clark, R. A. & Lowell, F. L. 1953. *The Achievement Motive*. New York.

Mahl, G. F. 1956. Disturbances and silences in the patient's speech in psychotherapy. *Journal of Abnormal and Social Psychology*, 53, 1–15.

Mahl, G. F. & Schulze, G. 1964. Psychological research in the extralinguistic area. In T. A. Sebeok, A. S. Hayes & M. C. Bateson (eds.) *Approaches to Semiotics*. The Hague.

Mallory, E. & Miller, V. A. 1958. A possible basis for the association of voice characteristics and personality traits. *Speech Monographs*, 25, 255–60.

Malmo, R. B. 1975. *On Emotions, Needs, and our Archaic Brain*. New York.

Markel, N. N., Phillis, J. A., Vargas, R. & Harvard, K. 1972. Personality traits associated with voice types. *Journal of Psycholinguistic Research*, 1, 249–55.

Martin, B. 1971. *Anxiety and Neurotic Disorders*. New York.

Matarazzo, J. D. 1965. The interview. In B. B. Wolman (ed.) *Handbook of Clinical Psychology*. New York.

Mead, G. H. 1934. *Mind, Self, and Society*. Chicago, Ill.

Meltzer, L., Morris, W. N. & Hayes, D. P. 1971. Interruption outcomes and vocal amplitude: explorations in social psychophysics. *Journal of Personality and Social Psychology*, 18, 392–402.

Miller, G. A. 1951. *Language and Communication*. New York.

Mischel, W. 1968. *Personality and Assessment*. New York.

Moerk, E. 1972. Factors of style and personality. *Journal of Psycholinguistic Research*, 1, 257–68.

Moore, G. E. 1939. Personality traits and voice quality deficiencies. *Journal of Speech Disorders*, 4, 33–6.

Morris, C. G. & Hackman, J. R. 1969. Behavioral correlates of perceived leadership. *Journal of Personality and Social Psychology*, 13, 350–61.

Moses, P. 1954. *The Voice of Neurosis*. New York.

Murray, D. C. 1971. Talk, silence, and anxiety. *Psychological Bulletin*, 75, 244–60.

Nelson, W. M. & Groman, W. D. 1975. Neurotic verbalizations: an exploration of a Gestalt Therapy assumption. *Journal of Clinical Psychology*, 31, 732–7.

Osgood, C. E. & Walker, E. G. 1959. Motivation and language behavior. *Journal of Abnormal and Social Psychology*, 59, 58–67.

Ostwald, P. F. 1964. How the patient communicates about disease with the doctor. In T. A. Sebeok, A. S. Hayes & M. C. Bateson (eds.) *Approaches to Semiotics*. The Hague.

(ed.) 1973. *The Semiotics of Human Sound*. The Hague.

Patterson, M. & Holmes, D. S. 1966. Social interaction correlates of the MMPI extraversion–introversion scale. *American Psychologist*, 21, 724–5 (Abstract).

Pear, T. H. 1931. *Voice and Personality*. London.

Ramsay, R. W. 1966. Personality and speech. *Journal of Personality and Social Psychology*, 4, 116–18.

1968. Speech patterns and personality. *Language and Speech*, 11, 54–63.

Rochester, S. R. 1973. The significance of pauses in spontaneous speech. *Journal of Psycholinguistic Research*, 2, 51–81.

Rogers, P. L., Scherer, K. R. & Rosenthal, R. 1971. Content-filtering human speech: a simple electronic system. *Behavioral Research Methods and Instrumentation*, 3, 16–18.

Rosenthal, R. 1973. *On the Social Psychology of the Self-fulfilling Prophecy: further evidence for Pygmalion effects and their mediating mechanisms*. Mss Modular Publications, 53. New York.

Rosenthal, R. & Rubin, D. B. 1978. Interpersonal expectancy effects: the first 345 studies. *The Behavioral and Brain Sciences*, 1.

Rudert, J. 1965. Vom Ausdruck der Sprechstimme. In R. Kirchoff (ed.) *Ausdruckspsychologie*, vol. v, *Handbuch der Psychologie*. Göttingen.

Rutter, D. R., Morley, I. E. & Graham, J. C. 1972. Visual interaction in a group of introverts and extroverts. *European Journal of Social Psychology*, 2, 371–84.

Sandell, R. 1977. *Linguistic Style and Persuasion*. London.

Sanford, F. H. 1942. Speech and personality. *Psychological Bulletin*, 39, 811–45.

Scherer, K. R. 1970. Attribution of personality from voice: a cross-cultural study on the dynamics of interpersonal perception. PhD thesis, Harvard University.

1971. Randomized splicing: a simple technique for masking speech content. *Journal of Experimental Research in Personality*, 5, 155–9.

1972. Judging personality from voice: a cross-cultural approach to an old issue in interpersonal perception. *Journal of Personality*, 40, 191–210.

1974a. Acoustic concomitants of emotional dimensions: judging affect from synthesized tone sequences. In S. Weitz (ed.) *Nonverbal Communication*. New York.

1974b. Persönlichkeit, Stimmqualität und Persönlichkeitsattribution:

pfadanalytische Untersuchungen zu nonverbalen Kommunikationsprozessen. In L. H. Eckensberger & U. S. Eckensberger (eds.) *Bericht über den 28. Kongress der Deutschen Gesellschaft für Psychologie*, vol. III. Göttingen.

1974c. Voice quality analysis of American and German speakers. *Journal of Psycholinguistic Research*, 3, 281–90.

1977a. Die Funktionen des nonverbalen Verhaltens im Gespräch. In D. Wegner (ed.) *Gesprächsanalyse*. Hamburg.

1977b. The effect of stress on fundamental frequency of the voice. Acoustical Society of America Meeting, Miami, 1977. *Journal of the Acoustical Society of America*, 62, Supplement no. 1, 25–6 (Abstract).

1977c. Kommunikation. In T. Herrmann *et al.* (eds.) *Handbuch psychologischer Grundbegriffe*. Munich.

1978. Inference rules in personality attribution from voice quality: the loud voice of extroversion. *European Journal of Social Psychology*, 8, 467–87.

1979a. Non-linguistic vocal indicators of emotion and psychopathology. In C. E. Izard (ed.) *Emotions in Personality and Psychopathology*. New York.

1979b. Voice and speech correlates of perceived social influence. In H. Giles & R. St Clair (eds.) *Language and Social Psychology*. Oxford.

In preparation. *Speech and Personality: the juror study*. University of Giessen.

Scherer, K. R. & Oshinsky, J. 1977. Cue utilization in emotion attribution from auditory stimuli. *Motivation and Emotion*, 1, 331–46.

Scherer, K. R., Helfrich, H., Standke, R. & Wallbott, H. 1976. Psychoakustische und kinesische Verhaltensanalyse. Research report, University of Giessen.

Scherer, K. R., Koivumaki, J. & Rosenthal, R. 1972. Minimal cues in the vocal communication of affect: judging emotions from content-masked speech. *Journal of Psycholinguistic Research*, 1, 269–85.

Scherer, K. R., London, H. & Wolf, J. J. 1973. The voice of confidence: paralinguistic cues and audience evaluation. *Journal of Research in Personality*, 7, 31–44.

Scherer, K. R., Scherer, U., Hall, J. A. & Rosenthal, R. 1977. Differential attribution of personality based on multi-channel presentation of verbal and nonverbal cues. *Psychological Research*, 39, 221–47.

Schönbach, P. 1977. Sprachstrukturelle Einflüsse auf Personenbeurteilungen. MS, University of Bochum.

Siegman, A. W. 1978. The tell-tale voice: nonverbal messages of verbal communication. In A. W. Siegman & S. Feldstein (eds.) *Nonverbal Behavior and Communication*. Hillsdale, NJ.

Siegman, A. W. & Pope, B. 1965. Effects of question specificity and anxiety-producing messages on verbal fluency in the initial interview. *Journal of Personality and Social Psychology*, 2, 522–30.

Sinha, S. N. & Sinha, L. N. 1968. Positive and negative self-references in high and low anxious subjects during a free verbalization situation. *Journal of Psychological Researches*, 12, 71–4.

Spielberger, C. D. (ed.) 1972. *Anxiety*, vols. I and II. New York.

Stang, D. J. 1973. Effect of interaction rate on ratings of leadership and liking. *Journal of Personality and Social Psychology*, 27, 405–8.

Stein, R. T., Geis, F. L. & Damarin, F. 1973. Perception of emergent leadership hierarchies in task groups. *Journal of Personality and Social Psychology*, 28, 77–87.

Steingart, I., Freedmann, N., Grand, S. & Buchwald, C. 1975. Personality organization and language behavior: the imprint of psychological differentiation on language behavior in varying communication conditions. *Journal of Psycholinguistic Research*, *4*, 241–55.

Streeter, L. A., Krauss, R. M., Geller, V., Olson, C. & Apple, W. 1977. Pitch changes during attempted deception. *Journal of Personality and Social Psychology*, *35*, 345–50.

Terango, L. 1966. Pitch and duration characteristics of the oral reading of males on a masculinity–femininity dimension. *Journal of Speech and Hearing Research*, *9*, 590–5.

Thorne, J. P. 1970. Generative grammar and stylistic analysis. In J. Lyons (ed.) *New Horizons in Linguistics*. Harmondsworth, Middx.

Trimboli, F. 1973. Changes in voice characteristics as a function of trait and state personality variables. *Dissertation Abstracts International*, *33*, 3965.

Trojan, F. 1975. *Biophonetik*. Zürich.

Uldall, E. 1960. Attitudinal meanings conveyed by intonation contours. *Language and Speech*, *3*, 223–34.

1964. Dimensions of meaning in intonation. In D. Abercrombie, D. B. Fry *et al.* (eds.) *In Honour of Daniel Jones*. London.

Vetter, H. 1969. *Language Behavior and Psychopathology*. Chicago, Ill.

Weinstein, M. S. & Hanson, R. G. 1975. Personality trait correlates of verbal interaction levels in an encounter group context. *Canadian Journal of Behavioral Science*, *7*, 192–200.

Whitaker, H. A. 1976. Neurobiology of language. In E. C. Carterette & M. P. Friedman (eds.) *Handbook of Perception*, vol. VII. New York.

Wiener, M. & Mehrabian, A. 1968. *Language within Language: immediacy, a channel in verbal communication*. New York.

Wiggins, J. S. 1973. *Personality and Prediction: principles of personality assessment*. Reading, Mass.

Witkin, H. A. & Goodenough, D. R. 1977. Field dependence and interpersonal behavior. *Psychological Bulletin*, *84*, 661–89.

Zipf, G. K. 1935. *The Psycho-biology of Language*. Boston.

6. Speech markers and social class[1]

W. PETER ROBINSON

Systematic studies of the associations between the use of language and socioeconomic status (SES) stretch back to the beginning of the century. During the first three decades reports were made of the differential production of various linguistic features by members of different SES groups, mainly children (see McCarthy 1930). The facts were recorded and left. By the 1950s and 1960s however, these and more recently collected data began to be included in educational arguments, particularly those addressed to issues of equality of opportunity in schools. Explanations and remedies for the facts of low SES underachievement were proffered, and at times it seemed that differential mastery of school language was the only remaining important variable responsible for distributing the average educational attainments of the various SES groups. In most of this work the research effort was directed to the exposure of differences in the production rather than in the comprehension or perception of speech and writing (see Robinson 1978: 112–17, for the exceptions). Almost no one working in educational contexts explored an alternative hypothetical sequence of events in which teachers used the speech of their students as one of the variables for identifying SES (among other variables of presumed educational significance) with the possible consequence of differential expectations and treatment leading to differences in the ultimate attainments of the students; no one was pursuing speech as a social marker.

This possibility was voiced by Lambert (pers. comm.), and its potential power could no doubt be traced beyond Shaw's *Pygmalion*. (It is noteworthy that Eliza claimed that it was not so much the induction into Received Pronunciation and Standard English that made her into a 'lady', as the fact that Colonel Pickering had always treated her as one.) It was

[1] The author is pleased to acknowledge the considerable constructive advice of Howard Giles and Klaus Scherer for the improvement of this chapter.

from the phoneticians in particular (e.g. Labov 1966) that the marking of social identity through speech came to the fore as a possible mediator of differential educational attainment, although this idea has yet to gather strength. Recent work by Williams (1976) may help to accelerate interest, although, as the studies in that volume show, SES does not operate as a single independent variable; it can interact with and can be confounded with other components of social identity. For example, much of the work of Lambert (1972) and his colleagues has been presented in terms of speech and ethnic identity, but ethnicity is not independent of social stratification in Canada, or anywhere else that has been studied. The many studies by Giles and others (see Giles 1977; Giles & Powesland 1975) which have examined inferences from accent to traits are clearly not independent of SES. Received Pronunciation (RP) in English English carries a prestige correlated with SES; broader regional accents are associated with membership of lower SES groups. However, since these studies seldom mention SES explicitly, they will be reviewed only when it is clear that the author is treating 'social class' or SES as a variable; a mention of 'status' unmodified or unqualified cannot be presumed to refer to SES.

Neither will we attempt to embrace the full range of questions about language and social stratification. No mention will be made of the historical or sociological origins of similarities and differences in the language use of SES groups. No concern will be shown for the developmental origins of similarities and differences in individuals in terms of socialization. Neither shall we address questions about the sociological consequences of people's speech being used to identify their SES; the psychological consequences of such identification will be explored only for their immediate social significance. We shall be primarily concerned with face-to-face encounters, where presumed or real associations between speech and SES could be or are relevant to decisions made in those encounters. (To avoid the repetition of the cumbersome phrase 'speech or writing', 'speech' will frequently be used alone, but this should not be taken to imply that writing does not present comparable problems and information, *mutatis mutandis*. The recent assertion of the historical primacy of speaking has tended to minimize the significance of writing to an unnecessary and invalid extent.)

While the problems of defining 'marker' are handled by Giles, Scherer & Taylor, (this volume: ch. 9, 3.2), there must be other conceptual wood-clearing before we can examine the empirical data themselves and finally pose some of the questions about explanations for the phenomena observed. We first note that 'marking' is not the sole function of language, worry briefly that 'social class' and SES are not synonymous, and ask whether it is appropriate to assume that there is a unidimensional scale of prestige in western societies. Passing by these issues with reluctant perfunctoriness, we then focus upon the distinction between 'knowing how' and 'knowing that' and between etic and emic marking of SES. And thence to the data.

1. Conceptual woodclearing

The word 'marker' in the title will be treated with respect and will contain the discussion; it will be used in its simpler sense to refer to any feature that could be or is used by people to identify its emitter as a member of some socially significant category. By concentrating upon this one function of language we ignore the many others also served by that vehicle (Halliday 1975; Robinson, 1972). Further, within the marking function, the starkness of the term 'marker' encourages us to attend to the immediate identificatory relevance of that speech for listeners rather than, for example, its longer-term relevance to the self-concept of the speaker. One important question which might be assumed to underlie the conjunction of 'social class' with 'marker' is, 'What are the distinguishing features of the speech and writing of each social class in a society that could be or are used by members of that society to identify who belongs to which class?' While this question does not explicitly exclude the idea of people categorizing themselves as well as others, it does not point overtly to the possibility that they may deliberately choose to fit their speech to the norms of a preferred or imposed identity. It does not hint at the idea that a person's speech may vary by role and context of situation, and that this variation might represent unsteady compromises and conflicts among the roles and identities of an individual. There is no suggestion that we may not hear ourselves as we really are, even though most of us have probably heard aspirants to more cultivated voices deny the validity of tape-recordings of their own. The question half-presupposes that there are social classes and that this is a relevant aspect of social stratification to study in relation to speech. It suggests we might reasonably expect markers of it to exist. While not presuming to deny the possibility that all significant social variation is marked linguistically in some way, *social class* itself may not be the most useful concept for sociolinguists interested in the relevance of social hierarchies to interpersonal behaviour, and, as the opening paragraphs exemplify, the phrase 'socioeconomic status' (SES) will be used here, since that is what workers in the field have normally measured in their studies.

In their studies of language and its use, sociologists, as well as linguists and social psychologists, have used 'social class' with a casualness that cannot be excused. We (and on this occasion it includes 'I' but may not embrace 'you') have taken *own occupation* or *father's occupation* as an index and then written about social class. Sometimes, in the misleading tradition of Hollingshead & Redlich (1958), we have refined our measurements with supplementary information about the occupations of other persons in the nuclear family, the education of family members, and the district of residence. This is doubly delusive. It seduces us towards imagining that we are approaching some real single status hierarchy ever more closely, and that is not so. The other is to imagine we are measuring *class*, which we are not. In none of its theories does sociology equate class with father's occupation. Marx would require us to measure a group's (not an individual's) power relationship to the means of production and distribution and write in terms of potential rather than realized class. Weber would insist that we separate *class*, *status* and *power*. If this separation is accepted in the terms that Weber set out, all the empirical work to be discussed has been concerned with *status* rather than *class* or *power*. In this case *status* means *prestige*.

But what does 'prestige' mean? We may choose to follow the recommendations of the dictionary and accept that it implies influence, or at least the potential for influence. Presumably this has to be conceptually distinguished from both physical force (power) and economic sanctions (class) if it is to function as Weber suggested. In what sense then have doctors more influence than primary school teachers, foremen more influence than printers, or train drivers more influence than lorry drivers? In what areas is this influence exercised and how? And if we want to know answers to these questions, why do we not conduct the appropriate investigations rather than sample averaged opinions of the uninformed (Hall & Caradog-Jones 1950)? Is it ecologically valid to abstract a unitary scale of occupational prestige in our societies or is this a fiction created by social scientists, and one that members of society have then helped to reinforce? Once we have learned the rules of the game, and our media help to keep us informed, we can then provide the rankings required and help the social sciences forward, but is this simply a process of generating and regenerating categories for a rhetoric roundabout (see p. 217 below)?

While there is no doubt that there are differential life chances associated with the occupation of different locations in the social structure and that various indices of vertical social stratification capture some of this variance, the manner in which these in fact operate remains somewhat of a mystery, and a single status hierarchy based on occupation may obscure more than it describes. Unconfident of the meaning, meaningfulness and measurement of SES, we may proceed.

'Marking' does not differentiate between potential and realized knowledge, between the etic and the emic (cf. Brown & Fraser, this volume: ch. 2, 1.2; Giles, Scherer & Taylor: ch. 9, 3.4). There may be speech features that covary strongly with other psychological and sociological characteristics of speakers and listeners, but which no one knows about or uses. Neither professional students nor amateur performers may yet have discovered the existence of these features, but once identified they could become available for exploitation.

Contrariwise people may in fact use features that are not valid markers of categories: the correlations assumed by their behaviour may be false or exaggerated. One can imagine English listeners having some difficulty with their identifications of the SES of Americans for those features of speech whose reported prestige values are reversed in the two societies (e.g. postvocalic /r/; Labov 1966): perhaps they would be tempted to reverse reality in their judgements. Exaggeration may be a more common problem: this is the case, for example, where the true association between the use of a speech feature in a given situation and SES is represented by a correlation of 0.4, but the listener reports beliefs or behaves as though this correlation is 1.0. While propensities to overestimate true values of correlations could be examples of 'stereotyping' by judges, they can also be the best provisional estimates on the information available, especially in those experimental studies in which no further relevant information about stimulus 'people' is provided. These distinctions between potential markers and used markers, and among imagined, genuine and exaggerated variants of the latter, have to be made if we are to avoid muddles in our descriptions and explanations.

1.1. The etics and emics of marking

'Etic' will be used here to refer to those features of speech or writing that are available at any moment of time for better than chance identification of SES membership – regardless of whether or not these features are so used or even whether or not more than one person is aware of their existence. Features which are etic in particular places at particular times, may not be so in other places at the same time or other times in the same place. They may be discriminatory only for certain subclasses of persons within SES groupings and may operate only in limited contexts for these. Any discriminable feature of a language is potentially etic, whether or not it is a distinctive feature in a linguist's catalogue. Which features are etic for SES has to be investigated empirically, and there is always the possibility that there are others of which we are contemporaneously unaware. (What will be fascinating for diachronic sociolinguists will be the search for the means by which particular features are selected in and out for marking SES and the reasons why these are preferred and subsequently rejected.) How to define 'emic' presents some difficulty. Emic features are those which serve for discriminatory behaviour, either unconscious or conscious. But should both genuine and imagined features be included within the definition? If the definition is to be in terms of how the hearer or reader actually discriminates then both have to be included; it is the phenomenological and not the objective reality which is important. However, if the definition is to draw attention to the genuine marking of the speaker or writer, the features used for invalid inferences should be excluded. The issue can be avoided by referring to real and imagined emic features, with an unmodified 'emic' being undifferentiated in this respect. We shall also have occasion to mention 'exaggerated' assumptions, which we have already referred to as those cases where there is a measure of correlation between the feature and SES but the behaviour of perceivers overestimates the size of the correlation. Large size of boots might be associated with being a policeman, but to assume that most men wearing size 11 shoes are policemen would be to overestimate the reality of the matter.

The distinction between phenomenological and objective reality is further complicated in the area of interest here by the possibility of the phenomenological becoming the real. For example, if teacher folklore associates characteristic X with expectations of scholastic ineptitude and teachers then provide inferior pedagogical facilities to children with characteristic X, then we might reasonably expect that the children will learn less. While it might be that X is genuinely predictive of low learning ability, it could also be the case that it is predictive only because relevant controllers of the situation believe it to be so and act to make it so. The approach in social science encouraged by Goffman's introduction of the concept 'stigma' (Goffman 1970) is underpinned by the fact that human beings can define their own social reality. The 'pleasantness' of the sound of the RP accent and the 'ugliness' of the regional urban accents are not necessarily appreciated by non-English-speaking listeners. We have some measure of self-seducing discretion in the manufacture of our own evaluations.

Some layers of reality are schematized in figure 1. The rings in this figure add to the distinctions introduced above. The outermost ring, labelled the *rhetoric roundabout*, is what people say they believe to be true about the relationships between language and SES in the course of their everyday conversations and other acts of speaking and writing. They may not say the same things to different audiences, and they may not believe what they say. And neither of these necessarily relates to what their behaviour *vis-à-vis* members of different SES groups implies. Dinner party chatter or taproom gossip may insist that hiring and firing decisions are made independently of consciously or unconsciously mediated associations between SES and language use, but those same people may discriminate on that basis when in such situations. (The reverse could also be true.)

Observers and investigators who try to find out what these facts are may distort the facets of reality through the instruments and procedures they use to collect their data. We are now familiar with some of the ways in which *task demands* can structure the behaviour of respondents (Orne 1969). To ask whether Russians are tall or short is to presuppose and presume beyond the bounds of sense. The answers that respondents give

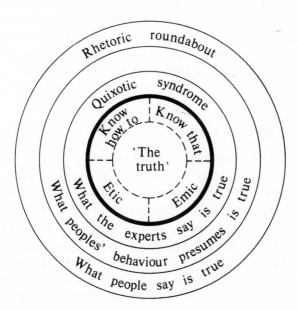

Figure 1. Some layers of reality

within the categories established for them may not reveal how those respondents behave, how they think, or what they say in the course of their everyday activities. Experts report their interpretations of their observations to yield another important layer within reality. It is an important layer, both because it tends to generate a life of its own in the academic community and because it can impinge upon the beliefs and behaviour already referred to in the other rings. Certain questions become the popular research pursuits to the exclusion of other questions. At various times in my life I have been discouraged from continuing to ask how awareness of self might influence behaviour (undergraduate), how far one might gain useful information through direct questioning of people (postgraduate), and whether communication with caretakers might not have some relevance to children learning to master language (assistant lecturer). Each was outside the framework of legitimacy at the time, and so it can be with any field: the experts define the frame of reference for research, and their definition may well limit the vision of other members of society, to the disadvantage of all. This layer deserves the label *quixotic syndrome* because academics are trapped too frequently by their failures to observe the reality associated with the phenomena they are supposed to be studying. (In this volume there is a risk that readers may assume that speech is perceived by academics to be the sole marker of age, sex, ethnicity or SES.)

The world of what might mark SES (etics) and what does mark SES (emics), and whether this knowledge is realized only through action (know how to) or symbolically/iconically (know that) or both, is portrayed as, and in fact is, encapsulated within the outer rings of belief and behaviour.

1.2. Knowing how and knowing that

The speech features treated as markers are *known* in two different ways: *knowing how to* and *knowing that* (Ryle 1949). We can know how to do things without being able to express this knowledge verbally: that we know how to do something does not entail that we know how to talk about how we do it. Conversely, we may be able to represent knowledge verbally without being able to exploit it either in experiment or in real life. We can know how without 'that' and we can know that without 'how'. *Knowing that* means being able to talk accurately about a matter. *Knowing how to* means being able to achieve something through action of some kind. People who become deaf may remember their International Phonetic Alphabet and may continue to speak Standard Average European, even though they will no longer be able to check their own pronunciation. Some people may be masterful in their descriptions of sociolinguistic phenomena, but be impotent at spotting who is what.

If we accept the usefulness of this distinction between *knowing how to* and *knowing that*, and if we allow ourselves the luxury of a measure of philosophical innocence, it is probably safe to propose that, in the everyday world that we experience, *knowing how to* is often ahead of *knowing that*. Men have been able to utter and hear linguistically differentiating sounds and sequences of sounds without benefit of a knowledge of phonology, grammar, lexis, semantics or pragmatics. One reason why *knowing that* is liable to lag is that man has to devise and diffuse new technical jargons for talking about matters not previously systematically investigated, described and discussed. We have difficulties in constructing descriptions and explanations, and we can then find it even harder to persuade colleagues and the rest of the world that our taxonomic enterprise is worthwhile and valid. Within the area of the intersect of language and behaviour, one illustration of this is of ironic relevance to the Whorf–Sapir hypothesis. In a succession of studies in which victims have recognized, remembered and communicated colour hues with varying degrees of efficiency, the experimenters have happily referred to the hues utilized with the nomenclature devised by Farnsworth and Munsell. They, the experimenters, have been able to comment on the errors of their subjects only because they have access to a powerful notational system which allows millions of discrete identifications, a system whose very existence precludes the possibility of our accepting too strong a version of the hypothesis it has been utilized to test (e.g. Brown & Lenneberg 1954; Lantz & de Stefflre 1964). For colour hue, the Farnsworth–Munsell notation has come to approximate to the original everyday nonverbal *knowing how* for successful discrimination, but it has at the same time well exceeded everyday verbal facilities for identification and labelling.

With respect to language and its use, the relative weights of *knowing how to* and *knowing that* for students and participants vary greatly from one linguistic level of analysis to the next. For example, the student's ability to talk about phonology and grammar far exceeds everyday knowledge about the same topics, but at present the difference for pragmatics is probably not that great. Within sociolinguistics generally the performance *know how* of both students and participants is considerably ahead of the *knowing that*. We are much better at switching our speech appropriately in real life than we are at describing what we are doing or why.

For the present topic, assuming that SES is marked linguistically, we have the possibility of people being able to identify SES membership on the basis of speech but being unable to represent this *know how* verbally. The verbal inadequacy could stem from personal ignorance of the facts and an associated technical terminology that has been developed, but it could also represent a universal ignorance at the present point in time. Practical experts in phonology are qualitatively superior to ordinary mortals in this regard, and it would be most instructive to see how well a sample of these linguists could sort voices accurately into SES groupings. In terms of the field's development it is the capacities of the informed rather than those of the ignorant that are of most immediate interest. Unfortunately such investigations have yet to be prosecuted. The observers would of course need to be informed about SES, its categories and likely character. It is also conceivable that people react to SES related speech markers without knowing they do so.

1.3. Realities

Reality is the whole of figure 1, and to proceed to point out that the nuclear circle is objective reality is not to deny the existence and power of the layers of social reality. It does not deny that the social can become the objective. We may however note two points about the rings. It has been argued that inconsistencies between belief and action and between either and reality are an impetus to the experience of conflict and that equilibrium is restored most effectively by accommodating to reality. If that is true then we should expect there to be pressures towards the contents of the outer rings becoming increasingly determined by the core truths, where these exist. In an omniscient society the etic and emic would be coterminous and *knowing how* and *knowing that* would be balanced. These points accept the validity of a Piagetian interactionist view of development and the realism of a Popper (1972), but they are in no way inconsistent with a phenomenological approach.

A brief expansion of the rings of the rhetoric roundabout and the quixotic syndrome may show why.

'The most important vehicle of reality-maintenance is conversation.' (Berger & Luckman 1967: 172)

'One will readily see that the great part, if not all, of everyday conversation maintains subjective reality.' (*ibid.*)

'In order to maintain subjective reality effectively, the conversational apparatus must be continual and consistent.' (*ibid*. 174)

'One extreme possibility . . ., sometimes approximated in primitive societies, is the definition of *everything* as social reality . . .' (*ibid*. 120)

If Berger & Luckman are correct, groups should be able to maintain fictions about these matters, both about other groups and about their own, by holding appropriate conversations with sufficient frequency. SES itself, and the relationships between it and speech, are the subject of conversations as well as possible determinants of behaviour. What the folk myths are about SES and speech we do not know. We do not yet know what functions they serve or how they serve these. Do upper and middle SES groups talk more about these matters than do the lower SES groups? If so, does this take the form of enhancing or emphasizing the superiority of the in-group at the expense of pretenders? 'Don't you catch a trace of Liverpool in Sir Alfred, my dear? Is it his ugly /u/ sounds that "let him down" and "give him away"?' (Why do we refer to such diagnoses with phrases also used for detected criminals?) Do such conversations exist? Does the conversation serve as an impetus to exclude aspiring members of out-groups? Does the mere threat of its possible occurrence keep the pretentious in their places, lest they find themselves unable to follow norms inappropriate to their station?

This issue is a wider one than the relationship between speech and SES, but speech may be expected to play a double role in the rhetoric, both as a possible marker and as a vehicle for creating and maintaining stories. If such conversations can take place when necessary, are they based on convenient fictions or do the presumed associations have a measure of validity, and if so how great a measure? If we rely on accounts and verbal judgements in our data collection, are we the investigators capturing reality or lies and, if lies, are these really untrue or does their repeated telling change their truth value?

The methodological implications for the investigator are clear in what they proscribe. A reliance upon single techniques applied at a single level of analysis cannot yield more than hints of possibilities. Collecting accounts and observing behaviour, participant observation and experimental intervention, will need to be combined if we are to capture the realities, at least for a moment of time. Comprehensive approaches may unravel the complexities; abuse of those who do not follow one's own preferred techniques will not.

The quixotic syndrome is a special case of the rhetoric roundabout, and it is appropriate to note its possible relevance to some of the discourse developed for discussing SES and speech. We have already wondered about the status of SES. Our analysis of language may well suffer from similar distortions.

We fail to observe facts that might cause us to reflect more critically upon our beliefs. We retreat behind abstractions and generalizations rather than ask whether these can be translated into particular cases – and occasionally we use particular cases to make general statements where we needed to base our conclusions upon observed generalizations.

Within education in particular, both SES and language individually, and the presumed associations between them, have been used to create extraordinary fictions intended to explain differential academic performances of children. These fictions have then been denied through the assertion of other propositions just as strange. Much of the debate is conducted without recourse to detailed evaluations of evidence (see Williams (1970) for examples of both sides of the language deficit vs. difference debate). Academics can therefore be seen to be tilting at windmills, and they have certainly made claims far beyond, and indeed independent of, the evidence. Why does not matter. What is important is that we concentrate our attention upon what has been observed rather than upon those strings of words that sometimes are full of sound and fury, but too often signify nothing about SES and speech.

2. Inductive empiricism

Theoretically we could devise an infinite number of studies to examine an infinite number of questions pertinent to the contents of figure 1. For any given society at a given time, once we had defined SES, both in theory and operation, we could sample the natural speech of representative samples of each grouping, including variations due to other parameters such as age, sex, audience, context, etc. The implementation of comprehensive Brunswikian designs (1956) would provide the raw material for examination and judgement. The corpuses collected could be subjected to machine and expert human analysis in order to plot which characteristics of speech are shared by and discriminate among members of the various SES groupings. Conducted at *all* levels of linguistic analysis, the results could be processed to say with what measure of predictive validity and confidence SES could be inferred from particular indicators singly and in combination (cf. Scherer, this volume: ch. 5, 1.2). This would provide an etic description of the phenomena. It is a grander

endeavour in several ways than the traditional activities of dialectologists, in that it would have to extend its scope beyond pronunciation and
the listing of unique lexical items or grammatical rarities known mainly
only to specially selected informants.

Essentially it would be an encyclopaedic dialectology that took cogni-
zance of vertical as well as horizontal social stratification, at the same time
recognizing the existence of situational and other variations in speaking
and writing – it would certainly not hypostasize a unitary, idealized
system of dialects. It is also certainly possible that the similarities
observed would oblige us to ask whether 'dialect' was not too strong a
word for referring to some of the differences found. This dialectology
would become more urban than its traditional ancestor in its domain of
operation, more taxonomic and less historical in its perspectives. It would
do for SES what Labov, Fasold, Wolfram and others have begun to try to
do for some components of Black English Vernacular (see, for example,
chapters in De Stefano 1973). The collection of at least subsets of this data
base is a prerequisite for answering either etic or emic questions about the
possible and actual relationships between speech markers and SES.

Questions about the rhetoric roundabout aspect of the problem do not
require the accumulation of such raw material. They require systematic
sampling of the *accounts* of the members of socially significant subgroups
of the society about the phenomena in question. To find out whether
respondents can identify SES from extracts of speech and writing
requires them to pass appropriate judgements when presented with
extracts; discriminations in their behaviour towards others based on
consciously or unconsciously held associations between speech and SES
are to be *observed* and *tested experimentally*. These studies should yield
further information about the emics. To date we are ill-informed about
most of these perspectives, and the lack of relevant empirical work
obliges this account to be more a review of what needs to be done than
one of what has been. The relationships between accounts people give
and the behaviour they exhibit will be more readily examined when we
have more data to consider.

3. Etics of SES markers: evidence

3.1. Phonology

Arising from dialectological work in the USA, Levine & Crockett (1967)
pointed to SES differences in the use of a small number of phonological

features in a rural township. Criticism can be made of the index of SES used, the sampling of respondents and other features of the design, and in the circumstances it might be hazardous to generalize from the results beyond the Piedmont community where the data were collected. Subsequently, Labov (1966) initiated a grander series of studies that could have been developed into a comprehensive description of the similarities and differences between the pronunciation of the various SES groups in New York City. However, only five of the many possible sounds of English were studied, and certain weaknesses of method leave some doubts in the mind about some of the conclusions drawn: a sceptical psychologist would have felt obliged to break up the recordings of speech in such a way that the judgements about particular sounds could not be influenced by previous judgements of sounds made by the same person, one of the several weaknesses pointed out by Giles (1973). Not only would precautions have had to be taken to ensure that measurements were independent of each other, but the identity of the speakers would also have to have been unknown to the scorer. In a work of this stature it would have been wise to include estimates of the reliability of scoring across judges as well as through time. Levine & Crockett (1967) did calculate interjudge reliabilities, but it is difficult to interpret their results. Across time their main scorer agreed with herself on 98 per cent of her scoring of post vocalic /r/s. Agreement with the second judge was less impressive. While it reached 88 per cent across twelve of the seventeen words for the twenty-eight respondents selected, for the other five words it dropped to 43 per cent; in 97 per cent of cases the second scorer omitted to register an instance when the first did. This does begin to answer the question of what expert scorers can achieve. Presumably Labov treated the issue as an unimportant one, which it may well be. We simply lack the relevant data processing to confirm or refute this.

In addition, the histograms of the variation by SES and situation found by Labov are shown only as gross percentages; there are no indications of variance. Estimates of variance are as critical to judgements of differences between groups as are differences between means, so that strictly speaking we are taking unnecessary and unknown risks if we accept that the trends depicted are more than chance variations. Given the strength of the particular displays, this is unlikely to be the case. The uncertainty and ambiguity could still be resolved by the publication of the appropriate statistical analyses. Very similar criticism must be applied to Trudgill's (1974) replication of Labov's study of New York City in Norwich, England; a persuasive picture, but suffering from the same crucial methodological weaknesses. While the discussion here will treat the results of both authors as reliable and valid, it must be recognized that this could prove to be an invalid act of faith.

Both Labov and Trudgill also show how situation interacts with SES to shift the proportions of phonological realizations of particular kinds. Both use a dimension for situation that runs from casual to formal and then show that low SES respondents are prone to increase the proportion of high SES variants as the situation becomes more formal. For some features this gradient is shallow, for others it is steep. For some the differentiation is greatest in the formal situations, for others in the casual. Some intermediate SES groups reveal *hypercorrection*, becoming more like the high SES than the high SES are themselves. At present we have no idea why these varieties of relationship exist. Both authors argue for a major boundary between manual and nonmanual SES groups. Trudgill's data reveal particularly impressive discriminations in this respect.

More detailed examinations by ethnic origin (Labov) and age and sex (Trudgill) are used to demonstrate that SES is not the only source of variation relevant to particular phonological realizations. Trudgill also uses his data to argue for changes in the system being initiated by different SES groups, but since all the data were collected at a single point in time, the hypotheses stand in need of further evidence if they are to become more than speculations. This evidence could be collected simply by repeating relevant sections of the study at a subsequent time.

Even with the few phonological features examined, the maps become delicately differentiated for New York City and Norwich. Glasgow yields an apparently comparable fineness of discrimination (Macaulay & Trevelyan 1973). Perhaps it is indeed true that *all* socially significant attributes are marked phonologically. Perhaps the etic markers waiting to be discovered will provide comprehensive possibilities of identification of SES. To know which of the particular features are actually used to identify and discriminate, it is necessary to study the judgements and behaviour of the members of the perceiving communities. (Oddly, no one has seriously pursued an analysis of the extent to which the phonological features of low SES groups in New York City, Norwich and Glasgow are alike in ways that distinguish them from those of the high SES groups in all three societies. A specification of any such similarities and a defensible explanation for their character would be a significant advance in knowledge.)

Neither Labov nor Trudgill proceeded to find out if professional phoneticians were able and willing to identify SES as such from speech, but again it would be a simple step to use their tape-recordings for this purpose.

3.2. Other levels of linguistic analysis

Many studies examining other SES differences in speech or writing have generated simple contrastive descriptions. Among these, Templin's (1957) descriptions of SES differences in children covered a wide variety of phonological, grammatical and lexical features. Fries' (1940) analysis of letters by SES of writer pointed to many potentially differentiating features, most simply summarized by referring to low SES writings as including many grammatical forms different from Standard American English forms and a higher incidence of certain lexical items, e.g. *get, do, would, can, awful, mighty, pretty, and, but,* . . . and the like. McCarthy (1930) showed that middle SES children asked more questions than low SES children. Numerous investigations could be mentioned that have reported differences: some have simply noted them; others have been concerned with the educational backwardness of low SES children. References to such studies can be found in Hess (1970: 516–27) and Zigler & Child (1969). None of them asked whether the indices measured could be used to identify SES membership.

The data from these earlier studies are just as relevant to questions about the relationship between language management and SES as the more recent work arising either in sympathy with or in antipathy to the theoretical suggestions of Bernstein (1971/1973), who has made many assertions about the relationships between language and SES; his collected papers reveal the full variety of these. He has offered various linguistic and sociolinguistic definitions of the 'restricted code' to which the lowest SES group are alleged to be confined. Unfortunately these have been contrastive only in the weakest sense. We are told how this code contrasts with the 'elaborated code' in terms of exhibiting more or fewer of certain linguistic features, but this is not sufficient for any form of positive identification; and early encouraging lists of such features (Bernstein 1961: 169) have more recently been condemned: 'I certainly would not wish to defend the indices created in those two lists' (Bernstein 1973: 264). Contrasts of any kind would not suffice. To know that the wavelength of green light is longer than that of red light does not tell us sufficient about either for us to be able to recognize either when we see them. Features that would enable us to identify speech as generated by a restricted code, even within specified contexts, have not been offered, in spite of the claim once made by Bernstein that 'Operationally it is more accurate to use the linguistic forms to distinguish the groups [of people] rather than a class affiliation' (1961: 168). (This would certainly imply possible marking of SES by others.) It has never been made clear just what proportion of the lower working class are supposed to be confined to the restricted code, nor do we ever find out what the fate is of such other important SES groupings in the culture as the skilled working class and the upper class. We may however ignore the weaknesses of Bernstein's theory, which are not immediately germane to the present concerns (see Dittmar 1976; Edwards 1976; Oevermann 1970; Robinson 1978; Rosen 1972; Stubbs 1976, for detailed evaluations), and we can still examine the evidence collected that may be relevant: the empirical data stand in their own right. We can bypass the theory itself and do not even need to define the codes. It is sufficient to note that investigators testing the thesis examined SES differences. Whether the SES differences demonstrated could be said to *mark* the SES of their producers is testable but untested, at least within that research tradition. (Fortunately other researchers have pursued that question.) To date, only one person has examined whether or not transcripts of corpuses of different origins can be sorted into SES categories with more than chance accuracy either by experts or by the man in the street. Callary (1974) used written versions of the Putnam & O'Hern (1955) materials (see below), eliminating deviant grammatical forms, and using correct spelling throughout. The rank order of the mean placements by seventy-six White undergraduates of the transcripts into high and low status categories produced rank order correlations (rho) with the true SES order of greater than 0.7 for both male and female judges. This represents an impressive measure of accuracy for amateurs operating with reduced scripts. Such a result certainly renders premature any accusation that such judgements are to be interpreted as revealing more about the psychology of the judge than about the social identity of the speaker. To be fair to Bernstein, it should be pointed out that he has never been concerned with speech as a marker of SES.

Empirical evidence collected within the Bernstein framework has not invariably yielded SES differences, and some of those that have been claimed to exist could be explained in terms of factors other than those connected directly with language and its use.

A number of the investigations which have failed to find SES differences have suffered from errors of method in sampling, scoring, and other aspects of design, that vitiate the validity of the conclusions drawn. Shriner & Miner (1968) found no differences in the ability of young children to apply certain morphological rules to nonsense syllables; but although their two social-class groups were matched on age and Peabody Picture Vocabulary Test scores, this was on mean scores only. The age range was two and a quarter years, and since age was a relevant source of variance, a matched-pairs design, at least, would have been necessary to provide a sensible test. La Civita, Kean & Yamamoto (1966) also reported no SES differences in the use of morphological and syntactic cues to identify parts of speech; but since their analysis was in fact by school, and the middle SES schools had only 58 per cent middle SES pupils and the low SES school only 76 per cent low SES pupils, the conclusion is hardly warranted. Both studies have been reported (e.g. Cazden 1970) as though they provide evidence relevant to the issues of the relationship between language and social class. Edwards (1979) has more recently made exactly the same error, defining 'disadvantaged' by characteristics of the school, and then referring to both the children and their speech as 'disadvantaged'. Half of his 'nondisadvantaged' children were not middle SES and a quarter of his low SES were not children of unskilled or semiskilled workers.

Cook-Gumperz (1973) correlated indices of restricted code with those of elaborated code in the speech of mothers and found significant *positive* correlations between the two. Since all her linguistic indices correlated positively with the total amount of speech with six of the fourteen above 0.5, she needed to remove the influence of this common factor before proceeding further with her descriptions of SES differences.

Small speech samples, small number of subjects, and other defects mar some studies reporting no differences. It is noteworthy that none of the investigations which yielded results of no difference checked the reliability or validity of their data either directly with statistical calculations or indirectly by including some known correlate of SES and demonstrating that its association held up in their investigation. There are many other reasons why *false negatives* may be obtained, and each investigation has to be scrutinized for its potential inadequacies. Such criticisms cannot, however, be made of all studies which have failed to find differences. As a single example we might quote Bruck & Tucker's (1974) demonstration of the disappearance of certain SES differences in grammatical mistakes with increasing age among kindergarten children; the pretest results showing differences enhanced the credibility of the posttest data which revealed that certain of these had disappeared.

Of those SES differences found which may be *false positives* in terms of the interpretations offered by their authors, the most common are probably those where middle and low SES participants have interpreted the task set differently. In these situations it may be more likely that the behaviour of the middle SES participants meshes with normative expectations of the experimenter. Hawkins (1969) reported a higher incidence of exophoric reference in the narrative speech of low SES children, that is, reference whose nature needs extratextual information to render the referent unambiguous. What is often omitted in secondary accounts of this investigation is that both experimenter and child could see the pictures. With no record of the nonverbal behaviour exhibited we have no way of ascertaining whether or not the exophoric references were validated by pointing, and we must pronounce the experimental findings as being uninterpretable, especially since Francis (1974) failed to find SES differences with comparable children in what she assumed to be a comparable situation where pointing was not possible. Did the middle SES children of Hawkins interpret the task as one where pointing would be inappropriate, even if perfectly sensible? Williams & Naremore (1969) claimed that substantial SES differences revealed in first responses to 'naming' questions disappeared after probing for 'elaborations'. In one of their tasks, low SES children were more likely to treat 'Did you watch TV last night?' at its face value, and answer 'Yes!' whereas middle SES children answered *in extenso* about the programmes seen without further encouragement. These conventions, especially those associated with *classroqmese*, may well be better known to more middle than lower SES children. Again however, these interpretive aspects have yet to be investigated.

Even the original study of Schatzman & Strauss (1955), in which interviewees gave accounts of a tornado, could be as readily explained by appeals to different perceptions of the task by the respondents: the authors reported that, relative to middle SES respondents, low SES interviewees were more likely to use one perspective only (their own), to ignore the fact that the listener had not been present and to give concrete and particular information (rather than more abstracted and generalized), and that they were more prone to follow a relatively incohesive linear structure. Did the low SES respondents think that the interviewer was demanding their personal account rather than a general one; that was after all what they are reported as having been asked for? Did they try to re-create their experience for the interviewer by making him feel frightened, confused and disorganized, and is that why their accounts were as they were? This may be unlikely, but it is feasible. While it is interesting and important if members of different SES groups interpret tasks differently and if their speech is consequently different, this does not inform us about what they would say or write when their interpretations were the same.

Even when their interpretations are basically the same, knowledge of the standards of good performance may not be equivalent. Many investigators have required students to write essays (e.g. Lawton 1968; Poole 1976; Rushton & Young 1975). While the writers were not instructed to write 'bad' or 'good' essays, custom dictates that aspiration should normally be towards the second. Do students differ in their beliefs about the nature of a good essay? Again it may be low SES students who have a lesser idea of the rules of the game. My own impression is that English teaching is stronger on assigning marks than it is on teaching children how to achieve better writing. For example, teachers do not write good and bad essays and show children how one can be transformed to the other; there is little exemplification with explanation. In so far as 'good' includes a fair measure of grammatical and lexical elaboration (everyday meaning) and diversity, and low SES are less aware of these norms or how to achieve them in a manner that appears to be sincere and coherent, they will tend to make lower scores on many of the linguistic measures normally included in SES comparisons. When, however, low SES students are writing on technical subjects with which they are familiar (Rushton & Young 1975), the normally found SES differences can be reversed.

My personal suspicion is that these two factors may account for much of the variance in a number of the empirical investigations conducted. Labov mentions or implies the operation of two further influences: unwillingness to conform to norms and intimidation by interviewers. While there is no systematic demonstration of the former at work, the principle is unexceptionable. In schools, for example, one might expect low SES older secondary boys who have been subjected to a history of failure and disrespect to be particularly likely to be uncooperative, especially in everyday school settings. Certainly I have seen experimenters whose behaviour should have reduced cooperativeness of pupils. Inadequately explained procedures can be foisted upon children in a nervously authoritarian manner. For myself, I have been surprised by the willingness of low SES pupils to be cooperative with visiting strangers and do not believe that their rebelliousness has affected most of the studies I have seen or conducted, but that is an unsupported opinion only. Clearly, adolescent Black English Vernacular speakers in the USA may feel strongly about using Standard American English in standard school exercises; the extent to which the use of a particular dialect or language is an issue of identity must be relevant in this context (see Giles, this volume: ch. 7, 1; Brown & Levinson: ch. 8, 2).

Labov (1969) illustrates how a large White interviewer enjoining a solitary Black child to 'Tell me about this picture' may intimidate him into silence and mumbling, whereas a friendly Black interviewer sitting on the floor with two Black children devouring coke and crisps may be able to elicit a wealth of speech. Again, we have no way of retrospectively estimating the extent to which this kind of influence has affected the results published.

Given this array of difficulties and reservations associated with the empirical work in this field, it is tempting to retreat into agnosticism, but that may not be necessary. If we survey the range of studies conducted (see the ten volumes in the series 'Primary Socialization, Language and Education' edited by Bernstein and published by Routledge; the review of the substantial Australian contribution by Robinson 1978; the bibliographies in Bruck & Tucker 1974; Dittmar 1976; Heider 1971; Williams 1970), we may be prepared to conclude that SES differences in language use on a substantial number of grammatical, lexical, semantic and pragmatic indices can be believed to exist. Qualifications are necessary: these have been demonstrated mostly in contexts which required language to be used mainly in its representational function, and the differences have been most obvious when respondents have been under pressure to use language at the limits of their skills. Even then the differences are not that great, and are confounded by developmental lags, so that particular differences at one age can have disappeared at a later point in time (see Bruck & Tucker 1974). It is somewhat hazardous to specify what these differences are, partly because they are generally small in size and have to be exposed by counting and the application of analytical statistics (Robinson 1978) and partly because they may well be context specific (Adlam 1977).

Nevertheless, if one were to risk a summary generalization about SES differences in speech and writing it might take the following form: given that the contextual demands are explicit, interpreted similarly and accepted by all participants, and given also that these demands stretch the speakers' skill with the representational function of language, then, relative to higher SES groups, members of low SES groupings will use more complex syntax less often (e.g. deeper levels of subordination, complicated nominal, verbal and adjunctive structures) and will exhibit a lesser diversity of lexis in nouns, verbs, adjectives and adverbs – provided the task demands such diversity. It would be even more hazardous to offer any general suggestions about semantics, but if the risk is to be taken, then it would have to be said that low SES are less likely than middle SES to raise the generality and abstractness of accounts above what commonsense would treat as the concrete and specific. A Piagetian might be tempted to express the difference in terms of less formal operational and more concrete operational and intuitive thinking being manifest in low SES speech and writing, within the representational function; it is still an open question whether or not he would be correct. Pragmatically, in the light of the evidence of Bruck & Tucker (1974), Heider (1971), Rackstraw & Robinson (1967), and Schatzman & Strauss (1955), we would have to argue that low SES children and adults are less effective communicators of referential information: as yet we do not know whether this results from an inability to analyse the listener's requirements, from a failure to see the need to do so in particular situations, or from a weakness in solving and maintaining the particular psychological or linguistic requirements of the problem presented. These discriminanda certainly have etic possibilities, but their emic role is as yet unknown, and it will be argued below that they are in fact unlikely to be exploited in everyday encounters.

There are some other simpler issues yet to be investigated that may be more likely to have emic significance. Do certain lexical items have typically different meanings in different SES groups and do different objects have typically different lexical items to refer to them, e.g. lavatories, meals? Ross's (1954) sketch of U and non-U English was directed to the borders between the middle and the upper classes, but the same questions could be posed in a systematic fashion across the whole SES spectrum. Who eats lunch, dinner, tea and supper when? Who swears how? Who uses which evaluative terms, especially those splendid and super superlatives? Who peppers speech with minimizers and mitigators (Robinson & Rackstraw, 1972)? What is surprising is that this elementary ground work has not been done.

Neither have there been any systematic comparative studies of the grammar of SES differences. The picture emerging of the differences in grammatical rules between Black English Vernacular and Standard American English (Fasold & Wolfram 1973; also Labov & Cohen 1973) is one of something less than fifty rules discriminating between the two, and these are mainly associated with verbs. British dialectologists have preferred not to do this kind of work, concentrating rather upon rural variations of pronunciation and lexis among pensioner males (Orton &

Dieth 1962). In fact the respondents in these surveys were probably almost entirely low SES, and the maps could be seen in terms of geographical variations within low SES. For example, Trudgill (1974) argued that in Norwich English the third-person singular nonpast tense, noncontinuous aspects of verbs (*he loves*, *it goes*) is identical to the first and second person (*he love*, *it go*), except in the case of *to be*. He notes that although this was common, it was not universally present, was not used by all speakers, and its incidence varied from verb to verb. One suspects however that such features could be entirely absent from upper or middle SES speech, except as occasional mistakes. That being so, the occurrence of such features would be sufficient to mark low SES status, but they would not necessarily be present in all samples of such speech. The presence marks, the absence does not. Presumably a list could be drawn up of stigmatized morphological and syntactical features likely to discriminate between low SES and middle and upper SES speech. Its validity could then be tested.

4. Emics of SES markers: evidence

The investigations set up to examine who can and does spot SES from speech are rare, and how their reactions are affected by their diagnoses are rarer. We have a substantial body of studies, mainly very recent, that have examined the kinds of inferences people draw about dispositions and traits from accents and dialects (see Giles & Powesland 1975), but these are not specifically linked to SES and have yet to be shown to be related to real-life activities, with some exceptions. Investigations by Giles have asked respondents for their opinions about the prestige associated with accents, but they have not required subjects to comment upon the SES of users nor have they examined whether the inferences drawn were mediated by any identification of the probable SES of the speakers. Bourhis & Giles (1978) have shown that requests for cooperation from bilingual members of a Welsh audience are less likely to be met if voiced in English RP than if uttered in Welsh, but such ideas have not been extended to SES variables.

We have already seen that Labov's study is an improvement on the methodological weaknesses of earlier dialectologists (e.g. Kurath & McDavid 1961; Levine & Crockett 1967), but we are a long way still from having a comprehensive portrait of covariations of SES with phonology in any society. Part of Labov's early work (1966: ch. 11) also marks the first attempt to see whether listeners were prepared to make judgements about the suitability for occupations of people whose voices exhibited the phonological variations linked to SES. They were so willing and were generally agreed in their assessments, albeit somewhat weakly. SES, sex, and ethnic identity each affected judgements made, as did the relationship between the sound being judged and the speaker's group's value for that sound. Whether the respondents were revealing capacities and preferences that affected their daily behaviour we have still to learn. SES was not specifically mentioned.

In their large Detroit survey Shuy, Baratz & Wolfram (1969) included SES as well as ethnicity and other variables in their identification studies, and, using selected half-minute speech samples, found considerable accuracy of judgement, regardless of the age, sex, ethnicity and SES of listeners, within the range sampled. Middle SES judges were more accurate than low SES, and the lower the SES of the speaker the more accurate the identification regardless of the SES of the listener. It was suggested that the presence of specific stigmatized grammatical and phonological features mediated these judgements.

Earlier work in the United States by Putnam & O'Hern (1955) had described (evaluated) lower SES Negro speech as characterized by weakened articulation of consonants, aberrant vowel and diphthong allophones, and unsophisticated (!) vocabulary and sentence structure. Judges were agreed about the SES ranking of twelve speakers ranging from low to high SES, and their assessment correlated highly (0.80) with an objective index of SES. Harms (1961) showed that comparable judgements were made by members of different SES groups, even when they were students in the Mid-West with little experience of Negroes (Harms 1963). Interviews with the students yielded no evidence that they identified the speakers as Negroes. In this work rankings were both reliable and valid. Moe (1972) found that minimal phonological differences were sufficient for judgements of some validity to be achieved. As mentioned earlier, much of the work in the United Kingdom focusing upon inferences from accents (see Giles & Powesland 1975 for a summary) is related to SES in so far as many of the geographically distinguishable accents are likely to be spoken in broader form mainly by low SES speakers. Since the measure of this association has not been actually demonstrated however, the work cannot be incorporated here at this time. Nevertheless, there seems to be little doubt that brief extracts of speech suffice for the assignment of SES and that these judgements are generally valid, at least in the United States.

Shuy (1970) also examined employers' reactions to speech. These men claimed that speech was largely irrelevant to their decisions in interviews, but located the speech of Negro professionals in the same category as the speech of Negro skilled manual workers. Williams (1976) reports an unpublished study by Finley purporting to show that employers relied on the presence, type and frequency of nonstandard features but not on structural complexity in assessing employability. Macaulay & Trevelyan (1973) are reported by Trudgill (1975) as having found that a sample of Glaswegian personnel selectors said they were indifferent to accent. To say this is misleading on the data presented. Twenty-eight assorted personnel selectors were asked eight questions of which one was 'To what extent are you interested in accent [when interviewing for a job]?' The analysis comprises a list of some examples of replies, with the only unsupported quantification being 'Most of the informants rejected the notion that accent was ever an important factor' (Macaulay & Trevelyan: 162). No conclusion could be drawn from the data as they are presented.

Fielding & Evered (1979) analysed judgements made of various features of a ten-minute doctor–patient diagnostic interview by preclinical medical students. The patient had been suffering from chest pains; he also revealed that he was anxious and tense, had both marital and drink problems and was experiencing other difficulties. From the associated literature, the authors derived an expectation that doctors lean towards psychosomatic diagnosis if they identify the patient as middle class and physical if working class. The version of the tape heard by one batch of students presented the speaker in an RP accent guise, the other in a rural regional one (RR). While tests revealed that the RP voice was more likely to be seen as belonging to someone of higher status ($p < 0.001$), only one of the other 16 scales was reported as discriminating between the voices: the RP voice being associated with a bias towards psychosomatic diagnosis ($t = 1.89$, $df = 41$, $p < 0.05$, one-tailed). This is interpreted as supporting the main hypothesis, and a subsequent factor analysis of all the ratings was used to mount and discuss a presumed association between high SES and 'emotionality'. The possible explanations offered are interesting in that they attempt to tease out some of the thinking processes involved in judgements, but the results seem to be too weak to sustain any of these.

Since the data presented do not include either mean scores for the ratings of the two voices or the correlation matrix on which the factor analysis is based, we cannot examine evidence necessary to evaluate the interpretations offered. How can such apparently slender differences be used to suggest that real participating doctors (as contrasted with the observing medical students) would be more likely to assign a psychosomatic origin to the symptoms of an RP speaker? Would follow-up behaviour have been different in the cases? While it is true that the first factor looks like SES, this may well be a direct consequence of the particular constellation of items included in the questionnaire. It is noteworthy that the following speech variables loaded at higher than 0.40 on this factor: sophisticated vocabulary, good grammar, fluency, incidence of complex elaborated sentences, effective use of language and use of complete sentences. Since only the accent in fact discriminated between the tapes, these loadings are superficially surprising, but without knowing the actual correlations with perceived SES we cannot proceed further. Factor 4 is identified as 'emotionality' and this is also surprising. The highest loading is on 'unusual–usual'; other loadings above 0.40 are on disorderly, weak, foolish, fast, excitable (unsuccessful). However, since the loading with SES is only −0.04 and with poor educational background +0.16, there are no grounds given for tying 'emotionality' to SES. It appears to be the case of the classic error of assuming a correlation between B and C when both are correlated with A. Nevertheless, this study presents the essence of a methodology that needs to be employed if we are to make headway in our study of linguistic markers of SES.

Educational settings provide the context of most of the remaining relevant work. Lambert once suggested that the performance of low SES children in school might be explained in large measure in terms of teachers' perceptions and differential treatment, with the speech of children serving as a marker for perception. Prosodic features of rate, pitch and range of intonation were included in the studies of Frender, Brown & Lambert (1970), Seligman, Tucker & Lambert (1972) and Frender & Lambert (1972). Slow speech at a low pitch with flat intonation in young school children was judged by teachers to be predictive of school failure. The second study showed that within the range of variation sampled, and for a small sample of trainee teachers (N = 19), voice characteristics were assigned more predictive validity of educational success than were compositions and drawings or photographs. The link with SES was established by showing that academically successful low SES pupils *in fact* differed in their speech from their unsuccessful peers in using a higher pitch, less volume and more appropriate intonation. This work is as close as we can come to a triangular linkage of speech, estimated SES and judged or achieved attributes. We do not as yet know about the sequence and structure of the thinking of the teachers, although there is evidence of differentiated treatment of pupils.

Brophy & Good (1974) have reviewed the evidence that teachers do distribute their time and treatment unevenly across children, have shown that this distribution is relevant to learning by the children, and have demonstrated that its nature varies with the values of the teachers. Most studies have shown that estimated ability was a significant determinant of the rationing and that in most, but not in all cases, more time was spent with those judged to be more able. We have already seen that the Canadian work finds teachers associating ability and SES, and relating both to prosodic features of speech.

We are not that well-informed as to the nature of teachers' thinking about children, and what we do know may only be an example of the rhetoric roundabout (Hargreaves 1977). The extent to which estimated or observed SES of pupils enters into teachers' decisions about pupils remains unknown, but there is now sufficient evidence that the performance of low SES pupils is underestimated (see Brophy & Good (1974) for a bibliography) to imply that it is probably an important influence.

We cannot expect all teachers to be alike in their thinking and behaviour about SES and pupils' behaviour. It must be noted that Seligman *et al.* (1972) used trainee teachers in their original demonstration that inferences could be made about pupils from certain speech characteristics. Eltis (1978) extended this work in Australia. He found that similar links existed between predicted success and personal characteristics and accent of speech. (According to Mitchell & Delbridge (1965) Australian pronunciation is not importantly differentiated by region, and most linguists argue for three varieties of accent: cultivated, general, broad.) However, the accent was less important for experienced than for trainee teachers. Experienced teachers placed greater reliance on written products, i.e. form and content, rather than voice. Nevertheless, all teachers and trainees, however partitioned in terms of sex, subject and type of school attended, were able to agree very closely to which streams the owners of a further twelve voices should be assigned. While their judgements were positively associated with known intelligence test scores, the teachers significantly exaggerated the true correlation. What this shows is that, in the absence of other information, teachers can invoke inference systems for utilizing voice as a basis for judgement; it does not yet show either that they normally do so or that perceived SES is a mediating concept. Neither does the contribution of Edwards (1979) which is methodologically too weak for substantive conclusions to be drawn. Not only was the 'disadvantaged' state of the children defined by school independently of home background (see above), but only fourteen second-year trainee teachers were used as judges, and the statistical analyses report main effects without first eliminating the effects of significant two-way and three-way interactions. It seems to be assumed in the paper that the judgements made were 'stereotypic', but there was no check run on the validity of the judgements to see whether this was indeed so.

Williams (1976) has recently collated a number of research papers by himself and his colleagues concerned with teachers' judgements of pupils' speech; the work is easier read than summarized, partly because the combination of factor analysis, regression and discriminant analysis applied to multifactorial designs generates a complexity that defies simple generalizations. It is clear in the data that teachers assessed SES from speech variables and that it is possible to list discriminating features at various levels of linguistic analysis that they use to this purpose. Sounding low SES was associated with the use of features heard as symptomatic of a lack of confidence and eagerness, but even more so with the presence of ethnicity and nonstandardness. Salient predictors were the incidence of silent pausing, the articulation of particular phonemes and certain departures from standard grammar, for example in main verb construction and pronominal apposition.

These broad statements can be given much more detailed linguistic underpinning. The studies reveal that judgements about speech and SES are compounded and confounded with judgements of ethnicity, and that these complex associations vary as a function of the ethnicity of the judge. For example, Black teachers separated their assessments of ethnicity and SES more than White teachers did. Teachers could be classified into types that relied on different speech variables to make their judgements of SES and into types that emphasized different SES × ethnicity × speech associations in their judgements.

It could be that the statistical treatment of these data has generated phenomenologically unreal complications of the contents and processes of judgement; it could also be the case, however, that in the real world where people possess other attributes in addition to SES, the picture is genuinely more complicated than the earlier Labov analyses might be assumed to suggest.

Sometimes it is assumed that those people who are prepared to assess SES on minute extracts of speech are using 'stereotypes' of doubtful validity. On the evidence presented here this is not so: among the samples studied, judgements of identity made have been generally both reliable and valid. Whether or not the further or direct inferences to other characteristics of the speaker are reliable and valid is a separate matter and should not be confused with the initial identification. Respondents can and do know how to recognize SES from speech.

Outside the educational context, we have mentioned that Labov (1966) showed that people who heard speech with different proportions of certain phonological realizations were prepared to sort the owners of various voices as being differentially suitable for a variety of occupations. But would they have made similar judgements in the presence of other information? How important would the variations have been to real personnel selectors, and under what conditions would SES have been a mediating variable?

Unfortunately, more substantial work of this kind, incorporating explicit reference to SES, is a necessary step to take before the examination of who in fact validly uses which markers to what ends. With a data base of representative speech samples, one could find out how variability in the sociological and psychological characteristics of judges related to the probability of their thinking of speech in terms of SES, the reliability and validity of their identifications, and the kinds of systematic bias in errors made. Eventually we would need to complement natural observations and survey work with experimental studies that mixed up the sources of information in ways that would enable us to determine the manner or operation and strength of the components of influence. Nonverbal aspects of behaviour would need to be included to find out how speech data were integrated into the more general judgemental process, perhaps including such techniques as those introduced by Frender *et al*. (1970) and Seligman *et al*. (1972) in Canada, and those used in studies of mainly nonverbal communication in the UK and USA (Argyle 1975; Mehrabian 1972). As yet these investigations have not been concerned with judgements of social identity *per se*, either as a mediating or as a dependent variable, and they have not given judges a free response array that would have allowed them to make such judgements had they wished.

The perspective so far adopted on these empirical activities reflects the bias of a realist and an objectivist. This is entirely valid and sensible, but is only partial. The phenomenology referred to earlier must not be omitted, and neither must the rhetoric, which may be dissociated from the nonverbal behaviour in important ways. We must be equally interested in what people believe about speech and SES, why they hold these beliefs, and what the consequences are for their actions and reactions. We must attend also to what people say they believe about the relationship between speech and SES, and how and why they talk as they do (if they do) about the subject. The answers to the 'why' questions posed about these issues will not be easy to construct and test. While it is trite to state that people behave in the light of their beliefs rather than of reality, reality sets limits to which beliefs can be sustained, notwithstanding the final quotation above taken from Berger & Luckman (1967). In a progressing society the phenomenological should move towards becoming a construction of reality.

The results of these activities will have to be integrated into appropriate theoretical accounts of the structure of beliefs and attitudes and how these relate to behaviour, as well as into theories of intergroup conflict (Tajfel 1978) and what develops out of attribution theory and its associates.

Traditionally in the field of beliefs and attitudes more attention has been devoted to inferences from race and nationality to traits and behaviour rather than from SES to other characteristics. Once into this second stage of studying inferences from SES to values, motives, traits or whatever (if such a stage exists), most of the questions will become psychological and will generally cease to be sociolinguistic. Those that will remain relevant to sociolinguistics are those that relate to verbal behaviour *per se*, as for example the questions that might be posed about convergence or contrast of speech styles (see Giles & Powesland 1975). Before we ask about the thinking processes linking speech, SES and other behaviour, it may be useful to suggest which of the many speech variables discriminating among SES groups are likely to be important as emic markers in addition to being etic possibilities.

5. Emics of SES markers: hypotheses

We can hypothesize that if features of speech are to serve as discriminating markers for interpersonal behaviour, then their efficiency will be greater the *earlier* in any interaction the signs become evident, the more *salient* these signs are, and the more *invariant* their occurrence is across a range of contexts. If perceived SES is an important determinant of the likelihood and quality of interactions among members of a society, it had best be marked obviously at the outset of most encounters. Five features of speech immediately commend themselves as candidates for such a role: pronunciation, prosody, endemic grammar, greetings and lexical preferences. We have already seen how even a small number of phonological variations discriminate between SES groups in the USA and the UK. Prosodic features of intonation and pitch have figured in a school context. We have pointed to the probability of certain very basic and therefore common syntactic structures and morphological features acting in similar fashion. Since one cannot begin to speak without pronunciation, prosody, or grammar, preferred realizations of these are manifested immediately an encounter begins. The same is true of greetings. There seem to be no data specifying SES variation in these within or across situations, if such exists. Some personally but casually collected Australian data certainly pointed to SES differences in both form and manner of sufficient magnitude and generality for greetings to be potential markers of SES. These four, along with the use of conjunctions of forms and meanings in particular words and phrases (Ross 1954), would appear to be much more useful candidates for marking SES than the Loban Index of Subordination or the mean length of the preverb stem. The unconscious or conscious reckoning of the values of these latter variables requires a workload of frightening complexity that may be as unnecessary as it would be difficult and time-consuming to calculate. That valid judgements of SES can be made after hearing only short extracts of speech points to the lack of any necessity to make counts of features across extended corpuses. If that line of argument is followed through, the data generated in response to Bernstein's thesis may have a relevance for linguistics, psychology and sociology, but not to judgements of SES in initial encounters. Those differentiating characteristics may have significance for the quality of cross-SES and within-SES interactions in the long term, but they are unlikely to be the basis of initial impressions and consequential decisions. The same will be true of the earlier catalogues of discriminanda at these levels of linguistic analysis, except where they can be categorized as deviant from standard norms in some readily perceptible way.

6. Processes of inference

We have asked whether etic and emic markers of SES are carried by speech and writing, and have concluded that on the evidence available for the samples studied, they are. The lists of such features that could be presented are woefully incomplete, but even so the respondents involved have succeeded in making accurate judgements. While the development of further systematic knowledge about such markers is one priority and, given the frame of reference of the title of the chapter, could be viewed as *the* priority, social psychologists must also be interested in how such identifications embed themselves in behaviour and whether they embrace all discriminatory behaviour based on a linkage of speech and SES (cf. Scherer, this volume: ch. 5, 5.3; Brown & Levinson, ch. 8, 3.3).

We can conceive of several sequences of discriminating processes:

(1) Analysis of features of speech → Conscious identification of SES → Assignment of traits, etc.

(2) Analysis of features of speech → Unconscious discrimination of SES → Assignment of traits, etc.

(3) Analysis of features of speech → Assignment of traits, etc.

These are only the simplest possibilities, and all models can be confounded by filtering them through the rings of figure 1. The first sequence is clearly consistent with the evidence cited. It has been objected (Ryan & Carranza 1975) that the second stage of inference may be moderated by considerations of context of situation, and there is no reason to dispute that suggestion. Ryan, Carranza and Moffie (cited in Giles & Powesland 1975) also reported that small increments in accentedness of speech were associated monotonically with less favourable impressions of the speaker, and this is interpreted to be inconsistent with sequence (1). Why remains unclear. Is their belief that the identification implies the use of a crude and rigid stereotype? The identification could involve a stereotype, but it might involve tentative and complex categorization. Identification does not entail the use of categories with rigid borders. Some Welshmen are more Welsh than others. Similarly there are doubtless some families which are low SES *par excellence*, others which are typical and yet others which are marginal (Rosch 1973). To posit an intermediate stage of marking social identity should not be taken to mean that the respondent makes a single simple unequivocal classificatory act, although the data do suggest this can be achieved with accuracy and ease. Edwards (1979) would add that it can be made with confidence as well. Whether similar results would be found in other societies with other languages and with all varieties of respondents remains to be discovered.

Whether or not an allocation to an SES category acts as an intermediate stage in an inference process may be contingent upon both the characteristics of the judge and the identity assigned. Closed-minded judges may be more inclined to assign people to clear categories and make strong inferences than are open-minded judges. Whereas Eltis (1978) found no differences in assessments of accents attributable to this variable, Giles (1971) had earlier shown that small extreme groups differed on an ethnocentrism scale, the highly ethnocentric being less favourably disposed towards regional accents and more favourably disposed towards RP.

The possibility of the validity of sequence (2) should not be ruled out. Peter Schönbach (pers. comm.) has correctly pointed out that sequence (1) assumes that all discriminatory behaviour is mediated consciously. It is possible that such discriminations have been and continue to be mediated by classical or operant conditioning processes that have never achieved conscious realization. It is equally possible that such behaviour was once a conscious process but ceased to remain accessible, having achieved an automated status similar to that exhibited by complex sensory-motor skills. Experiments would be necessary to tease out these issues; of especial use would be those that created composites for judgement out of characteristics that did not normally covary.

Sequence (3) would not appear to be directly relevant to the issues in hand, but the operation of the quixotic syndrome could render it relevant. Inferences from speech and writing to personality characteristics can be direct (see Scherer, this volume: ch. 5). In that chapter various speech disruptions are mentioned as being indicative of anxiety, for example. Frender, Brown & Lambert (1970) showed that slow speech at a low pitch with little intonation was perceived as indicative of low intelligence. They also showed that it was. Such beliefs might be mediated by an SES categorization, but that has to be investigated rather than assumed, again presumably exploiting experiments that combined attributes in ways in which they were not generally combined in the environment at large. Similarly the employment of Standard English may also be associated in people's minds with certain levels of intelligence or education rather than with SES, and perhaps the judgements of perceived intelligence of RP speakers reported by Giles (1971) are mediated in this way. Perhaps SES is an accidental covariate rather than an explanatory intermediary. We need to find out whether RP speakers are in fact more ambitious, intelligent, self-confident, determined and industrious. Too much of the work on prejudice (Allport 1954; Brown 1965; Katz & Braly 1933) concerned itself with explanations of the invalidity and inconsistency of respondents' thinking and too little focused upon the inadequacies and oddities of the experimenters' procedures and inferences. We will avoid the same mistakes only if we check in detail how inferences or discriminations involving SES are made and if we do so with more careful conceptual analyses than we have generally used heretofore.

When two-stage inferences are involved, then we should be interested, as behavioural scientists, more particularly if either stage involves invalid or exaggerated beliefs. If there are in fact very high correlations between speech markers and SES and between SES and other characteristics, we may wish to know how people come to learn this information, but we would not be overly interested in why they believed the associations to be real. In so far as any exaggeration in respondents' behaviour is simply an artefact of a methodology that is less than representative of reality, it is likewise of little interest. It will only be when the presumed speech markers of SES are invalid that the bases of thinking processes begin to be of either academic or practical psychological interest.

7. Concluding remarks

It is my suspicion that we need at present to operate with variables that are either more specific or more general than socioeconomic status for the study of interpersonal behaviour. An In-group/Out-group terminology (Tajfel 1978) may be more appropriate for the general problems, whereas for describing and explaining particular alliances and conflicts it will be necessary to specify particular situations in terms of participants, current problems and history. While the enemy of my enemy may be my friend, the same two persons may enjoy a variety of relationships contingent upon the roles they have to play. The jovial contempt in which Lancastrians and Yorkshiremen are alleged to hold each other is equalled only by the united contempt they both feel for southerners. But all three cooperate sympathetically in the face of a common enemy – foreigners. When events dictate that SES groupings become sociologically functional categories, then speech markers of SES may be used to decide who is likely to be friend and foe. In the meantime perhaps we should be a little more circumspect in our use of such categories.

We may begin to demystify the processes involved more rapidly if we return to an examination of particular interpersonal interactions and the decision-making that occurs within these. A study of the activities of gatekeepers to opportunities and services could provide us with a rewarding re-entry into the problems. There are several distinguishable kinds of role relationship in which relevant discriminations might be made. Those who operate at the counters of central and local government agencies as well as those behind the counters of shops may vary their interaction as a function of the inferred SES of the client. Minor functionaries of lower middle SES may behave differently from those of higher professional status. How are clients whose speech is seen to identify them as members of particular SES groups differently treated by police constables, clerks and nurses, on the one hand, and by judges, police inspectors and doctors, on the other? What form does the differentiation take? Are low SES people made conscious of their social identity, and what consequences does this have for their subsequent behaviour? While the general processes of convergence and divergence of accents (Giles & Powesland 1975) could be expected to occur, what consequential modifications to other behaviour and thinking occur?

A special case of these encounters would be those where the client is about to use some facility normally used by members of an SES group of which his speech is not typical. Do hotel commissionaires, head waiters and railway ticket clerks register surprise or disdain when confronted by atypical voices? Do they ask questions ('Was it first class you asked for?') or make suggestions ('The Public bar is round the corner')? Are anomalous aspirants treated in such a way as to discourage them from exercising their legal rights?

While these interfaces are of interest, perhaps particularly for reinforcing identities and maintaining social distinctions, the most obvious initial focus of attention would be the gatekeepers who control the chances of people changing their SES identity. In education we have seen that teachers make inferences to educationally relevant attributes on the basis of the accents and prosodic features of children's voices. Canadian and Australian data referred to above suggest that these inferences do not represent inaccurate or arbitrary judgements so much as exaggerations of real but lower correlations. We have yet to check whether such reported first impressions in laboratories also occur in the same form in the classroom. We have yet to examine whether first impressions are modified in the face of subsequent incongruent information. We have yet to explore when and how treatment of such pupils is consequentially discriminatory in a manner that disadvantages low SES children.

While probing the ecological validity of these ideas will require experiments and other investigations of considerable complexity, decisions about selection for employment can be categorical and final. Personnel selection in industry, commerce and government service is readily amenable to investigation. How does SES attributed variation in speech affect decisions of employing agents? The selection situation can in fact be readily exploited for well-controlled natural experiments for either downwardly or upwardly aspiring people. It is as important to know whether speakers identified as nonmanual middle SES are excluded from various manual occupations as it is to know the converse. Exclusiveness is not necessarily a prerogative of high SES organizations.

If such effects could be shown to operate we would at last have examples of situations where accredited SES was seen to be directly responsible for significant discrimination in a genuinely important context. To date so much of the work reporting SES as a cause of differential life chances is wrong in its conceptual analysis. Too often SES is several levels of analysis away from the on-going behaviour. In those studies it probably ought to be seen not as a distal link in a causal chain, but as an aspect of settings where probabilities of other events occurring differ. To begin to show its direct relevance to behavioural decisions would mark an excellent point of departure for work in this field.

References

Adlam, D. S. 1977. *Codes in Context*. London.

Allport, G. W. 1954. *The Nature of Prejudice*. Cambridge, Mass.

Argyle, M. 1975. *Bodily Communication*. London.

Berger, P. L. & Luckman, T. 1967. *The Social Construction of Reality*. London.

Bernstein, B. 1961. Social structure, language, and learning. *Educational Research*, 3, 163–76.

  1971. *Class, Codes and Control*, vol. i. London. Paperback ed. London, 1973.

Bourhis, R. Y. & Giles, H. 1976. The language of cooperation in Wales. *Language Sciences*, 42, 13–16.

Brophy, J. E. & Good, T. L. 1974 *Teacher–Student Relationships*. New York.

Brown, R. 1965. *Social Psychology*. Glencoe, Ill.

Brown, R. & Lenneberg, E. H. 1954. A study in language and cognition. *Journal of Abnormal Social Psychology*, 49, 454–62.

Bruck, M. & Tucker, G. R. 1974. Social class differences in the acquisition of school language. *Merrill-Palmer Quarterly*, 20, 205–20.

Brunswik, E. 1956. *Perception and the Representative Design of Psychological Experiments*. Berkeley, Calif.

Callary, P. E. 1974. Status perception through syntax, *Language and Speech, 17*, 187–92.

Cazden, C. B. 1970. The neglected situation in child language research and education. In F. Williams (ed.) *Language and Poverty*. Chicago.

Cook-Gumperz, J. 1973. *Social Control and Socialization*. London.

De Stefano, J. S. (ed.) 1973. *Language, Society and Education*. Worthington, Ohio.

Dittmar, N. 1976. *Sociolinguistics*. London.

Edwards, A. D. 1976. *Language in Culture and Class*. London.

Edwards, J. R. 1979. Judgements and confidence in reactions to disadvantaged speech. In H. Giles and R. St Clair (eds.) *Language and Social Psychology*. Oxford.

Eltis, K. 1978. *The Ascription of Attributes to Pupils*. PhD thesis, Macquarie University, Australia.

Fasold, R. W. & Wolfram, W. 1973. Some linguistic features of Negro dialect. In J. S. De Stefano (ed.) *Language, Society and Education*. Worthington, Ohio.

Fielding, G. & Evered, C. 1979. The influence of patients' speech upon doctors: the diagnostic interview. In R. St Clair & H. Giles (eds.) *The Social and Psychological Contexts of Language*. Hillsdale, NJ.

Francis, H. 1974. Social class, reference and context. *Language and Speech*, 17, 193–8.

Frender, R. & Lambert, W. E. 1972. Speech style and scholastic success. *Monographs in Language and Linguistics*, 25, 237–71.

Frender, R., Brown, B. L. & Lambert, W. E. 1970. The role of speech characteristics in scholastic success. *Canadian Journal of Behavioral Sciences*, 2, 299–306.

Fries, C. C. 1940. *American English Grammar*. New York.

Giles, H. 1971. Ethnocentrism and the evaluation of accented speech, *British Journal of Social and Clinical Psychology*, 10, 187–8.

1973. Accent mobility: a model and some data. *Anthropological Linguistics*, 1, 87–105.

(ed.) 1977. *Language, Ethnicity and Intergroup Relations*. London.

Giles, H. & Powesland, P. F. 1975. *Speech Style and Social Evaluation*. London.

Goffman, E. 1970. *Stigma*. Harmondsworth, Middx.

Hall, J. & Caradog-Jones, D. 1950. Social grading of occupation. *British Journal of Sociology*, 1, 31–55.

Halliday, M. A. K. 1975. *Learning How to Mean*. London.

Hargreaves, D. H. 1977. The process of typification in classroom interaction: models and methods. *British Journal of Educational Psychology*, 47, 274–84.

Harms, L. S. 1961. Listener judgments of status cues in speech. *Quarterly Journal of Speech*, 47, 164–8.

1963. Status cues in speech. *Lingua*, 12, 300–6.

Hawkins, P. R. 1969. Social class, the nominal group, and reference. *Language and Speech*, 12, 125–55.

Heider, E. R. 1971. Style and accuracy of verbal communications within and between social classes. *Journal of Personality and Social Psychology*, 18, 33–47.

Hess, R. D. 1970. Social class and ethnic influences on socialization. In P. H. Mussen (ed.) *Carmichael's Manual of Child Psychology*, vol. II. New York.

Hollingshead, A. B. & Redlich, F. C. 1958. *Social Class and Mental Illness*. New York.

Katz, D. C. & Braly, K. W. 1933. Racial stereotypes of one hundred college students. *Journal of Abnormal and Social Psychology*, 28, 280–90.

Kurath, H. & McDavid, R. A. 1961. *The Pronunciation of English in the Atlantic States*. Ann Arbor, Mich.

Labov, W. 1966. *The Social Stratification of English in New York City*. Center for Applied Linguistics, Washington, DC.

1969. The logic of non-standard English. In *Monograph Series on Language and Linguistics*, 22, 1–31. Georgetown University, Washington, DC.

Labov, W. & Cohen, P. 1973. Systematic relations of standard and non-standard rules in the grammars of Negro speakers. In J. S. De Stefano (ed.) *Language, Society and Education*. Worthington, Ohio.

La Civita, A. F., Kean, J. M. & Yamamoto, K. 1966. Socio-economic status of children and acquisition of grammar. *Journal of Educational Research*, 60, 71–4.

Lambert, W. 1972. *Language, Psychology and Culture*. Stanford, Calif.

Lantz, D. & de Stefflre, V. 1964. Language and cognition revisited. *Journal of Abnormal Social Psychology*, 69, 472–81.

Lawton, D. 1968. *Social Class, Language and Education*. London.

Levine, L. & Crockett, H. J. 1967. Speech variation in a Piedmont community: postvocalic /r/. *International Journal of American Linguistics*, 33, 76–98.

Also in S. Lieberson (ed.) *Explorations in Sociolinguistics*. Bloomington, Ind., 1967.

Macaulay, R. K. S. & Trevelyan, G. D. 1973. *Language, Education and Employment in Glasgow*. Social Science Research Report (HR2311).

McCarthy, D. 1930. *Language Development of the Preschool Child*. Institute of Child Welfare Monograph, *4*. Minneapolis.

Mehrabian, A. 1972. *Non-verbal Communication*. Chicago.

Mitchell, A. G. & Delbridge, A. 1965. *The Pronunciation of English in Australia*. Sydney.

Moe, J. D. 1972. Listener judgments of status cues in speech. *Speech Monographs*, *39*, 144–7.

Oevermann, U. 1970. *Sprache und Soziale Herkunft*. Berlin.

Orne, M. T. 1969. On the social psychology of the psychological experiment. In W. J. Gephart & R. B Ingle (eds.) *Educational Research*. Columbus, Ohio.

Orton, H. & Dieth, E. 1962. *Survey of English Dialects*. Leeds.

Poole, M. E. 1976. *Social Class and Language Utilization at the Tertiary Level*. Brisbane.

Popper, K. R. 1972. *Objective Knowledge*. London.

Putnam, G. N. & O'Hern, E. 1955. The status significance of an isolated urban dialect. *Language*, *31*, 1–32.

Rackstraw, S. J. & Robinson, W. P. 1967. Social and psychological factors related to variability of answering behaviour in five-year-old children. *Language and Speech*, *10*, 88–106.

Robinson, W. P. 1972. *Language and Social Behaviour*. Harmondsworth, Middx. 1978. *Language Management in Education: the Australian context*. Sydney.

Robinson, W. P. & Rackstraw, S. J. 1972. *A Question of Answers*. London.

Rosch, E. H. 1973. On the internal structure of perceptual and semantic categories. In T. E. Moore (ed.) *Cognitive Development and the Acquisition of Language*. New York.

Rosen, H. 1972. *Language and Social Class: a critical look at the theories of Basil Bernstein*. Bristol.

Ross, A. C. 1954. Linguistic indicators in present-day English. *Bulletin de la Societé Néo-philologique de Helsinki*.

Rushton, J. & Young, G. 1975. Context and complexity in working class language. *Language and Speech*, *18*, 366–87.

Ryan, E. B. & Carranza, M. A. 1975. Evaluative reactions of adolescents towards speakers of different language varieties. *Journal of Personality and Social Psychology*, *31*, 855–63.

Ryle, G. 1949. *The Concept of Mind*. London.

Schatzman, L. & Strauss, A. 1955. Class and modes of communication. *American Journal of Sociology*, *60*, 329–38.

Seligman, C. R., Tucker, G. R. & Lambert, W. E. 1972. The effects of speech style and other attributes on teachers' attitudes towards pupils. *Language in Society*, *1*, 131–42.

Shriner, T. H. & Miner, L. 1968. Morphological structures in the language of disadvantaged and advantaged children. *Journal of Speech and Hearing Research*, *11*, 605–10.

Shuy, R. W. 1970. Employee selection, training, promotion. CAL-NCTE Conference, Education and Training, February.

Shuy, R. W. Baratz, J. C. & Wolfram, W. A. 1969. Sociolinguistic factors in speech identification. NIMHR Project MH-15048-01. Center for Applied Linguistics, Washington, DC.

Stubbs, M. 1976. *Language, Schools and Classrooms*. London.

Tajfel, H. (ed.) 1978. *Differentiation between Social Groups*. London.

Templin, M. C. 1957. *Certain Language Skills in Children*. Minneapolis.

Trudgill, P. 1974. *The Social Differentiation of English in Norwich*. Cambridge.
 1975. *Accent, Dialect and the School*. London.

Williams, F. (ed.) 1970. *Language and Poverty*. Chicago.
 1976. *Explorations of the Linguistic Attitudes of Teachers*. Rowley, Mass.

Williams, F. & Naremore, R. C. 1969. On the functional analysis of social class differences in modes of speech. *Speech Monographs, 36*, 77–102.

Zigler, E. & Child, I. L. 1969. Socialization. In G. Lindzey & E. Aronson (eds.) *Handbook of Social Psychology*, vol. III. Reading, Mass.

7. Ethnicity markers in speech[1]

HOWARD GILES

An examination of the ways in which people mark their ethnic group membership in speech is perhaps a more awesome undertaking than a review of how many other social categories are indicated in speech. This may be so for at least two reasons. First, although males and females for example differ in their social relations across different ethnolinguistic cultures the dimensions along which they vary are probably far less in number and complexity than those which differentiate ethnic groups; the same point can also be made with respect to age and social class groupings. Thus, one can, with due caution, make certain valid generalizations about the manner in which females and young children speak from an examination of a very few situations. Not so with the thousands of distinct ethnic groups around the world which vary simultaneously on a vast range of dimensions, including history, territory, demography, institutional support and their economic and political relationships with other contrasting ethnic groups. Second, and perhaps arising because of the former, there are no coherent reviews of literature on differences in speech between ethnic groups. Admittedly, there is a significant body of knowledge concerning the relationship between language and ethnicity (e.g. Fishman 1972; Giles 1977a) and the factors affecting language maintenance amongst ethnic groups (e.g. Anderson 1979; Fishman 1966), yet these are separate, albeit related, issues. No attempt will be made in this chapter to describe exhaustively all the isolated studies in different parts of the world pertaining to ethnic speech markers. Given the heterogeneity of methodologies, findings, ethnolinguistic groups and subgroups of individuals within them, such a task in the present context would be doomed to failure through its endless catalogues of unrelated ethnic features. While it is of course essential to reflect the flavour of the

[1] I am extremely grateful to Philip M. Smith for his critical and insightful comments during the preparation of this chapter.

nature of ethnic speech markers, the author feels that our energies at this time ought to be expended elsewhere. It would seem a priority now to develop a predictive theory which will allow us to understand the social psychological processes which affect individuals who identify them- selves as members of ethnic groups and hence which influence their language behaviour. It is only when we have the beginnings of a viable theoretical framework that we can understand how and why for instance certain Malays may be using a given speech marker in particular interethnic contexts and be able to relate this to how and why Catalans are adopting another in their interethnic contexts. In other words, quite dissimilar linguistic mechanisms may be adopted for quite similar psychological reasons.

In the first section of this chapter, we shall examine what ethnic speech markers are used in some 'typical' interethnic contexts. In the second, we shall consider when and why these markers are adopted within the developing framework of a recent theory of language and ethnic rela- tions. Finally, this approach will be extended by considering when speech markers in an outgroup language assume salience over other nonlinguistic characteristics for subordinate ethnic groups in what will be termed a 'boundary perspective'.

1. Ethnic groups and their speech markers: a selective review

Before examining the nature of ethnic speech markers, let us briefly define our orientation towards ethnic groups and the types of ethnoling- uistic contact situations with which we will be dealing.

1.1. Definitions and typologies

The adequacy of different criteria for defining a collectivity as an 'ethnic group' has been discussed for decades (Glaser 1958; Narroll 1964; Moer- man 1965; Rose 1972; Cohen 1974; Isajiw 1974; Dashefsky 1975) as has its distinctiveness from a 'racial group' (Bram 1955; Potter 1960; Fishman 1972; Trudgill 1974), and this does not seem to be the appropriate context in which to continue this debate. My own perspective derives much from the work of Barth (1969) and of Turner (1978a). The former suggested a nonlinguistic, social psychological definition of an ethnic unit as those individuals who say they belong to ethnic group A rather than B and are willing to be treated and allow their behaviour to be interpreted and judged as As and not Bs. Turner also argues for a cognitive definition of any social group (ethnic or otherwise) as 'two or more people who share a common social identification of themselves or, which is nearly the same thing, perceive themselves to be members of the same social category'. The value of defining an ethnic group in cognitive terms is threefold. First, it allows one to highlight those who self-identify with that category rather than those who are externally allotted to it by means of supposedly objective criteria. Indeed, some of the latter may feel little identification with that ethnic identity and therefore may not act in accord with it.[2] Second, it does not rely upon the notion that the individual has to be physically close to, or even like, his ethnic ingroup in order to act in terms of this group membership. Third, it allows implicitly for the possibility that there could be certain conditions under which the same individual will self-identify in ethnic terms but not in others. Therefore, our own preferred definition of ethnic group is those individuals who perceive themselves to belong to the same ethnic category. Sometimes such group identifications are thought to be based on a common set of ancestral cultural traditions, othertimes they will stimulate the creation of a unique set of cultural traditions (Fishman 1977).

Having established our orientation towards ethnic group membership, it remains to distinguish between various interethnic contact situations. As Giles (1978) pointed out, one of the important sources of variance existing between different ethnic group contexts is the baseline linguistic repertoires of the groups concerned. Thus, for instance, some ethnic minorities are incapable of speaking the majority group's tongue (most Ceylon Tamil speakers in Sri Lanka), others however, only speak the dominant group's language (most Scots in the United Kingdom), while still others are bilingual in their own and the outgroup's language (many French Canadians in Canada). In order to illustrate the complexity of the possibilities existing for the language repertoires of ethnic in- and out-groups, Giles (1978) proposed a 4 × 4 matrix of sixteen interethnic contact situations. In the model, the possibilities rendered for both in- and outgroup were being (i) monolingual in the ingroup language, (ii) mono-lingual in the outgroup language, (iii) bilingual in the in- and outgroup languages, and (iv) bilingual in the ingroup language and a lingua franca. Although the typology is useful in specifying potential mono- and bilin-gual combinations of both groups, it is cumbersome as a heuristic particu-larly when exemplars are difficult to locate in a number of instances. In an attempt to provide a more manageable framework, the three types of

[2] This is not of course to deny the importance of those individuals who do not self-identify with a particular ethnic group membership yet may be attributed as members of that social category anyway; it is just that these involve a different set of theoretical assumptions.

contact situations relatively well-researched in the previous typology are considered here.

The classic example of interethnic communication has been omitted where two ethnic groups are monolingual in their separate languages. Language in this case can be regarded as the ethnic speech marker *par excellence*. However, given that verbal and vocal communication between the two groups is severely restricted, and more often than not breaks down when attempted (except when pidgins develop out of economic necessity), it has been relegated in importance for our present purposes. The three 'typical' ethnolinguistic contact situations appear in figure 1 and are labelled as the language choice, accommodation and assimilation paradigms. The *language choice* paradigm exists in many multi-ethnic societies where there are a large number of ethnic groups coexisting in the same social space who possess their own often mutually unintelligible tongues but have one or more languages in common; sometimes they are each others' (e.g. many ethnic groups in Singapore). A prime research concern with such contact situations has been: Which language does each group choose, and do they maintain it or switch during the length of an encounter? The accommodation and assimilation models (after a distinction introduced by Anderson 1979) side-step this problem as one ethnic group (usually the economic, social and political subordinate; Group B in figure 1) has either opted from choice or necessity to use the language of the other in interethnic contacts. In the *accommodation* paradigm, Group B (in figure 1) has often chosen to become bilingual so as to function more effectively in a Group A-dominated society but maintained its own ethnic tongue (b in figure 1) diglossically for within-group interactions (e.g. many Hispanic groups in the United States). In the *assimilation* paradigm, Group B has been, to varying degrees, deliberately de-ethnicized (cf. Giles 1978: 366) by the policies of Group A (e.g. as happened to many Welsh and Breton speakers), or has voluntarily assimilated into the dominant society at least linguistically (e.g. many West Indians in the United Kingdom). A prime research concern with both models has been: What intralinguistic speech markers characterize the two ethnic groups in contact, if any?

Besides limiting our review of ethnic speech markers to an implicit consideration of these three contact situations, we shall have to focus our attention, given the present state-of-the-art, on only those features of speech which would appear to characterize intergroup communication between representatives of two ethnic groups. This is not intended to gloss over the fact that interethnic communication occurs in multi-ethnic situations between more than two groups in an encounter nor that ethnic speech markers can occur in within-group situations for solidarity or other reasons. In sections 1.2 and 1.3, ethnic speech markers will be examined according to the languages of two ethnic groups in contact (mainly considered within the language choice paradigm), and the characteristics of their speech in terms of phonology, grammar, lexicon, paralanguage and prosody when they are using the same language (mainly considered within the accommodation and assimilation paradigms).

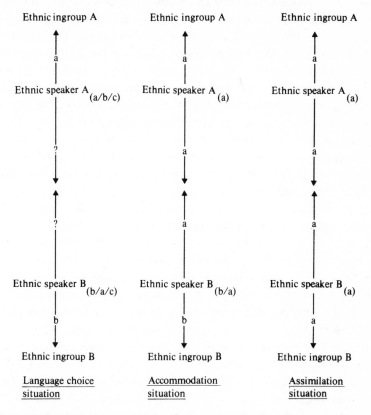

Figure 1. Typical language use in interethnic contact situations (lower case letters refer to the language(s) in which the speaker is fluent)

1.2. Language

When members of two ethnolinguistic groups wish to converse they will attempt to find a common language in which to communicate. Perhaps because of lack of motivation and mutual negative intergroup attitudes, it is usually only in formal, institutionalized settings that members of different ethnic groups encounter one another (cf. Taylor & Simard 1975). In most bicultural societies, there are quite explicit norms regarding the appropriate language to be used in formal contexts (Brown & Fraser, this volume: ch. 2; Herman 1961; Hymes 1972) and, more often than not, it is the higher prestige language of the dominant ethnic group that is spoken by both parties. In other words, even when members of both groups have the same languages in common, as was the case traditionally with many English and French Canadians in Quebec, it is usually the subordinate group that concedes to the dominant group in terms of the language used in interethnic communication (cf. Ros & Giles, in press); there is little room for bilingual negotiation. Indeed, Aboud (1978) has shown that such unidirectional tendencies for language accommodation exist even at the age of 6 years amongst Anglo and Chicano bilinguals in the United States in the sense that far more Chicanos would accommodate to Anglos via language than vice versa. Nevertheless, despite this general rule of language choice differences between ethnic groups in favour of the dominant one, exceptions can be found. First, there are of course instances where members of the dominant ethnic group will use the language of the subordinate group member (otherwise his or her bilingual proficiency would become dysfunctional) when the latter has been favourably perceived as an individual person rather than as a representative of an ethnic outgroup (cf. Giles, Taylor & Bourhis 1973). Such a language choice by the speaker is favourably viewed by the recipient when the intent of the converging shift is attributed positively (Simard, Taylor & Giles 1976). Second, cases have now been recorded, particularly in contexts where an ethnic group is redefining in a more positive direction its ethnolinguistic identity, where certain subordinate group members refuse to adopt the outgroup language with its bilingual (and sometimes even monolingual) representatives (cf. Giles, Bourhis & Taylor 1977: 330–1). Thus, for example, a number of French Canadians in Quebec have over the years refused to use English at all, despite their biliguality, in the presence of an English Canadian. Such patterns of language choice can exist in either the language choice or accommodation paradigms for Group B (see figure 1).

It has been proposed by Lambert (1974) that learning or using the language of a dominant ethnic group could be experienced as subtractive or threatening to a subordinate group's sense of identity and value system (Botha 1970; Ervin 1964); data now exist to support this contention (Taylor, Meynard & Rheault 1977). Nevertheless, it has been found that the use of an outgroup language, but with a distinctive ethnic accent, does not detract from the speaker's *perceived* ethnicity in the eyes of others (Giles *et al.* 1973). It would seem that many ethnic speech markers, perhaps particularly a distinctive dialect or accent, can serve to support an individual's sense of ethnic belongingness when an outgroup language has to be adopted (Bourhis, Giles & Tajfel 1973; Ryan 1979). Moreover, such differentiation in the outgroup tongue could be achieved by a variety of other means including the use of a formal, nominal style (Segalowitz 1977; see Brown & Fraser, this volume: ch. 2, 2.3), restricted code and paralinguistic patterns indicating distance and disinterest. Unfortunately, most of the work on bilingual code-switching has paid little attention to the specific linguistic features of the language once chosen by the different interlocutors.

The language choice paradigm is also exemplified in those situations where neither Group A nor B can speak each other's mother tongue but nevertheless share a third or even fourth language in common. Such a situation exists in Singapore where Platt (1977) has described how Malays, Tamils and Chinese speakers when interacting with each other keep selecting from their multilingual repertoires a language (or variety of a language) until they find one in common. In this society, because of the need for ease of interethnic communication at least for economic transactions (cf. Jones 1973), a lingua franca termed 'Singlish' has developed (or perhaps more accurately is *still* developing) which is a particular variety of English having incorporated a number of Malay, Tamil and Chinese linguistic features. Platt (1975) has coined the term 'creoloid' for a language variety which develops under these conditions. Obviously, lingua francas have been used throughout the ages as a means whereby ethnic groups who do not have command of each other's vernaculars can communicate (e.g. the use of Hausa in West Africa, and English in India and the Philippines). Scotton (1976) has described the situation in Kenya, a multi-ethnic society, which has two lingua francas (Swahili and English) each with their own particular connotations. Thus, when a Luo meets a Kikuyu, their choice of a lingua franca is determined by the impressions they want to convey based on their definitions of the situation. Scotton suggests that should the individual wish to stress his common African roots with the other and establish some form of transethnic solidarity, then he or she would choose Swahili. If, on the other hand, the speaker wanted to establish the notion that he was educated and in a position of authority he might choose English. In an attempt to capture both of these atmospheres, a speaker might easily switch from one lingua franca to the other. Indeed, Scotton & Ury (in press) have discussed the manner in which a speaker might switch back and forth between three languages during a thirty-second dialogue in an attempt to locate the interaction in the appropriate social arena (cf. Blom & Gumperz 1972; Bourhis 1979; Clyne 1967). However, as shown by Bourhis, Giles, Leyens & Tajfel (1979), when relations between ethnic groups become salient, and group members have negative views of the other and feel that their ethnic identity is being threatened, they might revert to their own ingroup language when speaking to members of the other group.

Once again, the emphasis in such work has been on analysing interactions in terms of the language chosen rather than on specifying the linguistic features of those languages. It might well be for instance that once the superordinate goal of a viable transethnic creoloid has been achieved, certain groups in Singapore (and elsewhere) might develop it in their own ethnolinguistic ways. Similarly, although lingua francas tend to be treated as homogenous wholes, it could be that different Kenyan groups for instance introduce vernacular, or even prestige (Scotton, 1978), speech markers into Swahili and English for purposes of ethnic differentiation in certain situations.

Summary. In this section, language has been shown to be an ethnic speech marker in two respects. First, it can act as a marker of ethnic identity such as when a minority group member deliberately maintains his or her ingroup language, or switches back into it when implicit norms require the use of the majority group's language in interethnic communication. Second, it can act as a marker of the relationship existing between ethnic groups (see Brown & Levinson (this volume: ch. 8) for a discussion of relationship markers) such as when the frequent adoption of the dominant group's language by both parties in formal contexts reflects the subordinate and dominant power positions of one group *vis-à-vis* the other. However, implicit in the foregoing has been the notion that language choice is not an all-or-none phenomenon in interethnic situations in the sense that either a 'pure' form of language a or a 'pure' form of language b is necessarily selected. It is more common that certain linguistic features of the ingroup can be found to 'intrude' into the outgroup language to varying degrees; at one extreme would be the mixing or interlarding of the two varieties (Agheyisi 1977; Shaffer 1976), while at the other would be the imposition of one or more ingroup phonological or lexical variants. Hence, language choice is more often than not a continuous rather than a discrete ethnic speech marker (see Giles, Scherer & Taylor, this volume: ch. 9, 3.2). Therefore, the use of an ingroup language does not necessarily have to be the most powerful indicator of ethnic group belongingness (Anderson 1979; Fishman 1977; Giles, Bourhis & Taylor, 1977). Rather, ethnic speech markers at the phonological, grammatical, lexical and paralinguistic/prosodic levels may often ably compensate for loss of ethnic identity when an outgroup language or lingua franca is used. In other words, the need to attenuate group differences at the level of language choice can often give rise to the accentuation of them at other levels of intralingual analysis. It is to a consideration of these ethnic speech markers that we now turn.

1.3. Intralingual markers

Phonological markers. Phonological differences between two ethnic groups who use supposedly the same language in interethnic communication have been examined in a number of societies. Perhaps the most well-documented situation is that of Black–White speech differences in the United States (e.g. Shuy, Baratz & Wolfram 1969; Wolfram 1971). Trudgill (1974) points to a range of phonological features which characterize American Black speakers, four of which will be considered here. First, there is an absence of the phoneme /r/ in a number of verbal contexts such as the postvocalic variant in a word like *far*, the intervocalic in a word like *carrot*, and after certain initial consonants in a word like *from*. Second, American Blacks do not possess the phonemes /θ/ and /ð/ as in *thought* and *then* so that in initial positions they are realized as [t] and [d] as in *tought* and *den*, whereas in other positions they are realized as [f] and [v] respectively as in *Afur* (Arthur) and *cloving* (clothing). Third, Black speakers do not pronounce certain final consonant clusters such as *-st*, *-sp* and *sk*, so that *risk* and its plural are pronounced as *ris* and *risses* respectively. Fourth, there is the absence of final /d/ such that *load* and *low* would be homophonous. It is important to note that each of these ethnic speech markers is not characteristic of all Black speakers in the United States nor of any one person on all occasions. The origins of these speech markers, as well as the Black grammatical markers to be introduced subsequently, are at the centre of a controversy in dialectology with one school claiming that they are not really different forms of English but that they are the result of an English (possibly Caribbean) Creole being de-creolized (Trudgill 1974: 73–7). Nevertheless, whatever the true origins of Black English phonological markers, most Americans would conceive of both groups as speaking a common language but with different dialects, and data now exist suggesting that such differences are socially significant for Blacks and Whites by the age of 3 years (Rosenthal 1974).

The origins of the phonological markers of other minority groups in the United States and elsewhere are less controversial. Thus for instance, the features peculiar to Polish, German and Norwegian accents[3] of American English can be directly attributed to intrusions from their substratum varieties or mother tongues. However, caution should be exercised in regarding such intrusions *simply* as instances of interlingual *interferences*, particularly in the cases of second and third generations of immigrants, as they may often be adopted by them deliberately as ethnic speech markers to establish a distinctive linguistic identity as proposed in the previous section. Indeed, Segalowitz & Gatbonton (1977) found that those French Canadians who identified more closely with Quebecois nationalism used more Francophone phonological features when pronouncing their English than those who sympathized to a lesser degree with separatist ideals (cf. Labov 1963). Moreover, these authors claimed that 'some features of speech [viz. /θ/ and /ð/] may matter more than others, that is they may carry the symbolic load of signalling ethnic affiliation more heavily than do other features'. Just as different individuals self-identify with their ethnic group membership to varying degrees and reflect this by means of speech markers, so too can different *contexts* arouse feelings of ethnic identity more than others which should also be manifest linguistically. The latter phenomenon was demonstrated in an experimental study by Bourhis & Giles (1977a). They found that when an English speaker moved from asking an emotively neutral question of Welshmen who valued their ethnolinguistic identity to threatening their Welsh identity in another question, the Welshmen broadened their accents; that is they *diverged* from the Englishman (Giles 1973, 1977b; Giles & Powesland 1975) in reply to the second question. Not so with Welshmen who did not value their Welsh ethnolinguistic identity. Instead their accents became more English; that is they *converged* towards the Englishman.

Ethnic speech markers at the phonological level then are continuous rather than discrete linguistic forms (Giles *et al.* this volume: ch. 9, 3.2). Indeed, Brennan, Ryan & Dawson (1975) found nine identifiable degrees of Spanish influence in the English accents of Mexican Americans, all of which were detected by linguistically naive listeners. Moreover, Ryan, Carranza & Moffie (in press) found that these small increments in Mexi-

---

[3] It is somewhat dubious to consider the notion of accent under the rubric of phonological markers in that it is undoubtedly built up out of prosodic and paralinguistic features as well, including rhythm, intonation and pitch (John Laver, pers. comm.).

can features in English were associated with gradually less favourable impressions of the speaker. Generally, speakers from minority ethnic groups who use ethnic phonological variants in their speech are downgraded not only by members of the dominant outgroup on scales relating to socioeconomic success such as self-confidence, ambitiousness and intelligence, but also by many members of their ethnic ingroup as well (Biondi 1975; Giles & Powesland 1975; Ryan & Carranza 1977; Williams 1976). On other evaluative dimensions however, these ethnic varieties are highly valued particularly on dimensions relating to solidarity and integrity (Ryan 1979). The value placed on such ethnic speech markers varies between different subordinate ethnic groups (Bourhis, Giles & Lambert 1975) and also between members of any one ingroup. As regards the latter, Mexican Americans who adopt the self-referent 'Chicano' are amongst the few who favourably perceive the use of many Mexican phonological markers in English (Flores & Hopper 1975).

However, some second generation Italian, Jewish and Mexican Americans in the United States, in their attempts to differentiate themselves from substratum influences in their parents' English, overcompensate on certain vowel sounds (Labov 1966; Sawyer 1973). As Trudgill (1974: 63) states, 'Native speakers of Italian tend to use an /a/ type vowel, more open than the English sound, in English words of this type, and their children, in wishing to avoid this pronunciation, may have selected the highest variants of this vowel available to them, i.e. the ones most unlike the typically Italian vowel.' Such 'hypercorrections' themselves soon become recognized and probably stigmatized as speech markers of the ethnic group involved.

They are a few situations where an ethnic group apparently does not mark its speech phonologically (Escure 1979). One such situation has been reported amongst West Indians in Cardiff, Britain, where no ethnic speech markers of any type were in evidence. In a series of studies, it was found that about 80 per cent of second and third generation West Indians had assimilated to such an extent that tape-recordings of their speech were labelled as 'White' (Bourhis & Giles 1977b; Giles & Bourhis 1975, 1976). This is in complete opposition to the American situation where, although Blacks have resided in the United States for many more generations than the British Black immigrants, they are still ethnically labelled accurately from speech cues alone 80 per cent of the time (Shuy, Baratz & Wolfram 1969). Giles & Bourhis (1976) suggested that one of the reasons for the Cardiff Blacks attenuating their ethnic speech markers more than their Black counterparts in the United States was their greater desire to assimilate into the host culture. It can however be proposed that, should members of a dominant group not perceive 'enough' ethnic speech markers in the speech of the subordinate group which they could stigmatize and avoid (Sawyer 1973), they may well have a tendency to invent them perceptually. In indirect support of this contention, Williams, Whitehead & Miller (1971) found that, when Whites in the United States were shown a videotape of a Black child playing with a toy, they downgraded the child as sounding ethnic and nonstandard, despite the fact that the voice-over was that of a superimposed, prestige-sounding White child. As suggested by Giles (1978: 369) if Group B (see figure 1) 'convincingly and inescapably adopts the defining speech markers of . . . Group A . . . the latter may react by creating new speech characteristics to mark off their distinctiveness. It would be interesting to determine if subordinate groups desiring the positive regard of the dominant group would respond in such an instance in terms of linguistic "pursuit".'

Grammatical markers. Intralingual grammatical markers between two ethnic groups are again perhaps best well-documented in the Black–White speech situation of the United States (Burling 1972; Dillard 1972; Wolfram & Clarke 1971). Four grammatical markers of American Black English are worthy of mention here. First, an important grammatical feature of Black English is the 'invariant *be*' which is used to refer to some repeated but noncontinuous actions, e.g. *Sometimes he be shopping*. Second, American Blacks delete the copula, the verb *to be*, in the present tense, e.g. *She big girl*. Third, there is the absence of -*s* in third-person singular present-tense forms, e.g. *She hate him*. Fourth, Blacks often use the negativized auxiliary pre-position (Trudgill 1974: 73): 'If a sentence has a negative indefinite like *nobody, nothing*, then the negative auxiliary (*doesn't, can't*) can be placed at the beginning of the sentence: *Can't nobody do nothing about it; Wasn't nothing wrong with that.*' Once again, such grammatical markers are not characteristic of all American Black speakers nor of any one of them in all contexts.

The substratum influence can be most clearly observed in the grammatical markers of many non-Black minorities in the United States. Many studies have examined the syntactical and lexical characteristics of English there as spoken for example by Mexicans (Ornstein & Dubois 1977), Hungarians (Janda 1976) and Portugese (Rameh 1977). Indeed, when sufficient grammatical speech markers have a certain amount of stability and longevity, they are often accorded the status of a distinctive variety with its own label, as has happened with Engañol or Puerto Rican English

(Nash 1976). Obviously the charting of varieties of English (and other colonial languages) as spoken by minority groups is a common activity of sociolinguists and dialectologists, and many other grammatical varieties have been documented outside the United States including the markers of Indian English in Britain (Gumperz 1977; Kachru 1965) and the use (and acquisition) of German (termed *Gastarbeiterdeutsch*) by different ethnic groups of foreign workers in West Germany (Dittmar 1977; Little-wood 1976; Meisel, in press). These attributes, like the phonological ones described earlier, are regarded by many dominant and subordinate ethnic groups as stigmatized linguistic features.

It has been found that American Blacks mark their speech grammatically by the lack of complex subordinate clauses and the use of sociocentric phrases far more when talking to Whites than talking to other Blacks (Ledvinka, 1971; Sattler 1970). Indeed, such speech markers may be a feature of any social group who finds itself in a subordinate relationship with another and is aroused by feelings of threat (e.g. see Robinson, this volume: ch. 6). From the other side of the coin, Lukens (1979) has made the point that 'just as speech used with foreigners often is stylized, that used by members of a dominant culture conversing with members of minority groups also may be stylized'. In this vein, Fanon (1961) and Shuy (1977) have discussed the manner in which Whites can adopt patronizing and seemingly contemptuous speech with Blacks, often making the latter feel child-like. It is characterized by grammatical simplification such as the deletion of articles and the increased use of infinitives in place of other forms, as well as by exaggerated pronunciations and slow and loud speech (cf. Ferguson 1975). Although such linguistic features may be described as attentuation markers (see Giles *et al*. this volume: ch. 9, 3.4) linguistically, they are nevertheless decoded by the recipients as accentuation markers because of their dissociative character psychologically; they are sometimes intentionally encoded for this purpose also. Therefore, while there are many grammatical devices available for interethnic differentiation, dominant group overaccommodation (Giles & Smith 1979) and subordinate group lack of grammatical sophistication are not ethnic speech markers *per se* (as they are often taken for in the latter case), but are markers of the role relationship established between the two groups (for a discussion of relationship speech markers, see Brown & Levinson, this volume: ch. 8).

Lexical markers. Ethnic groups can also possess a large range of distinctive lexical markers. Trudgill (1974) provides a series of examples of how

Moslems, Croats and Serbs, who all speak the same Yugoslav language (Serbo-Croat), have different words for the same semantic concept, e.g. *čaršija*, *grad* and *varos* respectively for the word, *train*. As Trudgill commented, 'It must be emphasized too, that this list does not supply any hard and fast rules for usage by different groups, it merely gives indications of general trends. In most cases speakers from all three groups can and do use the other forms on occasions (except that Serbs and Croats are unlikely to use the Moslem words for love or window)' (1974: 62). Moreover, even when two ethnic groups use the same lexical item, it does not of necessity imply that they share a common semantic content. In this regard, Holt (1972) has introduced the term 'linguistic inversion' where a word connotes exactly the opposite for one group than it does for the other. Such an example would be the word *nigger* which is negatively valued when spoken by American Whites but positively valued when used by Blacks. In this instance, Blacks have creatively redefined this negative referent of their group more favourably, thereby disallowing self-debasing terms in their vocabulary (Kochman 1975).

Lexical markers are of particular social significance when they are used as such intergroup referents and descriptions (Gearing 1970; Geuder 1979; Khleif 1979). Thus, for example, Group A may change its label for Group B (see figure 1) based upon how it feels about that group and may adopt it in many of the media contexts it controls (Husband 1979). Husband (1977) has described how the terms for Romany travellers in Britain changed over a seven-year period as the latter were perceived as more of a threat. The terms adopted became increasingly more derogatory, moving from *nomads* to *itinerants* to *gipsies* to *tinkers*. Indeed, Wescott (1971) proposed that in the United States there is a strong negative correlation between the number of derogatory labels adopted for use against an ethnic minority and its status in that society. Kochman (1975) also points out that the nature of such derisory labels used by a dominant group against the subordinate one (at least in the context of the American Black case) often centres around the physical characteristics of the group (e.g. *burrhead*), whereas the subordinate group does not use such physical attributes of Whites but is more discriminatory in its referents by means of depicting their social attitudes (e.g. (racist) *honky* vs. (nonracist) *brother*). Similarly, Rollman (1978) has shown that Blacks were better able than White observers to determine accurately which Whites in a series of vision-only videotapes were prejudiced and who were not prejudiced in recorded Black–White interviews.

The type of adjective a group uses to describe another is very often a subtle cue as to how that group is perceived simply because most so-called descriptions are in fact quite evaluative (Peabody 1970). Thus an outgroup's action might be described as 'rebellious' rather than 'questioning', or 'permissive' rather than 'open-minded' (cf. Eiser & Ross, in press). Moreover, a systematic study of intergroup differentiation in terms of discourse and negotiative styles (cf. Daniel 1970; Morley & Stephenson 1976), phrases adopted (Bourhis & Giles 1977a; McConahay & Hough 1976; Rich 1974) as well as verbal humour (Chapman, Smith & Foot 1977; Dundes 1971; Martineau 1972) might be a useful extension of this type of work.

Prosodic and paralinguistic markers. Prosody according to Gumperz (1978) refers to three basic signalling mechanisms, namely tone grouping; nucleus placement within a tone group; and tune (the direction of the tonal change characterizing the nucleus). The following sentence is broken into two tone groupings by means of an oblique line which is cued in speech through intonation and stress thereby supposedly indicating two separable pieces of information:

I am feeling fine / leave me alone

The nucleus placing occurs on the word *fine* by means of a low-rise tonal shift giving its so-called tune. If that word had received any other tune (say a low fall or high rise) it would have sounded 'odd' given our cooccurrence expectations in native English. From an analysis of West Indians talking to each other and to British Whites, Gumperz (1977, 1978) was able to suggest that the former adopt different prosodic rules than members of the host community, presumably because of substratum influences. He finds that 'West Indians can split a sentence into much smaller tone group units than British English speakers can. Furthermore, their use of a rising tone to indicate inter-sentence boundaries is much more restricted. Moreover, once a tone group has been established, nucleus placement is syntactically rather than semantically constrained.' As Gumperz shows, such prosodic differences lead to the wrong conversational inferences being drawn about the speaker's intent, the West Indian speaker is often perceived by a White as rude or impolite, and the former cannot understand the cause of negative feedback in response to his statement other than in discriminatory terms (for a discussion of certain interethnic communication breakdowns, see also Segalowitz 1977; Taylor & Simard, 1975; von Raffler-Engel 1979).

Gumperz also points to differences between the two ethnic groups mentioned above in terms of paralanguage: those features which apply to the tone grouping as a whole rather than to components of it such as pitch register, rhythm, loudness and tempo. West Indians will apparently in normal calm interethnic discussion suddenly and dramatically change pitch and increase loudness on tone groupings they wish to emphasize. This for members of the host community would have been signalled prosodically in their own speech and they consider such untoward para-linguistic changes as emotional outbursts by West Indians. Paralinguistic differences between ethnic groups are often quite salient although little research attention has been paid to them (Lass, Mertz & Kimmel 1978). Dickens & Sawyer (1962) found that American Blacks and Whites could be accurately distinguished from tape-recordings of them reading a stan-dard passage of prose which supposedly kept dialectal features at a minimum. In other words, ethnic categorization was to all intents and purposes largely determined by paralinguistic (or even prosodic) cues; perhaps absolute pitch, although no data were made available on this issue.

Summary. In this section, it has been suggested that speech markers of a subordinate group do not exist (or at the very least are greatly attenuated) when that group has a very strong desire to assimilate into the dominant group. The effect of speech marker attenuation on the speech of the dominant group, the new markers it may create in response, and the manner and the media through which it legitimizes and standardizes them (Husband 1979) are worthy of much further empirical consideration (cf. Scotton 1978; Ullrich, 1971). Indeed, this particular aspect of inter-group differentiation may be an important component of linguistic change throughout the community. More common however, is the occurrence of many intralingual speech markers of subordinate ethnic groups which arise, due either to voluntary or to involuntary substratum influences, or to subsequent phonological hypercorrection. Interestingly, most of these are continuous in form and are probabilistic in the sense that they do not occur with respect to all members of the ethnic group con-cerned nor for any one individual member on all occasions. Thus, ethnic speech markers at these intralingual levels can be used to varying degrees whenever the individual feels himself a representative of his or her ethnic group or perceives an interaction with an outgroup member more in *intergroup* rather than interindividual terms (Tajfel 1974; Taylor & Giles 1979). Unfortunately, little research has touched upon which set of mar-kers and combinations of them are necessary under which social condi-tions to provide the speaker with an adequate sense of ethnic identity.

Similarly, there are too few data for us to predict precisely to which speech markers a listener pays attention and affords social significance. It would seem useful to determine the subjective dimensions which underlie different types of interethnic encounters for both speakers and hearers (cf. Wish & Kaplan 1977), and to determine which set of markers become operative from the encoding perspective, and which become potentially salient from the decoding end. In other words, we need far more information from a variety of interethnic contexts as to which markers are accentuated and attenuated in intergroup encounters by whom in *both* Groups A and B (see figure 1) and for what purposes, and how these strategies are reacted to in turn by the recipients, in a continuing feedback loop.

2. A theoretical framework

Although the manner in which speech markers are used and valued differ between and within ethnic groups, a fairly clear notion emerges from the previous review That is, an ethnic group's perception and use of speech markers may be important indicators and communicators of social differentiation from, as well as social integration with, a contrasting ethnic group. In section 2, a social psychological framework will be outlined which will allow us to specify the social conditions under which the accentuation and attenuation of ethnic speech markers may occur. The theory, which has predictive value, is built from notions of social structure, intergroup relations (Tajfel 1974, 1978a) and speech accommodation (Giles 1973, 1977b). The theory will be presented here in its *integrative* form, details of its component parts appear elsewhere (Bourhis 1979; Giles 1978; Giles, Bourhis & Taylor 1977).

2.1. Speech and intergroup behaviour

The theory takes its starting-point from current notions in the social psychology of intergroup behaviour (Tajfel 1974, 1978a; Tajfel & Turner 1978). It is proposed that when members of different groups are in contact, they compare themselves with each other on dimensions which are important to them, such as abilities, physical characteristics, material possessions, etc. Such intergroup social comparisons will lead individuals to search for or even create dimensions on which they can make themselves positively distinct from the outgroup. The perception of a positive distinctiveness by the ingroup will ensure that they have an adequate social identity. In other words, people experience satisfaction in the knowledge that they belong to groups which enjoy some superiority over others. Thus, when ethnic group affiliation is important for an individual and interaction with members of a relevant outgroup occurs, he or she will attempt to make themselves distinctive from the other on valued dimensions. Given that language and ethnic speech markers are for many ethnic groups salient and valued dimensions of their social identity (Giles, Taylor & Bourhis 1977; Giles, Taylor, Lambert & Albert 1976; Taylor, Bassili & Aboud 1973), it may well be that the accentuation of ingroup speech markers is an important strategy for making oneself psychologically and favourably distinct from outgroup members. This process of enhancing ingroup speech markers in search of a positive ethnic identity has been termed 'psycholinguistic distinctiveness' (Giles, Bourhis & Taylor 1977). Illustrations of this, from section 1, are language-switching to an ingroup variety, the use of phonological, grammatical, paralinguistic/prosodic and lexical markers in the outgroup language, and the emphasis or *divergence* (Giles 1973, 1977b; Giles & Powesland 1975) of these markers in interethnic encounters. There could be a hierarchy of psycholinguistic distinctiveness in the use of speech markers where some (e.g., language-switching) might be more symbolic of ethnic differentiation than others (e.g. use of ingroup lexical items in outgroup language). Thus, the more ethnic group identity becomes salient for an individual, the more ethnic speech markers might be called into existence. The exact linguistic nature of this process is of course worthy of empirical investigation (cf. Lukens 1979).

Speech accentuation by means of ethnic speech markers is therefore *one* tactic designed to maximize the differences between ethnic groups on a valued dimension in search of a positive group identity. An important aspect of the present theoretical framework is its dynamic character and ability to account for ethnolinguistic *change*. It can be suggested that ethnic groups who command a dominant position in society will not be motivated to change the status quo along many dimensions, linguistic or otherwise. In other words, such groups experience a positive social identity under the existing, satisfactory, social conditions. It could perhaps be argued that the possession of an inadequate ethnic identity and speech characteristics marking that inferiority, such as often exists among subordinate ethnic groups, should motivate groups to implement changes in order to achieve a more satisfactory group identity. However, as can be seen from an observation of the ethnolinguistic scene, having an inadequate social identity *per se* is not sufficient for advocating and provoking social (or linguistic) change (Turner & Brown 1978). Many subordinate ethnic groups have for generations accepted without question their low status on linguistic dimensions (Lambert, Hodgson, Gardner & Fillenbaum 1960; Ryan & Carranza 1977). The present theory predicts that changes will only come about when dominant and subordinate groups become aware of *cognitive alternatives* to the existing interethnic status hierarchy. Turner & Brown (1978) propose that two independent factors contribute to this awareness of cognitive alternatives, namely the perceived legitimacy–illegitimacy and stability–instability of the intergroup situation. The former distinction refers to the extent to which individuals construe their group's position in the status hierarchy to be fair and just, whereas the latter refers to the extent they believe their group's status position can be changed, or even reversed.

Many subordinate ethnic group members who have an inadequate ethnic identity have not been aware of cognitive alternatives to their group position. That is, they have considered their own position *vis-à-vis* the outgroup as stable and legitimate, and tend to attribute the blame for their low status in society to themselves (internally in attribution terms) as a group because of their inferior characteristics. In order to achieve a more positive sense of identity, individuals may attempt one of at least three *self*-oriented strategies. One might be to attempt to leave the ethnic group which is causing so much dissatisfaction and pass (physical and other characteristics allowing) into the outgroup. An important tactic for achieving this successfully is the adoption of the speech markers of the dominant group. Individuals who adopt this tactic of social mobility are often considered cultural traitors by other members of the ingroup and uncomplimentary labels are often attached to them (Kochman 1975; Sawyer 1973). Another strategy (not discussed in other sources) might be to identify more closely with another type of social group which could contribute more favourably to one's sense of social identity. Given that speech markers of a subordinate ethnic group often enable one to qualify easily for membership of other oppressed social groups, the individual might redefine his or her ethnic speech markers along for instance *class* lines (cf. G. Williams 1979). Thus, a Welshman's use of ethnic speech markers in English with an Englishman might not be a reflection of ethnic differentiation as much as a symbol of his dissociation from him in terms of class. Finally, the individual might not make many social comparisons with members or the outgroup which causes feelings of inadequacy but might attempt to make comparisons on dimensions within the group which allow him a sense of positive distinctiveness, i.e. he will make intragroup, interindividual comparisons (cf. Williams & Giles 1978).

Once subordinate group members do perceive cognitive alternatives to the existing status relationship with the dominant group (i.e. they perceive the position of their own group *vis-à-vis* the outgroup as unstable and as illegitimate and blame their low status on repressive measures of that other group), they will tend to achieve a more positive social identity by *group*-oriented, collective strategies rather than by individual means. This can be achieved by at least four group strategies. First, the group as a whole might attempt to assimilate into the dominant group culturally and linguistically as a method of securing parity with the latter on power dimensions (Fishman 1966). Second, the group may attempt to redefine existing linguistic characteristics (e.g. language and dialect) in a more favourable direction and increasingly use these speech patterns in more public contexts. Hence, we have the 'Black . . . Welsh . . . Frog (in Quebec) is beautiful' linguistic movements (cf. Andersson & Boyer 1970; Glazer & Moynihan 1975; Greeley & McCready 1974). Third, the group may search for dimensions of comparison with the outgroup where they create their own linguistic distinctiveness. Examples abound here, such as reintroducing old Amerindian languages into the school curricula (Eastman 1979), inventing new forms of a distinctive language as in the case of Israel and others (Fellman 1973; Nahir 1978), or a distinctive alphabet as was the case amongst Ukrainian immigrants in Canada (Anderson 1979). Finally, subordinate groups may engage in direct social competition with the outgroup (Turner 1975) and incite civil actions in order to fight for their linguistic rights in the media, legal system, school, etc.

The dominant group does not lie idle when its own positive distinctiveness is being chipped away. When it perceives cognitive alternatives to its stable and just superiority, it may adopt different strategies in order to retrieve its power position by the use of demeaning language and abrasive humour directed towards the subordinate group, by creating its own new linguistic forms, and by implementing language policies in favour of its own members (Verdoodt 1977; Kearney 1977; Husband 1979). At the moment, we have little information on which conditions induce which linguistic strategies from subordinate or dominant ethnic groups when they become aware of cognitive alternatives to the status hierarchy, or whether there is a developmental sequence for the emergence of different strategies as groups compete for their positive ethnic identities.

2.2. Ethnolinguistic vitality

Before we can propose predictions from the theory about the use of ethnic speech markers in interethnic situations, we need to call upon the final aspect of the theory, that of ethnolinguistic vitality. The social psychological processes mentioned above do not occur in a vacuum and must be influenced by the prevailing sociostructural conditions affecting ethnic relations. In an attempt to put order into the different structural conditions operating between different ethnic groups, Giles, Bourhis & Taylor (1977) attempted to compile a taxonomy of sociostructural factors affecting an ethnic group. They called these *ethnolinguistic vitality* factors, and the more of these groups had in their favour, the more vitality a group possessed, and the more likely it was to thrive and survive as a distinctive entity in an intergroup context.

These authors proposed that most of the structural variables influencing ethnolinguistic vitality could be derived from three factors: status, demographic and institutional support. The status factors (economic, social, historical and linguistic) pertain to the configuration of prestige variables an ethnic group holds in an intergroup context. The more a group has economic and political control over its destiny, consensual high esteem, pride in its past and a respected language of international repute, the more vitality it is said to possess as a collective entity. The demographic variables are those related to the sheer numbers of group members and their distributions throughout the territory (Anderson 1979; De Vries 1979; C. Williams 1979). Groups having high absolute numbers concentrating together in their own ancestral homeland, a positive ingroup–outgroup proportion, a high birth rate, low emigration and incidence of mixed marriages with the outgroup, are more likely to have a high vitality than groups low in these regards. Institutional support variables refer to the extent to which an ethnic group receives representation in the various institutions of the nation or territory (Breton 1971). The vitality of an ethnic group should then be related to the degree it has representation, and its language variety is used, in various institutions of the government, school, church, mass media and culture (Clyne 1976).

It was proposed that, only through combining the effects of the three (and possibly other) factors could the relative overall vitality of a group be determined. Although it is impossible to provide weightings for these factors at the present time, ethnic groups can be globally placed along a continuum from high to low vitality. Thus for instance, Albanian

Greeks may be considered to have a very low vitality in the sense that they have low status, low institutional support for their language and culture inside Greece, and their low numbers are dispersed within a territory they cannot call their own (Trudgill & Tzavaras 1977). Contrast this with dominant groups such as the Anglo-Americans in the United States, English Canadians in Canada, the Sinhalese in Sri Lanka, all of whom can be considered to have high vitality, given that they occupy relatively favourable positions on status, demographic and institutional support variables. It can be proposed that members of dominant and subordinate ethnic groups carry around with them cognitive representations of their own and of each other's perceived vitalities. Sometimes the objectively measured vitality of a group can be at odds with its subjective character as perceived by its members. Indeed, it might be important for a dominant group to feed its subordinate counterparts with false information which could induce them to consider their vitality as low. How members of groups consider the sociostructural forces affecting them is as yet a barren, yet potentially fruitful, field for social psychological inquiry. Moreover, it could be argued that it is precisely these *perceptions* rather than any objectively calculated sociological or demographic forces which mediate and determine whether individuals (and hence groups) concede use of their language, and whether ethnic speech markers are adopted.

2.3. Ethnic speech markers: some predictions of usage

On the basis of sections 2.1 and 2.2, the following three empirically testable hypotheses are proposed about the use of ethnic speech markers (Giles 1978). These are translated into the terms of figure 1 where it can be assumed in this instance that Groups A and B constitute dominant and subordinate positions in the intergroup hierarchy respectively. First, the less aware Group B is of cognitive alternatives to its social and linguistic inferiority, and the lower its self-reported vitality, the more likely it will be that group members will adopt the language and ethnic speech markers of Group A and attenuate those associated with Group B. In accommodation terms (Giles 1973, 1977b), such a linguistic process is called 'upward convergence'. It might be worthwhile to point out that it is rare that subordinate groups perceive absolutely no cognitive alternatives to the existing status position of their group. More likely, it is the case that situations are set up for the subordinate group to view its position as legitimate but nevertheless a *little* unstable. Interestingly, Turner &

Brown (1978) manipulated orthogonally the dimensions stability–instability and legitimacy–illegitimacy to determine their effects on intergroup discrimination with minimal social groups of high and low status in a laboratory setting. They found that outgroup favouritism was the highest for the low status group when the situation was defined as being legitimate but unstable. It has been suggested by Donald Taylor (see Taylor & Giles 1979) in his cyclic theory of intergroup relations that the security of a dominant group is best maintained when the subordinate group is allowed to feel that some of its members (if exceptional enough) can qualify for acceptance into the superior group, i.e. the situation is perceived to be unstable but legitimate. In order to facilitate such feelings, a *limited* number of the subordinate group are indeed granted entrance, albeit sometimes short-lived (Tajfel 1978b), but many aspirants who have entirely adequate qualifications are refused entry. Taylor proposes that it is just these latter individuals who are thus made aware of the *illegitimacy* of the intergroup situation and who attempt to mobilize group action on the part of the subordinate group to rectify their social identity. Therefore, it may well be that the above hypothesis is fully operative in situations perceived as legitimate but unstable.

Second, the greater the awareness of cognitive alternatives among Group B as regards its inferiority, and the more vitality they self-report, the more likely they will be to retain their own language and create or accentuate ethnic speech markers in Group A's language (or a lingua franca) should communicational constraints demand a particular tongue. In accommodation terms, such a linguistic process is termed 'downward divergence'. Following Bourhis (1979), the higher Group B's vitality, the more resources it has available for sanctioning (e.g. use of abuse, traitor labels, negative evaluations) or for rewarding (e.g. offers of help and positive evaluations) linguistic behaviour of ingroup members which conforms to speech marker accentuation in particularly public interethnic encounters.

Third, the greater the awareness of cognitive alternatives amongst Group A as to its social and linguistic superiority, and the greater the perceived vitality of Group B, the more likely members of the former group will be to differentiate linguistically from the latter by means of adopting more derogatory lexical markers of the outgroup and by creating new ingroup markers at other linguistic levels. In accommodation terms, such a linguistic process is termed 'upward divergence'. It can also be suggested that one of the important ways in which dominant groups become sensitive to the existence of cognitive alternatives amongst the subordinate group is the latter's overt use of linguistic differentiation strategies in intergroup encounters.

Although all of these hypotheses are obviously important and worthy of theoretical extension each in its own right, let us now focus most of our attention specifically on the second one (i.e. the case where subordinate groups are aware of cognitive alternatives to the existing intergroup status hierarchy), for it is arguably here that psychological conditions are most ripe for disrupting the status quo and initiating social and linguistic change (Tajfel 1974, 1978a). Given that the criterial attributes for ethnic group membership can include a whole range of *non*linguistic characteristics, such as skin colour, cultural traditions, etc., the accentuation of speech markers (as pointed out in section 2.1) is only one of the *many* ways in which ethnic differentiation between groups can occur (Tajfel 1978b). As Giles stressed, 'linguistic differentiation *vis-à-vis* a competing outgroup does not in itself mean that an ethnic group has achieved a satisfactory social identity. This might be particularly true in a situation where economic and power disparities still exist between the groups' (1978: 388). Furthermore, as Smith, Giles & Hewstone (1979) have stated, 'Unfortunately, sociolinguistic research and theory has given little attention to the conditions under which speech styles and content gain pre-eminence over other features of the environment. A more complete picture of the role of language in society must take into account such concerns and this seems a useful empirical priority for the future.' Hence, although the awareness of cognitive alternatives and the perception of a high vitality may be the necessary conditions for a subordinate group to accentuate its ethnic speech markers, they may not be sufficient for *this* type of intergroup differentiation to occur. In section 3, a set of factors will be elaborated which may allow us to predict a little more precisely when speech markers rather than other nonlinguistic markers would be highly valued as components of ethnic identity and hence accentuated by subordinate groups who are aware of cognitive alternatives in interethnic contact. More specifically, it will be argued for such groups that the softer the perceived linguistic and nonlinguistic boundaries existing between ethnic groups, the more likely speech markers will be adopted in order to accentuate ethnic categorization. As intergroup communication between subordinate and dominant groups is more often than not conducted in the latter's language, we will be considering this process in terms of the subordinate group's use of ethnic speech markers in the outgroup tongue with which it is fluent.

3. An ethnic boundary model

Guided by notions of Banton (1978) on boundary maintenance, ethnic groups may be considered as occupying different positions along a continuum from *perceived* hard to soft ethnic boundaries. Hard boundaries are those ethnic characteristics a group possesses which are so overt and consensually distinctive of the social category that interethnic mobility is virtually impossible. Such hard boundaries would include distinctive skin colours, physical sizes, facial features, dress styles, cultural traditions and values as well as language. Ethnic groups placed at this end of the continuum would consider that they had a whole range of exclusive attributes which were (i) difficult to acquire and (ii) often easily and frequently used for ethnic categorization with the minimum of cognitive effort. Therefore, ethnic groups which had soft boundaries *vis-à-vis* a relevant outgroup would have far fewer of these attributes which could differentiate them, and hence interethnic mobility would be potentially much easier.

In the present context, it seems important to distinguish between hard and soft linguistic *and* nonlinguistic boundary continua, which gives us the two-dimensional space shown in figure 2 below. In quadrant A are those ethnic groups which perceive themselves to have both hard linguistic and hard nonlinguistic boundaries. These would be represented in North America by, for example, the Hutterites who have a distinctive religion (hard nonlinguistic) as well as a distinctive language (hard linguistic). Examplars in Britain would be members of certain Pakistani communities, and in Malaysia members of the Chinese communities, both of

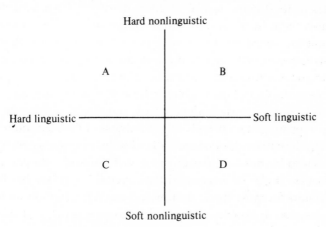

Figure 2. Perceived linguistic and nonlinguistic boundary continua

whom have distinctive cultural traditions, physiognomies and separate languages from members of the dominant cultures. In quadrant B are those ethnic groups which have a hard nonlinguistic boundary but a soft linguistic one. Representatives here would be those many ethnic minorities in North America such as certain Polynesian and Asian communities who have assimilated English with the loss of their own language (soft linguistic) but still have many distinctive features such as skin colour, cultural traditions, food, etc. (hard nonlinguistic). In quadrant C are those ethnic groups which have soft nonlinguistic boundaries but hard linguistic ones. To varying degrees, representatives would be many French Canadians and Welshmen who would consider that their use of French and Welsh respectively (hard linguistic) is virtually the only factor which distinguishes them from their relevant Anglophone outgroups, perhaps because they have assimilated the latter's values and traditions to a considerable degree and have a very similar physiognomy (soft nonlinguistic). Finally, in quadrant D are those ethnic groups which consider themselves at the softer end of both continua as there are few linguistic or nonlinguistic attributes they do not share with a relevant outgroup. Representatives here would be the many Bretons and Welshmen who have only a few values (soft nonlinguistic) and a slight accent in French and English respectively (soft linguistic) forming the boundary between themselves and the majority cultures.

It can be suggested that all individuals who self-identify with a particular ethnic category have some minimal nonlinguistic and linguistic characteristics with which to mark their ethnic affiliations. Thus, ethnic groups will at least think they have some differential values and abilities as well as at least some lexical ingroup markers (if not accents) which distinguish them from relevant ethnic outgroups. Hence, it can be proposed that the *overall* hardness–softness of the boundaries demarcating different ethnic groups will be a multiplicative function of their perceived linguistic and nonlinguistic hardness values. It would be interesting to explore empirically not only which ethnic attributes contribute most to perceived hardness along both continua, but also to determine whether ethnic groups in contact perceive the hardness of their boundaries in the same ways. It may be, for instance, that dominant groups perceive 'their' boundaries to be harder than those of their subordinate counterparts. Nevertheless, it can be suggested that overall boundary hardness is a desirable state for most ethnic groups and an optimal condition for which they may strive. It enables them to differentiate on valued dimensions between own and outgroup more clearly, thereby achieving a positive social identity (Tajfel 1978a) and allowing for the easier establishment of ingroup norms (Banton 1978).

The heuristic model presented in figure 2 is however intended to be *dynamic* in a number of respects. First, it allows for the location of different members of the same ethnic group to be located in different quadrants depending on how they *perceive* boundary hardness–softness. This is implicit in our examples of Welshmen cited previously, and in this sense the model is a truly social psychological one. Second, the model allows for the movement of ethnic groups from one quadrant to another. Thus, for instance, because of communication needs a subordinate group might have to soften its linguistic boundaries by accommodating or assimilating to the language of the outgroup (see figure 1). In other words, many ethnic groups through economic necessity might have to move from quadrant A into quadrant B. Should, however, this group be forced to concede in future some of its nonlinguistic boundaries due to the migration of some of its younger members, intermarriage, etc., i.e. feel they may be moving into quadrant D, they may react by attempting to restore overall boundary hardness by hardening their linguistic boundaries and moving into quadrant C. Third, the model allows for the reactions of the outgroup to such perceived movements of the ingroup from one quadrant to another both cognitively and behaviourally. For instance, in the cognitive domain, the loss of a distinct language by a group having to move from quadrant A to B may be viewed by the outgroup as an overt softening of ethnic identity by its members. (The latter may nevertheless compensate in any case by a hardening of its nonlinguistic dimensions.) Given that this group now looks apparently weaker, it appears more vulnerable to the outgroup who perceive their position as psychologically more secure and legitimate ('"They" moved towards "us" – "we" must be good and correct.') However, should the ingroup eventually move into quadrant D because of structural constraints as previously mentioned, the outgroup may feel *its* boundaries are becoming permeable. They may respond to such perceived boundary threats by creating linguistic differentiations, thereby *forcing* members of the ingroup into quadrant C. Thus, the perception of ethnic boundaries is in terms of social comparison so that both in- and outgroup perceive the stability of the hardness not only of their own, but also of the outgroup's, and react accordingly. Fourth, the model allows some insight into the complexities of intergroup categorization. Linguistic boundaries are intricately and interactively bound up with the accentuation *process* of ethnic categorization (Doise 1976; Tajfel 1972; Tajfel & Wilkes 1963). On certain occasions, the existence of ethnic boundaries at any one moment may be a consequence of social categorization (e.g. Parkin 1977; Wolff 1959), whilst, on others, they may be the antecedents setting in motion this process whereby an accentuation of group differences occurs on these and other evaluative dimensions (Giles & Powesland 1975; Lambert *et al*. 1960). In this sense, language can act as an independent as well as a dependent measure of interethnic relations.

The conditions under which subordinate ethnic groups who are aware of cognitive alternatives to the existing interethnic status hierarchy tend to accentuate speech markers the most, can now be made more explicit by means of the two propositions which follow.

Proposition 1. Members of a subordinate ethnic group who are talking in the outgroup language in interethnic interaction will accentuate their ethnic speech markers more in situations where they feel their linguistic boundaries are soft (quadrants B and D) rather than hard (quadrants A and C). In this regard, Bourhis *et al*. (1973) found that Welshmen who were learning Welsh (soft linguistic) considered themselves as having a stronger accent in their Welsh than those who could speak Welsh fluently (hard linguistic). Thus, subordinate group members will strengthen the linguistic boundaries in an outgroup tongue more when they do not have a distinct language within their repertoire to call their own (the assimilation paradigm in figure 1) than when they have (the accommodation paradigm in figure 1), in an attempt to achieve overall boundary hardness and distinctiveness.

Proposition 2. Members of a subordinate ethnic group who are talking in the outgroup language in interethnic interaction will accentuate their ethnic speech markers more in situations where they feel their nonlinguistic boundaries are soft (quadrants C and D) rather than hard (quadrants A and B). Thus, subordinate group members will strengthen the linguistic boundaries in an outgroup tongue more when they do not have many physical and cultural characteristics to call their own than when they have, in an attempt to achieve overall boundary hardness and distinctiveness. Conversely, the accentuation of ethnic speech markers may not be an important means of social differentiation between groups in those contexts where a large array of nonlinguistic dimensions already provide the group with a perceived hard boundary.

It can be argued, then, using an analysis of variance model, that the manipulation of the independent variables hardness vs. softness of linguistic boundary and hardness vs. softness of nonlinguistic boundary each has main effects on the dependent measure, use of ethnic speech markers. In figure 3, the degree of ethnic speech marker accentuation is schematized accordingly. Interestingly, the model suggests that the most linguistic differentiation occurs, paradoxically enough, with the very groups (quadrant D) which have the softest perceived overall ethnic boundaries and hence the greatest similarity with the ethnic outgroup (cf. Tajfel 1974). Support for this notion comes independently from the work of Turner (1978b). He suggested on the basis of cognitive dissonance and commitment principles (see Harvey & Smith 1977: 219–27) that when individuals voluntarily have chosen to take up membership of a social category, group cohesion will be greatest when the group fails on a task, but that for involuntary category members the reverse is true, i.e. group cohesion will be greatest when the group succeeds. Therefore, defeat in conditions of voluntary commitment to membership actually facilitates ingroup cohesion and outgroup differentiation. In quadrant D where both boundaries are perceived as soft, the individual has the choice of self-identifying with his ethnic ingroup or passing out of it to perhaps a greater extent than in any of the other quadrants. When the individual does commit himself to ethnic identification under these conditions, the 'failure' of the group in terms of the softness of its boundaries will mobilize the person to a greater sense of ingroup cohesion and collective

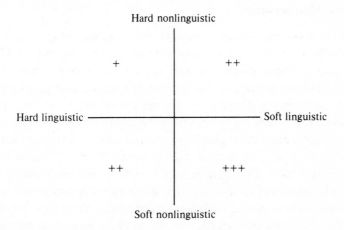

Figure 3. Degree of ethnic marker accentuation to perceived hardness–softness of linguistic and nonlinguistic boundaries (+ indicates the degree of ethnic speech marker accentuation)

action on behalf of the group than were the boundaries perceived to be more secure. Because ethnic speech markers can often be a more overt expression of social differentiation in interethnic interaction than their nonlinguistic counterparts (i.e. individuals can easily hear and monitor their distinctiveness tactics), it is the linguistic boundary that tends to become hardened. Indeed, such reasoning might in a small part help explain the rebirth of ethnicity in the last generation or so (Fishman 1977).

This discussion leads us to elaborate somewhat on the predictions made in section 2.3, but with respect to the use of ethnic speech markers in the dominant group's language. First, 'upward convergence' (an attenuation of speech markers by members of subordinate groups) will probably occur when there is (i) little awareness of cognitive alternatives and (ii) a low self-reported ingroup vitality. Second, 'downward divergence' (an accentuation of speech markers by members of subordinate groups) will probably occur when there is (i) an awareness of cognitive alternatives and (ii) a high self-reported vitality, *and* (iii) linguistic and nonlinguistic boundaries are perceived to be soft (quadrant D). Finally, it can be proposed that 'upward divergence' (an accentuation of speech markers by members of the dominant group) will probably occur when (i) an awareness amongst the subordinate group of cognitive alternatives is perceived, (ii) the greater is the perceived vitality of the subordinate group, *and* (iii) the subordinate group perceives ethnic boundaries to be linguistically and nonlinguistically soft.

4. Concluding remarks

The use of a separate ethnic language for a number of groups does not appear to be an essential component of their cultural identity (cf. Fishman 1972). Many ethnic groups appear to have a strong sense of ethnic identity without recourse to the use of a distinctive language such as the majority of Scots- and Irishmen, Guamanians and Albanian Greeks to name but a few (Riley 1975; Trudgill & Tzavaras 1977). Nevertheless, the possession of a distinct language can be a precious commodity for ethnic groups as was seen in section 1.2 (Fishman 1977). At the same time however, it is rare (although examples such as the assimilated Cardiff Blacks referred to earlier do exist) to find an ethnic group which does not have its own distinctive speech markers at some intralingual levels, even when they have lost their ethnic tongues as in the assimilation model (see figure 1). Indeed, implicit within this chapter has been the notion that intralingual ethnic speech markers in an outgroup tongue can be as important symbolizers of ingroup indentity as a distinctive language itself. This seems particularly evident when we recall the cognitive definition of ethnic group membership with which this chapter commenced; that is, only those individuals who self-identify with the ethnic category. As pointed out then, many individuals who, according to certain objective criterial attributes, would apparently qualify for ethnic group membership need not identify to any degree with that social category and hence with our sociolinguistic predictions. Such notions as these led Giles, Bourhis & Taylor (1977: 327) to claim that 'We must be careful of not taking a too restrictive view of "language". Perhaps we ought to substitute the term "ethnic speech style". . . . A distinctive language then need not be a necessary or sufficient symbol of one's ethnicity, but some speech style distinctiveness to one's group might be.' As suggested earlier, much research needs to be conducted to determine what are the important linguistic components of such an ethnic speech style at the phonological, grammatical, paralinguistic/prosodic and lexical levels.

One of the principal aims of this chapter, besides reviewing relevant work on ethnicity markers in speech, was to provide a coherent framework for social psychological work in this area which could be conducted with almost any ethnolinguistic contact situation. The theory proposed that linguistic behaviour (and probably many aspects of non-verbal behaviour; see von Raffler-Engel 1979), and particularly the use of ethnic (and *other* social) speech markers, can be understood in terms of (i) the relative status positions of the ethnic groups concerned, (ii) the group members' desire for a positive social identity and the degree of importance attached to ethnic group membership, (iii) the construal of the interethnic situation in terms of the awareness of cognitive alternatives or the lack of them, (iv) the subjective impression of ethnolinguistic vitality as high–low, and (v) the perception of ethnic boundaries on both linguistic and nonlinguistic dimensions as hard–soft. Ethnic groups are, as pointed out by Ryan & Carranza (1977) and others, not homogeneous wholes and hence individuals within them can be differentially considered along these dimensions. Given that some of the important (albeit undoubtedly not all) social psychological dimensions operating in an interethnic encounter have been specified, we may be better able to understand by means of the foregoing hypotheses when ethnic speech markers are adopted, by whom and to what degree in many cultural contexts. This is not of course to claim that the minimally sufficient conditions for the accentuation of ethnic speech markers have been discovered; obviously the theory is in its embryonic stages. Further work in this vein, particularly in relation to designing appropriate methodologies to explore empirically subjective vitality and boundary hardness, will enable not only deficiencies in the theory to be rectified but also specify more clearly which markers are used and why. It can be argued further that while social identity theory (Tajfel 1978a) itself helps explain to a considerable degree why certain language strategies are chosen in interethnic contexts rather than others, an examination of speech markers with real ethnic groups in contact can elucidate variables and processes which may provide a reciprocal input into social identity theory. For instance, perceived high–low ethnolinguistic vitality and boundary hardness–softness are variables implicitly held constant, but weakly, in the minimal intergroup categorization experiments (Tajfel 1978a; Tajfel, Flament, Billig & Bundy 1971). The predictions outlined above with respect to ethnic speech markers suggest that these two dimensions interact with group identification in important and predictable ways that could be manipulated within the confines of the laboratory setting. In any case, the present social psychological approach to language and ethnicity will not only allow us eventually to construct the ways in which linguistic markers of ethnicity are passive barometers, or dependent measures, of particular ethnic relations, but will also provide insight into the inevitable ways in which language acts as an *independent variable* creatively influencing those relations (Smith, Giles & Hewstone 1979; Taylor & Giles 1979).

References

Aboud, F. E. 1978. Social developmental aspects of language. *Papers in Linguistics*, 9, 15–37.

Agheyisi, R. 1977. Language interlarding in the speech of Nigerians. In P. F. A. Kotey & H. Der Houssikian (eds.) *Language and Linguistic Problems in Africa*. Columbia, SC.

Anderson, A. B. 1979. The survival of ethnolinguistic minorities. In H. Giles & B. Saint-Jacques (eds.) *Language and Ethnic Relations*. Oxford.

Andersson, T. & Boyer, M. 1970. *Bilingual Schooling in the United States*. Washington, DC.

Banton, M. 1978. *A Theory of Racial and Ethnic Relations: rational choice*. Working Papers on Ethnic Relations, 8. Research Unit on Ethnic Relations, University of Bristol.

Barth, F. 1969. *Ethnic Groups and Boundaries*. Boston.

Biondi, L. 1975. *The Italian-American Child: his sociolinguistic acculturation*. Georgetown University Monographs. Washington, DC.

Blom, J.-P. & Gumperz, J. J. 1972. Social meaning in linguistic structures: code-switching in Norway. In J. J. Gumperz & D. Hymes (eds.) *Directions in Sociolinguistics: the ethnography of communication*. New York.

Botha, E. 1970. The effect of language on values expressed by bilinguals. *Journal of Social Psychology*, *80*, 143–5.

Bourhis, R. Y. 1979. Language and ethnic interaction: a social psychological approach. In H. Giles & B. Saint-Jacques (eds.) *Language and Ethnic Relations*. Oxford.

Bourhis, R. Y. & Giles, H. 1977a. The language of intergroup distinctiveness. In H. Giles (ed.) *Language, Ethnicity and Intergroup Relations*. London.

1977b. Children's voice and ethnic categorization in Britain. *La monda lingvoproblemo*, *6*, 85–94.

Bourhis, R. Y., Giles, H. & Lambert, W. E. 1975. Social consequences of accommodating one's speech style: a cross-national investigation. *International Journal of the Sociology of Language*, *6*, 55–72.

Bourhis, R. Y., Giles, H. & Tajfel, H. 1973. Language as a determinant of ethnic identity. *European Journal of Social Psychology*, *3*, 447–60.

Bourhis, R. Y., Giles, H., Leyens, J. P. & Tajfel, H. 1979. Psycholinguistic distinctiveness: language divergence in Belgium. In H. Giles & R. St Clair (eds.) *Language and Social Psychology*. Oxford.

Bram, J. 1955. *Language and Society*. New York.

Brennan, E. M., Ryan, E. B. & Dawson, W. E. 1975. Scaling of apparent accentedness by magnitude estimation and sensory modality matching. *Journal of Psycholinguistic Research*, *4*, 27–36.

Breton, R. 1971. Institutional completeness of ethnic communities and personal relations of immigrants. In B. R. Blishen, F. E. Jones, K. D. Naegels & J. Porter (eds.) *Canadian Society: sociological perspectives*. Toronto.

Burling, R. 1972. *English in Black and White*. New York.

Chapman, A. J., Smith, J. R. & Foot, H. C. 1977. Language, humour and intergroup relations. In H. Giles (ed.) *Language, Ethnicity and Intergroup Relations*. London.

Clyne, M. G. 1967. *Transference and Triggering*. The Hague.

1976. Aspects of migrant language ecology in Australia. *Talanya*, *3*, 75–92.

Cohen, A. D. 1974. The Culver City Spanish immersion program. *Modern Language Journal*, *58*, 95–103.

Daniel, J. L. 1970. Facilitation of White–Black communication. *Journal of Communication*, *20*, 134–41.

Dashefsky, A. 1975. Theoretical frameworks in the study of ethnic identity: towards a social psychology of ethnicity. *Ethnicity*, *2*, 10–18.

De Vries, J. 1979. Towards a demography of language and ethnic relations. In H. Giles & B. Saint-Jacques (eds.) *Language and Ethnic Relations*. Oxford.

Dickens, M. & Sawyer, G. M. 1962. An experimental comparison of vocal quality among mixed groups of Whites and Negroes. *Southern Speech Journal*, *18*, 178–85.

Dillard, J. 1972. *Black English*. New York.

Dittmar, N. 1977. The acquisition of German syntax by foreign migrant workers. In D. Sankoff (ed.) *Linguistic Variation: models and methods*. New York.

Doise, W. 1976. *Groups and Individuals: explanations in social psychology*. Cambridge.

Dundes, A. 1971. A study of ethnic slurs: the Jew and the Pollack in the United States. *Journal of American Folklore*, *84*, 196–203.

Eastman, C. M. 1979. Language resurrection. In H. Giles & B. Saint-Jacques (eds.) *Language and Ethnic Relations*. Oxford.

Eiser, J. R. & Ross, M. A. In press. Partisan language, immediacy and attitude change. *European Journal of Social Psychology*.

Ervin, S. M. 1964. Language and TAT content in bilinguals. *Journal of Abnormal & Social Psychology, 68*, 500–7.

Escure, G. J. 1979. Linguistic variation and ethnic interaction in Belize: Creole/Carib. In H. Giles & B. Saint-Jacques (eds.) *Language and Ethnic Relations*. Oxford.

Fanon, F. 1961. *Black Skin, White Masks*. New York.

Fellman, J. 1973. Concerning the 'revival' of the Hebrew language. *Anthropological Linguistics, 15*, 250–7.

Ferguson, C. A. 1975. Towards a characterization of English 'foreigner talk.' *Anthropological Linguistics 17*, 1–14.

Fishman, J. A. 1966. *Language Loyalty in the United States*. The Hague.

1972. Varieties of ethnicity and varieties of language consciousness. In J. A. Fishman, *Language and Sociocultural Change: essays by Joshua Fishman*. Stanford, Calif. First published 1965.

1977. Language and ethnicity. In H. Giles (ed.) *Language, Ethnicity and Intergroup Relations*. London.

Flores, N. & Hopper, R. 1975. Mexican American's evaluations of spoken Spanish and English. *Speech Monographs, 42*, 91–8.

Gearing, F. O. 1970. *The Face of the Fox*. Chicago.

Geuder, P. 1979. Language and ethnic interaction in Rabbit Boss: a novel by Thomas Sanchez. In H. Giles & B. Saint-Jacques (eds.) *Language and Ethnic Relations*. Oxford.

Giles, H. 1973. Accent mobility: a model and some data. *Anthropological Linguistics, 15*, 87–105.

(ed.) 1977a. *Language, Ethnicity and Intergroup Relations*. London.

1977b. Social psychology and applied linguistics: towards an integrative approach. *ITL: Review of Applied Linguistics, 35*, 27–42.

1978. Linguistic differentiation in ethnic groups. In H. Tajfel (ed.) *Differentiation Between Social Groups*. London.

Giles, H. & Bourhis, R. Y. 1975. Linguistic assimilation: West Indians in Cardiff. *Language Sciences, 38*, 9–12.

1976. Voice and racial categorization in Britain. *Communication Monographs, 43*, 108–14.

Giles, H. & Powesland, P. F. 1975. *Speech Style and Social Evaluation*. London.

Giles, H. & Smith, P. M. 1979. Accommodation theory: optimal levels of convergence. In H. Giles & R. St Clair (eds.) *Language and Social Psychology*. Oxford.

Giles, H., Bourhis, R. Y. & Taylor, D. M. 1977. Towards a theory of language in ethnic group relations. In H. Giles (ed.) *Language, Ethnicity and Intergroup Relations*. London.

Giles, H., Taylor, D. M. & Bourhis, R. Y. 1973. Towards a theory of interpersonal accommodation through speech: some Canadian data. *Language in Society, 2*, 117–92.

1977. Dimensions of Welsh identity. *European Journal of Social Psychology, 7*, 29–39.

Giles, H., Taylor, D. M., Lambert, W. E. & Albert, G. 1976. Dimensions of ethnic identity: an example from Northern Maine. *Journal of Social Psychology, 100*, 11–19.

Glaser, D. 1958. Dynamics of ethnic identification. *American Sociological Review, 23*, 31–40.

Glazer, N. & Moynihan, D. P. 1975. *Ethnicity: theory and experience.* Cambridge, Mass.

Greeley, A. M. & McCready, W. C. 1974. Does ethnicity matter? *Ethnicity, 1*, 91–108.

Gumperz. J. J. 1977. Sociocultural knowledge in conversation inference. In *Georgetown University 28th Round Table on Languages and Linguistics.* Washington, DC.
　1978. The conversational analysis of interethnic communication. In E. L. Ross (ed.) *Interethnic Communication.* Proceedings of the Southern Anthropological Society. Atlanta, Georgia.

Harvey, J. H. & Smith, W. P. 1977. *Social Psychology: an attributional approach.* St Louis, Miss.

Herman, S. 1961. Explorations in the social psychology of language choice. *Human Relations, 14*, 149–64.

Holt, G. S. 1972. Inversion in Black communication. In T. Kochman (ed.) *Rappin' and Stylin' Out: communication in urban Black America.* Champaign, Ill.

Husband, C. 1977. News media, language and race relations: a case study in identity maintenance. In H. Giles (ed.) *Language, Ethnicity and Intergroup Relations.* London.
　1979. English language, media and Britain's immigration problem. In H. Giles & B. Saint-Jacques (eds.) *Language and Ethnic Relations.* Oxford.

Hymes, D. 1972. Models of the interaction of language and social life. In J. J. Gumperz & D. Hymes (eds.) *Directions in Sociolinguistics: the ethnography of communication.* New York.

Isajiw, W. W. 1974. Definitions of ethnicity. *Ethnicity, 1*, 111–24.

Janda, I. H. 1976. English–Hungarian and Hungarian–English language interference phenomena in Chicago. In P. A. Reich (ed.) *Second Lacus Forum, 1975.* Columbia, SC.

Jones, R. R. 1973. Linguistic standardization and national development. *International Journal of Psychology, 8*, 51–4.

Kachru, B. B. 1965. The *Indianness* in Indian English. *Word, 21*, 391–410.

Kearney, R. N. 1977. Language and the rise of Tamil separatism in Sri Lanka. Mimeo, Foreign Languages, Syracuse University, New York State.

Khleif, B. 1979. Insiders, outsiders and renegades: toward a classification of ethnolinguistic labels. In H. Giles & B. Saint-Jacques (eds.) *Language and Ethnic Relations.* Oxford.

Kochman, T. 1975. *Perceptions along the Power Axis: a cognitive residue of interracial encounters.* Southwest Educational Development Laboratory Working Papers in Sociolinguistics, *21*.

Labov, W. 1963. The social motivation of a sound change. *Word, 19*, 273–309.
　1966. *The Social Stratification of English in New York City.* Center for Applied Linguistics, Washington, DC.

Lambert, W. E. 1974. Culture and language as factors in learning and education.

In F. E. Aboud & R. D. Meade (eds.) *Cultural Factors in Learning and Education*. Bellington.

Lambert, W. E., Hodgson, R. C., Gardner, R. C. & Fillenbaum, S. 1960. Evaluational reactions to spoken language. *Journal of Abnormal and Social Psychology*, 60, 44–51.

Lass, J. N., Mertz, P. J. & Kimmel, K. L. 1978. The effect of temporal speech alterations on speaker race and sex identifications. *Language and Speech*, 21, 279–90.

Ledvinka, J. 1971. Race of interviewer and the language elaboration of Black interviewees. *Journal of Social Issues*, 27, 185–97.

Littlewood, W. T. 1976. 'Gastarbeiterdeutsch' and its significance for German teaching. *Audio-Visual Journal*, 3, 155–8.

Lukens, J. 1979. Inter-ethnic conflict and communicative distances. In H. Giles & B. Saint-Jacques (eds.) *Language and Ethnic Relations*. Oxford.

McConahay, J. B. & Hough, J. C. Jr. 1976. Symbolic racism. *Journal of Social Issues*, 32, 23–45.

Martineau, W. H. 1972. A model of the social functions of humor. In J. H. Goldstein & P. E. McGhee (eds.) *The Psychology of Humour: theoretical and empirical issues*. New York.

Meisel, J. M. In press. Linguistic simplication: a study of immigrant workers' speech and foreigner talk. In P. Corder & E. Roulet (eds.) *A Reader on Interlanguage*. Geneva.

Moerman, M. 1965. Ethnic identification in a complex civilization: Who are the Lue? *American Anthropologist*, 67, 1215–27.

Morley, I. & Stephenson. G. 1976. *The Social Psychology of Bargaining*. London.

Nahir, M. 1978. Language planning in Modern Hebrew. Mimeo, University of Manitoba.

Narroll, R. 1964. On ethnic unit classification. *Current Anthropology*, 5, 283–91.

Nash, R. 1976. Phantom cognates and other curiosities in Puerto Rican Engañol. *La Monda linguo problemo*, 5, 157–67.

Ornstein, J. & Dubois, B. L. 1977. Mexican-American English: prolegomena to a neglected regional variety. In R. J. Di Pietro & E. L. Blansitt (eds.) *Third Lacus Forum, 1976*. Columbia, SC.

Parkin, D. 1977. Emergent and stabilised multilingualism: poly-ethnic peer groups in urban Kenya. In H. Giles (ed.) *Language, Ethnicity and Intergroup Relations*. London.

Peabody, D. 1970. Evaluative and descriptive aspects in personality perception: a reappraisal. *Journal of Personality and Social Psychology*, 16, 639–46.

Platt, J. T. 1975. The Singapore English speech continuum and its basilect 'Singlish' as a 'Creoloid'. *Anthropological Linguistics*, 17, 363–74.

    1977. Code selection in a multilingual-polyglossic society. *Talanya*, 4, 64–75.

Potter, S. 1960. *Language in the Modern World*. Harmondsworth, Middx.

Rameh, C. 1977. The Portugese–English language contact in the United States. In R. J. Di Pietro & E. L. Blansitt (eds.) *Third Lacus Forum, 1976*. Columbia, SC.

Rich, A. L. 1974. *Interracial Communication*. New York.

Riley, G. A. 1975. Language loyalty and ethnocentrism in the Guamanian speech community. *Anthropological Linguistics*, 17, 286–92.

Rollman, S. A. 1978. The sensitivity of Black and White Americans in non-verbal cues of prejudice. *Journal of Social Issues*, 105, 73–7.

Ros, M. & Giles, H. In press. The Valencian language situation: an accommodation theory perspective. *ITL: Review of Applied Linguistics*.

Rose, A. M. 1972. Minorities. In D. Sills (ed.) *International Encyclopedia of the Social Sciences*. New York.

Rosenthal, M. S. 1974. The magic boxes: preschool children's attitudes toward Black and Standard English. *Florida FL Reporter*, Spring/Fall, 56–62, 92–3.

Ryan, E. B. 1979. Why do nonstandard dialects persist? In H. Giles & R. St Clair (eds.) *Language and Social Psychology*. Oxford.

Ryan, E. B. & Carranza, M. A. 1977. Ingroup and outgroup reactions to Mexican American language varieties. In H. Giles (ed.) *Language, Ethnicity and Intergroup Relations*. London.

Ryan, E. B., Carranza, M. A. & Moffie, R. W. In press. Reactions toward varying degrees of accentedness in the speech of Spanish–English bilinguals. *Language and Speech*.

Sattler, J. M. 1970. Racial experimenter effects in experimentation, testing, interviewing and psychotherapy. *Psychological Bulletin*, 73, 137–60.

Sawyer, J. B. 1973. Social aspects of bilingualism in San Antonio, Texas. In R. W. Bailey & J. L. Robinson (eds.) *Varieties of Present-Day English*. New York.

Scotton, C. M. 1976. Strategies of neutrality: language choice in uncertain situations. *Language*, 52, 919–41.

1978. 'Elite closure' and language policy in Africa. Paper presented at the Symposium on African Language Policies, Linguistics Institute, University of Illinois, 6–8 July.

Scotton, C. M. & Ury, W. In press. Bilingual strategies: the social functions of code-switching. *International Journal of the Sociology of Language*.

Segalowitz, N. 1977. Bilingualism and social behaviour. In W. H. Coons, D. M. Taylor & M.-A. Tremblay (eds.) *Individual, Language and Society*. Ottawa.

Segalowitz, N. & Gatbonton, E. 1977. Studies of the non-fluent bilingual. In P. Hornby (ed.) *Bilingualism: psychological and social implications*. New York.

Shaffer, D. 1976. The place of code-switching in linguistic contacts. In P. A. Reich (ed.) *Second Lacus Forum, 1975*. Columbia, SC.

Shuy, R. W. 1977. Problems of communication in the cross-cultural medical interview. *ITL: Review of Applied Linguistics*, 35.

Shuy, R. W., Baratz, J. C. & Wolfram, W. A. 1969. Sociolinguistic factors in speech identification. NIMHR Project MH 15048-01, Center for Applied Linguistics, Washington, DC.

Simard, L. Taylor, D. M. & Giles, H. 1976. Attribution processes and interpersonal accommodation in a bilingual setting. *Language and Speech*, 19, 374–87.

Smith, P. M., Giles, H. & Hewstone, M. 1979. Sociolinguistics: a social psychological perspective. In R. St Clair & H. Giles (eds.) *The Social and Psychological Contexts of Language*. Hillsdale, NJ.

Tajfel, H. 1972. La catégorisation sociale. In S. Moscovici (ed.) *Introduction à la psychologie sociale*. Paris.

1974. Social identity and intergroup behaviour. *Social Science Information*, 13, 65–93.

(ed.) 1978a. *Differentiation Between Social Groups*. London.

1978b. *The Social Psychology of Minorities*. London.

Tajfel, H. & Turner, J. 1978. An integrative theory of intergroup conflict. In W. G. Austin & S. Worchel (eds.) *The Social Psychology of Intergroup Relations.* Monterey, Calif.

Tajfel, H. & Wilkes, A. L. 1963. Classification and quantitative judgment. *British Journal of Psychology, 54,* 101–14.

Tajfel, H., Flament, C., Billig, M. & Bundy, R. 1971. Social categorization and intergroup behaviour. *European Journal of Social Psychology, 1,* 149–78.

Taylor, D. M. & Giles, H. 1979. At the crossroads of research into language and ethnicity. In H. Giles & B. Saint-Jacques (eds.) *Language and Ethnic Relations.* Oxford.

Taylor, D. M. & Simard, L. 1975. Social interaction in a bilingual setting. *Canadian Psychological Review, 16,* 240–54.

Taylor, D. M., Bassili, J. & Aboud, F. E. 1973. Dimensions of ethnic identity: an example from Quebec. *Journal of Social Psychology, 89,* 185–92.

Taylor, D. M., Meynard, R. & Rheault, E. 1977. Threat to ethnic identity and second language learning. In H. Giles (ed.) *Language, Ethnicity and Intergroup Relations.* London.

Trudgill, P. 1974. *Sociolinguistics.* Harmondsworth, Middx.

Trudgill, P. & Tzavaras, G. A. 1977. Why Albanian-Greeks are not Albanians: language shift and ethnicity in Attica and Biotia. In H. Giles (ed.) *Language, Ethnicity and Intergroup Relations.* London.

Turner, J. 1975. Social comparison and social identity: some prospects for intergroup behaviour. *European Journal of Social Psychology, 5,* 5–34.

1978a. Towards a cognitive redefinition of the social group. Paper presented at the Colloquium on Social Identity at the European Laboratory of Social Psychology, at Université de Haute Bretagne, Rennes, France.

1978b. Social identification and intergroup behaviour: some emerging issues in the social psychology of intergroup behaviour. Research proposal, University of Bristol.

Turner, J. & Brown, R. 1978. Social status, cognitive alternatives and intergroup behaviour. In H. Tajfel (ed.) *Differentiation Between Social Groups.* London.

Ullrich, H. E. 1971. Linguistic aspects of antiquity: a dialect study. *Anthropological Linguistics, 13,* 106–13.

Verdoodt, A. 1977. Educational policies on languages: the case of the children of migrant workers. In H. Giles (ed.) *Language, Ethnicity and Intergroup Relations.* London.

von Raffler-Engel, W. 1979. The unconscious element in intercultural communication. In R. St Clair & H. Giles (eds.) *The Social and Psychological Contexts of Language.* Hillsdale, NJ.

Wescott, R. 1971. Labio-velarity and derogation in English: a study in phonosemic correlation. *American Speech,* Spring, 123–37.

Williams, C. 1979. Ecological and behavioural approaches to language change. In H. Giles & B. Saint-Jacques (eds.) *Language and Ethnic Relations.* Oxford.

Williams, F. 1976. *Explorations of the Linguistic Attitudes of Teachers.* Rowley, Mass.

Williams, F., Whitehead, J. L. & Miller, L. M. 1971. Ethnic stereotyping and judgments of children's speech. *Speech Monographs, 38,* 166–70.

Williams. G. 1979. The political economy of language erosion. In H. Giles & B. Saint-Jacques (eds.) *Language and Ethnic Relations.* Oxford.

Williams, J. A. & Giles, H. 1978. The changing status of women in society: an intergroup perspective. In H. Tajfel (ed.) *Differentiation Between Social Groups*. London.

Wish, M. & Kaplan, S. J. 1977. Toward an implicit theory of communication. *Sociometry*, 40, 234–46.

Wolff, H. 1959. Intelligibility and inter-ethnic attitudes. *Anthropological Linguistics*, 1, 34–41.

Wolfram, W. 1971. Black–White speech differences revisited. In W. Wolfram & N. Clarke (eds.) *Black–White Speech Relationships*. Center for Applied Linguistics, Washington, DC.

Wolfram, W. & Clarke, N. (eds.) 1971. *Black–White Speech Relationships*. Center for Applied Linguistics, Washington, DC.

8. Social structure, groups and interaction[1]

PENELOPE BROWN and STEPHEN LEVINSON

1. Introduction

In this chapter we have two main concerns. The first is to examine how matters of large-scale social structure are related to aspects of verbal interaction, especially through the mediation of participants' membership in social groups. Examining the relation between group membership and its reflection in speech, we shall see that to a large extent this relation itself is mediated by the intervening variable of social relationships. A subsidiary theme is then how, through these interrelations, linguistic markers of one social variable can convey information about other social variables.

It would be impossible within the scope of this chapter to review all the kinds of relations between social structure and aspects of verbal interaction – that would involve a survey of the whole of sociolinguistics, the sociology of language, and much of the social psychology of language use, not to mention the ethnography of speaking and cognitive anthropology.[2] This chapter does not purport then to be a complete survey of the literature; we have chosen instead to focus on some exemplary phenomena that illustrate the complex nature of the interrelations between social structure, groups, social relationships, interaction and language usage.

[1] We are indebted to the following people who read and commented on the first draft of this chapter: Colin Fraser, Howard Giles, Uli Jorns, Thomas Luckman, Peter Robinson and Klaus Scherer. We hasten to add, however, that they would not necessarily agree with the final version.

[2] For a survey of views about the relation between language structure and social structure see Grimshaw 1970; for specific claims about the relationship between social structures and the kinds of communicative codes they support see Gumperz 1962; for general surveys of these fields see Ervin-Tripp 1969; Fishman 1972, 1974; Giles & Powesland 1975; Hymes 1974; Labov 1972a: chs. 8 and 9; Trudgill 1974b. Cf. also collections of essays in Bailey & Shuy 1973; Bauman & Sherzer 1975; Fishman 1968, 1971–2; Giglioli 1972; Gumperz 1971; Gumperz & Hymes 1972; Hymes 1964; Pride & Holmes 1972; Sanches & Blount 1976; Shuy 1973; and issues of the journal *Language and Society*.

Arising out of that first concern – how matters of social structure are reflected in verbal interaction especially through the mediation of group membership – our second major concern is to make some basic theoretical observations about the ways in which social information is communicated in verbal interaction. Essentially we shall argue that it would be easy to be misled, partly by some of the methods and implicit assumptions of social psychology, towards an oversimple view of how social information is conveyed in speech.

Although we shall return to these theoretical observations in section 3, it will be helpful at the outset to have an indication of the theoretical direction of the chapter. This we provide in section 1. In section 2 we return to the empirical questions about how membership in social groups is reflected in speech, taking different kinds of linguistic marker in turn. From this a number of further questions arise, which we attempt to answer in section 3.

1.1. Approaches to relations between verbal interaction and social facts

In interaction, information about participants' social identities and relationships, and about the nature of the social context, are clearly conveyed by aspects of the speech exchanged. An attractively simple model of how this information is communicated would be this: linguistic variables are sometimes correlated with social variables, each such correlation being a *marker* in the sense of this volume, so that in interaction such linguistic variables act as direct signals of the correlated social variable. In interaction, then, social information is basically conveyed by the presence of such markers in speech.

Throughout the chapter we shall provide many examples of socially significant aspects of speech that do not fit this scheme, and we shall conclude that this picture is essentially misleading. As will become clear, this is because interactants do not generally treat socially significant linguistic features as simple signals of social facts – but rather take into account the interactional and social context in their evaluation of these features in highly complex ways. Nevertheless, there are a number of reasons why social psychologists might be predisposed to adopt such a model of how social information of this sort is encoded in speech. The reasons lie in discernable tendencies in the discipline. First, there tends to be an assumption that processes of interaction can be isolated from matters of social structure in a relatively unproblematic way. Secondly, arising from the traditional reliance on experimental methods, there is an emphasis on the concept of correlation; given a correlation between a linguistic and a social variable it is tempting to think that the linguistic variable acts for participants directly as a signal of the social variable. Thirdly, there is a tendency to think of interaction as constituted by an unstructured exchange of such signals (which we may call the *barrage-of-signals* view of interaction), even though a barrage of signals patently does not add up to the highly structured event that any interaction is. Fourthly, and relatedly, there tends to be an underemphasis or even a neglect of the notion of *structure*, either as holding among linguistic variables or among social variables. Finally, there is an overwhelming concentration on nonverbal communication, an area where the barrage-of-signals view of communication may possibly be more appropriate.[3]

[3] Some of these tendencies are much easier to document than others. There is no problem finding an array of basic introductory social psychology texts in which there is a total absence of the notion of social structure (and of structure in general), and in which interaction is treated in what for sociologists would be a social vacuum (see, e.g., Baron, Byrne & Griffitt 1974; Freedman, Carlsmith & Sears 1970; Jones & Gerard 1967). Views on the nature of communication systems are harder to document – in fact it is remarkable how many basic texts on social psychology and interaction have nothing at all to say about the structure of communication systems in the sense that, say, a linguist would understand that phrase (see, e.g., McClintock 1972; Secord & Backman 1974). But where views are expressed explicitly, they often seem to convey that disturbing picture to which we object – namely the view that interaction consists of a barrage of unstructured signals. Consider for example Newcomb's A-B-X system, as described by Sahakian (1974: 368): 'In speaking of social interaction, Newcomb does so in communicative terms, that is, social interaction (a process lasting a lifetime) he describes as virtually an exchange of information. . . . An interaction unit, the *communicative* act, is defined as "any observable behavior by which information, consisting of discriminative stimuli, is transmitted from a human source to a human recipient (Newcomb, 1953, p. 141)".' To be fair, the barrage-of-signals view of interaction, and the correlational view of a signal, seems to have another source in work done in kinesics and paralanguage by ethologists, phoneticians and others besides social psychologists. It seems for example to underlie the discussion of *indexical* information by Abercrombie (1968), Laver (1968), Laver & Hutcheson (1972), and although the model may be applicable to such domains (although this needs to be demonstrated rather than assumed – for counter-evidence see Good 1978), it certainly must not be generalized to all aspects of verbal or nonverbal communication systems. The basic distinction to be made here is that between what Lyons (1972: 71) calls *communicative* signals, those intended to inform by an exercise of choice by the sender, and noncommunicative but nevertheless *informative* signals that were not intended to convey information (cf. Laver & Trudgill, this volume: ch. 1, 1). The structureless barrage-of-signals view is only, if then, adequate for the latter kind of information transfer.

For some reason social psychologists have shied away from studying central aspects of linguistic communication, even when they claim to be studying interaction; we find instead a concentration on proxemics, kinesics, paralanguage – i.e. nonverbal communication (see e.g., Secord & Backman (1974), with a short discussion of nonverbal communication and none of verbal communication, or Argyle's (1969) text on interaction with only four pages centrally concerned with verbal interaction). Because of this concentration there is a considerable danger that the barrage-of-signals view of communication, more appropriate to the nonintentional aspects of nonverbal communication, will be generalized to the much more structured field of intentional verbal communication.

If the diagnosis is correct, these tendencies threaten to lead social psychologists towards a simple model of the sort sketched, and away from a more complex one that treats interaction systems and social systems as structures interlocked in such a way that, given aspects of the one, participants have strong expectations about aspects of the other. Such a more complex model is certainly what is required if the way in which participants themselves perceive and manage their interactions is to be adequately captured.[4]

It is instructive to contrast anthropologists' approach to interaction. To them patterns of interaction are very largely a reflex of social structure. They attempt to tie aspects of interaction, as dependent variables, back to aspects of social structure; so for example, particular principles of kinship structure are held to lie behind the systematic distribution of respect, avoidance, familiarity and joking behaviour among specific kinds of kin in particular societies (see, e.g., Lévi-Strauss 1968; Radcliffe-Brown 1952 and discussion in Brown & Levinson 1978: 243ff.). Indeed the interrelations between social organization and the structure of interaction become much clearer when one varies the social and interactional variables in cross-cultural work. Further, anthropologists treat communication systems as organized along strictly structural lines, whereby the values of symbols are seen to derive from contrast and juxtaposition with other symbols rather than from intrinsic connections to social variables (see, e.g., Leach 1976). And when anthropologists study verbal interaction in detail, they do not isolate linguistic variables, but explore instead how they cohere into a structured event that ties into social structure in a number of detailed ways (vide the ethnography of speaking, as exemplified in Bauman & Sherzer 1975). While anthropological analysis generally lacks the rigour and replicability of social psychological methods, the

---

[4] We raise here the problem of emic vs. etic analyses. We take the uncompromising position that the only facts relevant to interaction are emic ones, ones that are perceived (or at least perceivable) by participants and so can potentially play a communicative role in the interaction (cf. Giles, Scherer & Taylor, this volume: ch. 9, 3.4). We are not committed to the view that emic facts are explicitly statable by participants or even that they are conscious of them. How then are emic facts to be distinguished from etic ones? First, to be candidates for emic status they must be facts at thresholds that humans can perceive. Second, they should be shown to be attended to by participants. There are various ways of showing this, both directly and indirectly. An example is to be found in the work of Labov, discussed below. Labov showed that rates of /r/ production correlated with the social class of speakers in New York City. So far the result was etic, with no evidence that New Yorkers pay any attention to this fact or even notice it. But Labov went on to show, via the matched-guise technique, that New Yorkers can perceive different rates of production, and apparently do attend to them, and on the basis of these relative rates assign class and occupational potential (Labov 1972a). It was only the latter study that showed this social marker of class to be of any interactional significance.

emphasis on how the parts fit together to form a whole has important application to the study of social interaction.

The emphasis on one concept in particular is worth borrowing from anthropologists, namely the concept of *structure*. We may isolate two rather different concepts of structure, one relatively weak, the other stronger. The weak one involves the interdependencies and interrelations between the component parts of a whole; the dominant metaphor used here is an analogy to a mechanical or organic system where each part functions in relation to the other parts to produce the behaviour of the whole. The stronger notion of structure – as for example in Saussurian linguistics – maintains that components can only be isolated and defined, and their significance assessed, in relation to their role in the whole. So, for example, phonemes are only isolable by contrast to all the other phonemes of the language. The stronger notion seems generally appropriate to communication systems, and when we talk of *interactional structure* we may generally be taken to imply the stronger concept at least in part. In talking of social systems some theorists (e.g. Nadel 1957: 7ff.) employ only the weaker concept, while others (e.g. Leach 1961) use the stronger notion in that domain as well. When we talk of *social structure* we frankly equivocate, although in some cases at least the stronger notion does indeed seem appropriate (e.g. in the isolation of significant social groups – see below).

We shall argue that the notion of structural dependency is crucial to an understanding of how social information is conveyed in speech. It operates both to structure the relations between social variables and to structure the relations between linguistic and other interactional variables. As a consequence we shall show that for participants to understand the social significance of linguistic items, they must have a prior understanding of the social structures within which interaction takes place and a knowledge of the structural relations between aspects of interactional organization. These points can best be exemplified by a single extended example, which now follows.

1.2. Case study: T/V pronominal usage in a Tamil village

In a Tamil village in the middle of South India the population is exhaustively assigned to a set of about twenty castes (for the sociological details of this case see Beck 1972; for the sociolinguistic facts see Levinson 1977). Members operate a Tu/Vous type of pronominal system (Brown & Gilman 1960), where an asymmetric use of a T and a V pronoun indicates the superiority of the T-giver and the inferiority of the V-giver. Looking for social variables that correlate with the use of each pronoun, we would soon isolate caste membership. Correlating speaker's caste with T or V usage we could get quite strong correlations for individuals at either end of the caste hierarchy, for high-caste speakers would tend to use T and low-caste speakers would tend to use V. We would of course be wrong to conclude that T and V are therefore markers of caste – for the correlations are actually a contingent matter, contingent in part on the demographic facts that if our speaker is a top-caste member then the chances are that a random interlocutor will be of a lower caste, and will thus receive T. Let's assume that we avoid this pitfall, and realize that the asymmetric use of T and V are markers of *relative* status only. But still we cannot conclude from an instance of, say, T that the speaker is superior to the addressee, for that depends (mostly) on whether the addressee returns V. If he returns T, the two will seem rather to be exchanging markers of solidary equality. So here is a case where to ignore an elementary structure of interaction (an *exchange* of address forms) would hopelessly confuse the picture of what is going on. We conclude therefore that a giving of T *relative to a receiving of V* is a marker of the relative superiority of speaker over addressee. There is no direct correlation with caste, as we find out when we examine the speech of middle-caste members who will of course be giving T to those below and V to those above. Caste is therefore no longer a variable in our account of T/V pronouns as markers.

But that is absurd. Because caste in fact lies behind the assignment of relative status to any pair of interlocutors, and in order for members to decide appropriate usage they need to know the caste of the addressee. For they know that the social structure of the village assigns the local population exhaustively to a (almost) linear rank of castes, so that for two members drawn from different castes one can nearly always assign a relative rank to the dyad. This fact about social structure underlies members' use of pronouns even if caste is not a significant variable when correlated directly with the T/V marker.

But for members to use the T/V pronouns appropriately they need to know a lot in addition to all this. In particular they need to know more about both interactional structure and social structure. For example, they need to know that when requesting favours from particular alters it behooves them to be more polite than they otherwise would (see Brown & Levinson 1978), and this may shift their pronoun usage.[5] In addition, they

[5] The fact that T/V usage in some languages is sometimes situationally manipulable for particular interactional ends may come as a surprise to speakers of languages where the

would not fall into the trap of thinking that the reciprocal exchange of T between members of four castes of intermediate status is an expression of solidarity, for they would know that these castes find themselves in a structural position of extreme delicacy on the border of an important bipartite distinction between high and low castes. Consequently, none dares give an inch for fear of falling into the low category; if none can therefore give the others V, they must all give each other T. The reciprocal T is thus here a sign of bitter stalemate.

This example we hope points out the potential dependencies of any observable pattern of language use on the structural properties of events and their encompassing social structures. For example, we have shown that the significance (or 'social meaning') of a pronominal choice depends on a number of aspects of interactional structure: first it depends critically on the reciprocal usage, and secondly on a distinction between a normal and a marked usage, as in the extra politeness (and switch to V) involved in certain requests. We have also shown that the significance of a pattern of pronominal usage can only be properly understood against a background of social structural facts: in this case we have to appreciate that the caste hierarchy imposes a status relationship on an intercaste dyad, so that caste is only indirectly reflected and not directly marked in T/V usage. In addition, only social structural information could lead us to know that the symmetrical exchange of T among members of the four intermediate castes mentioned above is not an expression of mutual solidarity. The social and interactional significance of a particular pronominal usage is thus relative to other features of these two levels of organization: in order to understand a given pattern, we must refer back to these structural features, just as the members who produced the pattern referred to the same features in their production and interpretation of it.

In the rest of the chapter our concern is to trace out some of the (not always obvious) connections between patterns of language usage and the particular social systems in which they occur.

---

use of a T or V pronoun is more rigidly determined only by relatively permanent features of social relationships, such as status. Brown & Gilman (1960) note that this situational and attitudinal flexibility clearly existed in the past in French and English. Friedrich (1972) documents the same for Russian (for further details see Levinson 1978). In Tamil the switch from T to V to mark extra politeness in requests only occurs in social relationships where the decision to use T or V is borderline in any case; however, the switch from V to an extra-polite pronoun ('super-V') is very common in many kinds of relationships (Levinson 1977).

2. Social groups and interaction

The term 'social structure' is used in a great number of different ways by social scientists,[6] but most would probably agree that a description of a social structure should include a description of the structural relations between the major segments of a society. Such segments are often groups. Now group membership plays an important role in social interaction presumably for the following simple reason. To the extent that there are social regularities in interaction these are due in large measure to some typing or classification of significant classes of persons; rules for appropriate behaviour can then be attached to such classes. Group membership provides one such useful categorization, and so group membership often plays an important role in linking overall social structure to the details of social interaction.

After explaining what we shall mean by 'group' in section 2.1, we examine in 2.2. some cases of relatively direct linguistic markers of social group membership. We shall see, however, that in many cases the understanding of these markers requires reference both to social structure and to the structure of interaction. In section 2.3 we show how markers of social relationships in many cases are derivatively clues to group membership, and we therefore (in 2.4) review some basic markers of social relationships. In section 2.5 we describe some even more indirect ways in which social structure can affect group patterns of interaction, and in section 2.6 we draw together and discuss the different types of markers of relations between groups and language.

2.1. Group

Social scientists use the word 'group' in so many ways, as for example in the phrases *small group*, *reference group*, *corporate group*, *ethnic group*, *interest group*, that we are unlikely to find any common core that means more than 'set'. Social scientists who adopt the weak concept of structure outlined above are likely to think of groups in relatively concrete terms, as independently isolable units of social structure – perhaps in terms of Deutsch's (1968: 265) definition as 'an entity that consists of interacting people who are aware of being bound together in terms of mutually linked interests'. On the other hand, social theorists who adopt the stronger concept of structure are more likely to think of groups as relative

---

[6] For a set of contrasting views of anthropologists, see Fortes 1969; Leach 1954: 4; Lévi-Strauss 1968: 279; Nadel 1957: 5; Radcliffe-Brown 1952: 192.

concepts, each group being a unit that is relevant only in relation to units of like size that for immediate purposes are contrasted with it. Thus for a man who lives in Cambridge, his territorial identification will be with Cambridge when contrasted with Newmarket, with Cambridgeshire when contrasted with Lancashire, with England when contrasted with Scotland, with the United Kingdom when contrasted with Germany, and so on. Evans-Pritchard's (1940) classic description of the 'segmentary structure' of Nuer lineages showed that this relative concept can be the basis of coordinated group action over common interests, so that it is not necessarily inconsistent with the more concrete concept of an interest-based, potentially co-active group. In many respects this relative concept of a group, as a contrastive category, seems to fit the 'native' intuitions better: for example in India there is no lexeme that unequivocally denotes the western sociologists' units of caste or endogamous subcaste; instead the word *jaati* (adopted by western sociologists for their units of analysis) can denote any category from a lineage to an animal species. Such conceptual relativity to opposed units may also explain the elusive nature of the western folk notion of 'social class'.[7]

An interest in the linguistic correlates of group membership itself directs attention to certain kinds and levels of social unit. While with enough ingenuity a few linguistic reflexes of even the smallest and most transitory of groups can probably be found, deep discontinuities in a number of aspects of communicative competence seem to be found on the whole only in the larger groups of the sort we call ethnic groups, sectarian groups, social classes, caste categories, and so on. Such units are, at least to some extent, culture-bearing units, and the linguistic discontinuities exist because there are independent bodies of norms governing the use of speech in each such unit, maintained by the kind of internal social network that can sustain such linguistic subcultures (see Giles, this volume: ch. 7; Gumperz 1958). For those who wish to retain some more concrete concept of group, these units can be thought of as categories from which actual interest groups can be drawn in particular localized situations – in a small town, for example. But the communication networks that sustain the linguistic differentiation of the larger categories must clearly stretch beyond these localized instantiations.

Just how these networks operate is still quite unclear – Gumperz (1958) has provided evidence that discontinuities in social dialect, for instance, are not always attributable directly to discontinuities in networks of

[7] For an ethnosemantic study of Hawaiian terms for race and class along similar lines, see Kay 1975.

interaction as Bloomfield (1933) had argued. This makes untenable the view (as implied, e.g., in Trudgill 1974b: 34) that the analogues of the rivers and mountains that typically serve to divide regional dialects are, in the case of social dialects, fundamental divides in social networks (i.e. interaction barriers between groups).

However they are maintained, such basic discontinuities in language can, and are likely to, show up at all levels of the grammar (in which case we talk of *social dialects*) as well as in the norms that govern use of language – in short, in all aspects of what Hymes (1972) has termed *communicative competence*. There have in fact been relatively few studies of subcultural differences in the use of language, but this is likely to be a growing and important field of research that will complement studies of social dialect. Apart from Bernstein's work (1971), some suggestions can be found in Brown & Levinson (1978: 247–60), and some empirical work in Gumperz (1976, 1977, 1978) and Gumperz, Agrawal & Aulakh (n.d.).

Smaller groups are unlikely to maintain these fundamental discontinuities in communicative norms. Nevertheless, differences of repertoire, social deixis, but above all differences in vocabulary – and consequently in *register*, *argot*, *slang*, and so on – can still be distinctive amongst small groups. Thus in India only large categories of castes are likely to have distinctive dialects and communicative competences, while the smaller units of caste and subcaste are likely to display some lexical isoglosses. We shall touch on each of these distinctive aspects of language below.

2.2. Markers of group membership

Dialect. One of the most direct ways in which groups play a role in verbal interaction is that when we speak we tend to betray, sometimes by design and sometimes whether we like it or not, details of our group memberships. This information is carried above all in the particular variety of the code that we speak. Dialect, both regional and social, plays a key role here, and has been the subject of an immense amount of linguistic and sociolinguistic work. By dialect we understand a variety of a language distinguished from other varieties by features cross-cutting the grammar, including phonological, syntactic, lexical and prosodic features, which can be specified as a distinctive subset of the linguistic rules of a language. This will not quite serve to distinguish dialect from some related phenomena, but it will distinguish dialect from *accent* (phonological and phonetic features only), *register* and *argot* (features of lexis, predominantly), and *style* (a distinctive usage of linguistic resources within a dialect).[8] Regional dialect can be a marker of social group membership insofar as regional boundaries are coterminous with social group boundaries but, given migration and invasion, the correspondence of regional and group boundaries is not usually one to one. Regional dialect can be deepened to accentuate linguistic differences between a local group and invading outsiders (Labov's report of linguistic change in Martha's Vineyard (Labov 1972a: ch. 1) is a case in point). And frequently regional dialect becomes a marker of social group membership as a social dialect, when a group migrates into a favourable or unfavourable social niche in another area (for example the Irish in New York; the Jews in Germany (Weinreich 1968); and dialects typical of other regions often typify the speech of particular castes in India).

But it is social dialects, especially dialects associated with ranked social strata, that tend to be the most significant markers of group membership within a single speech community. There is an ever-accumulating amount of information on social dialects in western cities, of which the most important is still probably the work of Labov on New York City English (Labov 1966, 1972a, 1972c; but see also Trudgill (1974a) on Norwich English; and Shuy, Wolfram & Riley (1967), Wolfram & Fasold (1974) on Detroit English; as well as the work of Sankoff (1973, 1975), Sankoff & Cedergren (1971), Sankoff, Sarrasin & Cedergren (1971) on Montreal French). Labov's work on social dialects in New York City reveals that in the continuously graded social strata of the White population, the 'dialects' are themselves continua distinguished by a relatively small number of sociolinguistic variables (mostly phonological), that are more often distinctive by relative quantity than by absolute absence or presence.[9] It is apparently the relative frequency of these variables that

---

[8] Usage of these terms in the literature is in fact varied and confused, in part because the phenomena themselves are not clearly discrete. Both structural and functional criteria are necessary to distinguish them. For example, diglossic variants are structurally the same phenomena as dialects, but functionally different: for the high diglossic variant is not the vernacular (basic casual speech level) of any speakers. *Style* is used in many ways, but two usages are especially significant for the sociolinguist: one (adopted in the text) views style as distinctive choices (usually related to social contexts) within the grammatical options provided by a dialect; another much broader (and purely functional) view takes style to be *any* distinctive language variant (including diglossic level, dialect, register, etc.) that is chosen from a speaker's repertoire in response to the social situation. As for the distinction between two dialects of a language and two distinct but closely related languages, Trudgill (1974b) gives a good exposition of the sociopolitical nature of such distinctions.

[9] Both Labov's and Trudgill's work has concentrated on phonological aspects of dialect, but the same kinds of results have been found for syntactic features of Black English (see, e.g., Labov 1972c: ch. 3) and of Montreal French (Sankoff 1973). Choice between lexical alternates (for example, *ta/thanks*, or *sweet/pudding/dessert/afters*, in English English) has

lies behind the perception of a speaker's class (although there may also be some discrete variables, double negation for example); and matched-guise tests show that this perception is associated by members with the attribution of occupational potential (Labov 1972a: ch. 6; see also social psychological status attribution studies, reviewed in Giles & Powesland 1975: 38–9). Labov did find that Black English in New York is less continuous with White dialects, as one would expect from the nature of the Black community as an enclave in the city (the differences are also due to historical factors: southern regional features and, possibly, traces of Creole origins in Black English; see Labov 1972c: ch. 2). But even here, most differences are not of the discrete kind.[10]

The work of Labov suggests that dialect is not then as clear-cut a marker of social groups as one might imagine. Indeed recent sociolinguistic studies in general make it clear that neither languages nor dialects are the homogeneous and discrete entities that laymen and even some dialectologists had imagined (cf. Laver & Trudgill, this volume: ch. 1, 2.3). When the dialectologist elicits, what he tends to get is paradigmatical ideal–typical responses, while tape-recordings of actual situated speech reveal that dialects tend in fact to be much less distinct from other local varieties than the elicitations suggest (see, e.g., Blom & Gumperz 1972). Furthermore, the picture that emerges from the study of situated speech is that local varieties tend to be distinguished by gradient phenomena – such as degrees of articulation on some phonetic dimension (e.g. vowel quality), or relative frequency of some syntactic construction (e.g. copula deletion) – rather than categorical (absolute) differences in grammatical rules (Blom & Gumperz 1972; Labov 1972a, 1972c). These studies suggest that the student in search of categorical markers of class, ethnic or other group identities in speech is likely to be largely disappointed (cf. Giles *et al*. this volume: ch. 9, 3.2). What one is likely to find is that social group

hardly been studied in the same systematic way as yet, but is likely to show in some instances at least the same kind of variability coupled with class-based preferences. There are probably also instances of the same lexeme being used to denote different things, which are less likely to be variable (a case might be *dinner* in English, which is variously used to describe either the midday or the evening meal, or alternatively the chief meal of the day whenever it occurs).

[10] Even where the features are distinctive of Black English, they can be shown to be much more closely related to White English variants than might at first be supposed. For example, deletion of the copula (as in *He bad*) is considered to be a characteristic grammatical feature of Black English, but Labov has elegantly demonstrated that it is an inherently variable feature of Black English, which in function parallels the contraction of the copula (*He's bad*) in White dialects, and which itself varies with contraction in the Black dialect. Of the rules governing contraction and deletion in the Black English Vernacular, then, only a few are peculiar to Black English; the rest are shared with White dialects of English.

membership will be marked by a handful of categorical rules (e.g. in upper-class British English double negation with the semantics of single negation seems never to occur) and a large number of rules that are distinctive only by degree of application or use. This seems to be true for both regional and social dialects of a language (cf. Trudgill 1974b), and even sometimes for languages themselves, as evidenced by language studies in communities on the border of different language areas (Gumperz & Wilson 1971).

Two other important points for the notion of group markers in speech emerge from the work of Labov. One key proposition of Labov's is that after the age of about 23 (1972a: 103–6) the ability to control the production of sociolinguistic variables is restricted to some reduction in frequency in formal contexts (including situations where persons from different classes or from outside the local group are present) if the variables are stigmatized, and some increase in frequency if they are prestigious.[11] The reason why speakers are unlikely to be able to control two vernaculars (i.e. the casual styles of two dialects) is to be found in the nature of dialect differences: the two dialects will differ in part in subtle conditions on applications of the same linguistic rules, and such subtle distinctions in applicability conditions are not amenable to conscious control to a very large extent (Labov 1972a: 215). The point is important not only because Labov's historical reconstructions of the speech community (1972a: ch. 9) rest on it, but also because – if it is true – persons bear the marks of their social class in their speech permanently if they have not escaped their own social group before early adulthood. If correct, this suggests limitations to the degree of possible assimilation or accommodation of the sort envisaged by Giles & Powesland (1975: 157–80).

This 'freezing' of dialect during the maturation of the individual accounts of course for the relative reliability of dialect as a marker of group membership. But it is important to emphasize that Labov's finding will not always have this consequence: it seems to be perfectly possible for whole communities to be bidialectal, providing all individuals have sufficient exposure to both dialects at an early age (see, e.g., Blom & Gumperz 1972; and discussion below). More common perhaps will be the situation

[11] Independent support for this claim of Labov's is provided by a number of social psychological studies of status evaluations of the tape-recorded speech of speakers from different SES backgrounds (cf. Robinson, this volume: ch. 6). Ellis (1967), for example, found that judges can with a high degree of accuracy assign SES to speakers reading a text, both in their vernacular style and even when the readers have been instructed to role-play and speak with as 'upper-class' an accent as they can – thus showing that status evaluations based on speech are apparently immune from attempts to disguise them. (The cues utilized by the judges, however, may be paralinguistic rather than dialect features.)

where a number of individuals come to be at least in part bidialectal through geographical or social mobility at an appropriate age (and here educational establishments and the media can play a crucial role). Labov has argued (1972a: 99–109, 215) that even here individuals can only produce a gross impression of one of the dialects, but we need considerably more evidence before we know just what the limits to bidialectalism are – and by implication just how reliable social dialects are as indicators of group membership.[12]

A second important point that emerges from Labov's studies is that sociolinguistic variables, while being sensitive markers of speaker identity in terms of class membership, are not on the whole reliable means of class attribution *unless* contextual factors are taken into account. For most sociolinguistic variables have distinctive rates of production in speech in relation to both speaker identity and to 'style', defined by Labov as degree of attention to speech.[13] So a pipe-fitter being formal in New York may produce sociolinguistic markers at a rate that would be equally typical of a salesman being casual (Labov 1972a: 240). The implication is that even those markers of speaker identity that seem most clear and unequivocal prove on close analysis to require contextual information for their correct interpretation. Attribution of class on the basis of these sociolinguistic variables can be made only if the systematic interactional effect of formal and informal contexts (aspects of interactional structure; see Brown & Fraser, this volume: ch. 2) is taken into account.[14]

---

[12] Ability to control two dialects may be related to just how discrete those dialects are. Thus Blom & Gumperz (1972: 416) note that in the Norwegian bidialectal community they studied there were relatively strict cooccurrence constraints that served (except for some students who were in the process of losing their local identification) to keep the two dialects apart and unmixed, in contrast to the New York social dialects studied by Labov. Other kinds of relatively discrete language variants, diglossic levels for example, can be acquired after an individual's acquisition of his vernacular without difficulty.

[13] Labov distinguishes 'indicators', which vary only in relation to speaker identity, from 'markers', which vary in relation to both speaker identity and style. Labov's views on style are specific and unusual and should be consulted directly (1972a: 70–110).

[14] We have discussed Labov's work in a largely uncritical way, as the empirical findings by him and his colleagues remain the most detailed factual evidence about class dialects that we possess. But one may accept the findings without the general theory that accompanies them – a theory that minimizes the structural properties of interaction (subsumed within an impoverished view of 'style'; see Labov 1972a: ch. 3), and emphasizes the role of correlation as a source of sociolinguistic significance in speech. As the whole thrust of this chapter emphasizes the inadequacy of this point of view for the broad range of phenomena that we are considering, we may omit detailed criticism of it here; in the conclusions we attack a class of models of how social significance is conveyed in speech, into which some of Labov's view seems to fall as a particular instance. For critical remarks on the Labovian approach from different angles, many of which we would go along with, see Bickerton 1971, 1973; Dittmar 1976; Gazdar 1976; Levinson 1977; Robinson, this volume: ch. 6).

The kind of sociolinguistic variables isolated by Labov and others may be a very general phenomenon (see similar studies in Panama by Cedergren (1970), in England by Trudgill (1974a), and in Quebec by Sankoff (1973, 1975), Sankoff & Cedergren (1971) and Sankoff *et al.* (1971)), but they do not seem to be universally associated with stratified speech communities. Even within European urban communities, it seems (on the basis of native speaker reports) that speakers do not betray class affiliation by the use of markers of this sort in Zurich, Switzerland, for example, or in Madrid, Spain (B. Comrie & J. Moore, pers. comms.). And in what must surely rank as one of the world's most closely stratified set of speech communities, social dialects in India appear to be really rather different phenomena from those in the west.

The Indian facts are worth considering in detail because one might think that the lack of absolute markers of speaker's group identity in Europe was a correlate of the continuously graded stratification of western class systems and their associated social mobility (cf. Robinson, this volume: ch. 6). One might then turn to the Indian data expecting to find absolute markers of caste status correlated with the rigid hierarchies of Indian communities. But despite the proliferation of the term 'caste dialect' in the literature (see, e.g., Pillai 1972; Ramanujan 1968; Southworth 1975), with one or two exceptions (notably Brahman dialect in the south) there are no phenomena that match that description, i.e. it is not the case that a speaker can be assigned rigorously to an endogamous group or occupational category – a caste or subcaste – simply by reference to grammatical features of his speech. The general pattern seems to be rather that members of local communities of twenty castes and more are assignable to two or three gross categories only, on the basis of phonological or syntactic variables.[15] In the north of India the categories seem to be Touchable castes (the great majority) vs. Untouchable, while in the south one genuine caste dialect – that of the Brahmans – is superimposed on this distinction. McCormack (1960) played tapes of speakers of various castes in South India to local persons who were able to distinguish Brahmans, Non-Brahmans, and Untouchables with some measure of success (87 per cent correct recognition of Brahmans, but only a maximum of 25 per cent for Untouchables). An informal replication by Levinson (1977) in a Tamil

[15] It is true that castes, and even subcastes, are sometimes distinguishable by distinctive lexical items for a few ritual and cultural concepts, including kinship terms. But distinctive lexis in a few domains does not alone constitute a dialect – the phenomena here are closer to register (discussed below). Besides, these distinctive lexical items are avoided in intercaste interaction (usually by replacement with terms used by the locally dominant caste), so they do not serve to indicate group membership except within the group.

village showed no more definite results, and when the identification clues were tracked down, some of them turned out to be purely pragmatic and paralinguistic (for instance, members of the dominant caste spoke more 'forcefully', and used more swear words). Some groups that had immigrated to the region within the last hundred years were distinctive by virtue of regional dialect, and groups who maintained Telegu as a domestic language had some detectable transferred accent (but both sets of groups contained subgroups from opposite ends of the hierarchy). Now by virtue of this and other background information, informants could go some way towards speaker identification, but to do so they had to integrate a lot of information about the local social structure beyond dialectal clues. For example, the castes are divided between those (formerly called the 'right-hand' castes) who are fully integrated into the rural economy and were the first settlers in the region, and apparently later arrivals (formerly known as 'left-hand' castes) who maintain urban ties. The former tend to have stronger regional dialects, the latter have dialects closer to standard colloquial Tamil; the former avoided Brahmanical lexical items and English loan words, the latter adopted them. Since this distinction cuts the caste hierarchy vertically down the middle, while the Brahman/Non-Brahman/Untouchable one cuts it horizontally into ranked sections, the ingenious collater of information may be able to locate a speaker fairly closely in this two-dimensional social space. This suggests that in many cases even where speaker identity as a member of Group X is not directly encoded in social dialect, it may be inductively inferred from a large number of heterogeneous message components together with knowledge of the local social structure. And even where social dialect is clearly associated with a social group – as in the case of the Brahman dialect in the south – it may not have the interactional significance that one might imagine. For example, in isolated rural areas Brahmans in fact speak to Non-Brahmans without any recognizable trace of Brahman dialect, switching into the latter only when talking to other Brahmans (see Levinson 1977:29ff.), thus eliminating the one clear case of caste dialect as a factor in intercaste interaction.

Once again, then, in the case of Indian castes we do not generally find direct and context-insensitive markers of speaker's group membership. Rather we find that precise speaker identification is based on a large set of indirect clues ('forceful pronunciation', the use of swear words, etc., which are perhaps direct indications of personality or social relationship) along with detailed social structural information (right-hand castes vs.

left-hand ones, Telegu-speaking minorities, etc.) which together yield strong inferences.

Dialects can mark other kinds of social groups in addition to class and caste. In the Arab world, for instance, distinctive dialects can be found associated with religions and religious sects. In Bahrain, for example, members of Sunni and Shi'i sects have markedly different dialects of Arabic (Clive Holes, pers. comm.), while Jews, Christians and Moslems spoke different dialects of Arabic in prewar Baghdad (Blanc 1964). These kinds of dialects seem to be considerably more discrete than class dialects in the west. Just what are the conditions promoting maintenance of discrete dialects among interacting groups remains something of a sociolinguistic mystery. In certain social conditions dialects tend to become assimilated into a single prestige continuum (as described by Labov for New York City, and also, *mutatis mutandis*, for Creole dialects and their respective Standards; see Bickerton 1975; Hymes 1971). In other social conditions distinctive dialects are actually accentuated (see Labov 1972b: ch. 1).

Language. If dialect is one way in which a speaker signals his group or category affiliations, language itself can be another in multilingual societies. The particular way in which language can function as a group marker will be constrained by the nature of the multilingualism, to what extent it is diglossic, to what extent multilingualism is pervasive in the society, and so on (see Fishman 1974). We can imagine some limiting cases. In one, members of different groups speak different languages and do not understand at all (although they may recognize) the other languages; here language could signal group membership to members of other groups, but there would hardly be any point in using it in inter-group interaction. In another, members of different groups all speak all the available languages in just the same circumstances, so choice of language would not be a signal of group membership at all. A weak approximation to the first case would be some parts of ethnic groups in a large western city (e.g. older or female Pakistanis and Cypriots in London); an approximation to the second situation can be found where there is widespread multilingualism in a speech community and shared norms for usage of the different languages – a case would be the use of Spanish and Guarani in Paraguay (see Garvin & Mathiot 1968; Rubin 1968). But in general we tend to find situations falling somewhere between these two extremes, and in these intermediate situations language choice can function as a marker of group identity. A typical situation, found for example in communities from village to city size in India, is where there are a number of groups using minority languages strictly for intragroup communication, and switching to the single majority language for intergroup communication. There language choice does not signal group membership in intergroup relations, although it does serve to mark the shared group membership of those speaking minority languages to one another (cf. Giles, this volume: ch. 7). There will be some further remarks on the significance of this below.

Clearly, very special conditions are required to allow language choice to function as a marker of group membership in intergroup interaction. Specifically, this would require that members of the society have comprehension of a number of languages, but productive competence shared with other group members in only one (or alternatively that this behaviour is normatively enforced). An approximation to this is provided perhaps by the remarkable case of multilingualism reported by Jackson. (1975) and others for the Vaupés basin in Colombia. There in a population of less than 10,000 more than twenty mutually unintelligible languages are maintained, each individual speaking at least three of these but identifying with one in particular (his 'father language').[16] In this situation language can function to signal speaker identity, some significant social groups and categories being coextensive with language boundaries: 'Each individual initially speaks in his own father-language during a conversation in order to assert his tribal affiliation' (Sorensen 1967: 678, quoted in Jackson 1975: 61), although, as Jackson points out, in most interactions such identifications have already been made, allowing other factors to enter into the choice of which language to speak in.

Situations like the Colombian one are rare enough to restrict the main function of language choice *per se* to marking ingroup vs. outgroup social relations (and some finer distinctions within ingroup relations) which will be discussed below. This is not to say that traces of a native language in speech in another language (most significantly, traces of accent) do not mark group membership – indeed, the volume by Giles & Powesland (1975), as well as chapter 7 in this volume by Giles, amply document the ways in which they do. Such traces are perhaps the most important way

---

[16] Since in this society there is a rule of linguistic exogamy – i.e. that one must marry someone from a group that speaks a different language from one's own – the language of a person's father will be different from his mother's language. Speakers may learn their mother's language first, but identify with the second-learned language of their father because of the patrilineal kinship system. With ethnic group boundaries thus splitting the family unit, the identification of ingroup vs. outgroup (and its linguistic correlates) becomes extremely problematic.

in which membership in an ethnic minority group is marked in speech in intergroup interaction. Interference from the native tongue in the use of the dominant language can be very subtle, and there is growing work in this area (see, e.g., Gumperz 1977, 1978, and Gumperz, *et al*. n.d., on prosodic patterns in the English of Londoners of Indian extraction). Most of this material is covered in detail by Giles (this volume: ch. 7), and we may omit it here.

Repertoire. A rather different way in which group or category affiliation can be signalled by the code that a speaker utilizes derives from the fact that different groups within a speech community may command different subsets of the total linguistic resources available in the community. That is, their *linguistic repertoires* (Gumperz 1972: 20) may be different. This is well illustrated by the Javanese case reported by Geertz (1960). Here the language provides three levels of addressee honorifics and two levels of referent honorifics (see below) and six allowable combinations of these to form six distinct named varieties of the language. But no persons have productive control of all of these (or at least none can use them all); rather the varieties are unequally distributed across the three 'estates' (strata, groups) of aristocrats, townsmen and peasants. Thus the aristocrats control levels 3a, 3, 1b and 1 (Geertz's labels), townsmen control levels 3a, 3, 2, 1a and 1, and peasants control levels 2a, 1a, 1b and 1. This allows various inferences about a speaker's identity: if he is speaking levels 3, 3a, or 3b he cannot be a peasant, if he is speaking level 2 he must be a townsman or peasant, or if 1b either an aristocrat or a peasant, and so on. However, in intergroup interactions an aristocrat uses only level 1, a peasant only level 2, while a townsman may use 1, occasionally 1a, 3, or 3a, depending on the category of the addressee. This entire system has as its *raison d'être* something entirely different from the signalling of speaker identity – namely, the signalling of appropriate deference or power in relationships (i.e. the variables are markers of speaker–addressee relationship, not of speaker identity). Nevertheless, given the uneven distribution of competence, the system also indirectly acts to signal ranges of speaker identity.

What is really involved here is the fact that repertoire restrictions can carry clues to speaker identity. The different ways in which such clues may operate may be very large, but probably differential control of specific *registers* (see Brown & Fraser, this volume: ch. 2; Halliday 1968) is in general the most important. Thus an upper-class Englishman is unlikely to know the language of darts playing, and a lower-class

Englishman the jargon of horse breeding. Indeed, some registers are specifically designed to make them unintelligible to nonmembers of the group – for example argots used by members of the underworld (cf. Agar 1973; Halliday 1976). Sometimes these can be stable and linked to respectable occupations, as is apparently the case for the ship-builders' and goldsmiths' distinct argots in Bahrain, which are totally opaque to other local Arabic speakers (Clive Holes, pers. comm.).

A related source of information about speaker's group membership is provided by what we may call *pragmatic resources*. In talking of speech markers, analysts generally focus on features of the linguistic code, but equally and possibly even more revealing of speaker identity are aspects of what Hymes (1972) has called 'communicative competence', or rules for the utilization of a code in appropriate ways in social situations. Relevant here is a great deal of work in the ethnography of speaking, exemplified in the papers in Bauman & Sherzer (1975), Gumperz & Hymes (1972) and Sanches & Blount (1976). Some examples of the way in which the knowledge of how to utilize linguistic repertoires is differentially distributed in social structures, thereby allowing speaker's group identification, are the following. Labov (1972b) describes some special uses of language among Black youths in New York which involve exchanges of ritual insults as a competitive game for prestige. Amongst the rules for such insults are some that specify the use of phrases like *Your mother so X that P*, where X is an abusive category and P is obviously false (thus: *Your mother so old she fart dust*). If P is true then the rules are broken, and the ritual insults are just plain insults. Outsiders or group marginals are unlikely to understand the rules, and the correct employment of the rules in a verbal contest is then an indication of membership in the Black community.

Another set of cases involves the widespread reports that in rigidly hierarchical societies not everyone equally controls specific genres of speaking. Thus in Burundi (Albert 1972) only the top-ranking ethnic group is educated in oratory and related verbal skills.[17] Here control of part of the linguistic repertoire (namely oratory) is importantly linked to social structure, including political control – and is used as an excuse for that control (see also Bloch 1975). The employment of such oratorical skills is a marker not only of membership in the elite group, but of legitimate authority.

---

[17] In the same society (as equally in South India), low-ranking persons have to display verbal noncoordination, bumbling and hesitation, but this is in fact a marker not of speaker identity, since it is adopted only before high-ranking alters, but rather of speaker–addressee relationship.

Social deixis. Finally, there are some rather unusual markers of the identity of participants in interaction, markers that are truly unequivocal, categorical (rather than probabilistic) and determinate. These are linguistic items that encode social deixis. Deixis is a term linguists use to refer to the ways in which linguistic elements can refer to, or can only be interpreted by knowing, certain aspects of the communicative event in which those elements are used. Simple examples are words like *I* which refers to the current speaker, *now* which refers to the time of speaking (in some usages), *here* which refers to the place where the speaker is at the time of speaking, and so on. Analogously, there are linguistic elements that instead of referring to temporal/physical properties of the speech event, refer to its social properties: T/V pronominal alternates, for example, honorifics, address forms, and so on (for remarks on the scope of social deixis see Fillmore 1975; Levinson 1977). Most aspects of social deixis are relational, and have to do especially with speaker–addressee or speaker–referent relationships (see below), but just a few are absolute indicators of participant identity. There are a few forms in most languages that are restricted to *authorized speakers*. For instance the term *Gringo* is restricted to Latin Americans referring to North Americans (Fillmore 1975). Similarly, Chinese emperors alone used the pronoun *chin* for 'I', while in Koasati and Chukchee certain morphological alternates are reserved for each sex (Haas 1964; Comrie, pers. comm.). In the same way there are also forms reserved for *authorized recipients*. Not only are second-person pronouns distinguished for sex of referent in some languages (Serbo-Croatian, Basque, Japanese), but in Tunica (an American Indian language formerly spoken in Louisiana) third-person pronouns were also distinguished for sex of addressee (so there would be two words for 'they', one meaning 'they when speaker is addressing a man' and the other meaning 'they when speaker is addressing a woman' (Haas 1964)). Much more familiar, of course, are titles of address of the kind that are specialized to certain types of recipient. Thus in Modern English only a judge is addressed as *Your Honour* and only members of the royal family are addressed as *Your Highness*. Sometimes such terms do indicate group membership directly; in the Tamil village described above, the title *esamaanka* 'Lord', is more or less reserved for landed members of the high castes, while another, *caami* 'Lord', is reserved by high-caste members for Brahmans and gods while lowest-caste members generalize it to a number of high castes (Levinson 1977: 314ff.). Another good example of titles reserved for members of each major group in the society is reported by Goody (1972: 51) for Gonjaland in Ghana.

Prosodic and paralinguistic markers of group. The term *prosodics* is generally understood to include matters of intonation, stress and timing, while features of *paralanguage* 'differ from prosodic features in not being so closely integrated into the grammatical structure of utterances' (Lyons 1972: 53). Idiosyncratic person-identifying voice quality is often excluded from paralanguage (see Crystal 1975: 51ff.), while group-identifying voice setting can more reasonably be included (Crystal 1975: 62–4). What is involved in the latter is a habitual configuration of the speech organs within certain ranges that, due to processes of norm and socialization, group members tend to share, and the result can be distinctive and relatively determinate markers of group membership. There is evidence that class background is sometimes effectively indicated by such voice settings (see, e.g., Laver 1968; and social psychological work reviewed by Giles & Powesland (1975)). More curiously, an experiment by Brown, Strong & Rencher (1975) suggests that some such associations have cross-cultural validity: Americans with no knowledge of French could apparently assign Canadian French speakers to their correct social strata (although exactly what cues were attended to by subjects in the experiment is not clear; see discussion in Giles & Powesland 1975: 13–15). Prosodic and paralinguistic features are likely to prove some of the most reliable and direct markers of social information, particularly group membership; Crystal (1975: 84–95) indicates many areas for future research. Features like pitch range, loudness, tempo, rhythm and voice setting are all likely to be sources of indexical information about the speaker's group affiliations (cf. Laver & Trudgill, this volume: ch. 1, 2).

It is important to stress, however, that like all the linguistic features that we have described above, these too are subject to systematic variations in particular social contexts, and to manipulative exploitations. Indeed, prosodic and paralinguistic features play an important role in style (see Crystal & Davy 1969). They can also be more specifically communicative: features like falsetto pitch and nasalization have been reported as honorific markers of deference (or social distance) in, respectively, the Mayan language Tzeltal (Brown, in press) and the Bolivian language Coyavava (Key 1967: 19, cited in Crystal 1975). The researcher cannot therefore assume that paralinguistic or prosodic features will turn out to be much less problematic as markers of social group membership than dialect, repertoire and so on. It is likely that in many cases such markers will, like the others, be relative to situations and to other aspects of interactional structure, and require social structural information for their correct interpretation.

2.3. Clues to group membership provided by markers of social relationships

We have been considering some of the ways in which group membership is indicated in speech in relatively direct ways. It has been necessary to point out, though, that such markers are hardly ever context independent correlations between group membership and linguistic features. Moreover, the inference to group membership from these specific aspects of language often requires detailed knowledge about encompassing social structures, the total communicative repertoires of different categories of speaker and so on. It is important to remember, too, that a great deal of exploitation of such markers, or simulations of group membership, is likely to go on in interaction. Nevertheless, with these caveats, it is clear that members of social groups in many cases do command distinctive ranges of communicative competence – languages, dialects, registers, styles – that are a basic source of inferences about speakers' group identity.

But besides limiting ranges of communicative competence, group membership determines aspects of interaction in a number of other ways, which can then serve to provide indirect clues to participants' group membership. It is important to grasp the distinction between the direct kinds of marker of group membership reviewed above, and the indirect clues to group membership we shall discuss here. The direct markers are *indexical* in the sense of Laver (1968) – i.e. indicative (with all the caveats noted above) of the speaker's affiliation to a particular identifiable group – to the 'working class', say, or to the New York City Jewish community, or to the Brahmans of a particular area of South India. Such indexes to a person's group affiliation occur perhaps largely unintentionally, often without the speaker's conscious control and indeed often despite his attempts to mask them. The indirect clues to group membership to which we now turn are quite different in nature, for they tell us not *what* group a speaker is from, but rather what kind of social relationship obtains between speaker and addressee. From this information it is possible, as we shall see, to infer whether the relationship is 'ingroup' or 'outgroup', and armed with this knowledge plus knowledge of the relevant groups in the speech community and their respective social structural loci, it is often possible to infer what group the speaker is from. The inferences involved are often subtle and complex in themselves, and greatly complicated by the fact that the expression of social relationships is open to a great deal of intentional manipulation.

We shall concentrate on markers of social relationships as indirect clues to group membership, for these, we suggest, provide the most important indirect clues on the basis of which members make inferences about speakers' group memberships. The importance of social relationships for this task derives from the way in which, for any pair of participants, group membership restricts and even selects the social relationships that may be enacted. As for the concept of social relationship itself, we understand this in the standard sociological and anthropological way to denote 'determinate ways of acting toward or in regard to one another', with the emphasis on expectations concerning rights, duties and the manner of behaviour (see, e.g., Beattie 1966: 34ff.; Goodenough 1969; Nadel 1957: 8ff.). Most theorists agree in seeing in social relationships the basic and smallest unit of social structure; for this reason social relationships and their markers provide an important connection between the levels of social structure and interaction.

In considering the relationship between groups and social relationships, a crucial distinction that immediately arises is that between ingroup (that is, *intra*group) and outgroup (that is *inter*group) interaction. Here we are concerned with the broad characteristics of interaction across groups as opposed to that within a group, regardless of the nature of the particular groups involved (whether class-based, kin-based, task-based, or whatever). Considerable social psychological research has been devoted to features of ingroup vs. outgroup interaction: see, for example, Campbell (1965); Cartwright & Zander (1960); Sherif *et al*. (1961); Tajfel (1974). It seems a reasonable hypothesis that if both parties to an interaction are drawn from one group then it is likely that the social relationship obtaining between them will be organized around nongroup (or subgroup) identities – sex, kinship, role, personality, or whatever the relevant criteria may be. On the other hand, if the parties belong to different groups, then their group identities are likely to be the ones that (at least in large part) determine their relationship. So the distinction between ingroup and outgroup relationships is one which is fundamental to the organization of interaction for any two parties (cf. Giles, this volume: ch. 7).

The group boundary thus looms large in interaction, and it is expressed in the verbal channels in a great range of (largely redundant) ways. First, there are code differences: if A perceives B as a co-member of a group he belongs to, then he may use a language or a dialect or a register appropriate to their shared group, or even just a few markers that are retained for such ingroup addressees. Many of the simpler aspects of code-switching are determined by this; for example in the north of Norway the local dialect (Ranamål) will be used only between 'members of the local team' (Blom & Gumperz 1972). Gumperz has shown in a number of cases that in plural societies where code-switching is rampant, the languages switched between tend to converge systematically, so that syntactic structures can become isomorphic in two languages of quite distinct language families (Gumperz & Wilson 1971). The interesting questions then are these: Why are the two codes maintained as distinct entities? Why is the merging process halted, instead of going to completion? The codes may be distinguished by no more than a few lexical items and phonological correspondences (see, e.g., Gumperz's (1964) description of Punjabi and Hindi in Delhi). Gumperz's answer is that the token differences are maintained just where there are two distinct domains of use, within the group on the one hand, and for intergroup interaction on the other. It seems that the desire to mark the group boundary in interaction is sufficient to keep the two codes at least minimally distinct.

Secondly, in addition to code differences, there are attitudinal markers of many different kinds that function as signals of ingroup membership between interlocutors. For example there are the signs of ease and relaxation (allegro speech, kinds of laughter and the like), some of which have been described by Labov as being associated with or constituting 'vernacular speech' or 'casual style' (Labov 1972a: ch. 3). In addition there are a great number of verbal strategies typical of ingroup relations which have been catalogued and discussed under the rubric 'positive politeness' in Brown & Levinson (1978). These range from familiar address forms (T pronouns, nicknames, endearments) to the rhetoric of exaggerated statements (*How fabulous your roses are, Gertie!*), immediacy (. . . *and so he comes over and says to me, '. . .'*) and presumptive request forms (*I've come to borrow a cup of flour*). As we shall discuss below, many of these strategies seem to be universally employed in ingroup encounters.

Beyond the group boundary, when members of a dyad are drawn from different groups (or when whatever groups they may share are not significant in the context) and they have thus selected codes and attitudes typical of extragroup relations, group membership still continues to play a further role in structuring interaction. Often, if the groups have a characteristic and definable relationship one to the other, a dyad that is drawn from them will inherit that relationship. Thus, to return to the Tamil example we used in section 1.2, if caste A is higher than caste B, then a member *a* of A will be higher than *b*, a member of B. So *a* will typically give *b* the T pronoun, and *b* will typically give the V pronoun in exchange. It is certainly an important observation that the kinds of relations that can hold between groups (rank, rivalry, alliance, etc.) are precisely the kinds of relations that can hold between members of them. It is because of this parallelism that we can often infer the group membership of *a* and *b* by observing their interaction, given further background information.[18]

We may have given the impression in this discussion that every individual is assimilated to only one group, which would have the implication that indicators of ingroup and outgroup relationships are more or less automatic reflexes of the group membership of each participant. This is clearly not the case. Not only can individuals be members of many different kinds of well-established groups, and members of different orders of the same kind of group (as in 'segmentary' group structures), they can even invent groups to cover new interactional situations (as when strangers from neighbouring lands meet up far abroad). The result of course is that group membership is often negotiable or selectable in actual interactional situations, and when this is so it will often be selected and signalled by linguistic indicators of ingroup/outgroup relations (this is clearest, perhaps, in studies of code-switching). The noteworthy thing about membership in ranked social groups, whether ethnic, class-based, or caste-based, is that negotiability tends to be highly constrained (by the interests of the higher-ranked groups). Even here, though, the interactional relevance of such memberships can be held in abeyance in the formation of special interest groups (e.g. co-gamblers in an Indian village may ignore caste memberships while gambling, in a way they normally cannot).

2.4. Some markers of social relationships

So far we have indicated how group memberships (at least once they have been selected in interaction) can determine gross features of social relationships, namely those we associate with ingroup and outgroup interaction. But there are of course much finer-grained distinctions within these broad categories that can be marked in speech. For example, it may

---

[18] Of course many factors other than group memberships can determine the nature of a social relationship, including role relations, personal attractions and so on. But the potential importance of these other factors is itself likely to be determined by social structural constraints. It is only when social groups have an overriding effect on the nature of a social relationship that we may be able to infer backwards from that relationship to particular group memberships (given further information about the number and relations of such groups). But class, caste and ethnic group memberships, for instance, often seem to have such an overriding effect.

be that members of some groups other than one's own can be treated as rank inferiors, while members of others must be treated as rank superiors. So degrees of deference can indicate for an observer which of a number of ranked groups an addressee is likely to be associated with. Moreover, within ingroup relations, the same degrees of deference (now expressed in conjuction with ingroup markers) may distinguish different kinds of kinsmen, for example (see, e.g., Levinson 1977: ch. 5). So how persons treat other persons interactionally, together with a great deal of knowledge about the relevant structures, can be the basis for inferred attributions of precise group or subgroup membership.

Rather than describe what must inevitably be culture-specific details of such attribution processes, it will be more useful to describe the kinds of markers of social relationship that sociolinguists have found to recur in speech across different cultures. Each of these categories of markers may yield inferences about group memberships, but they are only likely to do so relative to a great deal of background information. In reviewing some of the most important ways in which social relationships are marked in speech we may seem to deviate from the main topics of this chapter. But markers of social relationships play such an important role in indirectly conveying group memberships that they should not be ignored in this connection. Moreover, there is reason to believe, as we shall make clear in the concluding remarks, that markers of social relationships have a very special and central role to play in the conveying of many different kinds of social information in interaction.

There seem to be two basic ways in which the social relationship obtaining between speaker and addressee is marked in speech. One is through the direct encoding of kind of social relationship in the grammatical system, in which case we talk of *social deixis* (Fillmore 1975; Levinson 1977). The other is by the way of putting things, the particular choice of linguistic expression, governed we suggest by *strategies*. We shall take these in turn.

Socially deictic markers. We have already mentioned how social deixis can mark features of speaker or addressee *identity*, but it is far more commonly the case that it is the social *relationship* between speaker and addressee (or between speaker and some referent) that is thus grammatically encoded. The relationship encoded may be one of asymmetrical rank disparity, in which case we may talk of honorifics; and it is important here to distinguish *addressee honorifics*, where respect to the addressee can be conveyed by choice of linguistic form regardless of the content of the message, from *referent honorifics*, where respect can only be given to things or persons (including the addressee) that are actually referred to (for justifications of the distinction see Brown & Levinson 1978; Comrie 1976). The implication of the distinction is that in some languages – those with addressee honorifics – it is possible to say a sentence like *The soup is hot* and by choice of lexical item convey deference or the reverse to the addressee, whereas in other languages (those which only have referent honorifics) one would have to add some title like *Your Honour*.

The distinction between these two kinds of honorific is important because they are not encoded in the same way in grammatical structure. Referent honorifics are necessarily confined to referring expressions, and morphological agreements with them, and empirically they tend to turn up in titles of address, verb endings, words for persons and their body parts and belongings. Addressee honorifics, on the other hand, could theoretically turn up in any part of the linguistic system, and empirically tend to be found in lexical alternates for common words (including function words, auxiliary verbs, and so on), aspects of morphology, special particles that are otherwise without meaning, and aspects of prosodics and paralinguistics.

The two kinds of honorific are also differently distributed in the world's languages. Addressee honorifics are relatively rare and exotic; the really elaborate reported systems all come from Southeast Asia (in Japanese, Javanese, Madurese, Korean and so on).[19] The Javanese case is familar to sociolinguists through Geertz's (1960) well-known description; we have mentioned above that six named levels of honorific speech were distinguished by the Javanese. These levels were made up in fact of three levels of addressee honorific combining with two levels of referent honorific. It is interesting that Indian languages, despite the even more hierarchical societies in which they are used, do not display the same richness of addressee honorifics, although they tend to have at least some particles that function in this way (see Levinson 1977). Addressee honorifics encoded in prosody and paralanguage are probably much more widespread; in the Mayan language Tzeltal, for example, the use of sustained falsetto gives deference to the addressee (Brown & Levinson 1978), and in English we seem to have a few special polite intonation contours for use in requests and the like.

Referent honorifics, on the other hand, include titles, and are thus almost certainly universally available to some degree in all languages.

[19] Japanese has been extensively described for its elaborate honorifics systems. See, e.g., Harada 1976; Martin 1964; Miller 1967; O'Neill 1966; Uyeno 1971; Yamanashi 1974.

They also include the familiar T/V systems, since the choice of the polite alternative requires that the sentence refers to the addressee. These systems are in fact extremely widespread, and probably to be found in most language families (see Levinson 1978). Since Brown & Gilman's (1960) classic study there has been a growing amount of work on European T/V systems (see, e.g., Hollos 1975; Lambert & Tucker 1976; Paulston 1975; Slobin 1963; for discussion and further references, see Levinson 1978; for an Indian case, Levinson 1977). The ways in which patterns of T/V usage can provide inferences to group memberships have already been illustrated in the Tamil examples in section 1.2. In English, though we now lack the pronominal choice, the choices amongst titles and names (*sir*, *Professor*, *Your Honour*, *Madam*, first name, last name, title plus last name, etc.) can pattern in usage in a precisely similar way to T/V pronouns (see Brown & Ford 1964; Ervin-Tripp 1972). Here we can see clearly how group membership can indirectly determine linguistic usage (which can thus in turn indirectly mark group membership): a labourer or a porter or a college servant may say 'sir' or 'guv'ner' to someone whom he takes to be of a higher-ranking group, and while a doctor is unlikely to address another doctor as 'doctor', a patient, nurse or visitor – or even outside that context, the doctor's garage mechanic – may feel obliged to do so.

Honorifics are not the only kind of socially deictic marker of social relationships; social relations other than relative rank can be encoded in the structure of a language. Kinship terms, for example, indicate what kind of genealogical relationship persons are in, together with the associated prescribed behaviours, including altruism, respect and joking behaviour. In many societies (especially those of simple technology typically studied by anthropologists), kinship is the basis for membership in the most enduring social groups, and the use of kin terms in such a context would function directly as recognitions of group membership.

Strategies of language use. Let us turn now to the second major way in which social relationships are indicated in speech, namely by means of strategies of language usage. Again, from the relationships indicated, indirect inferences can sometimes be made to the group memberships of participants; but here the markers of social relationship are themselves inferential. A certain way of putting things, i.e. the strategic choice of message form, can indirectly imply the nature of the social relationship between speaker and addressee. To take a simple example, in English we vary the ways in which we request things partly in relation to what we are requesting, but partly in relation to whom we are requesting from. So for instance to a close friend one may say, 'Lend us five bob, Bill', while to a more distant acquaintance one is more likely to say something like 'Could you by any chance lend me twenty-five pence?' Such variations in the way in which one expresses a particular speech act turn out to be highly systematic, based on a large but delimitable set of constructional principles, many of which are investigated in Brown & Levinson (1978). There it is argued that the motivations for modifying the expression of speech acts are visible in the particular modifications that are chosen, and on the basis of these we can identify the strategies that actors are pursuing in their speech. For example, contrast the strategies involved in:

(1) You'll lend us a fiver, won't you mate.
(2) You wouldn't by any chance be able to lend me five pounds, would you?

The first intuitively involves interactional *optimism*, the second interactional *pessimism*, and the particular constellation of negative, subjunctive and remote possibility features in the second can be seen to derive rationally from the corresponding strategy.

The choice of one strategy rather than another clearly depends crucially on the relationship between interlocutors. In this way, a choice of strategy conveys an assessment of the relationship, or, in other words, it is a *marker* of that relationship. Thus an interlocutor, by saying (2), is indicating via his choice of language that his social relationship to the addressee is not intimate. In this way strategies of language usage can be markers of social relationships, via a chain of reasoning and inference, in a way that parallels the more straightforward markers of social relationship that are found in the use of socially deictic linguistic forms such as address terms and honorifics.[20]

Other ways in which language usage strategies are tied to social relationships, and ultimately back to group memberships, have emerged from work in the ethnography of speaking (see Bauman & Sherzer 1975; Sanches & Blount 1976). We may take as an example Irvine's (1975) description of greetings among the Wolof of Senegal. Here the one who initiates the greeting is the lower in status, and the more elaborate the

[20] Indirect speech acts play an important role in politeness strategies of this sort, and have received a good deal of attention recently from linguists. Among the most important studies of the usage of indirect speech acts in context, which shed light on how one can use them to analyse the expression of social relationships in speech, are a case study of interactors in a university office (Shimanoff 1977), where the use of many of the strategies described in Brown & Levinson (1978) was tested, and a number of studies of the acquisition and use of some of these in actual contexts (Bates 1976; Ervin-Tripp 1976; Shatz 1975).

greeting, the greater the deference given. Given that there are some four or more ranked 'castes' or estates in this society, the mode of greeting can indirectly convey the group memberships of the participants. Moreover, there are distinct styles of speaking that convey deference or superiority, and these are especially associated with caste membership (Irvine 1975). However, although the mode and style of greeting can effectively convey participants' membership in the ranked groups to a bystander (and alter's perception of ego's membership to a participant), the whole performance is subject to manipulation: high-status has its price (gift-giving, in particular) and is often effectively denied by assuming the lower-status role (Irvine 1975: 175–6). These strategies for greeting are first and foremost markers of social relationship, and thus open to any manipulations that social relationships are subject to; they are only indirect, and uncertain, clues to group membership, although nevertheless an important potential source of such information.[21]

2.5. Further connections between groups and language: stratification and social network

So far we have emphasized the point that even apparently simple markers of group membership on close examination soon turn out to be less than simple 'signals'; in fact, in many cases, we have argued, group membership is indicated in speech only indirectly through markers of social relationships, which in turn are partly structured by group memberships. However, there are even more indirect relations between group membership and features of language employed by group members which in the long run are no less significant. One such indirect relationship that we shall concentrate on here is the recurrent association of distinct patterns of language usage with high or low groups (or strata) in stratified social systems.

Consider for instance the following interesting and hitherto unexplained fact: it is regularly reported that in stratified societies where a

---

[21] Another African study is worth reporting for the light it throws on the notion of a linguistic marker. Goody (1978) reports that among the Gonja of Ghana, sentences that are syntactically questions are interpreted very differently according to the relationship between speaker and addressee. If the speaker is lower in rank than the addressee, questions will tend (when possible) to be interpreted as polite suggestions, while if the speaker is higher in rank they will tend to be interpreted as assertions of control. Since there are three ranked estates that are one source of rank disparities in the society (see Goody 1972), a question with its interpretation (as revealed in the response) may serve to indicate group memberships. Here the linguistic form is a marker of social relationship only when paired with a particular kind of interpretation.

Tu/Vous type opposition in singular second-person pronouns is employed, there is a tendency for the reciprocal exchange of the T pronoun to be associated with the lower groups, classes or castes in their ingroup interactions, and a tendency for the reciprocal use of V to be associated with upper strata (for a full discussion, the statement of a tentative sociolinguistic universal, and some apparent counterexamples, see Levinson 1978).

For instance in the Tamil village mentioned above, there are different patterns of T/V usage within castes depending in part on the status of each caste in the local hierarchy. The lower the caste, the more internal reciprocal T exchange is used, while in the upper castes such usage is increasingly replaced by symmetrical V exchange and asymmetrical T/V usage (see Levinson 1977 for details). There is some evidence that reciprocal T exchange within the family is a nonprestigious feature of language usage in the village, while the increased use of V is prestigious. Can we *explain* the distribution of intracaste usages by identifying reciprocal T as a stigmatized variable, reciprocal V or asymmetrical T/V as a prestige one? Or, equivalently, by identifying the usages as markers of, respectively, low-group membership and high-group membership?

A moment's reflection will show that the notion of marker in this context would be nonexplanatory. In the case of socially deictic items or aspects of social dialect, their functions as direct markers of social features will generally provide an account of their *raison d'être*, or at least of the reasons for their maintenance. But we cannot think of these T/V patterns in the same sort of way, as (at least synchronically) arbitrary markers of group prestige or stigma, for the following reasons. First, they are intrinsically tied to particular kinds of social relationship, and so cannot simply be adopted for reasons of prestige without also adopting something as fundamental as the basic quality of ingroup social relationships. Secondly, since the usages in question only occur in ingroup interactions, the supposed claiming of prestige *vis-à-vis* other groups will pass largely unnoticed by those other groups. Thirdly, if the basic motivation for the use of reciprocal V (or at least the avoidance of reciprocal T) in high-status groups was simply that that usage was a marker of prestige, then we should expect the usage to be arbitrarily prestigious (like certain phonological variables are in class dialects) and thus expect to find the pattern reversed in some other society – which never seems to be the case. So some deeper explanations of the patterns and their distribution are required.

The explanation for this association of reciprocal T-giving with low-status groups follows the same chain of reasoning that native observers are likely to follow in trying to make sense of the patterns they may perceive. T/V usage is tied primarily to kinds of social relationship, and the association of T-exchange with low-status groups in stratified societies is due to the way that stratification affects the nature of intra-group social relations. Specifically we may suggest that segments of lower social strata constitute communities where people interact intensely with one another in many different roles and capacities often involving diffuse debt; in such circumstances relations of equality and solidarity are likely to arise between adults, appropriately symbolized by mutual T-exchange. Correspondingly, social networks in high social strata tend to be fragmented for many reasons: smaller units (like families) vie for prestige, and do not rely on each other for support or services (provided instead by lower-status service personnel), with the consequence that relations between these units tend to be socially distant, and appropriately symbolized by V-exchange. There tends also to be an emphasis on hierarchy within the family, which precludes T-exchange (see Brown, in press; Levinson 1978). Given knowledge of the ranked groups and their internal social organization, a native observer of a particular pattern of intragroup T/V exchange can in this sort of way use it as an indirect clue to group membership.

There are other recurring patterns of language usage associated with high- and low-status groups in stratified societies that are probably best thought of in much the same sort of way – i.e. as indirect manifestations of group status that come about through the ways in which stratification affects social networks and thus social relationships. For example, there appear to be different kinds and levels of politeness typically used in different social strata (Brown & Levinson 1978: 247–60), and speech styles tend to polarize into a plain 'low' style (used by lower strata) and a structurally and rhetorically elaborated 'high' style used by elites (see Levinson 1978). Bernstein's (1971) well-known work on class-stratified patterns of language usage also seems to fit in here: he claims to find distinctive styles of talking ('codes') associated with the working and the middle classes in England. His particular view of these differences as due to a radically distinctive psychological orientation inculcated through different patterns of socialization has come under severe criticism in recent years (see, e.g., Dittmar 1976), but that there are stylistic differ-ences in the speech of members of different classes is very likely. Such differences however are likely to be tied to qualities of social relation-ships, which are in turn tied to social networks, which in turn are partly determined by social rank (for some empirical work here see Bott 1957) – without necessarily involving deep psychological variables.

2.6. Linguistic markers of group membership: some important distinctions

We have ranged over a number of very different ways in which group membership can be indicated in speech, and it may be helpful to draw together the observations about the various kinds of 'markers' we have been examining. Recollect that a marker is, in the terminology of this volume, a systematic correlation between a speech variable and a social variable; and we have suggested (as have some other authors in this volume) that the concept should be restricted to *emic* correlations – that is to correlations at least potentially observable by interactants in such a way that they could play a role in interaction (cf. Brown & Fraser: ch. 2, 1.2; Robinson: ch. 6, 1.1). The markers we are interested in then are markers for interactants rather than markers for observers. As we proceeded we found that on close examination simple correlations of the sort that the term 'marker' at least connotes are the exception – group membership tends to be encoded in speech in rather complex and often indirect ways. It is useful, therefore, to distinguish between direct markers and indirect clues, where the latter are direct markers of some social variable other than the one in focus, but are empirically related to it. So, for example, markers of social relationship are indirect clues to social group memberships insofar as the social relationship is determined by those group memberships. There is an underlying idea here that language features are primarily tied to some particular social variables, and only derivatively to others; the difference would emerge clearly when one considered what would count as an explanation of the occurrence of those features.

Thus, so far we have considered two important distinctions: correlations discernible by the analyst vs. associations used by participants, on the one hand, and direct markers vs. indirect clues to group membership, on the other. However, in considering the concept of a social marker in speech there are a number of other important distinctions that we have not made, possibly at the cost of some confusion. The first set of distinctions has to do with the *intentionality* of markers. Although the importance of the distinction between intended and unintended signals has been noted in discussions of communication (e.g. by Lyons 1972), the distinction is not often rigorously applied (see, e.g., Argyle (1975), where the distinction is made, but then ignored in the search for general properties of nonverbal communication). In any case more is required than that. Crucially at least the following three-way distinction is required: (i) unintended or natural signs; (ii) intended signs produced in such a way as to appear to be unintended – i.e. exploited 'natural' signs; and (iii) communicative signs proper, that are not only intended, but are intended to be seen to be intended. Only the last are truly communicative, as Grice (1971) has pointed out. Now communication *systems* are only constructed from type (iii) signs (although not all such signs are necessarily part of a system). Further the barrage-of-signals view of interaction that we outlined in the introduction is only legitimate for type (i) signs, and it is especially inadequate for signs of type (iii).

A single piece of verbal behaviour can function in different circumstances in each of these three ways. Suppose, for example, that there is a correlation between a deep voice and the speaker's personal confidence (for some such examples see Scherer this volume: ch. 5). A speaker may thereby be judged confident by a knowing observer. Strictly, the signal here is no more communicative than black clouds can be said to be communicating forthcoming rain; it is in this sense a natural sign. However, knowing this, a politician may purposefully lower the natural tone of his voice to induce belief in his self-confidence – he is then intentionally *exploiting* a 'natural' sign. In a third situation, someone may jokingly advise a friend to jump in a lake in the same low tone, where his intention is to convey his intention to sound mock-authoritative and confident.

The three-way distinction has application to the material reviewed above in the following sorts of ways. Some aspects of dialect, those that are relatively hard to change, can function as type (i) 'natural' signs – a case in point would be what Labov calls *indicators* (1972a: ch. 8), sociolinguistic variables correlating firmly and only with the socioeconomic status of the speaker. Similarly, aspects of repertoire restriction are likely to signal a speaker's group affiliations whether he likes it or not. Other aspects of dialect can function more like type (ii) signs, for example what Labov calls in his terminology (a different usage from the one in this volume) *markers*, that is, sociolinguistic variables that are within the manipulation of the speaker so that he is likely to use them to claim higher prestige in intergroup, formal transactions. So can aspects of repertoire, as when a prestigious register is used to impress or influence. But aspects of social deixis are mostly not like these; they are communicative signals of the third type. An intimate pronoun of address, for instance, is part of a communicative system of address where it contrasts with a polite plural used to a singular addressee; and a choice within such a system will always be read as intentionally significant and intended to be recognized as such. Nevertheless, signs can be both communicative and natural signs simultaneously: for example, the Javanese honorific levels mentioned above are constructed of communicative signs that convey degrees of respect to the addressee and to certain referents, yet a particular repertoire of these levels can be a distinctive natural sign of membership in one of the three Javanese estates.

The picture that emerges is a confusing and complex one: natural signs get exploited as communicative resources (see, e.g., Good 1978 on hesitation), while communicative signs can be distinctive of speaker's identity and thus function as natural signs. The web of interconnections between linguistic and social variables allows both a wealth of unintended inferences and intended exploitations for communicative and other purposes.

Another distinction, related but not quite the same, is that between markers whose existence can be attributed to their signalling function, and those that exist for independent historical reasons and just happen to be correlated with social variables. A case of the former would be the T/V pronominal systems, a case of the latter would be social dialects that derive directly from regional ones (as when an urban proletariat is recruited from a distinct rural area). In many cases these are very different kinds of phenomena, but the interesting observation perhaps is that markers that start off as correlations due to historical chance rapidly become integrated into a symbolic system where they function as sensitive signals of social variables (as the work of Labov has demonstrated in detail).

Finally, we have indicated that, as far as we can see, only emic markers of social variables will be of interest to the study of the principles which persons use to conduct social interaction. What are 'markers' for analysts may not be markers for participants, and we must be careful not to prejudge the emic status of, say, dialect as a marker of group membership, just because it functions in a number of particular societies in that way. We have used the terms 'emic marker or clue' to cover all cases where the information associated with the relevant speech variables is available to participants; we could make a further distinction between that information actually employed by participants in governing a particular occasion of interaction, and that which although potentially available to them is not used in a particular interaction. Interestingly, information not used by actually interacting individuals might well be utilized by nonparticipating bystanders (native analysts, if you like) to make sense of the observed interaction. The interactional importance of any emic marker will clearly depend on how, and how often, it is used to guide actual occasions of interaction, or make sense of them to native bystanders. In reviewing types of markers of group membership and social relationship, and more indirect sources of social information in speech, we have followed the authors' own indications of emic status in the particular societies on which they have reported. But, apart from the avowedly emic status of socially deictic markers, the interactional relevance of each kind of marker is something that has to be empirically investigated in each culture. Nevertheless, the kinds of linguistic features we have reviewed are, judging from the available evidence, especially good candidates for emic markers of (or clues to) group membership or social relationship, and would be a good starting-point for research in a new social locus.

3. Concluding remarks

We have pursued two main themes. One is that social structure serves to link social variables in such a way that linguistic correlates with one such variable can provide important clues to the values of other such variables. In particular we have argued that group membership is not often directly marked in an unequivocal or unambiguous way in speech, and that in interaction there is much reliance on indirect clues to group membership The other main theme is that interaction is organized in such a way that linguistic variables are dependent for their social significance on other aspects of interaction, including states of other linguistic variables.

Sections 3.1 and 3.2 follow up these two themes respectively. Section 3.3. addresses the theoretical problem that arises most directly from them: What would be an adequate model of the ways in which social information (especially about participant identities and relationships) is conveyed in speech?

3.1. Social variables and speech markers

We have argued that straightforward and direct markers of group membership are few and far between, and that the bulk of the ways in which social group membership is indicated in speech are indirect and involve a number of intervening social variables – especially the variable of social relationship. This indirect 'marking' is possible because social structural determinants, which structure the relations between groups, penetrate right down into the organization of social relationships. There is thus a connection between the degree of interrelation between different social variables and the extent to which they are marked simply and directly in speech; the more interrelation, the greater the possibility of indirect marking.

It may be that other social variables (e.g. those examined in the other chapters in this volume) correlate with linguistic variables in a more straightforward fashion than social group. But we doubt this. And we suspect that, as is the case with markers of group membership, the overall social structure will determine the importance of the social variable in question, its relations to other variables, and hence the possibility of indirect 'marking' in speech. We would like briefly to review some of these other variables and to ask of each (i) to what extent its corresponding markers in speech are really direct, and (ii) to what extent the social variables themselves vary in their significance and in their connections with other variables due to social structural differences in different societies.

To some extent, due to our broad definition of group, we have already reviewed some of these other variables – in particular, class and ethnicity. But turning to markers of sex in speech, we can see that except for some paralinguistic features and some rare instances of linguistic features categorically reserved for one sex or the other, the linguistic markers of sex derive from one of two sources (cf. Smith, this volume: ch. 4). Either they are markers indicating the hierarchical relationship between the sexes, and so only indirectly markers of sex *per se* (and directly markers of deference or power), or they stem from the different social networks or activities in which members of the two sexes are involved in some societies (see Brown (in press) for a Mexican Indian case where usages of politeness strategies are tied to networks of relationships unique to each sex). The social structural determinants of the importance of sex as a social variable, and thus perhaps the likelihood of direct markers, do not always act in a simple way. Consider for instance that in South India women are markedly lower in status than men of their own caste and sex roles are sharply differentiated, yet there are very few direct markers of sex in their speech. The reason seems to be that the social hierarchies based on age within caste, and on caste-status in intercaste interaction, override the status asymmetry based on sex.

Another important social variable is age, but again simple direct markers of age are not common (cf. Helfrich, this volume: ch. 3). Thus in speech communities we have studied in England, Mexico and India, apart from certain paralinguistic features (voice set) and perhaps the age stratification of repertoire and slang,[22] markers of age are indirect; what is directly marked most conspicuously is the relative status that age confers. Furthermore, the degree of relative superiority thus conferred differs radically in the three societies due to the differing role that age plays as a criterion for authority and office, as determined by each social structure.

Even the most idiosyncratic of social variables, personality, is subject to broad social influences. Indeed this is the premiss of the work done in the 'culture and personality' school of American anthropology (see Kaplan 1961), wherein relations between cultural traits, child-rearing practices and the basic range of personality type in a culture are explored. A good feeling for the empirical basis of this kind of work can be gained from Carstairs' (1967) account of Hindu character; a more familiar example of such interconnections is provided by the belief held by many that the function of the elite English 'public schools' is as much to breed a certain kind of character as it is to educate (Scherer (this volume: ch. 5) makes a similar point concerning 'Prussian' personality). There is a special problem for markers of personality, namely that it seems that a great many of the dimensions on which personalities are usually thought to differ (at least by the layman) – e.g. aloof/friendly, leader/follower, confident/insecure, outgoing/shy, and so on – are also and perhaps primarily dimensions on which the qualities of social relationship differ. It would be possible, then, to claim that the markers in question are directly markers of social relationships and only secondarily expressions of personality. The point of course is that personality is expressed in the conduct of social relations, and particular ways of conducting them are the source of many if not most personality attributions.

Situation as a social variable is subject to the same kinds of observation (cf. Brown & Fraser, this volume: ch. 2). Clearly, social structure determines to what extent and how many emic locales and activities are distinguished. And again, markers of situation are often more directly markers of other things. Consider for example the switch from first names to titles plus last names by two English academics as they move from an informal situation (e.g. a chat in the common room) to a formal one (e.g. a faculty meeting). Such usages are primarily markers of social relation-

[22] Labov's (1972a) studies of markers of social class have shown that these too stratify by age of speaker. This comes about because the sociolinguistic variables in question are subject to continuous processes of change. The result is that a certain phonetic realization, for example, that was once prestigious may within a generation become stigmatized, and vice versa. But since an individual's usage will tend to be frozen by his middle twenties, his speech will contain markers that may contrast with those of both younger and older members of his own class. We draw attention to this because it is yet another way in which such markers of social class also function as markers of a number of other social variables.

ships (indicating degree of intimacy or distance), but it so happens that in formal situations the display of intimacy is not appropriate.

In sum, we have argued here that group membership is not exceptional in being largely indirectly indicated in speech via inferences from markers of other social variables. In these other cases too, social structural determinants link the variable in focus to other social variables, thus allowing indirect marking. But if markers of most social variables tend to be indirect then there must be some social variables that are key, and carry the bulk of the direct marking. Our study of group markers and our short review of markers of other social variables suggest strongly that there is one key social variable that is more heavily and directly marked in speech than any other – namely, kinds and qualities of social relationship. (Indeed in 1967 Gumperz expressed a similar view (1971: 226).) It is as if markers of other social variables tend to be compressed into markers of social relationships, and thus into indirect status. We do not have to look far to see why this is so: the arena for social interaction is the social relationship – it is within the social relationship that other social variables have to be communicated – the social relationship *is* (at least in large part) the communication context. By linguistic modulations that vary the kind and quality of social relationships expressed, social variables on many other dimensions can be indirectly conveyed.

Because the social relationship constitutes the situation of communication to such a large extent and involves the recognition of, and adaptation to, a large variety of potential alters, we would expect markers of this variable to be of the intentionally communicative, voluntary kind. And this seems largely to be the case. For direct markers of other social variables are more often (though not exclusively of course) involuntary – like voice set as a marker of sex or age (taken indeed by laymen to be 'natural signs' of the same), and also many features of dialect. By contrast, the key markers of social relationships, such as address forms and politeness levels, are within voluntary, even sometimes conscious, control.

The heavy reliance on markers of social relationship to convey indirectly other pertinent social variables thus comes to have another significance: such indirect markers are likely to be of the voluntary kind. They are thus likely to be subject to manipulation, impression-management, strategic deployment. And the extent to which social markers in speech tend to be that way may be an important feature of human societies. If by birth we inherited inalienable markers of identity on all dimensions, then human social organization could be considerably more like that of ants.

3.2. Interactional structure and the interdependence of linguistic variables

We have argued that the social significance of markers in speech cannot be adequately assessed without reference to other aspects of interaction, including other such markers and various background assumptions made by participants about the nature of the interaction. We can isolate one basic set of problems concerning the notion of marker that will exemplify the point.

The problems have to do with what Brown & Fraser (this volume: ch. 2, 3.2) have termed the multiple ambiguity of social markers. This property seems to be more common than not, and it raises fundamental difficulties with analysis, especially of a quantitative kind. We may distinguish various ways in which markers can be ambiguous, that is, signal different kinds of things in different circumstances:

Markers with vector values. Examples are provided by Labov's variables (for example, New York City /r/) which are sensitive both to speaker's class membership and what Labov calls 'style', namely aspects of context that induce more or less attention to speech. Any particular rate of final or postvocalic /r/ pronunciation will be (in Labov's analysis) a function of the values on the two dimensions of speaker's social stratum and style.

Markers with dyadic interpretations only. The simple example here is the use of T/V pronouns, where the social valuation depends both on what pronoun is given and on what is received: a reciprocal T indicating solidarity, a T given and a V received indicating a nonsolidary power relation. This may be a much more general phenomenon than we now know. For example, in Giles' theory of dialect accommodation, if only one party accommodates there may be implications that the other is of higher status, if both accommodate they may seem to be striving for a degree of solidarity. Consider too code-switching phenomena: the social significance of a choice of language is likely to be at least partially dependent on what language other participants are using.

The neutralization of social information in linguistic markers. Again, T/V pronouns are illustrative here, but the remarks hold equally for the choice between any two sociolinguistic alternates (address forms, honorifics, styles, diglossic levels, even languages). Sociolinguists, following Geoghegan's pioneering work (see Geoghegan 1971; Ervin-Tripp 1972;

and discussion in Levinson 1977), have used flow-chart formalisms to represent the choices underlying uses of address forms. In such flow charts, a number of distinct pathways through a series of assessments of the social situation lead to the choice of a pronoun or address form. For example, in Ervin-Tripp's (1972: 226) representation of nineteenth-century Russian pronoun usage there are six pathways leading to choice of the V pronoun. Any instance of a pronoun usage is thus, when decontextualized, multiply 'ambiguous', although in context, given the available information about whether the addressee is or is not adult, whether the social context is formal or informal, etc., there is no such ambiguity for participants, who can reconstruct exactly what assessments lie behind a usage, i.e. its social significance. Thus a pronominal choice is only a marker of detailed social information relative to a great deal of other social information.

The 're-use' of contrasting markers to signal further social information. An example should make the notion clear. In a northern Norwegian situation described by Blom & Gumperz (1972), two rigidly separated dialects (perceptually, perhaps, distinct languages), Ranamål and Bokmål, are associated primarily with members of the local fishing population and members of the southern elite, respectively. For locals, ingroup trans-actions are primarily in Ranamål, outgroup transactions in Bokmål, and this is perhaps the primary social significance of the codes employed. But given this, the opposition can be *re-used* within ingroup transactions to signal other secondary social significances – for example, it can be used to distinguish between kinds of social role. Thus two locals will conduct official business in Bokmål, and neighbourly transactions in Ranamål. And then *within* the conduct of official business the opposition can be re-used yet again to signal attitudes to the topics under discussion. We cannot then simply say of one or other code that it is a marker of such and such; it depends critically on the interactional context (see Brown & Fraser, this volume: ch. 2, for additional examples).

Significances dependent on syntagmatic relations between markers. Clearly the address form *sir* in English has quite different significance when used alone, and when followed by a name as in *Sir Arthur*. Similarly, it has been reported for the Swedish pronouns of address *du* (T) and *ni* (V) that their social significance depends critically on the presence or absence of other address forms in the utterance: thus *du* plus first name conveys intimacy, *du* without first name conveys nonintimate solidarity, *ni* plus first name is a rural form of respect, *ni* without address form can be considered rude, while *ni* with title plus last name indicates personal reserve (Paulston 1975). There is reason to suspect that this is a general, if largely unexplored, phenomenon.

'Marked' usages of markers. Here the term 'marked' is used in a distinct and technical sense to refer to the unexpected usage that contrasts with the basic or fundamental usage (see Geoghegan 1973). A simple case of marked usage would be the use of a T pronoun to insult where a V pronoun would be the expected 'unmarked' usage, or the use of a V pronoun to indicate withdrawal of affection where a reciprocal use of T is normal. One can find marked usage of all kinds of sociolinguistic alternates, including the languages used in code-switching. Their correct interpretation relies on a rejection of the 'face value' of the marked usage and the identification of the contrasting expected unmarked usage.

All these different kinds of usage of markers in speech are sources of 'ambiguity', and they indicate that one cannot attribute a particular social significance to a linguistic variable without a large amount of knowledge about other aspects of the interaction. In insisting on the importance of attention to structure in interaction, it is these kinds of phenomena that we have in mind. Any linguistic variable has a structural relation to other such variables with which it contrasts, or with which it forms a significant unit as a reciprocal or syntagm. Moreover, the social significance of a social marker can vary according to the overall 'frame' attributed to an interaction: to the same interlocutor a T pronoun or a first name may be unmarked in an informal setting while a V pronoun or a title plus last name may be unmarked in a formal setting. The full significance of a social marker can only be assessed against a body of information about the interaction situation and the values of other interaction variables.

The straightforward implication is that social markers cannot be simply identified by correlating linguistic variables with social variables: different instances of the same linguistic variable may have quite different social significances. Quantitative techniques can only sensibly be applied after a prior examination of the dependencies that a linguistic variable's significance has on other aspects of interaction structure and process.

3.3. Towards a model of how social information is conveyed in speech

In section 1 we indicated dissatisfaction with a simple and initially beguiling model of how social information, especially about speaker and addressee identities and relationships, is conveyed in social interaction (cf. Robinson, this volume: ch. 6, 6; Scherer: ch. 5, 5.3). The model that we argued against can be characterized by the following assumptions:

(1) a. There are simple and direct correlations between isolated social variables and linguistic variables, each such correlation constituting a social marker in speech.

b. Some such markers are perceived by participants in interaction (are of emic status), thus effectively functioning as signals of the relevant social variables.

c. A theory of how social information is conveyed in speech will essentially consist of an inventory of such markers.

We think that the model has a certain *prima facie* plausibility, and moreover suspect that certain aspects of social psychological methodology will predispose social psychologists to adopt it implicitly. Nevertheless, in our detailed discussions of how group memberships are marked in speech, as a general model of the ways in which social information is conveyed in speech we have shown it to be untenable. Collecting together our reasons for rejecting the model, we may state them as follows:

(2) a. Direct markers seem to be relatively rare and not the most important way in which social information is conveyed in speech.

b. Because social structure links diverse social variables, a marker of one such variable can serve to mark another, and this proves to be an equally important source of social information.

c. Even when direct markers can be found they tend to be multiply ambiguous in their social significance. Their actual significance on an occasion of use can only be ascertained by examining their relations to other aspects of the interaction.

d. Because it relies crucially on the concepts of marker and correlation, the model is atomistic. The notion of structure is required to make clear how the linguistic variables cohere into an interactional system and the social variables into a social system. Instead of an inventory of simple signals, what seems to be involved is a complex web of interconnecting and interdependent variables that allow complex chains of inference.

There is an additional danger associated with the model, namely that any strong correlation between linguistic and social variables will be taken to constitute a marker. But as we illustrated in section 1, such correlations can be epiphenomenal and misleading, so that the emic status of such correlations cannot be taken for granted and must be independently demonstrated, if we are to suppose that they play any role in the conduct of interaction by participants.

Finally, the notion of a social marker lumps together phenomena of very different kinds: there are markers (like address forms) that are under voluntary control, others (like voice set) that are usually not; there are linguistic items that are so to speak designed to be social markers (honorifics, for instance), and those that for one historical reason or another just happen to indicate social information (like regional dialect). There is reason to suppose that not all these kinds of markers are utilized by participants in exactly the same kind of way as sources of social information.

It would almost certainly be premature to offer in place of the model in (1) any general theory that purported to account for all ways in which language usage can convey information concerning the social properties of aspects of the speech event (including of course participant identities and relationships). But our discussion has made it clear, we hope, that an adequate model would have at least the following characteristics:

(3) a. It should incorporate a model of interactional structure, which would provide an account of the context dependency of the significance of linguistic signals of social information.

b. It should incorporate models of social structure that describe the interrelations between social variables of different kinds, and provide accounts of their relative significance to participants.

c. It should provide an account of the complex interrelations between social structures and interactional structures, such that participants using their knowledge of these structures and their interrelations can *infer* – often in involved and indirect ways – the social information from situated speech that they can empirically be shown to infer.

We therefore conclude that correlation, and the concept of marker that relies on it, can only be a useful method of locating potentially rewarding research sites, and cannot be the basis for an adequate general model of the ways in which participants themselves extract social information from speech. To do that they generally seem to utilize structural information about both interactional and linguistic systems on the one hand, and about social systems on the other.

336   Penelope Brown and Stephen Levinson

References

Abercrombie, D. 1968. Paralanguage. *British Journal of Disorders of Communication*, 3, 55–9.
Agar, M. 1973. *Ripping and Running: a formal ethnography of urban heroin addicts.* New York.
Albert, E. 1972. Culture patterning of speech behavior in Burundi. In J. J. Gumperz & D. Hymes (eds.) *Directions in Sociolinguistics: the ethnography of communication.* New York.
Argyle, M. 1969. *Social Interaction.* London.
1975. *Bodily Communication.* London.
Bailey, C.-J. & Shuy, R. N. (eds.) 1973. *New Ways of Analyzing Variation in English.* Washington, DC.
Baron, R., Byrne, D. & Griffitt, W. 1974. *Social Psychology: understanding human interaction.* Boston.
Bates, E. 1976. *Language and Context: the acquisition of pragmatics.* New York.
Bauman, R. & Sherzer, J. (eds.) 1975. *Explorations in the Ethnography of Speaking.* Cambridge.
Beattie, J. 1966. *Other Cultures.* London.
Beck, B. 1972. *Peasant Society in Koṅku.* Vancouver.
Bernstein, B. 1971. *Class, Codes and Control*, vol. i. London.
Bickerton, D. 1971. Inherent variability and variable rules. *Foundations of Language*, 7, 457–92.
1973. Quantitative versus dynamic paradigms: the case of Montreal *que*. In C.-J. Bailey & R. N. Shuy (eds.) *New Ways of Analyzing Variation in English.* Washington, DC.
1975. *Dynamics of a Creole System.* Cambridge.
Blanc, H. 1964. *Communal Dialects in Baghdad.* Center for Middle Eastern Studies, Cambridge, Mass.
Bloch, M. (ed.) 1975. *Political Language and Oratory in Traditional Society.* New York.
Blom, J.-P. & Gumperz, J. J. 1972. Social meaning in linguistic structures: code-switching in Norway. In J. J. Gumperz & D. Hymes (eds.) *Directions in Sociolinguistics: the ethnography of communication.* New York.
Bloomfield, L. 1933. *Language.* New York.
Bott, E. 1957. *Family and Social Network.* New York.
Brown, B. L., Strong, W. J. & Rencher, A. C. 1975. Acoustic determinants of the perceptions of personality from speech. *International Journal of the Sociology of Language*, 6, 11–33.
Brown, P. In press. How and why are women more polite?: some evidence from a Mayan community. To appear in R. Borker, N. Furman & S. McConnell-Ginet (eds.) *Language and Women's Lives: a feminist perspective.* Ithaca, NY.
Brown, P. & Levinson, S. 1978. Universals in language usage: politeness phenomena. In E. Goody (ed.) *Questions and Politeness: strategies in social interaction.* Cambridge Papers in Social Anthropology, 8. Cambridge.
Brown, R. & Ford, M. 1964. Address in American English. In D. Hymes (ed.) *Language in Culture and Society.* New York.
Brown, R. & Gilman, A. 1960. The pronouns of power and solidarity. In T. Sebeok (ed.) *Style in Language.* Cambridge, Mass.

Campbell, D. T. 1965. Ethnocentric and other altruistic motives. In *Nebraska Symposium on Motivation*, vol. xiii. Lincoln, Nebr.

Carstairs, G. M. 1967. *The Twice-Born*. Bloomington, Ind.

Cartwright, D. & Zander, A. (eds.) 1960. *Group Dynamics: research and theory*. Evanston, Ill.

Cedergren, H. 1970. Patterns of free variation: the language variable. Mimeo, University of Montreal.

Comrie, B. 1976. Linguistic politeness axes: speaker–addressee, speaker–referent, speaker–bystander. *Pragmatics Microfiche* 1.7, A3-B1. Department of Linguistics, University of Cambridge.

Crystal, D. 1975. *The English Tone of Voice*. London.

Crystal, D. & Davy, D. 1969. *Investigating English Style*. London.

Deutsch, M. 1968. Group behaviour. In D. Sills (ed.) *International Encyclopaedia of the Social Sciences*, vol. vi. New York.

Dittmar, N. 1976. *Sociolinguistics: a critical survey of theory and application*. London.

Ellis, D. S. 1967. Speech and social status in America. *Social Forces*, 45, 431–7.

Ervin-Tripp, S. 1969. Sociolinguistics. In L. Berkowitz (ed.) *Advances in Experimental Social Psychology*. New York.

　　1972. On sociolinguistic rules: alternation and co-occurrence. In J. J. Gumperz & D. Hymes (eds.) *Directions in Sociolinguistics: the ethnography of communication*. New York.

　　1976. Is Sybil there? The structure of some American English directives. *Language in Society*, 5, 25–66.

Evans-Pritchard, E. E. 1940. *The Nuer*. Oxford.

Fillmore, C. J. 1975. Santa Cruz lectures on deixis. *Indiana University Linguistics Club Papers*. Bloomington, Ind.

Fishman, J. A. (ed.) 1968. *Readings in the Sociology of Language*. The Hague.

　　(ed.) 1971–2. *Advances in the Sociology of Language*, vols. i and ii. The Hague.

　　1972. Domains and the relationship between micro- and macro-sociolinguistics. In J. J. Gumperz & D. Hymes (eds.) *Directions in Sociolinguistics: the ethnography of communication*. New York.

　　1974. The sociology of language: an interdisciplinary social science approach to language in society. In T. Sebeok (ed.) *Current Trends in Linguistics*, vol. xii. The Hague.

Fortes, M. 1969. *Kinship and the Social Order*. London.

Freedman, J., Carlsmith, J. M. & Sears, D. 1970. *Social Psychology*. Englewood Cliffs, NJ.

Friedrich, P. 1972. Social context and semantic feature: the Russian pronominal usage. In J. J. Gumperz & D. Hymes (eds.) *Directions in Sociolinguistics: the ethnography of communication*. New York.

Garvin, P. & Mathiot, M. 1968. The urbanization of the Guarani language: a problem in language and culture. In J. Fishman (ed.) *Readings in the Sociology of Language*. The Hague.

Gazdar, G. 1976. Quantifying context. *York Papers in Linguistics*, 6, 117–32.

Geertz, C. 1960. *The Religion of Java*. Glencoe, Ill.

Geoghegan, W. 1971. Information processing systems in culture. In P. Kay (ed.) *Explorations in Mathematical Anthropology*. Cambridge, Mass.

　　1973. A theory of marking rules. In K. Wexler & A. K. Romney (eds.) *Cognitive Organization and Psychological Processes*. Washington, DC.

Giglioli, P. P. (ed.) 1972. *Language and Social Context*. Harmondsworth, Middx.
Giles, H. & Powesland, P. F. 1975. *Speech Style and Social Evaluation*. London.
Good, D. 1978. On (doing) being hesitant. *Pragmatics Microfiche* 3.2, E1-F14. Department of Linguistics, University of Cambridge.
Goodenough, W. 1969. Rethinking 'status' and 'role': toward a general model of the cultural organization of social relationships. In S. A. Tyler (ed.) *Concepts and Assumptions in Contemporary Anthropology*. New York.
Goody, E. 1972. 'Greeting', 'begging', and the presentation of respect. In J. S. La Fontaine (ed.) *The Interpretation of Ritual: essays in honour of I. A. Richards*. London.
    1978. Towards a theory of questions. In E. Goody (ed.) *Questions and Politeness: strategies in social interaction*. Cambridge Papers in Social Anthropology, *8*. Cambridge.
Grice, H. P. 1971. Meaning. In D. Steinberg & L. A. Jakobovits (eds.) *Semantics: an interdisciplinary reader*. Cambridge.
Grimshaw, A. D. 1970. Sociolinguistics. In W. Schramm *et al.* (eds.) *Handbook of Communication*. New York.
Gumperz, J. J. 1958. Dialect differences and social stratification in a North Indian village. *American Anthropologist, 60*, 668–81. (Reprinted in Gumperz 1971.)
    1962. Types of linguistic communities. *Anthropological Linguistics, 4*, 28–40. (Reprinted in Gumperz 1971.)
    1964. Hindi-Punjabi code-switching in Delhi. In H. Lunt (ed.) *Proceedings of the Ninth International Congress of Linguistics*. The Hague. (Reprinted in Gumperz 1971.)
    1971. *Language in Social Groups*. Stanford, Calif.
    1972. Introduction. In J. J. Gumperz & D. Hymes (eds.) *Directions in Sociolinguistics: the ethnography of communication*. New York.
    1976. Language, communication and public negotiation. In P. R. Sanday (ed.) *Anthropology and the Public Interest: fieldwork and theory*. New York.
    1977. Sociocultural knowledge in conversational inference. In *Georgetown University 28th Round Table on Languages and Linguistics*. Washington, DC.
    1978.The conversational analysis of interethnic communication. In E. L. Ross (ed.) *Interethnic Communication*. Proceedings of the Southern Anthropological Society. Atlanta, Georgia.
Gumperz, J. J. & Hymes, D. (eds.) 1972. *Directions in Sociolinguistics*. New York.
Gumperz, J. J. & Wilson, R. 1971. Convergence and creolization: a case from the Indo-Aryan/Dravidian border. In D. Hymes (ed.) *Pidginization and Creolization of Languages*. Cambridge.
Gumperz, J. J., Agrawal, A. & Aulakh, G. n.d. Prosody, paralinguistics, and contextualization in Indian English. MS (1977), Language Behavior Research Laboratory, University of California, Berkeley.
Haas, M. 1964. Men's and women's speech in Koasati. In D. Hymes (ed.) *Language in Culture and Society*. New York.
Halliday, M. A. K. 1968. The uses and users of language. In J. Fishman (ed.) *Readings in the Sociology of Language*. The Hague.
    1976. Anti-languages. *American Anthropologist, 78*, 570–84.
Harada, S. I. 1976. Honorifics. In M. Shibatani (ed.) *Syntax and Semantics*, vol. v, *Japanese Generative Grammar*. New York.

Hollos, M. 1975. *Comprehension and Use of Social Rules in Pronoun Selection by Hungarian Children*. Working Papers in Sociolinguistics, 24. Southwest Educational Development Laboratory, Austin, Texas.

Hymes, D. (ed.) 1964. *Language in Culture and Society*. New York.

(ed.) 1971. *Pidginization and Creolization of Languages*. Cambridge.

1972. On communicative competence. In J. B. Pride & J. Holmes (eds.) *Sociolinguistics*. Harmondsworth, Middx.

1974. *Foundations in Sociolinguistics: an ethnographic approach*. Philadelphia.

Irvine, J. 1975. Strategies of status manipulation in the Wolof greeting. In R. Bauman & J. Sherzer (eds.) *Explorations in the Ethnography of Speaking*. Cambridge.

1975. *Wolof Speech Styles and Social Status*. Working Papers in Sociolinguistics, 23. Southwest Educational Development Laboratory, Austin, Texas.

Jackson, J. 1975. Language identity of the Colombian Vaupés Indians. In R. Bauman & J. Sherzer (eds.) *Explorations in the Ethnography of Speaking*. Cambridge.

Jones, S. C. & Gerard, H. B. 1967. *Foundations of Social Psychology*. New York.

Kaplan, B. (ed.) 1961. *Studying Personality Cross-culturally*. New York.

Kay, P. 1975. *Tahitian Words for Race and Class*. Working Paper, 40. Language Behavior Research Laboratory, University of California, Berkeley.

Key, H. 1967. *Morphology of Cayuvava*. The Hague.

Labov, W. 1966. *The Social Stratification of English in New York City*. Washington, DC.

1972a. *Sociolinguistic Patterns*. Philadelphia.

1972b. Rules for ritual insults. In D. Sudnow (ed.) *Studies in Social Interaction*. New York.

1972c. *Language in the Inner City*. Philadelphia.

Lambert, W. & Tucker, G. R. 1976. *Tu, Vous, Usted: a social-psychological study of address patterns*. Rowley, Mass.

Laver, J. 1968. Voice quality and indexical information. *British Journal of Disorders of Communication*, 3, 43–54.

Laver, J. & Hutcheson, S. (eds.) 1972. *Communication in Face-to-face Interaction*. Harmondsworth, Middx.

Leach, E. 1954. *Political Systems of Highland Burma*. Cambridge, Mass.

1961. *Pul Eliya: a village in Ceylon*. Cambridge.

1976. *Culture and Communication*. Cambridge.

Levinson, S. 1977. Social deixis in a Tamil village. PhD dissertation, Department of Anthropology, University of California, Berkeley.

1978. Universals in sociolinguistics. MS, University of Cambridge, Department of Linguistics.

Lévi-Strauss, C. 1968. *Structural Anthropology*. London.

Lyons, J. 1972. Human language. In R. A. Hinde (ed.) *Non-Verbal Communication*. Cambridge.

McClintock, C. G. 1972. *Experimental Social Psychology*. New York.

McCormack, W. 1960. Social dialects in Dharwar Kannada. In C. Ferguson & J. Gumperz (eds.) *Linguistic Diversity in South Asia*. University Research Center in Anthropology, Folklore, and Linguistics, Bloomington, Ind.

Martin, S. 1964. Speech levels in Japan and Korea. In D. Hymes (ed.) *Language in Culture and Society*. New York.

Miller, R. A. 1967. *The Japanese Language*. Chicago.

Nadel, S. F. 1957. *The Theory of Social Structure*. London.

Newcomb, T. M. 1953. Motivation in social behavior. In J. S. Brown *et al.* (eds.) *Current Theory and Research in Motivation: a symposium*. Lincoln, Nebr.

O'Neill, P. G. 1966. *A Programmed Guide to Respect Language in Modern Japanese*. London.

Paulston, C. B. 1975. *Language and Social Class: pronouns of address in Swedish*. Working Papers in Sociolinguistics, *29*. Southwest Educational Development Laboratory, Austin, Texas.

Pillai, M. Shanmukam, 1972. Tamil today. *Indian Linguistics, 33*, no. 1.

Pride, J. B. & Holmes, J. (eds.) 1972. *Sociolinguistics*. Harmondsworth, Middx.

Radcliffe-Brown, A. R. 1952. *Structure and Function in Primitive Society*. London.

Ramanujan, A. K. 1968. The structure of variation: a study in caste dialects. In M. Singer & B. Cohn (eds.) *Structure and Change in Indian Society*. Viking Fund Publications in Anthropology. New York.

Rubin, J. 1968. Bilingual usage in Paraguay. In J. Fishman (ed.) *Readings in the Sociology of Language*. The Hague.

Sahakian, W. S. 1974. *Systematic Social Psychology*. New York.

Sanches, M. & Blount, B. (eds.) 1976. *Social Dimensions of Language Use*. New York.

Sankoff, G. 1973. Above and beyond phonology in variable rules. In C.-J. Bailey & R. W. Shuy (eds.) *New Ways of Analyzing Variation in English*. Washington, DC.

  1975. A quantitative paradigm for the study of communicative competence. In R. Bauman & J. Sherzer (eds.) *Explorations in the Ethnography of Speaking*. Cambridge.

Sankoff, G. & Cedergren, H. 1971. Some results of a sociolinguistic study of Montreal French. In R. Darnell (ed.) *Linguistic Diversity in Canadian Society*. Champaign, Ill.

Sankoff, G., Sarrasin, R. & Cedergren, H. 1971. Quelques considérations sur la distribution sociolinguistique de la variable QUE dans le français de Montréal. Paper given at the 39th Congress, Association canadienne-française pour l'avancement des sciences.

Secord, P. F. & Backman, C. W. 1974. *Social Psychology*. New York.

Shatz, M. 1975. The comprehension of indirect directives: can two-year-olds shut the door? *Pragmatics Microfiche* 1.5, C3–D7. Department of Linguistics, University of Cambridge.

Sherif, M. *et al.* 1961. *Intergroup Conflict and Cooperation: the robber's cave experiment*. Norman, Oklahoma.

Shimanoff, S. 1977. Investigating politeness. In E. O. Keenan & T. L. Bennett (eds.) *Discourse Across Time and Space*. Southern California Occasional Papers in Linguistics, *5*. Department of Linguistics, University of Southern California, Los Angeles.

Shuy, R., (ed.) 1973. *Sociolinguistics: current trends and prospects*. Report of the 23rd Annual Round Table Meeting on Linguistics and Language Studies, Georgetown University. Washington, DC.

Shuy, R., Wolfram, W. & Riley, W. K. 1967. *A Study of Social Dialects in Detroit*. Final report, Project 6-1347. Washington, DC.

Slobin, D. 1963. Some aspects of the use of pronouns of address in Yiddish. *Word, 19*, 193–202.

Sorenson, A. 1967. Multilingualism in the Northwest Amazon. *American Anthropologist, 69*, no. 6, 670–82.

Southworth, F. C. 1975. Sociolinguistics research in South India: achievements and prospects. In B. Stein (ed.) *Essays on South India*. Asian studies at Hawaii, 15. The University Press of Hawaii.

Tajfel, H. 1974. Social identity and inter-group behaviour. *Social Science Information, 13*, 93ff.

Trudgill, P. 1974a. *The Social Differentiation of English in Norwich*. Cambridge.
1974b. *Sociolinguistics: an introduction*. Harmondsworth, Middx.

Uyeno, T. 1971. A study of Japanese modality: a performative analysis of sentence particles. PhD dissertation, Department of Linguistics, University of Michigan, Ann Arbor.

Weinreich, M. 1968. *Yidishkayt* and Yiddish: on the impact of religion on language in Ashkenazic Jewry. In J. Fishman (ed.) *Readings in the Sociology of Language*. The Hague.

Wolfram, W. & Fasold, R. W. 1974. *The Study of Social Dialects in American English*. Englewood Cliffs, NJ.

Yamanashi, M. 1974. On minding your p's and q's in Japanese: a case study from honorifics. In *Papers from the Tenth Regional Meeting of the Chicago Linguistic Society*. Chicago.

9. Speech markers in social interaction[1]

HOWARD GILES, KLAUS R. SCHERER and
DONALD M. TAYLOR

The concept of speech markers has only recently been incorporated into the domain of sociolinguistics (Abercrombie 1967; Labov 1970).[2] The present volume represents an attempt to assess the current state of knowledge about speech markers particularly, although not exclusively, from a social psychological perspective. This final chapter develops key recurring themes throughout the volume and offers a possible framework for future research on this embryonic concept.

From the detailed chapters in this volume, it would seem that speech markers operate at two different levels. At the most fundamental level, they serve as easily perceived auditory stimuli which permit speakers to reveal their association with broadly defined biological, social and psychological states, and listeners to categorize others accurately in these terms. Level 1 speech markers, then, serve the general function of maintaining the social system by identifying and recognizing members who occupy various roles and hierarchical positions within it. It is interesting to note that most individuals do not have voluntary control over their affiliation with the various biological, social and psychological categories referred to in this volume. For instance, people have little choice over the age, sex and ethnic group membership they present to others, or, albeit to a much lesser extent, their social class, personality, the situations in which they find themselves and the social structures in which these are embedded. Moreover, speech markers indicating these broad level 1 states are more often than not paralleled by other equally potent nonlinguistic cues. We need not attend to an individual's voice in order to decide his gender; in most contexts we can base our decision on cues of physical

[1] We are grateful to Penny Brown, Peter Robinson and Philip Smith for their insightful and valuable comments made in the preparation of this chapter.
[2] For a discussion of Abercrombie, see Laver & Trudgill (this volume: ch. 1, 1) and for Labov, see Brown & Levinson (this volume: ch. 8, 2.6).

appearance and dress style. Similarly, dramatic visual cues are often easily available for the assignment of individuals to an ethnic or racial group, socioeconomic status and age categories as well as for the classification of situations as public or private, formal or informal, and so forth. Despite the potential redundancy of level 1 speech markers, there are many instances when their operation at this level is crucial. There are certain contexts when speech markers are the sole means by which individuals socially categorize others and define the situation when other cues are either unavailable or uninformative. In this sense, level 1 speech markers may attain the status of an independent variable which determines our categorizations of, inferences about, and reactions towards another (cf. Smith, Giles & Hewstone 1979). In addition, level 1 speech markers assume salience when they appear inconsistent with competing nonlinguistic cues emanating from the other. Thus, although young Johnny may look like a 3-year-old, if he speaks 'with the mind' of a 10-year-old, this mode of expression may for the most part determine our behaviour towards him. Hence, the cognitive maps we possess concerning the associations between speech markers and various biological, social and psychological states perhaps constitute the more fundamental template against which others' characteristics and capabilities can be assessed. Similarly, a person may look Black and be 90 years of age and yet nevertheless *feel* 'White' and act 50. Although physiognomy undoubtedly influences considerably reactions to such an individual, greater weight may be attached to the processing of speech markers and other aspects of overt behaviour (cf. Seligman, Tucker & Lambert 1972; Scherer, Scherer, Hall & Rosenthal 1977). Indeed, it is the greater flexibility of speech to mark complex and dynamic states over other sensory channels and modalities which underlines its importance. Thus, level 1 speech markers are psychologically important as they represent an essential baseline for understanding the *dynamics* of speech markers in social interaction.

At a second and psychologically more important level, speech markers permit interlocutors indirectly to communicate important attitudes, beliefs, values and intentions about their own social states as well as processing the emotional significance of the social states of others. From a social psychological perspective, level 2 speech markers are important in social interaction in at least two ways. First, although our assignment to many social categories is largely involuntary, we do have some control over our overt feelings about them. Speech markers assume salience, then, in marking our beliefs about and attitudes towards these social categories. Therefore, it may be obvious which ethnic group a person

belongs to from cues of skin colour and the language spoken, but inferences about whether the person is proud or ashamed of the affiliation,
the person's attitudes towards other related social categories, and specific
anxieties about various categories and so forth can be communicated by
accentuating or attenuating speech markers characteristic of the particular social category in question (see section 3.4 below). Second, speech
markers assume salience in social interaction by indicating subtle,
perhaps *voluntary*, social and psychological states. In social interaction,
there are norms governing the emission and elicitation of information on
intimate issues. These might include how the other feels about you, his
relationships with others you dislike, and his views on trade unions and
socialism. Given that we do not interrogate people directly about their
feelings on such issues, and because they may be reluctant to self-disclose
particularly threatening information, the monitoring of various speech
markers is a singularly important means by which an individual can glean
such information (cf. Berger 1979). Moreover, while individuals may wish
to avoid verbalizing certain feelings and making specific information
about themselves more public, there may be other issues (e.g. their
achievements, kindnesses, power) which they would like to make more
explicit but about which they feel restrained from communicating
directly. Once again, the subtle use of speech markers indicative of these
psychological states may be the mechanism whereby these emotionally
charged ideas are brought inferentially to the attention of another more
appropriately. Speech markers at level 2, then, are characterized by more
voluntary linguistic features (although not by implication necessarily
intentionally adopted) which are not easily perceived and do not overlap
with parallel nonlinguistic cues. It is precisely because we often do not
exchange overt feelings (sometimes even in the most intimate, longstand-
ing relationships) about our social states, the situations in which we find
ourselves, and our sociopolitical beliefs that the study of speech markers
in social interaction assumes the utmost social psychological significance.
While there may be some ambiguity in operationalizing the two levels of
speech marking functions, they serve as useful conceptual anchorpoints
around which to organize our discussion of the nature of speech markers.

The present chapter addresses itself to the nature of speech markers in
three distinct parts. The first examines communication in various subhuman species with a view to delineating the basic functions of level 1
markers as they apply at the level of human interaction. In the second
part, the more complex psychological functions of speech markers are
organized into a framework comprising cognitive organization and iden-

tity maintenance. In the final part, key conceptual dimensions pertaining to the social significance of speech markers are elaborated.

1. Social markers in animal communication

In considering the possible origins and functions of level 1 markers, discussion will centre on the phenomena in subhuman species. The relevant behavioural repertoire in animals is usually smaller and less complex in organization, which makes it somewhat easier to gain insights into the operation of speech markers at the first level. At the same time, we have to beware of premature generalizations from mechanisms assumed to underlie animal behaviour to explanations of human behaviour. The comparison between animal and human behaviour has become somewhat suspect since some ethologists and sociobiologists have not been able to withstand the temptation to engage in premature and often questionable generalizations. Consequently, the following review of some examples of social markers in animal communication should be regarded as little more than an attempt to provide scope to the discussion of functions and uses of markers in human social interaction and to point to some considerations which make it likely that marking of biological, psychological and social categories is a basic mechanism for communication in any kind of social system. It should be quite clear, however, that we do not wish to suggest on the basis of the rather sketchy discussion which follows that human marking can be explained by the same mechanisms which we speculatively attribute to account for some of the examples of marking in animal species.

1.1. Examples of marking in animal species

Bird song, which is one of the most intensively studied phenomena in animal communication, shall serve as an example to illustrate the import-ance of social markers for social organization. It is now well-established that birds not only recognize their conspecifics on the basis of song patterns, but that they are also able to differentiate regional differences on the basis of 'dialects' (Thorpe 1972; Thielke 1969). This differentiation of local subgroups has important functions for the operation of territoriality and for the diversification and multiplication of species due to restriction of genetic variation (cf. Wilson 1975: 237–8). In addition to species and local subgroup recognition, some species of birds appear to be able to recognize individual identity (cf. Beer 1970). For example, in a study of the indigo bunting, Emlen (1972) has been able to isolate those aspects of the bird's song pattern that are indicative of species, individual identity, and motivational state respectively. The ability to recognize individuals allows, among other things, territorial birds to differentiate between neighbours and strangers. It is not surprising that social animals which are not organized according to a caste system as are the social insects (cf. Wilson 1975: ch. 20) require recognition of individuals. As soon as social organization is based on enduring relationships between individuals over time, such as in stable mating pairs or dominance hierarchies, the identifiability of individuals becomes essential. Thus, in many species with more than rudimentary social organization we find an ability to recognize individual identity – and, as a result of the social structure that is established over time, an ability to recognize caste, rank, and possibly roles via status signals (cf. Wilson 1975: ch. 8).

Given the importance of categorization and identification of individuals for reproduction and social organization, many species have developed a wide array of cues or markers. One of the most obvious cues is of course dimorphism or polymorphism which always differentiates species and which in many species differentiates sex and in some species caste (e.g. in many insect societies; cf. Wilson 1975: ch. 20). Size can serve as an index of age, sex, or both. In most species various aspects of outward appearance carry important cues as to categorical membership, individuality and other characteristics of an organism. For example, one of the most important markers for individual identity in primates (cf. Marler 1965) is facial physiognomy.

Clearly dimorphism or other aspects of outward appearance in themselves are not sufficient to guarantee an effective operation of the marking and recognition systems. This is because many species may not have appropriate visual sense organs, or they may need to identify and/or categorize one another at a distance. The particular signals and the sensory channels used for marking are determined by the communication systems that are predominantly utilized by a species. In species that are heavily dependent on chemical communication, like dogs, marking is achieved through the use of odour signals (pheromones). In species relying primarily on auditory and visual communication, as in most primates including humans, marking occurs via vocal patterning and movement. The relative advantages and disadvantages of these communication systems are discussed in Wilson (1975: ch. 10), and need not be taken up here. Thus, in addition to the static structural cues in appearance, most species utilize dynamic cues in communicative behaviour for marking and recognition. Smith (1969) listed identification as one of the important 'message types' in animal communication. It also seems to be true that there is rarely communication without identification of the sender or marking of sender characteristics. At the same time as the song of a male bird indicates his sexual availability, it also indexes his individual identity, sex, residence and species. A chimpanzee engaging in a threat display at the same time communicates information about his age, status and individual identity. The marking of individual identity, categorical membership and other characteristics of the sender is not only an unavoidable byproduct of any act of communication, in many cases it is necessary for the receiver to be able to interpret and adequately respond to the message conveyed by the sender. For example, a female bird will respond only to the song of a male conspecific and possibly only if he uses the right dialect (Thorpe 1972; Thielke 1969); the recipient of the chimpanzee threat will react quite differently according to whether it was the highest status (alpha) male or one of his equal status age mates who threatened him.

Thus, in many cases, the functions of identification and recognition which are most important for the establishment and maintenance of social organization in social species are achieved through marking of essential social categories and characteristics of individual organisms.

1.2. The functions of marking in social systems

While it is clear that identification and recognition are central functions of markers, the question of which categories or characteristics are marked and in what way this is achieved needs some further discussion. The role that the respective categories or characteristics play in serving the functions of the system they subserve – population, social group, or individual – seems to be of major importance. While this is not the place to engage in a functional analysis of socially organized species we shall try to sketch briefly the functions that markers serve on the level of the population as a system, the social group as a system and the individual as a system.

Without getting involved in the quarrels within biology and genetics, it seems reasonable to assume that on the level of the population as a system there are at least the following two attributes necessary for a successful species: nonrandom selective mating and adaptation of organisms to a changing environment. For social species, among the mechanisms that have evolved to serve these functions, territoriality and bonding and more generally grouping seem to be the most important ones. In order for these mechanisms to operate the members of the species must be able to recognize individual identity or at least categorical membership. As mentioned above, mating does seem to require that sex and age of the potential partner can be assessed; if, as postulated, selection for adaptive traits is involved, the female will have to process additional information such as whether the male owns a territory or is sufficiently high in the dominance hierarchy. In species organized by small groups of animals, e.g. groups of chimpanzees, the stability of the group depends on the ability to differentiate group members from strangers. In territoriality, owners of territory must be differentiated from nonowners and neighbours must be differentiated from total strangers. Thus, among the relevant categories to be marked if territoriality and bonding/grouping are to operate on the population level, are sex, age, individuality, area or home base and group membership. The animal communication literature abounds with examples of how these categories or characteristics are marked by specific features of signals or displays (Marler & Hamilton 1966; Sebeok 1968, 1977; Smith 1977).

On the level of the group as a system we can postulate at least the following two purposes of the system: continued existence of the group, which requires protection from external danger and avoidance of excessive internal conflict, and goal attainment such as obtaining food, rearing the young, and providing social stimulation. Some of the mechanisms that serve these purposes are the formation of relationships between individuals and a coordination of effort, the development of status ranking and dominance hierarchies, and the presence of group cohesion and xenophobia. Again, the minimal requirements for the operation of these mechanisms are the ability to recognize age, sex, individuality and group membership. It seems obvious that without the ability to recognize individual identity, no stable relationships of any kind can be formed. While the marking of these fundamental categories is necessary for the development of social structure in a group, the stability and maintenance of this structure require marking of the positions that individuals have attained on the basis of their past interactions with other individuals in the group. For example, a dominant male rhesus monkey walks around with a brisk, striding gait, with his tail held erect and curled back at the tip, gazing calmly and confidently at other monkeys catching his attention, while subordinate males display virtually a contrasting set of signals (Altman 1962; cf. also Wilson 1975: 191). Clearly, this type of status marking stabilizes the social structure in a group and renders the pattern of interaction much more predictable.

The interactions of individuals within groups in most species are not limited to mating and dominance fights. Consequently, who interacts with whom and how, may be dependent on a number of additional factors, one of which might well be individual differences in behaviour disposition, of which there is increasing evidence in many animal species. Reynolds (1975: 38) provides the following example: 'when you get to know a monkey group well, you eventually learn which vocalizations go with which individuals. Who says it is a major determinant of how it is responded to. Some individuals, for example, who are known to be nervous nellies, consistently have their alarm barks ignored.' Thus, the marking of individual differences in behaviour dispositions (for humans we will call this personality) in communicative signals may play an important role in the formation and maintenance of enduring relationships and types of interactions.

To specify in a few sentences the system purposes and the mechanisms required to serve them for the level of the individual is virtually impossible, considering the centuries of philosophical and psychological debate on this issue. Adopting a somewhat simplistic approach we can argue that the purposes of the individual as a system are personal survival and optimal satisfaction of personal needs. Out of the mechanisms that serve these functions two seem to be most closely connected to the functions of markers of social categories and other characteristics of individuals: processing of information about the social environment and the maintenance of an effective state for coping with the environment. Obviously, social markers have an important function for the information-processing mechanism: accurate recognition of species, age, sex, individuality, group membership, status, local origin, etc., of a sender will not only facilitate decoding and interpretation of the message but also reduce uncertainty about the receiver and his probable course of action, and will allow the individual to adjust accordingly his own strategy for the interaction (cf. also Berger 1979). Maintenance of an effective coping state is a much more complex mechanism, of which two aspects are particularly important for the issue of marking: maintenance and presentation of self identity. While the latter can be easily exemplified in humans and animals (e.g. a dominant ape can 'parade' his status in situations where potential contenders are present), the former is difficult to show in animal species. For this mechanism, markers contribute in establishing and maintaining the self-identity of an individual both for himself and for others in his social environment.

In summary, there are many instances of marking in animals which show remarkable parallels with markers in human interaction. Given that marking of important characteristics of individuals and social categories they belong to seems to fulfil important requirements for the functioning of living systems on the level of the individual, the group and population as systems, it seems rather likely that there is some degree of evolutionary continuity in marking. Thus, the comparative analysis of social markers in animal and human communication is a most promising area for further research.

2. Social psychological functions of markers in human speech

The animal literature makes it clear that through speech markers functionally important social categorizations are discriminated and that these have important implications for social organization. For humans, speech markers have clear parallels. From evidence presented in this volume, it is evident that social categories of age, sex, ethnicity, social class and situation can be clearly marked on the basis of speech, and that such categorization is fundamental to social organization even though many of the categories are also easily discriminated on other bases.

There are however fundamental ways in which human social categorization differs. Like animals, humans belong to social categories but in addition they have feelings and attitudes about belonging to these categories as well as about others who belong to these categories. It is precisely the emotional significance of the social categories which distinguish level 2 markers from those at level 1. For example, while it may be relatively easy to assign a person to the female sex on the basis of very primitive markers, a more subtle set of level 2 markers is needed to ascertain the person's emotional attachment to the category 'female' and perhaps their need to change the meaning of the category for themselves and others. Similarly, speech markers very easily categorize a person as an immigrant, but the immigrant who is made to feel ashamed of this category may very well wish to disguise the speech markers associated with it. Finally, certain categories may be too broad. A person may be socially categorized as English but may have more emotional commitment to being a certain class of English or from a more specified part of England and may well use level 2 speech markers to denote this emotional commitment to the finer category.

Clearly then, while level 1 human speech markers denote social categories and psychological states, there is a need to understand the more important and complex process of how the emotional significance of these categories is perceived and communicated by means of level 2 speech markers. The numerous functions of level 2 markers are categorized on the basis of two overriding functions: cognitive organization and identity maintenance.[3]

2.1. The cognitive organizational function

The manner in which people organize their perceptions of the social environment is a complex process. Although formal subcategories of the organization function are deemed premature at this stage, there are a number of components to this function which have been recognized. An excellent brief discussion of several of the features is provided by Triandis (1971) from whom we have drawn in the present chapter.

First, the organization function involves categorization. When social stimuli are categorized on the basis of speech markers, as for example when all members of a race, age or sex are placed in a category, all members of the category are treated in a similar fashion. On the one hand this form of categorization allows the complex social environment to be reduced to manageable units; however, in the process important information regarding individual differences within the category may be lost.

Following categorization, structures develop in the form of organized relations between categories. Triandis describes three such dimensions of organization. First, a *horizontal* dimension of discrimination in order to permit appropriate differential response patterns to different categories. Thus, Blacks, Whites and Orientals may be categories discriminated along such a dimension, and the utility of the category discrimination would lie in the person orienting him or herself differently to each category.

The second dimension is depicted as a *vertical* level of category abstraction. Someone wishing to make a very general statement about speech markers, for example, may refer to an abstract category (all speakers), whereas the same person may use a more concrete category when a more specific marker is referred to (English speakers) and so forth.

The third dimension of organization is the *centrality* of the category (see Rokeach 1967, 1968). The important implication of this dimension is that the more central categories are more resistant to change, and if change

---

[3] A variety of theorists in social psychology have included implictly within their frameworks of social perception notions similar to those we have referred to as the cognitive organizational and identity maintenance functions.

should occur in a central category, such as religious beliefs for some people, other vertically and horizontally related categories will be affected as well (see also Jones & Gerard 1967).

How then do horizontal category discrimination, vertical abstractness of category, and category centrality, assist in the process of perceptual organization? From the point of view of the *decoder* the organizational structures allow for more efficient interaction with the social environment. Without such structures it would be necessary for the decoder actively to seek out and interpret detailed information about every other stimulus person encountered in the course of social interaction; even for the most superficial and routine of interactions. A set of categories organized in terms of horizontal discrimination, abstractness and centrality places at the decoder's discretion a set of guiding principles for social behaviour. Clearly, for such cognitive structures to develop and then serve as a guide to behaviour, it is necessary for the decoder to process markers which will accurately reflect where in the organization scheme a specific stimulus person belongs. A number of attributes such as physical appearance, dress and situation are important in this process, but many significant markers are found in spoken language, the most important human communication system.

For routine interactions the decoder may well attend only to those speech markers that invoke relatively undifferentiated abstract categories, and act on that basis. For more intimate and important interactions the decoder may attend to more subtle speech markers with a view to invoking the appropriate category more precisely and concretely.

Using speech markers to invoke the correct category within the decoder's organizational structure does more than merely provide an automatic set of rules for behaviour. It provides for the decoder a functional 'understanding' of the social environment by identifying the social positions of the significant others, which allows him to make predictions about their interactive strategies. Current theories in social psychology emphasize the need people have to feel a sense of control over their environment. The term control is sometimes used by theorists in areas such as learned helplessness (Seligman 1975), the locus of control (Lefcourt 1976; Rotter 1966) and attribution (Kelly 1973) to refer to the opportunity for the person actively to manipulate others or create change in the environment. McKirnan (1977, 1978) has pointed out, however, that a more fundamental sense of control is derived from merely 'understanding' the cause–effect relationships in the social environment. This view is consistent with Kelly's assertion that attribution processes are motivated by a need people have to arrive at some 'meaning' of the world in cause–effect terms.

Thus, speech markers may serve to develop and then invoke appropriate categories within the decoder's cognitive structure and these may in turn provide the decoder both with a fundamental understanding of the environment as well as a set of guidelines for appropriate behaviour.

The second important aspect of the organizational function focuses upon the encoder. Not only does the receiver try to structure the incoming message in order to achieve communicational efficiency but, in addition, the sender monitors and organizes his output often to facilitate this process. In other words, speakers will, particularly in cooperative encounters, assess the communicational and emotional needs of their listeners and structure their message in an attempt to secure cognitive similarity by adopting speech markers they associate, rightly or wrongly, with the receiver. Indeed, some ways in which speakers adjust or accommodate to the level of their listeners have been observed with regard to many linguistic features in many dyadic situations, such as adult-to-child interactions (Ferguson 1964; Fraser & Roberts 1975), older-to-younger child (Shatz & Gelman 1973), one ethnic group to another (Giles, Taylor & Bourhis 1973), as well as to the specific requirements of the situation (cf. Brown & Fraser, this volume: ch. 2). Indeed, the study of this organizational function is related to the area of speech diversity – the 'hallmark of sociolinguistics' (Hymes 1972) – as well as being a central concern of all the chapters in this volume.

A number of hypotheses can be suggested regarding the organizational function of speech markers. First, it would be expected that amount of contact would be related to the way in which speech markers are encoded and decoded. Thus, for individuals representing groups which are not interacted with frequently or intimately, there would be little desire to do other than a very abstract and undifferentiated form of categorization on the basis of very salient speech markers. For example, some individuals may have so few international contacts that categorization is based on the very obvious marker – do they or don't they speak my language? Such individuals may even go so far as not to distinguish among foreign languages. Such an English speaker might place all speakers of Russian, Spanish, French, German, etc., under one abstract and undifferentiated category – 'different', or 'foreigner'. This form of categorization would not suggest anything about the intelligence of the decoder but only that making further distinctions might be unnecessary given the person's history of contact with such people.

With increased contact comes the need for more sophisticated categorization and structure, along with a greater need to be accurate in the assignment of people to such categories. In these conditions, the speech markers being emitted by the encoder and perceived by the decoder should be more differentiated. When a teacher orients him or herself to the child, it should not be sufficient to note merely markers of social class and ethnicity. Markers of personality, emotion, mood and relationship to authority may also be important for social evaluation and interaction outcomes.

A second issue related to the organization function of speech markers concerns the ambiguity of the situation. One of the important dimensions of situation is the extent to which the situation places normative constraints regarding speech (cf. Price & Bouffard, 1974). The advantage of constrained situations is that they require little guesswork on the part of interlocutors about appropriate speech styles. Participants know what is expected, for example at a church service or formal cocktail party, and execute their roles accordingly. There is however one important paradox. If a person chooses to use speech markers to communicate 'hidden' messages in a constrained situation, it will be necessary to employ very subtle cues, given the constraints of the situation.

Unconstrained situations pose a different difficulty. Since the situation defines the appropriate speech patterns less, it is left to the participants to define the situation for themselves. In this case the interlocutors must attend more carefully, and therefore use more particularistic categories. A meeting in an informal, unconstrained situation may become defined as an opportunity for idle chatter, ingratiation, a chance to engage in sensitive business matters, or as a means of appearing to others that one is socially active. Which one of these the situation evolves into may sometimes depend on the participants, the speech markers they employ, and the extent to which these are perceived, reciprocated, and jointly acted upon. Again, there exists the paradox that unconstrained situations may be so poorly defined that only very obvious speech markers can define the nature of the interaction. A person might, over a drink following a golf game, simply adopt an obviously formal speech style and openly announce 'let's get down to business'. In either case hypotheses centring around the ambiguity of the situation, and the use of speech markers, as well as their relationship to the organization function, can be generated and tested empirically.

A third set of hypotheses related to the organizational function can be derived, not from the ambiguity of the situation as in the last example, but rather from ambiguities related to the self. To a certain extent at least our 'selves' are defined socially: that is by how we are reacted to by significant others. In order for these reactions to be incorporated meaningfully as part of self-definition they must be attended to and then internalized. Thus, upon moving to a new neighbourhood, a teenage boy might well wish to become accepted into the local street gang. By monitoring the extent to which he is spoken to in the unique 'style' of the gang members, our newcomer will receive clear but implicit social indicators as to if and when he has been fully accepted as part of the gang.

Similarly, once a sense of social self has been articulated the person can use speech markers to signify that definition. Thus our newly accepted gang member can with assurance consistently reinforce his own identity as a gang member by adopting the gang's 'unique' aspect of speech both within and sometimes without the group.

It would seem reasonable to hypothesize that attention to and use of speech markers for the purposes of self-definition would be enhanced in contexts where ambiguities about the self emerge. Changes of role, occupation or status may be examples where attention to speech markers is enhanced. The foreman who has just been elevated to a position in management may have a need to overemploy those speech markers of his new role of which he is aware, while at the same time being particularly attentive to the other markers of his new reference group which he has not yet internalized. Similarly, encountering novel social or ethnic groups, especially outside one's normal sphere of relationships, may produce the same focus on speech markers. If one finds oneself in a dramatically different culture, for example, the normal speech markers which permit one to categorize others and more importantly categorize oneself in relation to others, may cease to be available. In extreme conditions this may lead to feelings of alienation and a total lack of social understanding.

2.2. The identity maintenance function

In terms of self-definition, precisely because the decoder orders the social world by attending to speech markers, the encoder is provided information about the self by being reacted to in an organized manner. As writers in the symbolic interaction theory tradition (Cooley 1902; Mead 1934) have persuasively argued, much of our understanding of self is derived – entirely or partially – from how others react to us. Self-definition is a dynamic process involving interpreting others' reactions to us and at the same time providing others with stable cues as to our self-identity. For the encoder speech markers provide one functional way of presenting one's 'self' to others in a stable and organized manner. For example, a person for whom ethnic group membership plays an important role in self-identity will ensure that speech markers associated with his or her ethnic group are emitted in the course of all interactions with others (see Giles, this volume: ch. 7). By so doing, others can meaningfully interpret the encoder's values, attitudes, beliefs and so forth, and interact accordingly. A secondary function is that the encoder's stable speech markers may evoke consistent reactions from others thereby reinforcing the encoder's definition of self.

The second important aspect of the identity maintenance function focuses on emotional needs rather than efficiency of interaction. A number of related but not identical concepts have been described in the social psychological literature including self-image, self-esteem, ego defence and positive social identity, to name a few. The underlying notion is that people are motivated to see themselves, and those whom they view favourably, in positive terms. It is conceivable then that decoders will actively seek out or attend to markers that positively reinforce that self or ego, and sometimes may even deliberately avoid or fail to process markers which convey unpleasant information about the self. Similarly, encoders will concentrate on emitting speech markers which they believe to present their self in the most favourable light.

The importance of the identity maintenance function should not be underestimated. People feel free to communicate about many topics, but the ones they guard jealously are those which may unveil threatening information about the self. The social psychological literature on self-disclosure (Cozby 1973; Jourard 1971) attests to the reluctance with which people provide personal information about themselves, and indeed extent of disclosure itself is a very good barometer of the intimacy of a relationship. The reasons for lack of disclosure are not clear but presumably self-disclosure renders the person vulnerable and hence the motivation for nondisclosure may be strongly linked to notions of ego protection and identity maintenance. Since disclosures are not communicated directly, they are inferred from subtle behaviours generally, and an important feature of these is level 2 speech markers. Thus, our fears, anxieties, affections and values are communicated and interpreted on the basis of subtle markers rather than direct statements.

A fundamental hypothesis regarding the identity maintenance function is that under conditions of threat the identity maintenance function will become more prominent with a corresponding lessening of attention to organizational needs. Thus, the threatened (and perhaps the upwardly mobile) individual will both emit and attend to others' speech markers that will serve to enhance his self-image and will attend less to markers that under normal circumstances may be useful cues for effective interaction. An example might be the case of a teacher, threatened by intelligent queries from the class, who adopts an exaggerated, prestigious style of speech himself while at the same time concentrating on markers of that student's inferior status. In the process of so doing, of course, the teacher is not attending to other markers (e.g. uncertainty, nervousness) which would render the interaction more effective as a learning experience.

Some empirical evidence already exists of the above formulation. Giles and his collegues have conducted two experiments which demonstrate shifts in speech markers as a function of introducing threat in the course of interaction. In one study (Bourhis & Giles 1977) the speech marker in question was accent: it was found that if a Welsh person, conscious of cultural identity, was threatened in this domain by an English interlocutor, the Welsh subject would diverge from his normal speech style and adopt a broader than usual accent when answering the English speaker's question. In a second study (Bourhis, Giles, Leyens & Tajfel 1979), the issue was choice of language: Flemish subjects who were threatened by a Walloon speaker about their ethnic identity chose more often to reply in Flemish than when they were not so threatened.

Although these studies were designed to test hypotheses derived from accommodation theory (Giles & Powesland 1975; Giles 1977), they do not bear directly on the present formulation. The evidence therefore is limited to accent and choice of language, and no direct interpretations regarding identity maintenance can be made. Nevertheless, it would seem that speech markers were affected under threat and, although speculation is required, it would seem that the nature of the speech shifts were consistent with the present formulations. That is, the adoption of a broader accent or choice of ingroup language would probably reduce communication efficiency (cognitive organizational function) and the motivation for the shift was probably related to group and personal pride (identity maintenance function).

More indirect evidence for the ability of identity maintenance functions to alter the perception of speech markers is to be found in the literature on perceptual defence. The so-called 'new look' in perception work which flourished in the 1950s subsequently received a good deal of criticism. In total, the evidence suggests that there is a vigilance in the perception of

positively valued stimuli and that negatively valued or threatened stimuli
are repressed as a defensive reaction or as a means of identity maintenance (Erdelyi 1974). If this is the case for stimuli such as the recognition
threshold of taboo words, then it would suggest these vigilant and defensive processes operate even more freely in the case of subtle speech
markers.

Finally, Scherer's discussion of personality markers (this volume: ch. 5)
supports the present view. He notes, for example, that one reason for the
faster speech rate of highly anxious subjects may be their 'greater sensitivity to listener response and/or greater need for social approval', explanations which evoke the concept of identity maintenance. Further,
Scherer suggests that the anxious (threatened, stressed) person's need
for positive self-presentation (identity maintenance) may also explain the
significantly shorter latency times for their responses. These two isolated
examples demonstrate that identity maintenance functions may also be
involved in speech markers such as voice quality and filled and unfilled
pauses. And, as the author notes, these particular speech marking
devices are often detrimental to communicational effectiveness.

In summary, the cognitive organizational and identity maintenance
functions of speech markers are both concerned with the encoding and
decoding processes as schematized in figure 1. However, there is little
doubt that both functions operate simultaneously. The use of any speech
marker either by the encoder or the decoder is serving a dual function and
these will be difficult to separate empirically. Theoretically, it may be
useful to imagine the relative importance of the two functions in a particular situation as lying on a hypothetical continuum defined at one end by
cognitive organization, and at the other by identity maintenance. It is
possible to imagine at one extreme someone employing speech markers
solely for their organizational value with zero attention to matters of
identity maintenance, as in the case of Professor Higgins, diagnosing

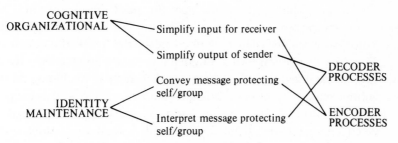

Figure 1. The functions of human speech marking

Eliza's birthplace from behind a column at Covent Garden. Conversely, at the other extreme of the continuum someone might process speech markers totally as a means of self-presentation with little or no regard for their organizational value as when Eliza tries to pass the test of ladylikeness at the tea party.

3. The nature of speech markers

In the remainder of this chapter, we will discuss the different types of markers that can be used by a speaker and the manner in which these are decoded by relying on a semiotic framework (Morris 1946; cf. also Laver & Trudgill, this volume: ch. 1). Throughout, we will attempt to amalgamate this orientation with the previous sections on functions.

3.1. Speech markers: a semiotic approach

Speech markers are defined as those extralinguistic, paralinguistic and linguistic cues which differentiate between various biological, social and psychological categories or characteristics of speakers which are important – actually or potentially – for social organization and social interaction. In other words, marking is concerned with the relationship between speech and social variables. As can be seen from Laver & Trudgill (this volume: ch. 1, 2.3), linguistic constraints over the production of speech sounds are not so great as to restrict to a mere handful the number of variables having social psychological significance. Indeed, the nature of speech variables having such surplus meanings is very wide, ranging from isolated phonological features, to lexical items, to pitch features, to styles of speaking and discourse types, and, in fact, to discrete languages and the manner in which they intermix. In this vein, we have the sociolinguistic notion of a 'speech repertoire' (see, e.g., Gumperz 1964; Hymes 1967) from which speakers can select speech markers appropriately to meet the needs of the specific social interaction and their cognitions concerning it. Similarly, the range of biological, social and psychological variables (which shall be called the 'marked' variables) is equally wide. In general terms, linguistic variables are available for the marking of the speaker's own characteristics such as his biological (see this volume: chs. 3, 4) and psychological states (ch. 5) as well as his place in the social structure (ch. 8). In addition, marking of the receiver's perceived characteristics (chs. 2, 7), together with the nature of the relationship between speaker and addressee (ch. 8) and the characteristics of the situation in which the interaction takes place (ch. 2), can also occur in speech.

Marking is, of course, a very complex process and the phenomenon can be examined by means of at least four orthogonal distinctions: namely, discrete vs. continuous; invariant vs. conditional/probabilistic; unique vs. equivocal; and extrinsic vs. intrinsic. These and other considerations will be discussed in terms of a semiotic framework of the semantic, syntactic and pragmatic aspects of marking.[4]

3.2. Semantic aspects of marking

In this section, we are concerned with the specific nature of the coding relationship between speech variables and marked variables in terms of its form, strength and origins respectively.

Coding form. One of the prime dimensions of the nature of a social marker is its linguistic form with regard to the dimension, discrete–continuous. Speech markers which are more *discrete* in form, i.e. either the speaker has it or does not, can be exemplified by means of the presence or absence of key lexical items or phrases, such as the use or not of curse words or tag questions. Most speech markers, however, appear to be more *continuous* in their composition, to the extent that there are various degrees of the linguistic feature in question. For instance, Brennan, Ryan & Dawson (1975) have shown that in the southwest of the United States, not only are there at least eight phonologically distinct degrees of Mexican accentedness identifiable across Spanish–English bilingual speakers' English, but that these points along the mild–broad continuum are also identifiable by linguistically untrained listeners. At other levels of linguistic analysis, we find speech markers which are continuous in form, such as pitch height and range, grammatical complexity, type-token ratios, etc. In all these cases, the possession of the linguistic feature is not an all-or-none matter; speakers use or adopt various degrees of it and thereby signal different degrees of the marked variable (cf. Laver & Trudgill, this volume ch. 1, 2.3). Linguistic forms can, however, be continuous in two senses. Some are intrinsically continuous (e.g. absolute pitch, loudness, rhythm) such that variations along the continuum are not aiming at a particular endpoint which has a structural locus in the linguistic system. Phonetic

---

[4] Parts of the conceptual distinctions introduced below are derived from a semiotic discussion of the functions of nonverbal behaviour in speech (Scherer 1977) which, in turn, was influenced by a conceptual scheme introduced by Ekman & Friesen (1969).

articulation, on the other hand, is continuous but varies around a focal point (the phoneme) which has structural meaningfulness. The distinction may be important because the former, being inherently continuous for all speakers, cannot carry social meanings (i.e. be markers) in the same way that Labovian-style continuous variables (e.g. New York /r/) can (Labov 1970); the latter are continuous for some speech communities but not for others.

The social, biological and psychological states to be marked by linguistic features can also be discrete or continuous. Thus, for example, membership of sex and ethnic categories are more discrete than continuous, whereas the formality of a situation and the fact you are angry are more continuous than discrete. Indeed, given that most situations, social structures and psychological states in which we are engaged are never clearly discrete, it is not surprising to discover that most speech markers are continuous in linguistic form. Nevertheless, it is possible to have discrete linguistic forms being associated with continuous marked states such as the occurrence of curse words at a certain level of expressed anger, and also to have continuous linguistic forms being associated with discrete marked states such as the use of different pitch ranges by the two sexes.

Coding strength. Let us now move away from aspects of the form of speech markers and marked states to the nature of the relationship between them in terms of the strength of their correspondence. Two independent sets of distinctions are important in this respect. The first relates to the proportion of correspondent occurrences between linguistic features and marked states; the invariant vs. condition/probabilistic distinction.[5] A speech marker is considered *invariant* when it is always associated with a particular marked variable, i.e. it is perfectly correlated with the marked state for all people in a given cultural context in all situations and in all linguistic environments. Instances of this are somewhat rare, although interethnic situations where monolingual groups in contact speak their own distinct languages might be illustrations *par excellence* of invariant markers. In fact, invariant markers can be subdivided into *universal* or *culturally specific*, where the former, of course, would be signalling biological, social or psychological states which are found irrespective of the cultural background of the speaker. Obviously, speech markers of the

---

[5] Cf. Brown & Fraser's discussion of invariant vs. probabilistic markers (this volume: ch. 2, 1.2) and Smith's discussion of sex-exclusiveness vs. sex-preferential usage (this volume: ch. 4, 1.2).

biological states would be better candidates for universality than other marked variables, and perhaps paralinguistic markers such as pitch height and range for males and females may be accorded this status after more cross-cultural work has been conducted.

Most speech markers are either probabilistic or conditional, and more the former than the latter. *Conditional* speech markers would be those where the relationship between a linguistic feature and a marked state appears only in specifiable situations, linguistic contexts, or for certain types of people.[6] Thus, for example, Labov's (1966) New York City /r/ would be conditional in that it is associated with certain social contexts and social classes in particular linguistic environments (cf. Laver & Trudgill, this volume: ch. 1, 2.3). In a similar vein, not all manual labourers use working-class speech markers (see Robinson, this volume: ch. 6), while speech markers of trait state anxiety are found only in threatening situations and not others (see Scherer, this volume: ch. 5); i.e. they are conditional on the type of person and situation involved respectively. *Probabilistic* speech markers would be those which mark a particular state some percentage of the time for some percentage of people without the actual determinants of its occurrence being known. Thus, for example, men and women differ in the use of prestige phonological variants (see Smith, this volume: ch. 4, 1.1). However, it is not that women use them whilst men do not, but rather that both use them with women adopting them far more often. At the moment, it is difficult to predict precisely the conditions under which women use more prestige variants during a conversation than men. When more information is known about the determinants of probabilistic speech markers, to such an extent that we can specify the conditions of their occurrence, they may then assume the status of conditional speech markers (cf. section 4 below).

The second distinction of interest concerning the strength of the covariation between a linguistic feature and a marked variable relates to whether the former marks one and exclusively one biological, social or psychological state, or whether it marks two or even more states. Examples of the former variety, which shall be termed *unique* speech markers, are very difficult to find although the use of a certain language or dialect by only one particular ethnic or racial group would qualify. Most speech markers seem to be of the latter variety and can be termed *equivocal* (see Brown & Fraser, this volume: ch. 2, 1.2, for their discussion of 'ambiguity'). Thus, for example, the use of low prestige phonological

[6] Cf. Smith's discussion of saturated vs. unsaturated usage (this volume: ch. 4, 1.2).

features could mark an informal context as well as be correlated with a low SES speaker. Similarly, a loud voice could be the marker of an extrovert, angry mood, noisy environment, or of a large physical distance between interlocutors. Although in many instances the correct social meaning attached to the speech marker will be seen as intended by the speaker if other nonlinguistic cues are available, sometimes attribution problems can arise. For instance, the introduction of low prestige features in another's speech during a conversation could either signal that the speaker wishes to make the situation more informal and relaxed or that his social origins had up till then been masked by the use of high prestige speech features.

Coding origins. Let us now consider our fourth dimension, intrinsic–extrinsic. As can be inferred from the earlier discussion, it must be the case that some of our speech markers are evolutionarily inherited and biologically determined; in other words, *intrinsically* derived. In this regard Scherer (this volume: ch. 5, 5.1) discusses the biophysical determinants of the speech production of different personality types, and other examples abound throughout this volume. For instance, sex is marked in males and females differently due to certain anatomical differences in vocal tract shape and elsewhere, and age is also marked by reference to certain biological (and cognitive) maturation processes (see Laver & Trudgill, this volume: ch. 1, 2.1).

However, the origins of many speech markers are best represented by an interaction of biological (intrinsic), and *extrinsic* factors at the psychological and sociostructural levels. Moreover, given the tendency for most speech markers to be probabilistic in nature, it can be argued that the emphasis in this intrinsic–extrinsic interaction should be laid at the latter door. Indeed, even some of the speech markers of the elderly, females and extroverts, which at first sight could be considered intrinsically derived, may in large part be extrinsically determined. For instance, it would seem reasonable to suppose that in most cultures, women, the elderly and extroverts are expected to speak in particular ways (the notion of speech stereotyping will be taken up below, section 3.4). It would not be surprising to discover then that members of these social categories are socialized into self-fulfilling these prophecies. Furthermore, the mere fact that there are cross-cultural differences in such supposedly similar cultures as West Germany and the United States in terms of personality speech markers (Scherer 1972, 1979, this volume: ch. 5) underlines the salience of extrinsic influences. The interface of the biological and the social psychological is obviously very difficult to disentangle empirically particularly as one mutually affects the other.

A particularly interesting set of extrinsic influences affecting the origins of speech markers in social interaction is sociostructural variables. Indeed, it may even be the case that different structures, hierarchical organizations and ideological perspectives induce their own particular speech markers (see Brown & Levinson, this volume: ch. 8, 1.2). Giles, Bourhis & Taylor's (1977) notion of 'vitality factors' may provide us with a means of classifying objective social structures and also of discovering how they are defined subjectively by the speaker (cf. Giles, this volume: ch. 7, 2.2). Nevertheless, particular social structures do impose constraints on interactive patterns particularly when participants in a social encounter derive from two social categories who occupy different positions in the status and or power hierarchy. Thus, women adopt a so-called 'powerless speech style' with men, ethnic minorities with majorities, children with adults and so on (see this volume: chs. 4, 2.2; 7, 1; 3, 4, respectively). In other words, many of the linguistic variables intuitively associated with social categories like sex, ethnicity and age are not intrinsically derived, but rather are determined by structural relations operating between the social categories. Hence, if the power positions between dominant and subordinate were changed or even reversed then one would expect a corresponding change in the linguistic variables associated with these categories. However, we must be cautious as to how we assign these linguistic variables the status of speech markers. Although these speech features may serve as *cues* to which member of a particular dyad is the man or woman, working- or middle-class person, subordinate or dominant (given background knowledge of the social structure), they are speech markers of a power *relationship* and not speech markers of the social category itself (see Brown & Levinson, this volume: ch. 8, 3.1). Indeed, the attribution of linguistic variables either to speech markers of a particular relationship or to a social category is of considerable pragmatic importance. Many inferences that have been made about the relationship between language and social class (see Robinson, this volume: ch. 6) may have been the result of a misunderstanding about the origins of speakers' linguistic patterns. Thus, if one explores the notion that the speech patterns of a working-class boy when being interviewed by a middle-class interviewer in a formal setting on an abstract topic are not class markers *per se*, but markers of his perceived position (subordinate) in a particular relationship, then quite different inferences can be made about the boy's capabilities, potential and competences, etc.

A final note of caution should be made about the identification of the origins of speech markers. Giles *et al.* (in press) in a couple of studies found that profeminism in women was associated with a particular speech style. However, a recent study by Giles & Nuttall (forthcoming) suggests that profeminism is not the determinant of these linguistic variables at all. Their study found that the same speech differences which exist between female profeminists and nonprofeminists are found in men as well. It also showed that profeminism in men correlated extremely highly (r = +0.93) with liberal ideologies. In other words, it is likely that profeminism in the original studies was only a smaller part of a larger sociopolitical constellation, and it was the latter that was being marked, not profeminism *per se*.

Our discussion of the semantics of speech markers has suggested that we have to be cautious in the appropriateness of which linguistic–social psychological covariations are assigned the status of speech markers, and when they are, which marked variables are correctly being referred to. This section has also pointed to the fact that many speech markers are more continuous than discrete in their linguistic form, more conditional or probabilistic than invariant in the proportion of their correspondent occurrences, more equivocal than unique in their associations with various marked states, and more extrinsic than intrinsic in origin. In the following section, we will examine the relationship between different speech markers.

3.3. Syntactic aspects of marking

It is the case, of course, that usually more than one speech marker is associated with a particular marked variable, i.e. different speech markers covary. For instance, formality is marked by syntactic structures, a nominal style, a high incidence of polite forms and of prestige phonological variants. Because of this and similar examples, it could be argued that the notion of 'style' could be favoured as that more meaningfully correlated with a marked variable than isolated, single speech markers. While this may be the case in many instances, one should also be open to the possibility that the isolated occurrence of a single speech marker associated with a particular psychological state may be socially significant for listeners. For instance, it has been suggested that just the 'drop' of one low prestige variant in an otherwise flawless middle-class speech style is enough for listeners to detect a speaker's background as working class (Mackay 1969; see section 4 below).

Speech markers are not only multicomponential in terms of the number of linguistic features involved, but also in the number of marked states that can be manifest at any one point in time. In other words, speakers may wish to – and undoubtedly do – communicate their youthfulness, personality traits, ethnicity, social class, sex, and definition of the situation simultaneously. Therefore, a speaker's message may include speech markers with the obvious implication, for example: 'I'm an outgoing young man brought up in a working-class district in Glasgow who sees this situation as quite informal.' Naturally enough, marked variables are marked not only by linguistic features but by visual ones as well. Ultimately then, the area of speech markers will need to be integrated with the area of nonverbal communication[7] if a complete picture of the complexity of marking is to emerge.

A number of empirical questions can be asked about the syntactic aspects of speech marking in social interaction. Does the encoder transmit all the necessary markers at one and the same time, or does he convey them hierarchically in terms of their centrality to the speaker at that point in time? Similarly, does the decoder process these markers simultaneously, or does he decode them according to his own priorities? In this latter sense, it is possible that the decoder will not detect certain markers if they are low on his receptive priorities. Once the listener has established a cognitive map of the speaker's states according to his central dimensions, he is liable to expend some energy making finer discriminations about these other markers if he wishes to understand the encoder better (cf. Berger 1979). Moreover, the decoder's knowledge of the encoder's understanding of the situation and social structure, and what he thinks the encoder believes it means to the decoder, is important in the attribution of speech markers. We have now moved on to the pragmatic aspects of speech marking and it is to this issue we now turn. Suffice it to say that at present we have not enough descriptive information about the linguistics nor the social psychology of speech marking to enable us to formulate an explanatory model of its syntax.

3.4. Pragmatic aspects of marking

In this section, the ways in which speech markers are encoded and decoded will be discussed in relation to the functions they were proposed to perform earlier, i.e. in terms of cognitive organization and identity maintenance.

---

[7] It is to be stressed that given the structural relations between kinesic, paralinguistic and linguistic systems, as they are all part of a communication system, one cannot study each in isolation and later expect to come up with a simplistic union.

Sender perspectives. An important distinction related to the sender's encoding of speech markers is the *informative–communicative* one (cf. Lyons 1972; see also Laver & Trudgill, this volume: ch. 1, 1). It refers to the extent to which speech markers are intentionally delivered (communicative) vs. being unintentionally conceived (informative).[8] Some speech markers are undoubtedly more of the latter type in that they are not deliberately managed or represented, but are nevertheless picked up by the listener as an identification cue without the knowledge of the speaker. The reasons for the occurrence of informative speech markers are at least threefold. First, the unintentionality may derive from the sender's attention being directed to other salient aspects of the communication (Labov 1970). For instance, he may be angry or depressed and thereby not be in a position to monitor certain, for example, class markers in his speech. Second, the sender may be ignorant about the existence of certain linguistic variables being correlated with a given marked state and hence be unaware of their social significance. Third, the sender may be aware of the fact that a linguistic feature is associated with a particular psychological state but may refuse to acknowledge the fact that *he* uses it in his speech. Wilkinson (1965) reports this phenomenon with regard to Birmingham secondary school pupils in Britain and states that 'very many English people who have not heard their voices on tape imagine they have R.P. whilst their neighbours have an "accent". Even when they have heard it themselves, the prestige of R.P. is so high that they are often unwilling to admit to themselves that they deviate from it.' There are methodological problems in determining whether a speech marker is informative or not, since simply to ask a speaker retrospectively about his awareness at the time concerning the use of a linguistic feature disposes him to think he must have used it otherwise he would not have been asked. Alternatively, some people may not want to admit having used a particular linguistic variable in an attempt to maintain a valued degree of cognitive and/or behavioural consistency.

The situation described above, albeit complex, is nevertheless too static to encompass the dynamics and richness of speech markers in social interaction. Hence, speech markers must be viewed as dynamic, meaningfully anchored to an underlying baseline but continually being modulated to meet changing circumstances. The nature of these modulations

---

[8] There has been much debate in the literature on the definition of intentionality and the concept's relationships with awareness and consciousness. Given that after decades, if not centuries, the issues remain largely unresolved, we will not complicate the discussion further by unveiling the problems inherent in the notion of intentionality.

will, of course, be reflections of the underlying organizational and identity maintenance functions.

At the outset of section 3, it was stated that linguistic variables exist which not only mark the speaker's states but which also mark aspects of the receiver's states as well. It has been found, for instance (see Helfrich, this volume: ch. 3, 4), that speakers take into account the fact that their listeners are younger or older than them and modify their speech appropriately. One of the ways of doing so is to make one's speech more like the person being addressed. In fact, such accommodations occur with regard to a wide variety of linguistic features and between members of a number of different social categories besides the age ones, e.g. different ethnolinguistic groups (see Giles, this volume: ch. 7). These 'convergences', as they have been called in other theoretical contexts (Giles & Powesland 1975; Jaffe & Feldstein 1970), occur in such a manner that the sender becomes linguistically more similar to his receiver, and hence they will be termed 'attentuation markers' because the differences between them are reduced. It can be argued that these linguistic variables are introduced – and in bilingual contexts this could involve a complete switch of language – to increase communicational effectiveness. In other words, the sender has adopted the speech patterns peculiar to his receiver which in all likelihood facilitates cognitive similarity and hence information flow and communicational satisfaction as well. The sender can then control his markers to the receiver by means of linguistic attenuation strategies in order to fulfil an organizational function of interactional efficiency.

Attenuation markers can often serve the dual function of both cognitive organization and identity maintenance. For instance, Giles (1977) claims that individuals adapt to one another, and ingroup speakers to outgroup speakers, because they wish to gain social approval or because they wish to be socially integrated. Indeed, the strategy of attenuation often results in positive reactions from the recipient when the reduction of linguistic dissimilarities is attributed positively and when the convergence is perceived to occur at an optimal level (Giles & Smith 1979; Simard, Taylor & Giles 1976). However, within the age context, one can also envisage situations where an adolescent would not adapt (or attenuate) to the speech of a younger or even older person, but would *diverge away* from it (cf. Bourhis & Giles 1977; Bourhis *et al*. 1979). Such a strategy, involving 'accentuation markers', could serve the dual identity maintenance function for the speaker of not only dissociating him from other individuals or members of outgroup categories but of associating him positively with speech markers characteristic of his own peer group (Giles *et al*. 1977).

Thus, receiver markers can function dynamically in terms of attenuation (where there is a move towards the receiver) or accentuation (where there is a move away from the receiver), depending on the sender's definition of the social interaction.

Both these types of receiver markers, and particularly the latter, can involve strategies of what Goffman (1959) calls 'self-presentation' (cf. Scherer, this volume: ch. 5, 5.3). Speech markers of self-presentation reflect the sender's need to mark a particular social category or psychological state in order to project a particular image of himself for the listener. Although self-presentation markers encapsulate the identity maintenance functions of attentuation and accentuation, conceptually they must stand on their own. For instance, a sender may wish to present a self- (or group) image of·a particular type, such as that of a confident, assured person, irrespective of whether this is similar to, or dissimilar from, that perceived to be apparent in the decoder. Interestingly, it is possible that a sender may wish to self-present his perspective on the social situation in a particular manner (e.g. markers of formality) so that he may control the interaction better for his self-interests given his perceived advantages at other linguistic levels (e.g. by means of middle-class speech markers). Moreover, such is the flexibility of human communicative behaviour that speakers may be able to attenuate, accentuate and self-present three quite distinct, and yet parallel, images at one and the same time. For instance, a speaker may attenuate his grammatical markers for a younger person and thereby appear a little more comprehensible and accommodating, yet also accentuate certain ethnic markers (e.g. phonological features) to emphasize the fact that he proudly claims membership of a particular minority group, while at the same time use speech markers (e.g. paralinguistic features) suggesting that he is a humble, flexible and negotiable person with whom to talk. In this sense then, the pragmatics of speech markers are intricately bound up with their syntax. Of course, the extent to which a sender can effectively adopt a particular representation of himself, whether it be by masking his social origins or his true abilities by attenuation markers or by means of self-presentation markers, depends on the extent of his speech repertoire and the linguistic flexibility he possesses within it. This now introduces us into the realm of the decoding of speech markers.

Receiver perspectives. Just as the sender may or may not be aware of marking his speech in particular ways, so too the decoder may or may not be aware of processing such speech markers. From the receiver's perspective, the dimension etic–emic seems important (Brown & Fraser, this volume: ch. 2, 1.2; Robinson: ch. 6, 1.1). Emic speech markers are those which have social meaningfulness, while etic markers refer to those which may be highly correlated with, for instance, a social category or psychological state yet are not used in any sense by listeners in terms of recognition, evaluation or behavioural response. While not all of the authors in this volume have used the etic–emic distinction, there seems to be general consensus on the importance of the issue, i.e. the usability or the effectiveness of speech differences for the attribution processes of naive actors in social interaction. The Brunswikian lens model introduced by Scherer (see this volume: ch. 5, 1) may serve to illustrate the distinctions that have been drawn by different authors. Figure 2 shows the different terms used in this volume in the context of the lens model.

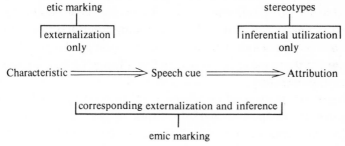

Figure 2

While most authors state or imply that there must be some degree of 'emicness' (or accurate inference by naive observers without the help of sophisticated apparatus and digital computers), it would be misleading to assume that some speech cues are always or are never an emic marker of a specific characteristic. As Scherer (see ch. 5, 6) has pointed out, externalization may *develop* due to self-presentation mechanisms, if there are sufficiently strong stereotypical inference rules. Furthermore, given that humans are excellent information processors, people may become aware of etic markers and start using them in attribution. Just because in the immediacy of the situation the receiver has given no indication (to the scientist at least) that he used a speech marker for recognition or evaluation does not mean that he has not stored it for future reference in a subsequent interaction. Indeed, in attribution terms, he may have noted it and judged that he required some cross-situational evidence before committing himself to an attribution of a particular sender state on the basis of these markers. Moreover, it is often not possible to be sensitive enough to all the relevant attitudinal and behavioural dimensions so that one can be confident that all the dimensions on which the marker might have emic relevance for the receiver have been tapped in a scientific investigation. Perhaps more importantly however, it is also the case that what is etic can be *potentially* emic in some future space or time. For instance, certain English speech markers of social class may not have achieved emic status in the middle of this century until other markers of group identity (e.g. nonlinguistic ones such as dress and housing) had dissipated somewhat. In other words, what are today's etic markers may be tomorrow's emic ones. Hence the social psychological processes underlying the shift from etic to emic status, particularly in the context of the dynamics of intergroup relations (cf. Giles, this volume: ch. 7, 2.1), might have important consequences for the processes of linguistic change (Labov 1970; Peng 1976). Added to this, the state of the art (even as reflected in the preceding chapters) is etic-biased, given that researchers have in the first place, understandably enough, tended to establish the objective existence of linguistic and social psychological correlations prior to testing for their social relevance across a range of evaluative dimensions for the decoder.

Having now established ourselves within decoding perspectives, let us discuss how speech markers function for the receiver pragmatically, in terms of the cognitive organization and identity maintenance functions.

Berger & Calabrese (1975) devised a theoretical framework for understanding the development of interpersonal relationships and accorded the notion of 'uncertainty' a central role within it. They argue that when two strangers meet for the first time their uncertainty levels are high in the sense that they are initially doubtful about the alternative behaviours and beliefs the other is likely to manifest or hold and, consequently, are uncertain themselves as to how to behave appropriately. Berger & Calabrese propose that acquaintanceship is concerned with reducing such uncertainty so that once the other is perceived to be more predictable, a decision can be made about the likelihood of future interactions, and the probable intimacy of them. In order to reduce uncertainty in first encounters, interactants need to elaborate a basis for predicting the other's behaviours and attitudes. Berger & Calabrese argue that these predictions, called 'proactive attributions', are made early on in the interaction and based on input cues from the situation and the behaviour of the other. Naturally enough, uncertainty reduction is a continuously developing process, and the construction of proactive attributions is but one of the strategies Berger proposes interactants adopt to increase predictability (Berger 1979).

One of the ways in which receivers can form such proactive attributions and thereby reduce cognitive uncertainty about the other and the validity of their own reactions in social interaction is by processing potential speech markers in the sender's stream of discourse. In other words, receivers use and are constantly modifying their interpretations of speech markers in order to organize cognitively the input cues from the sender. Speech markers then allow the receiver to place the sender on his cognitive map. How this process works more specifically is not yet well understood, and receivers undoubtedly make inferences from one set of speech markers for reducing uncertainty about a whole range of supposedly correlated sender states according to their implicit personality theories. Indeed, in terms of the unfolding of an interaction over time, processes of social comparison (Festinger 1954) and the reinterpretation of speech markers in the context of increasing information are very complex processes. Probably further understanding of the organizational functions of speech markers from the perspective of the receiver can only come about when existing and future work in the cognitive sciences concerning perceptual processes and higher cognitive functions are introduced into the theoretical framework. Needless to say, the receiver's interpretation of speech markers does not assume accuracy either in terms of correctly decoding underlying states of the sender, or in terms of correctly attributing states the sender intended to be projected. In other words, barring physical constraints such as interpersonal distance and ambient noise, speech markers are often cognitively organized in such a manner as to fulfil the identity maintenance function.

In general terms, receivers perceive speech markers according to certain evaluative biases laid down in their cognitive structures which maintain their own self-esteem or positive group identity (Aronson 1972; Tajfel 1974). In this regard, Smith (see this volume: ch. 4, 2.3) makes a distinction between speech markers and *speech stereotypes*. He suggests implicitly that people possess cognitive maps of what they think people ought to sound like when they derive from certain social categories, are entertaining particular psychological states, and/or are engaged in specific social situations. Indeed, the stereotypes that exist (for example, between the sexes, see Smith: ch. 4, 2.3) about how members of two social categories should speak do not always overlap objectively with the actual speech markers used by them. It is likely that some speech stereotypes and speech markers do overlap, hence the availability of self-presentation speech markers, whereas in others they may be completely contradictory as in the male–female situation (see Smith: ch. 4, 2.3). In this respect, Scherer (this volume: ch. 5, 4) also points to instances where inference rules regarding the relationships of voice to certain personality traits completely contradict the actual marking patterns.

A number of questions can be posed about the relationship between speech markers and speech stereotypes for all marked variables. For instance, when overlaps do not occur, is it due to receivers' ignorance concerning the conditionality of the occurrence of speech markers, or is it due to people wishing to differentiate themselves from relevant out-groups on valued dimensions (Giles *et al.* 1977)? What happens when speech stereotypes are in the receiver's cognitive map and yet are not confirmed in the sender's speech patterns? Does the receiver perceptually bias the behaviour in terms of the stereotype anyway? In this vein, although women may use more unassertive remarks (probabilistic marker) than men, a situation where men and women produced the same moderate amounts of unassertiveness could be seen as confirming the stereotype for the latter, whereas for the former it would be afforded no social relevance whatsoever; men are not assertive all of the time anyway! In addition, are there hierarchies of speech markers in people's speech stereotypes (as suggested implicitly earlier) such that some markers are associated more saliently with a particular marked variable than other markers? In such a case, then, the receiver, failing to find the 'top few', might simply go down the list and identify less salient ones, thereby perhaps enabling him to confirm his stereotype. Even if the receiver has to go further down the list and still cannot substantiate the speech stereotype, he may attribute the lack of markers externally in attribution terms, i.e. to situational constraints (to conditionality in our own terms). On other, more typical, occasions the receiver may imagine that the appropriate markers have been emitted (cf. Gardner & Taylor, 1968). Should the listener ultimately be incapable of escaping the fact that the sender does not conform to the stereotype, he may, in an attempt to maintain cognitive consistency, be attributed role deviance and a range of negative attributions.

It may be that the social significance of speech stereotypes is at least equal to the meaningfulness of naturally occurring speech markers. Certainly, that is the case if people perceive discourse in terms of their biases and the identity maintenance function anyway. Moreover, if one defines speech differences with respect to what people feel they hear rather than what actually occurs in their speech[9] then the former may well be psychologically more important. In short, then, receivers' not noticing, or their lack of attentiveness to, certain speech markers, let alone their creation of ones that do not exist, (see Williams 1976), functions in such a manner as to organize the speech input according to their own predetermined and valued cognitive structures.

4. Concluding remarks

This chapter has attempted to show that man reveals much information about his basic psychological dispositions through a range of level 1 and level 2 speech markers. Level 1 speech markers are in certain situations redundant because they yield information about biological, social and psychological states that can be arrived at by means of other, often more potent, cues. In this sense, level 1 speech markers function most often at a lower level of psychological complexity. Marking at level 2 has been shown to be determined by social psychological factors which provide a basis for the encoding of more complex states of the speaker. Indeed, in social interaction we spend a lot of time trying to understand the other person's intentions, attitudes and values, at the same time also attempting to present an appropriate image of ourselves. Yet it is clear that we do not do this explicitly. We do not approach a person and say, 'What is your political ideology?' or 'Why are you being my friend?', etc. In similar vein, we do not readily offer information about our achievements, or provide precise assessments about the other and his weaknesses. If we did these things and people actually believed the responses, there would be no need for speech markers. It is because we do not interrogate others on fundamental issues and do not divulge revealing statements about our true selves that level 2 speech markers are vitally important for our complex needs. At this higher functional level, then, level 2 speech markers provide the receiver with information that can be processed along with other knowledge available about the sender's social attitudes, group memberships and perspectives concerning the ongoing interaction. Just as importantly, man can communicate and organize his speech output for his receiver's efficient interpretation of it as well as presenting many complex and simultaneous messages about how he wants to be perceived on a number of dimensions, and how he wants to define the

[9] Cf. Giles & Powesland (1975: 6) for a similar social psychological perspective on language vs. dialect differences. Note also the relevance of this discussion to Robinson's notion of the 'rhetoric roundabout' (this volume: ch. 6, 1.1).

social relationships and tenor of the situation. In these senses, level 2 speech markers serve the functions of cognitive organization and identity maintenance.

From our review of the characteristics of speech markers it is clear that there is rarely a simple one-to-one relationship between a particular speech variable and a corresponding social group or psychological state. Rather, there are a host of linguistic and paralinguistic variables which tend to be continuous in nature and probabilistic with regard to their association with marked states. Attempts to discover clear-cut linguistic and social relationships, then, are not likely to be fruitful. However, conceptualizing speech markers as deviations from a community's speech norms may help to explain how, despite their complexity and irregularity, speech markers may be potent conveyors of social information. Presumably a community has latitudes of acceptable speech for different situations to which all members of the community are expected to adhere. Speakers will then attempt to comply with these norms by ensuring their speech falls within the acceptable latitude. Speech becomes marked in a level 2 sense when it deviates from these norms. As such, it is not necessary for the speaker to be antinormative all of the time in all situations on all linguistic variables. Often a single deviation will suffice. There are at least two important implications for deviation in terms of speech markers. Speakers may purposely deviate in order to present themselves in what they consider to be a more favourable light. For example, a person who wishes to present himself as highly educated need only introduce one or two appropriate linguistic features that deviate from normal speech requirements in a half-hour's conversation to convey this message. Secondly, a speaker may rigidly adhere to speech norms in order to disguise what he believes to be negatively valued information about himself. Thus, for example, one speech marker implying anxiety is often sufficient to convey a sense of the speaker's stress to the listener. Given that it may only require a *single* deviation from linguistic norms to communicate important information, it is understandable that speech markers are often only probabilistically associated with marked states. Viewed from this perspective, research directed at cataloguing invariant relationships between speech and social variables is not likely to be constructive. Rather, the aim should be to examine a community's speech norms and evaluate the effects of even single deviations from these.

It is, of course, essential for the future development of our understanding of the role of speech markers in social interaction that we work very closely with linguists and other social scientists; indeed, the present volume is an initial attempt in this direction. Throughout we have proposed, as have others in the preceding pages, potentially fruitful avenues of empirical work. Undoubtedly, this will move us on from albeit necessary descriptive systems of speech markers in social contexts to more fundamental *explanatory* ones. It is now in order to make a few suggestions concerning specific priorities to which workers in the field of speech markers (whether it be sex, ethnicity, personality, or whatever) should attend. First, we need to know far more about how speakers and listeners in an encounter define the situations they are in during the developing course of an interaction. For instance, how do they see the purpose of the interaction? What strategies of understanding are being introduced over the course of the development of the conversation? Is the interaction being viewed more as a confrontation of two representatives from two different social categories (intergroup situation), or as two different individuals discussing an issue (interindividual situation)? The work in progress by Wish & Kaplan (1977) on the dimensions of interpersonal relationships, by Berger (1979) on the strategies of uncertainty reduction in the development of interpersonal relations, and by Tajfel (1978) on the dynamics of intergroup behaviour and social change, are likely to provide useful guidelines for theoretical frameworks. Second, we need to be more adventurous and wide-ranging in our investigation of speech markers in a linguistic sense. Too many ('one-off') studies are being conducted exploring the relationship between one social and one linguistic variable. Investigations should not only aim to consider more than one social variable at a time but ensure that their linguistic analyses cover grammatical, paralinguistic and discourse parameters simultaneously. In this way, we might be able to explore the manner in which social and linguistic variables cluster together. Third, and more methodologically, we need to move beyond recognition and identification measures of speech markers in a 'behaviour dynamic' direction (Giles & Bourhis 1976). That is, we should investigate a greater range of attitudinal and behavioural dimensions in the reactions of listeners who are attending to the speech markers of their interlocutors, and determine the manner in which the latter respond to these in turn. In addition, the decoder significance of certain speech markers in many studies up till now has been determined by passive listeners evaluating a tape-recording. Such people do not have access to all variables salient at the time of the interaction to which they are listening, and, in any case, the message in which these markers are conveyed is not addressed to them personally. Indeed, the discrepancy in interpretation of messages by actors and observers has been clearly demonstrated by Storms (1973). It seems, therefore, important in future work to obtain decoders' evaluations of markers in the immediacy of the situation in which they themselves are participating. If we can refine future research in many different cultural settings more sophisticatedly on these three fronts, the resultant progress would surely move us towards our ultimate goal, namely, a viable 'marker theory'. In the meantime, it is to be hoped that this book will provide a much needed framework for understanding the nature and uses of speech markers in social interaction.

References

Abercrombie, D. 1967. *Elements of General Phonetics*. Edinburgh.

Altman, S. A. 1962. A field study of the sociobiology of rhesus monkeys, Macaca Mulatta. *Annals of the New York Academy of Sciences*, *102*, 338–435.

Aronson, E. 1972. *The Social Animal*. San Francisco.

Beer, C. G. 1970. Individual recognition in the social behavior of birds. *Advances in the Study of Behaviour*, *3*, 27–74.

Berger, C. 1979. Beyond initial interaction: uncertainty, understanding, and the development of interpersonal relationships. In H. Giles & R. St Clair (eds.) *Language and Social Psychology*. Oxford.

Berger, C. & Calabrese, R. J. 1975. Some explorations in initial interaction and beyond: toward a developmental theory of interpersonal communication. *Human Communication Research* ,*1*, 99–112.

Bourhis, R. Y. & Giles, H. 1977. The language of intergroup distinctiveness: In H. Giles (ed.) *Language, Ethnicity and Intergroup Relations*, London.

Bourhis, R. Y., Giles, H., Leyens, J.-P. & Tajfel, H. 1979. Psycholinguistic distinctiveness: language divergence in Belgium. In H. Giles & R. St Clair (eds.) *Language and Social Psychology*. Oxford.

Brennan, E. M., Ryan, E. B. & Dawson, W. E. 1975. Scaling of apparent accentedness by magnitude estimation and sensory modality matching. *Journal of Psycholinguistic Research*, *4*, 27–36.

Cooley, C. H. 1902. *Human Nature and the Social Order*. New York.

Cozby, P. C. 1973. Self-disclosure: a literature review. *Psychological Bulletin*, *79*, 73–91.

Ekman, P. & Friesen, W. V. 1969. The repertoire of nonverbal behavior: categories, origins, usage, and coding. *Semiotica*, *1*, 49–98.

Emlen, S. T. 1972. An experimental analysis of the parameters of bird song eliciting species recognition. *Behaviour*, *41*, 130–71.

Erdelyi, M. H. 1974. A new look at the New Look: perceptual defense and vigilance. *Psychological Review*, *81*, 1–25.

Ferguson, C. A. 1964. Baby talk in six languages. In *American Anthropologist*, *66* (Supplement no. 6), 103–14.

Festinger, L. 1954. A theory of social comparison processes. *Human Relations*, *7*, 117–40.

Fraser, C. & Roberts, N. 1975. Mothers' speech to children of four different ages. *Journal of Psycholinguistic Research*, *4*, 9–16.

Gardner, R. C. & Taylor, D. M. 1968. Ethnic stereotypes: their effects on person perception. *Canadian Journal of Psychology*, *22*, 267–74.

Giles, H. 1977. Social psychology and applied linguistics: toward an integrative approach. *ITL: a Review of Applied Linguistics*, *35*, 27–42.

Giles, H. & Bourhis, R. Y. 1976. Methodological issues in dialect perception: a social psychological perspective. *Anthropological Linguistics*, *19*, 294–304.

Giles, H. & Nuttal, Z. Forthcoming. The voice of feminism: a follow-up investigation.

Giles, H. & Powesland P. F. 1975. *Speech Style and Social Evaluation*. London.

Giles, H. & Smith, P. 1979. Accommodation theory: optimal levels of convergence. In H. Giles & R. St Clair (eds.) *Language and Social Psychology*. Oxford.

Giles, H., Bourhis, R. Y. & Taylor, D. M. 1977. Toward a theory of language in ethnic group relations. In H. Giles (ed.) *Language, Ethnicity and Intergroup Relations*. London.

Giles, H., Smith, P., Browne, C., Whiteman, S. & Williams, J. A. In press. The voice of feminism. In R. Borker, N. Furman & S. McConnell-Ginet (eds.) *Language and Women's Lives: a feminist perspective*. Ithaca, NY.

Giles, H., Taylor, D. M. & Bourhis, R. Y. 1973. Towards a theory of interpersonal accommodation through speech: some Canadian data. *Language in Society*, *2*, 117–92.

Goffman, E. 1959. *The Presentation of Self in Everyday Life*. New York.

Gumperz, J. J. 1964. Linguistic and social interaction in two communities. *American Anthropologist*, *66* (Supplement no. 6), 137–53.

Hymes, D. 1967. Models of the interaction of language and social setting. *Journal of Social Issues*, *23*, 8–28.

  1972. Models of the interaction of language and social life. In J. J. Gumperz & D. Hymes (eds.) *Directions in Sociolinguistics: the ethnography of communication*. New York.

Jaffe, J. & Feldstein, S. 1970. *Rhythms of Dialogue*. New York.

Jones, E. E. & Gerard, H. B. 1967. *Foundations of Social Psychology*. New York.

Jourard, S. 1971. *Self-Disclosure: an experimental analysis of the transparent self*. New York.

Kelly, H. H. 1973. The process of causal attribution. *American Psychologist*, *28*, 107–28.

Labov, W. 1966. *The Social Stratification of English in New York City*. Washington, DC.

  1970. The study of language in its social context. *Studium Generale*, *23*, 66–84.

Lefcourt, H. M. 1976. *Locus of Control: current trends in theory and research*. New York.

Lyons, J. 1972. Human language. In R. A. Hinde (ed.) *Non-Verbal Communication*. Cambridge.

Mackay, J. R. 1969. A partial analysis of a variety of nonstandard Negro English. Doctoral dissertation, University of California, Berkeley.

McKirnan, D. J. 1977. Some thoughts on the 'unit of analysis' in social psychology. Paper presented at the Canadian Psychological Association Meeting, Vancouver.

1978. Community perspectives on deviance: some factors in the definition of alcohol abuse. *American Journal of Community Psychology*, *6*, 219–38.

Marler, P. R. 1965. Communication in monkeys and apes. In I. De Vore (ed.) *Primate Behaviour: field studies of monkeys and apes.*

Marler, P. R. & Hamilton, W. J. III. 1966. *Mechanisms of Animal Behaviour.* New York.

Mead, G. H. 1934. *Mind, Self and Society: from the standpoint of a social behaviourist.* Chicago.

Morris, C. W. 1946. *Signs, Language and Behaviour.* New York.

Peng, F. 1976. Language change: a sociolinguistic approach. *Forum Linguisticum, 1.*

Price, R. H. & Bouffard, D. L. 1974. Behavioural appropriateness and situational constraints as dimensions of social behaviour. *Journal of Personality and Social Psychology*, *30*, 579–86.

Reynolds, P. 1975. Comments on Marler's paper. In J. F. Kavanagh & J. E. Cutting (eds.) *The Role of Speech in Language.* Cambridge, Mass.

Rokeach, M. 1967. Attitude change and behavioural change. *Public Opinion Quarterly*, *30*, 529–50.

1968. *Beliefs, Attitudes and Values.* San Francisco.

Rotter, J. B. 1966. Generalized expectancies for internal versus external control of reinforcement. *Psychological Monographs*, *80* (whole no. 609).

Scherer, K. R. 1972. Judging personality from voice: a cross-cultural approach to an old issue in interpersonal perception. *Journal of Personality*, *40*, 191–210.

1977. Kommunikation. In T. Herrmann *et al.* (eds.) *Handbuch psychologischer Grundbegriffe.* Munich.

1979. Voice and speech correlates of perceived social influence. In H. Giles & R. St Clair (eds.) *Language and Social Psychology.* Oxford.

Scherer, K. R., Scherer, U., Hall, J. A. & Rosenthal, R. 1977. Differential attribution of personality based on multi-channel presentation of verbal and non-verbal cues. *Psychological Research*, *39*, 221–47.

Sebeok, T. A. (ed.) 1968. *Animal Communication: techniques of study and results of research.* Bloomington, Ind.

(ed.) 1977. *How Animals Communicate.* Bloomington, Ind.

Seligman, C. R., Tucker, G. R. & Lambert, W. E. 1972. The effects of speech style and other attributes on teachers' attitudes toward pupils. *Language in Society*, *1*, 131–42.

Seligman, M. E. P. 1975. *Helplessness.* San Francisco.

Shatz, M. & Gelman, R. 1973. *The Development of Communication Skills: modifications in the speech of young children as a function of listeners.* Society for Research in Child Development Monographs, *38*.

Simard, L., Taylor, D. M. & Giles, H. 1976. Attribution processes and interpersonal accommodation in a bilingual setting. *Language and Speech*, *19*, 374–87.

Smith, P. M., Giles, H. & Hewstone, M. 1979. Sociolinguistics: a social psychological perspective. In R. N. St Clair & H. Giles (eds.) *The Social and Psychological Contexts of Language.* Hillsdale, NJ.

Smith, W. J. 1969. Messages of vertebrate communication. *Science*, *165*, 145–50.

1977. *The Behaviour of Communicating: the ethological approach.* Cambridge, Mass.

Storms, M. D. 1973. Videotape and the attribution process: reversing actors' and observers' points of view. *Journal of Personality and Social Psychology, 27*, 165–75.

Tajfel, H. 1974. Social identity and intergroup behaviour. *Social Science Information, 13*, 65–93.

(ed.) 1978. *Differentiation Between Social Groups: studies in the social psychology of intergroup relations*. London.

Thielke, G. 1969. Geographic variation in bird vocalizations. In R. A. Hinde (ed.) *Bird Vocalizations: their relation to current problems in biology and psychology*. Cambridge.

Thorpe, W. H. 1972. Vocal communication in birds. In R. A. Hinde (ed.) *Non-Verbal Communication*. Cambridge.

Triandis, H. C. 1971. *Attitude and Attitude Change*. New York.

Wilkinson, A. 1965. Spoken English. *Educational Review*, Supplement 17(2), Occasional Publication, no. 2.

Williams, F. 1976. *Explorations of the Language Attitudes of Teachers*. Rowley, Mass.

Wilson, E. O. 1975. *Sociobiology: the new synthesis*. Cambridge, Mass.

Wish, M. & Kaplan, S. J. 1977. Toward an implicit theory of communication. *Sociometry, 40*, 234–46.

Subject index

Author index